Mike Meyers' Certification
Passport ★

CompTIA
Network+®
Fourth Edition
(Exam N10-005)

MIKE MEYERS

SCOTT JERNIGAN

Mc
Graw
Hill

New York • Chicago • San Francisco
Lisbon • London • Madrid • Mexico City
Milan • New Delhi • San Juan
Seoul • Singapore • Sydney • Toronto

The McGraw·Hill Companies

Cataloging-in-Publication Data is on file with the Library of Congress

McGraw-Hill books are available at special quantity discounts to use as premiums and sales promotions, or for use in corporate training programs. To contact a representative, please e-mail us at bulksales@mcgraw-hill.com.

Mike Meyers' CompTIA Network+® Certification Passport, Fourth Edition (Exam N10-005)

1 2 3 4 5 6 7 8 9 0 DOC DOC 1 0 9 8 7 6 5 4 3 2

ISBN: Book p/n 978-0-07-178908-0 and CD p/n 978-0-07-178907-3
of set 978-0-07-178905-9

MHID: Book p/n 0-07-178908-1 and CD p/n 0-07-178907-3
of set 0-07-178905-7

Sponsoring Editor Tim Green	**Technical Editor** Jonathan Weissman	**Production Supervisor** James Kussow
Editorial Supervisor Jody McKenzie	**Copy Editor** Lisa McCoy	**Composition** Cenveo Publisher Services
Project Editor Emilia Thiuri (Fortuitous Publishing Services)	**Proofreader** Emilia Thiuri (Fortuitous Publishing Services)	**Illustration** Cenveo Publisher Services
Acquisitions Coordinator Stephanie Evans	**Indexer** Jack Lewis	**Art Director, Cover** Jeff Weeks
		Cover Series Design Ted Holladay

Dedication

We dedicate this book to our acquisitions editor at McGraw-Hill, Tim Green, who's been such an instrumental part of our success over the years.

Acknowledgments

The team at McGraw-Hill managed the process and kept us moving, jumping, skipping, (and other assorted mobility words that should be substituted for "writing"). So a big salute to Tim Green, Stephanie Evens, and Jody McKenzie. Project editor and proofreader Emilia Thiuri, copy editor Lisa McCoy, and compositor Cenveo did a fabulous job turning text into a printed book. It was great working with you again.

Our team at Total Seminars' Orbital HQ once again demonstrated creativity, professionalism, and self-deprecating humor during the usual tough process of creating a book. Thank you—Aaron Verber, Ford Pierson, and Michael Smyer—for the great work on writing, editing, illustrating, and photographing. Our networking instructors also played a big role as sounding boards and fellow networking enthusiasts. Thanks to Scott Strubberg, Doug Jones, and Dave Rush.

Our technical editor, Jonathan Weissman, did an outstanding job catching errors, flaws, imperfections, typos, and wacky grammar, and not being afraid to point it all out. Looking forward to the next project together!

About the Authors

Mike Meyers, lovingly called the "AlphaGeek" by those who know him, is the industry's leading authority on CompTIA Network+ certification. He is the president and co-founder of Total Seminars, LLC, a provider of PC and network repair seminars, books, videos, and courseware for thousands of organizations throughout the world. Mike has been involved in the computer and network repair industry since 1977 as a technician, instructor, author, consultant, and speaker. Author of numerous popular PC books and videos, including the best-selling *CompTIA Network+ Certification All-in-One Exam Guide*, Mike is also the series editor for the highly successful Mike Meyers' Certification Passport series, the Mike Meyers' Computer Skills series, and the Mike Meyers' Guide To series, all published by McGraw-Hill. As well as writing, Mike has personally taught (and continues to teach) thousands of students, including U.S. senators; U.S. Supreme Court justices; members of the United Nations; every branch of the U.S. Armed Forces; most branches of the U.S. Department of Justice; and hundreds of corporate clients, academic students at every level, prisoners, and pensioners.

Email: michaelm@totalsem.com
Facebook: Mike Meyers (Houston, TX)
Twitter/Skype/Most IMs: desweds
Web Forums: www.totalsem.com/forums

Scott Jernigan wields a mighty red pen as editor in chief for Total Seminars. With a master of arts degree in medieval history, Scott feels as much at home in the musty archives of London as he does in the warm computer glow of Total Seminars' Houston headquarters. After fleeing a purely academic life, he dove headfirst into IT, working as an instructor, editor, and writer. Scott has edited and contributed to dozens of books on computer literacy, hardware, operating systems, networking, and certification. His latest books are *CompTIA Strata IT Fundamentals All-in-One Exam Guide* (with Mike Meyers) and *Computer Literacy: Your Ticket to IC³ Certification*. Scott co-authored the best-selling *CompTIA A+ Certification All-in-One Exam Guide* and the *Mike Meyers' A+ Guide to Managing and Troubleshooting PCs* (both with Mike Meyers). He has taught computer classes all over the United States, including stints at the United Nations in New York and the FBI Academy in Quantico, Virginia.

About the Technical Editor

Jonathan S. Weissman earned his master's degree in computer and information science from Brooklyn College (CUNY), and holds 19 industry certifications, including Cisco CCNA, CompTIA Security+, CompTIA i-Net+, CompTIA Network+, CompTIA A+, CompTIA Linux+, Novell CNE, Novell CNA, Microsoft Office Master, Microsoft MCAS Word, Microsoft MCAS PowerPoint, Microsoft MCAS Excel, Microsoft MCAS Access, Microsoft MCAS Outlook, and Microsoft MCAS Vista.

Jonathan is a tenured assistant professor of computing sciences at Finger Lakes Community College (FLCC), in Canandaigua, New York, and also teaches graduate and undergraduate computer science courses at nearby Rochester Institute of Technology (RIT). In addition, Jonathan does computer, network, and security consulting for area businesses and individuals. Between FLCC and RIT, Jonathan has taught nearly two dozen different computer science courses, including networking, security, administration, forensics, programming, operating systems, hardware, and software courses.

About Total Seminars

Total Seminars provides certification training services to thousands of schools, corporations, and government agencies. Total Seminars produces the #1 selling CompTIA A+ and best-selling CompTIA Network+ certification books, and develops training materials such as the Total Tester for superior exam preparation. You can find Total Seminars on the Web at www.totalscm.com.

CompTIA.

CompTIA Network+

The CompTIA Network+ certification ensures that the successful candidate has the important knowledge and skills necessary to manage, maintain, trouble-shoot, install, operate, and configure basic network infrastructure, describe networking technologies, basic design principles, and adhere to wiring standards and use testing tools.

It Pays to Get Certified

In a digital world, digital literacy is an essential survival skill. Certification proves you have the knowledge and skill to solve business problems in virtually any business environment. Certifications are highly valued credentials that qualify you for jobs, increased compensation, and promotion.

CompTIA Network+ certification is held by many IT staffers across many organizations. Twenty-one percent of IT staff within a random sampling of U.S. organizations within a cross-section of industry verticals hold CompTIA Network+ certification.

- The CompTIA Network+ credential—proves knowledge of networking features and functions and is the leading vendor-neutral certification for networking professionals.
- Starting Salary—the average starting salary of network engineers can be up to $70,000.
- Career Pathway—CompTIA Network+ is the first step in starting a networking career, and is recognized by Microsoft as part of their MS program. Other corporations, such as Novell, Cisco, and HP, also recognize CompTIA Network+ as part of their certification tracks.
- More than 325,000—individuals worldwide are CompTIA Network+ certified.
- Mandated/recommended by organizations worldwide—Apple, Cisco, HP, Ricoh, the U.S. State Department, and U.S. government contractors such as EDS, General Dynamics, and Northrop Grumman recommend or mandate CompTIA Network+.

How Certification Helps Your Career

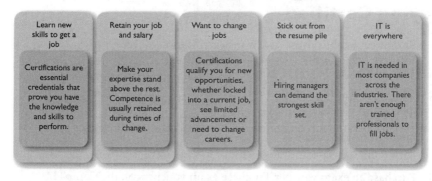

Learn new skills to get a job	Retain your job and salary	Want to change jobs	Stick out from the resume pile	IT is everywhere
Certifications are essential credentials that prove you have the knowledge and skills to perform.	Make your expertise stand above the rest. Competence is usually retained during times of change.	Certifications qualify you for new opportunities, whether locked into a current job, see limited advancement or need to change careers.	Hiring managers can demand the strongest skill set.	IT is needed in most companies across the industries. There aren't enough trained professionals to fill jobs.

CompTIA Career Pathway

CompTIA offers a number of credentials that form a foundation for your career in technology and that allow you to pursue specific areas of concentration. Depending on the path you choose, CompTIA certifications help you build upon your skills and knowledge, supporting learning throughout your career.

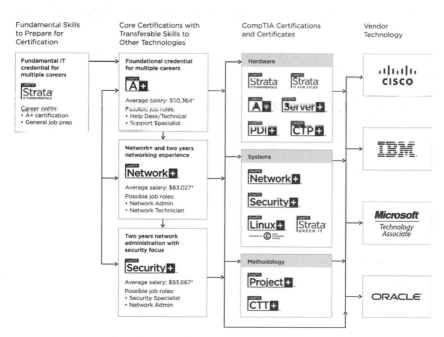

*Source: *Computerworld* Salary Survey 2010—U.S. salaries only

Steps to Getting Certified and Staying Certified

1. **Review exam objectives.** Review the certification objectives to make sure you know what is covered in the exam:
   www.comptia.org/certifications/testprep/examobjectives.aspx

2. **Practice for the exam.** After you have studied for the certification, take a free assessment and sample test to get an idea what type of questions might be on the exam:
   www.comptia.org/certifications/testprep/practicetests.aspx

3. **Purchase an exam voucher.** Purchase exam vouchers on the CompTIA Marketplace, which is located at: www.comptiastore.com

4. **Take the test!** Select a certification exam provider, and schedule a time to take your exam. You can find exam providers at the following link:
   www.comptia.org/certifications/testprep/testingcenters.aspx

5. **Stay Certified!** Continuing education is required. Effective January 1, 2011, CompTIA Network+ certifications are valid for three years from the date of certification. There are a number of ways the certification can be renewed. For more information go to: http://certification.comptia.org/getCertified/steps_to_certification/stayCertified.aspx

Join the Professional Community

The free online IT Pro Community provides valuable content to students and professionals. Join the IT Pro Community:

http://itpro.comptia.org

Career IT job resources include:

- Where to start in IT
- Career assessments
- Salary trends
- U.S. job board

Join the IT Pro Community and get access to:

- Forums on networking, security, computing, and cutting-edge technologies
- Access to blogs written by industry experts

- Current information on cutting-edge technologies
- Access to various industry resource links and articles related to IT and IT careers

 **AUTHORIZED**

Content Seal of Quality

This courseware bears the seal of CompTIA Approved Quality Content. This seal signifies this content covers 100 percent of the exam objectives and implements important instructional design principles. CompTIA recommends multiple learning tools to help increase coverage of the learning objectives.

Why CompTIA?

- **Global recognition** CompTIA is recognized globally as the leading IT nonprofit trade association and has enormous credibility. Plus, CompTIA's certifications are vendor-neutral and offer proof of foundational knowledge that translates across technologies.
- **Valued by hiring managers** Hiring managers value CompTIA certification because it is vendor- and technology-independent validation of your technical skills.
- **Recommended or required by government and businesses** Many government organizations and corporations (for example, Dell, Sharp, Ricoh, the U.S. Department of Defense, and many more) either recommend or require technical staff to be CompTIA certified.
- **Three CompTIA certifications ranked in the top 10** In a study by DICE of 17,000 technology professionals, certifications helped command higher salaries at all experience levels.

How to Obtain More Information

- **Visit CompTIA online** Go to www.comptia.org to learn more about getting CompTIA certified.
- **Contact CompTIA** Please call 866-835-8020, ext. 5 or e-mail questions@comptia.org.
- **Join the IT Pro Community** Go to http://itpro.comptia.org to join the IT community to get relevant career information.
- **Connect with CompTIA** Find us on Facebook, LinkedIn, Twitter, and YouTube.

CAQC Disclaimer

Contents

Check-In

May I See Your Passport?

What do you mean, you don't have a passport? Why, it's sitting right in your hands, even as you read! This book is your passport to a very special place. You're about to begin a journey, my friend: a journey toward that magical place called certification! You don't need a ticket, you don't need a suitcase—just snuggle up and read this passport. It's all you need to get there. Are you ready? Well then, let's go!

Your Travel Agent: Mike Meyers

Hello! I'm Mike Meyers, president of Total Seminars and author of a number of popular certification books. On any given day, you'll find me stringing network cable, setting up a website, or writing code. I love every aspect of this book you hold in your hands. It's part of a powerful new book series called the Mike Meyers' Certification Passports. Every book in this series combines easy readability with a condensed format—in other words, the kind of book I always wanted when I went for my own certifications. Putting a large amount of information in an accessible format is certainly a challenge, but I think we've achieved our goal, and I'm confident you'll agree.

I designed this series to do one thing and only one thing: to get you the information you need to achieve your certification. You won't find any fluff in here. I packed every page with nothing but the real nitty-gritty of the Network+ Certification exam. Every page has 100 percent pure concentrate of certification knowledge! But I didn't forget to make the book readable, so I hope you also enjoy the casual, friendly style.

My personal e-mail address is mikem@totalsem.com. Please feel free to contact me directly if you have any questions, complaints, or compliments.

Your Destination: CompTIA Network+ Certification

This book is your passport to CompTIA's Network+ Certification, the vendor-neutral industry-standard certification for basic networking skills. CompTIA Network+ Certification can be your ticket to a career in all-around networking or simply an excellent step in your certification pathway. This book is your passport to success on the CompTIA Network+ Certification exam.

Why the Travel Theme?

The steps in gaining a certification parallel closely the steps in planning and taking a trip. All of the elements are the same: preparation, an itinerary, a route, even mishaps along the way. Let me show you how it all works.

This book is divided into 12 chapters. Each chapter begins with an *Itinerary* section, which lists the objectives covered in that chapter, and an *ETA* section to give you an idea of the time involved in learning the skills in that chapter. Each chapter is organized by the objectives, which are either drawn from those officially stated by the certifying body or reflect our expert take on the best way to approach the topics. Also, each chapter contains a number of helpful items to highlight points of interest:

Exam Tip

Points out critical topics you're likely to see on the actual exam.

Travel Assistance

Lists additional sources, such as books and websites, to give you more information.

Local Lingo

Describes special terms in detail in a way you can easily understand.

Travel Advisory

Warns you of common pitfalls, misconceptions, and downright physical peril!

The end of each chapter gives you two handy tools. The *Checkpoint* reviews each objective covered in the chapter with a handy synopsis—a great way to review quickly. End-of-chapter *Review Questions* (and answers) test your newly acquired skills.

But the fun doesn't stop there! After you've read the book, pull out the CD and take advantage of the free practice questions! Use the full practice exam to hone your skills, and keep the book handy to check your answers.

When you find yourself acing the practice questions, you're ready to take the exam. Go get certified!

The End of the Trail

The IT industry changes and grows constantly, *and so should you.* Finishing one certification is only one step in an ongoing process of gaining more and more certifications to match your constantly changing and growing skills. Read Appendix A, "Career Flight Path," at the end of the book, to find out where this certification fits into your personal certification goals. Remember, in the IT business, if you're not moving forward, you're way behind!

Good luck on your certification! Stay in touch!

Mike Meyers
Series Editor
Mike Meyers' Certification Passport

Network
Fundamentals

	NEWBIE	SOME EXPERIENCE	EXPERT
ETA	4 hours	2 hours	1 hour

1

When you link computers together to share files and communicate and do all the things we like to do, you create a *network*. Networks range in size from the smallest and simplest network—two computers connected together—to the largest and most complex network of all—the Internet.

This chapter begins with an overview of all the pieces that come together to make a computer network, including the hardware needed to make the physical connections. The chapter then dives into two network models techs use to discuss network components and functions.

Objective 1.01   Overview of How Networks Work

Networks come in many sizes and vary widely in the number of computers attached to them. Some people connect two computers in their house so that they can share files and play games together—the smallest network you can have. Compare this to companies that have thousands of employees in dozens of countries and need to network their computers together to get work done. Network folks put most networks into one of two categories: LANs and WANs. You'll find a few other groupings as well.

A *local area network (LAN)* covers a small area and contains a modest number of computers (Figure 1.1). LANs are usually in a single building or group of nearby buildings. Typical LANs include home and school networks.

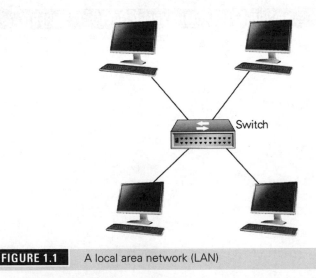

FIGURE 1.1   A local area network (LAN)

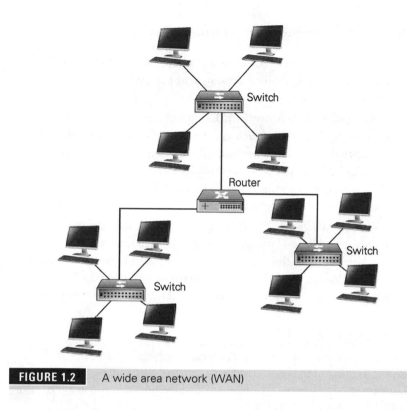

| FIGURE 1.2 | A wide area network (WAN) |

A *wide area network (WAN)* covers a large area and can have a substantial number of computers (Figure 1.2). Usually, a WAN is composed of two or more LANs connected together. All of the LANs in all of the schools in a city school district, for example, link together to form a WAN. Computers in a WAN usually connect through some type of public network, such as a telephone system, leased lines, or satellites. The largest WAN in existence is the *Internet*, which is a worldwide network that connects millions of computers and networks.

An *intranet*, in contrast, is essentially a private TCP/IP network that is a scaled-down version of the Internet for a very specific group of users. Just like the Internet, an intranet will offer various network services, such as websites, FTP access, Voice over IP, and so on. The key difference is that it's private rather than public.

Another similar term, *extranet*, is used to denote a private intranet that is also made accessible to a select group of outsiders using the Internet.

Here are a few other *x*ANs in use in various networks:

- A *campus area network (CAN)* is a group of interconnected LANs within a small geographical area, such as a school campus, university, hospital, or military base.

- A *metropolitan area network (MAN)* is a group of networks with a sociopolitical boundary, such as a network of district authority offices in a town or city. MANs can range in size from a few city blocks to entire cities. Sites on a MAN are usually interconnected using fiber-optic cable or some other high-speed digital circuit, and the MAN itself may carry voice as well as data traffic.

- A *global area network (GAN)* is a single network with connection points spread around the world. GANs are used mostly by large corporate organizations and consist of a series of networked, orbiting satellites. Note the subtle difference between a WAN and a GAN. The latter is a single network, not a number of interconnected networks.

Travel Advisory

The terms CAN and GAN don't exist as official standards, but their use and definitions have become generally accepted over time. A MAN is an official standard of the Institute of Electronics and Electrical Engineers (IEEE) as the IEEE 802.6 standard.

Servers and Clients

People use two types of devices in networks these days: servers and clients. In a nutshell, *servers* share things—such as files, folders, and printers—and *clients* request access to those shared things. Let's get one thing straight: Almost any personal computer can act as a server or a client or both! A lot of it has to do with how you set up the computer.

Computers running Windows, Macintosh, and the many varieties of Linux make up the vast majority of clients. You'll also find other devices that are clients, though, such as the following examples:

- Game consoles, like the Xbox 360
- Smartphones and tablets, such as the iPad
- DVRs, like TiVo and other set-top boxes

Server computers come in all shapes and sizes, but they serve—if you'll pardon the pun—a similar purpose. Servers manage *network resources* (like printers and

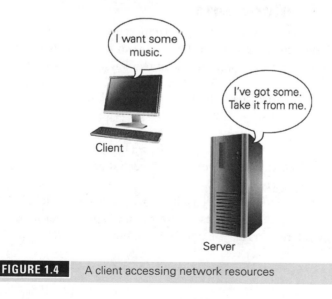

FIGURE 1.3   A server sharing network resources

e-mail—all the stuff that makes a network valuable), provide central storage of files, and provide services for users (such as the printer server telling the printer to print, or the e-mail server sending your e-mail). See Figure 1.3.

Client computers enable you to access the shared resources, programs, and services on server machines (Figure 1.4). Most users access servers via clients, although there's no law that says you can't access a server from another server machine. The latter machine, in that case, would be *acting* as a client regardless of the firepower of the box!

FIGURE 1.4   A client accessing network resources

Networks are traditionally classified into *client/server* and *peer-to-peer* *designations*, depending on the role played by each computer in the network. In a client/server network, one or more computer systems act as a server, while the remaining computers are clients that access resources from the server. On some home or small office networks, however, there may not be a separate server. Instead, every computer on the network acts as both a client and a server. Such networks are called peer-to-peer networks.

Exam Tip

The CompTIA Network+ exam uses the terms *client/server topology* and *peer-to-peer topology* to describe these two network arrangements. A *topology* more commonly refers to the way computers connect together rather than the roles they play on a network, but be prepared for the unusual use of the word on the exam. Chapter 3 covers the more commonly described network topologies.

Every operating system (OS) today can operate as a client, a server, or both, and many networks employ a mix. My network, for example, has a set of dedicated servers and each employee has one, two, or more computers in his or her office. Many of the office computers have shared folders, such as music or games, so they function as both clients and servers. This nice mishmash of machine roles creates a *hybrid* network.

Network Components

Whether you want to put together a LAN or connect a couple of LANs into a WAN, you need connectivity between the PCs and a way to handle communication. Computers connect to a network in one of two ways:

- Directly to a LAN via a cable from the computer to a LAN port
- Wirelessly to the LAN (this will be covered in Chapters 2 and 10)

A typical network client has a *network adapter* or *network interface card (NIC)* that connects to a cable that connects to a central network box, called a switch. Figure 1.5 shows a typical NIC.

Every NIC has a unique identifier called a *media access control (MAC) address*. I'll go into more detail on these addresses in Chapter 4. For now, just know that a MAC address acts like a name for a computer on a LAN.

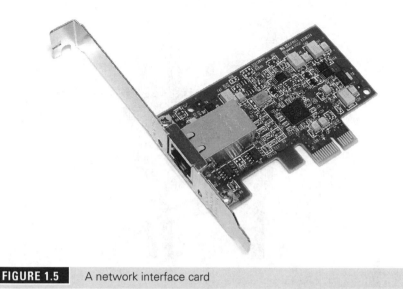

FIGURE 1.5   A network interface card

To make this into a nicely configured network, add another network client. Throw in a server. Don't add water, but turn on network sharing, and voilà! You have a network. Each machine attaches to a network cable that then connects at the other end to the switch. Any device attached to a network—client, server, printer, or whatnot—is called a *node*.

Ethernet

You might be wondering how you can tell what sort of cable to use for this network and how to determine the type of switch required for a network. Networking means communicating; the computers need to be able to speak the same language and follow the same technology.

The *Ethernet* standard defines everything about modern network hardware. Ethernet cables have standard connectors, for example, such as the *RJ-45 connectors* shown in Figure 1.6. Ethernet defines electrical signaling as well. That way, the sending NIC will break data down into little pieces and the receiving NIC will know exactly how to put them back together.

If two machines do not have the same kind of networking technology—a common problem in the early days of computer networks—then they can't network together. I won't bore you with a list of all the networking technologies that have had a brief moment of glory and market share in the past. Suffice it to say that today, Ethernet is king of the LAN.

FIGURE 1.6   RJ-45 connectors

Most modern Ethernet networks employ one of three technologies (and sometimes all three), *10BaseT, 100BaseT,* or *1000BaseT.* As the numbers in the names suggest, 10BaseT networks run at 10 Mbps, 100BaseT networks—called *Fast Ethernet*—run at 100 Mbps, and 1000BaseT networks—called *Gigabit Ethernet*—run at 1000 Mbps, or 1 Gbps.

Each Ethernet technology requires a specific kind of cabling that can handle its top speed. 100BaseT networks use Category 5 (CAT 5) or better Ethernet cables (Figure 1.7), while Gigabit Ethernet runs on Category 6 (CAT 6) or better Ethernet cables.

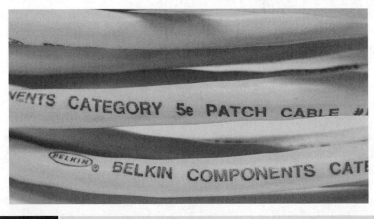

FIGURE 1.7   Category 5e (CAT 5e) cable

Hubs and Switches

Hubs and switches sit at the very center of networking, handling the tasks of receiving and sending packets of data to the connected computers. Each functions quite differently when it receives an Ethernet frame.

A *hub* repeats the frame down every network cable connected, hoping one of the computers connected is the recipient machine, such as Johan's laptop, for example (Figure 1.8).

A *switch,* in contrast, learns the network address of every machine connected to it, reads the recipient address on the frames, and sends them along only on the appropriate connection (Figure 1.9).

The radically more efficient switches now have completely replaced the earlier hubs in the marketplace.

Software

Of course it takes both hardware and software to make network communication work well. If Johan's computer requests an MP3 file from Michael's computer, Michael's operating system and other software take that MP3 file and break it into small, individually numbered units called *packets.* The NIC then takes the

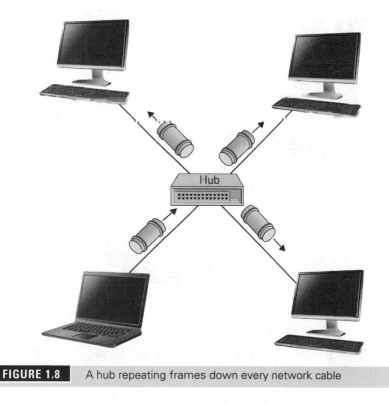

FIGURE 1.8   A hub repeating frames down every network cable

FIGURE 1.9   A switch sending frames only to the recipient

packets and, following the Ethernet standards, wraps up those packets into *network frames* that get sent out along the cable to the central network hub or switch (Figure 1.10).

All the machines on the network must use the same language—or *protocol*—for any sharing to happen. Over the years, various protocols have been developed, and you had to choose the protocol that worked best with a specific type of network or network needs. Today, that choice is easy because everybody uses

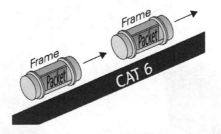

FIGURE 1.10   Packets wrapped in frames sent along an Ethernet CAT 6 cable

Transmission Control Protocol/Internet Protocol (TCP/IP), the language of the Internet. Chapter 5 covers TCP/IP in depth, so I won't go into the details here.

Applications

Finally, you need network-aware applications to accomplish things like accessing a shared file over a network. A commonly used network application is the web browser, such as Google Chrome, my personal favorite (Figure 1.11).

Connecting LANs

Enabling communication between two or more LANs requires several other pieces. First, you need a physical connection through cabling or radio waves. Second, you need special-purpose boxes to provide the intelligent direction so

FIGURE 1.11 Chrome web browser

that data can properly flow either within a LAN (switches) or between the LANs (*routers*). Finally, devices need an address that goes beyond the LAN and applies WAN-wide. Today, that address is an *IP address,* because everyone uses TCP/IP to communicate. Chapter 5 covers IP addresses.

Travel Advisory

All nodes on a TCP/IP network have two addresses. The MAC address is the physical address of a computer on a LAN. The IP address enables communication across routers and thus between LANs as well as within a LAN.

Objective 1.02 The OSI Seven-Layer Model

The *International Organization for Standardization (ISO)* created a framework into which the major network hardware and software components and protocols could be placed to give every item a common reference point. This framework, called the *Open Systems Interconnect (OSI) seven-layer model,* provides a means of relating the components and their functions to each other and a way of standardizing some of the components and protocols.

Travel Advisory

The letters used for the International Organization for Standardization—ISO—don't map to the initials in English, French, or Russian, the three official languages used by the body. Rumors abound that the word is derived from a Greek word that means equal, but those are just rumors.

The OSI model provides a critical common language that network hardware and software engineers can use to communicate and ensure that their equipment will function together. Each layer of the model represents a particular aspect of network function.

Exam Tip

The CompTIA Network+ exam expects you to know the layers by name (especially layers 1 through 4), how they function in relation to each other, and what they represent.

As well as helping to standardize the design elements of network components, the OSI model helps describe the relationships between network protocols. As you'll see, more than one protocol or action is needed to get your data onto a network.

The Layers and What They Represent

Let's run through the layers and an overview of their tasks and responsibilities. Figure 1.12 summarizes the layers and their functions.

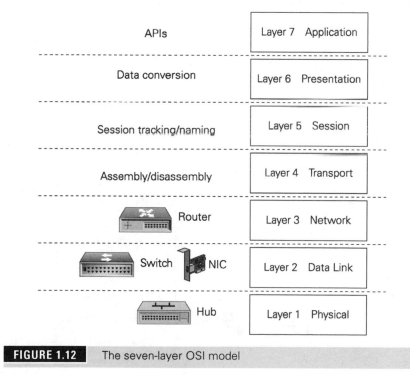

APIs	Layer 7 Application
Data conversion	Layer 6 Presentation
Session tracking/naming	Layer 5 Session
Assembly/disassembly	Layer 4 Transport
Router	Layer 3 Network
Switch NIC	Layer 2 Data Link
Hub	Layer 1 Physical

FIGURE 1.12   The seven-layer OSI model

Layer 1: Physical Layer

Layer 1 of the OSI model, the *Physical layer*, defines the network standards relating to the electrical signals that travel the network cables, the connectors, and the media types (cables) themselves. The Physical layer also determines the way that data is placed on the network media.

For the CompTIA Network+ exam, you need to know examples of components that run at each layer of the OSI. Examples of network components that are considered the Physical layer are cabling and hubs (Figure 1.13).

Layer 2: Data Link Layer

Layer 2, the *Data Link layer*, defines the rules for gathering and completing all the elements that make up a data frame and putting the whole thing together so that it can be passed to a Physical-layer device and on to the network. The exact components of the frame will vary depending on the data-link protocol being used, but would typically include the data being sent, an identifier for the sending machine, an identifier for the receiving machine, and an error-correction mechanism such as a frame check sequence (FCS).

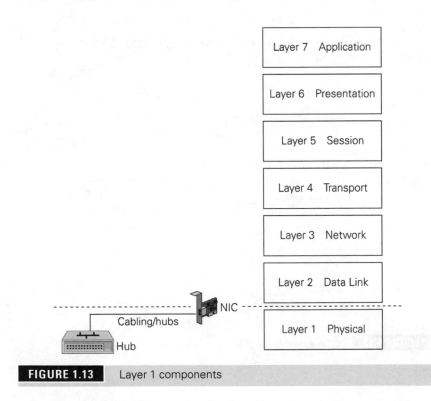

FIGURE 1.13   Layer 1 components

The Data Link layer on the sending machine assembles outgoing frames and calculates the FCS by applying a standard mathematical formula to the contents of the frame. The receiving machine performs the same calculation for incoming frames, enabling the receiving machine to verify the validity of the data by comparing its locally generated FCS value with that sent in the frame. If the values don't match, the frame is discarded and requested again.

The Data Link layer also determines how data is placed on the wire by using an access method. The wired access method is *carrier sense multiple access/ collision detection (CSMA/CD)*, used by all wired Ethernet networks.

The Data Link layer is divided into two sublayers:

- **Logical Link Control (LLC)** The LLC is the component layer responsible for error-correction and flow-control functions.
- **Media Access Control (MAC)** The MAC is responsible for addressing network devices by using the physical address—that's the MAC address that is burned into the ROM chip of each network card. This physical address is placed in the layer-2 header for the sending and receiving system.

Exam Tip

For the CompTIA Network+ exam, know that layer 2 is divided into two sublayers and is responsible for physical addressing. Any device, such as a switch, that works with a physical address runs at this layer.

Layer 3: Network Layer

Layer 3, the *Network layer*, is responsible for routing functions and logical addressing. The Network layer addresses identify not only a system, but also the network on which the system resides. The router uses this information to determine how to send data to the destination network. The IP address in a TCP/IP network is a layer-3 address; routers use this address to determine to which network and node to send a packet.

Exam Tip

Examples of layer-3 components are the IP protocol and a router. An IP address is considered a layer-3 address; a MAC address is a layer-2 address.

Layer 4: Transport Layer

If the data being sent is bigger than the packet size allowed by the lower-level protocols, layer 4, the *Transport layer,* breaks the data into smaller, manageable chunks that will fit inside two or more packets. Breaking up data into smaller chunks is known as *fragmentation.*

The Transport layer is also responsible for confirming whether transmitted packets have reached their destination intact and retransmitting them if they haven't. For incoming packets, the Transport layer reassembles the fragmented data, ensuring that received packets are processed in the right order.

Exam Tip

Examples of layer-4 protocols are Transmission Control Protocol (TCP) and User Data Protocol (UDP), which are part of the TCP/IP protocol suite.

Layer 5: Session Layer

Layer 5, the *Session layer,* is responsible for the session setup. The Session layer also manages and terminates the data connections (called *sessions*) between programs on networked devices. These sessions enable networked systems to exchange information.

Layer 6: Presentation Layer

Layer 6, the *Presentation layer,* is responsible for managing and translating the information into an understandable format that the Application layer can process further. In fact, many "Application-layer" protocols function at the Presentation layer too, taking datagrams and segments and turning them into formats programs can use.

Layer 7: Application Layer

Layer 7, the *Application layer,* represents the network-related program code and functions running on a computer system that either initiate the request (on the sending system) or service the request (on the receiving system).

Note that the Application layer does not refer to applications such as Microsoft Outlook. Instead, it refers to the protocols on which those programs rely. For example, Post Office Protocol 3 (POP3) and Simple Mail Transfer Protocol (SMTP) are important Application-layer protocols for e-mail, but many different end-user applications use those protocols (such as Outlook and Mozilla Thunderbird).

Using the Seven-Layer Model

The seven-layer model is only a theoretical representation of how networks function. Although knowing it inside-out won't change your life, it should help you pass the CompTIA Network+ exam. The conceptual use of the model assumes that an event on one computer system (for example, a user pressing ENTER on a login screen) creates some data that sets off a chain of events. The data runs down through the layers on the sending machine and then leaves the system, traveling across the network and then up through the layers on the receiving machine, until the data arrives intact at the Application layer and is processed by the receiving system. Later chapters in this book point out where certain key protocols and hardware fit into the model, and this can be useful stuff to know for both the CompTIA Network+ exam and real life.

Objective 1.03 The TCP/IP Model

The OSI model was developed as a reaction to a world of many different protocols made by different manufacturers that needed to play together. ISO created the OSI seven-layer model as the tool for manufacturers of networking equipment to find common ground between multiple protocols, enabling them to create standards for interoperability of networking software and hardware.

The adoption of TCP/IP as the sole protocol suite used in modern networks has rendered the OSI seven-layer model somewhat obsolete at the layers specific to TCP/IP. Many techs use a model specifically tailored to TCP/IP networks called, appropriately, the *TCP/IP model*.

Local Lingo

Internet model   A lot of techs and tech sites call the TCP/IP model the *Internet model*.

The TCP/IP model consists of four layers:

- Link/Network Interface
- Internet
- Transport
- Application

It's important to appreciate that the TCP/IP model doesn't have a standards body to define the layers. Because of this, there are a surprising number of variations on the TCP/IP model. Some even have it as five layers rather than four!

A great example of this lack of standardization is the Link layer. Without a standardizing body, we can't even agree on the name. While "Link layer" is extremely common, the term "Network Interface layer" is equally popular. A good tech knows both of these terms and understands that they are interchangeable. Notice also that, unlike the OSI model, the TCP/IP model does not identify each layer with a number.

CompTIA has chosen one popular version of the TCP/IP model for the CompTIA Network+ competencies and exam. That's the version you'll learn right here. It's concise, having only four layers, and many important companies, like Cisco and Microsoft, use it, although with a few variations in names as just described. The TCP/IP model gives each protocol in the TCP/IP protocol suite a clear home in one of the four layers.

The clarity of the TCP/IP model shows the flaws in the OSI model. The OSI model couldn't perfectly describe all the TCP/IP protocols. The TCP/IP model fixes this ambiguity, at least for TCP/IP.

The Link Layer

The TCP/IP model lumps together the OSI model's layer 1 and layer 2 into a single layer called the *Link layer* (or *Network Interface layer*).

A nice way to separate layers in the TCP/IP model is to think about packets and frames. Any part of the network that deals with complete frames is in the Link layer. The moment the frame information is stripped away from an IP packet, we move out of the Link layer and into the Internet layer.

Travel Advisory

At the Link layer, just about every network tech reverts back to the OSI model for troubleshooting. It's important to distinguish between problems happening at the Physical layer, with cabling, for example, and problems that reflect the Data Link layer, with switches and MAC addresses. That's why accomplished techs know both models!

The Internet Layer

The *Internet layer* should really be called the "IP packet" layer. Any device or protocol that deals with pure IP packets—getting an IP packet to its destination—sits in the Internet layer. IP addressing itself is also part of the Internet layer, as are routers and the magic they perform to get IP packets to the next router. IP packets are created at this layer.

The Transport Layer

The *Transport layer* combines features of the OSI Transport and Session layers with a dash of Application layer just for flavor. While the TCP/IP model is certainly involved with the assembly and disassembly of data, it also defines other functions, such as connection-oriented and connectionless communication.

Connection-oriented vs. Connectionless Communication

Some protocols, like the popular Post Office Protocol (POP) used for sending e-mail messages, require that the e-mail client and server verify that they have a good connection before a message is sent (Figure 1.14). This makes sense because you don't want your e-mail message to be a corrupted mess when it arrives.

Alternatively, a number of TCP/IP protocols simply send data without first waiting to verify that the receiving system is ready (Figure 1.15). When using Voice over IP (VoIP), for example, the call is made without verifying first whether another device is there.

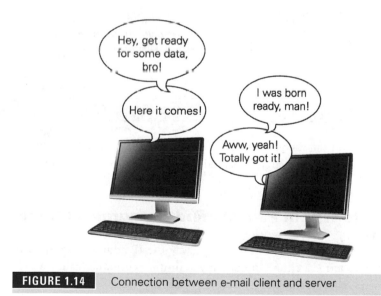

FIGURE 1.14　Connection between e-mail client and server

Here comes some data! Hope you're ready!

Connectionless communication

The connection-oriented protocol is called *Transmission Control Protocol (TCP)*. The connectionless protocol is called *User Datagram Protocol (UDP)*.

Travel Assistance

Chapter 5 covers TCP, UDP, and all sorts of other protocols in detail.

Everything you can do on the Internet, from web browsing to Skype phone calls to playing World of Warcraft, is predetermined to be either connection-oriented or connectionless.

Segments Within Packets and Datagrams Within Packets

To see the Transport layer in action, strip away the IP addresses from an IP packet. What's left is a chunk of data in yet another container called a *TCP segment* or a *UDP datagram*.

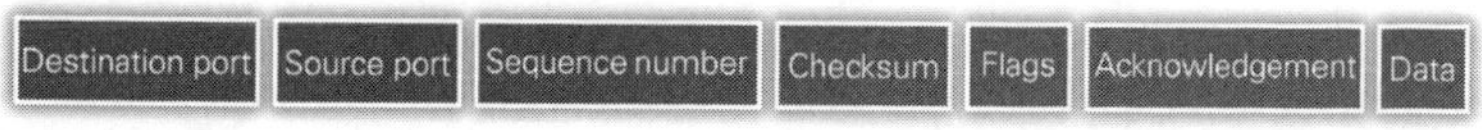

Destination port | Source port | Sequence number | Checksum | Flags | Acknowledgement | Data

FIGURE 1.16 TCP segment

TCP segments have many fields that ensure the data gets to its destination in good order. These fields have names such as Checksum, Flags, and Acknowledgement. Chapter 5 goes into more detail on TCP segments, but for now, just know that TCP segments have fields that ensure the connection-oriented communication works properly. Figure 1.16 shows a typical (although simplified) TCP segment.

Data comes from the Application-layer applications. The Transport layer breaks that data into chunks, adding port numbers and sequence numbers, creating the TCP segment. The Transport layer then hands the TCP segment to the Internet layer that, in turn, creates the IP packet, which encapsulates the segment.

UDP also gets data from the Application-layer programs and adds port and sequencing numbers to create a container called a *UDP datagram*. A UDP datagram lacks most of the extra fields found in TCP segments, simply because UDP doesn't care if the receiving computer gets its data. Figure 1.17 shows a UDP datagram.

Just like with TCP segments, when the Transport layer hands the UDP datagram to the Internet layer, it in turn creates the IP packet, which encapsulates the datagram.

The Application Layer

The TCP/IP *Application layer* combines features of the top three layers of the OSI model (Figure 1.18). Every application, especially connection-oriented applications, must know how to initiate, control, and disconnect from a remote system. No single method exists for doing this. Each TCP/IP application uses its own method.

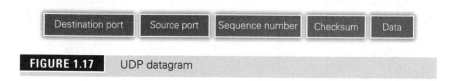

FIGURE 1.17 UDP datagram

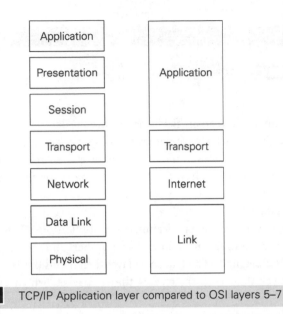

FIGURE 1.18   TCP/IP Application layer compared to OSI layers 5–7

TCP/IP uses a unique port-numbering system that gives each application a unique number between 1 and 65,535. Some of these port numbers are very well known. The protocol that makes webpages work, HTTP, uses port 80, for example.

Although we can say that the OSI model's Presentation layer fits inside the TCP/IP model's Application layer, no application requires any particular form of presentation as seen in the OSI model. Standard formats are part and parcel with TCP/IP protocols. For example, all e-mail messages use an extremely strict format called Multipurpose Internet Mail Extension (MIME). All e-mail servers and clients read MIME without exception.

In the OSI model, we describe the Application Programming Interface (API)—the smarts that make applications network aware—as being part of the Application layer. While this is still true for the TCP/IP model, all applications designed for TCP/IP are, by definition, network aware. There is no such thing as a "TCP/IP word processor" or a "TCP/IP image editor" that requires the added ability to know how to talk to a network—all TCP/IP applications can talk to the network, as long as they are part of a network. That's because they work directly with the APIs at the Application layer to send and receive data.

CHECKPOINT

✔**Objective 1.01: Overview of How Networks Work** The most obvious pieces of network hardware are the computers on the network. These are divided into client and server systems unless they are desktop systems that are sharing resources, in which case they are known as peer-to-peer systems. Corporate networks generally use dedicated servers because they offer higher performance, greater stability, and better security than peer-to-peer options. Your network won't be complete without some media—such as copper wiring, fiber optics, wireless, or infrared—to interconnect your systems, as well as a network interface card (NIC) to connect your system to the media. Other devices on the network—such as switches and routers—enable you to expand the system locally or to other sites.

✔**Objective 1.02: The OSI Seven-Layer Model** The OSI seven-layer model describes how data flows from one networked system to another—it's a theoretical model into which many of the standards, components, and functions of a network fit. The model promotes the use of recognized network standards and helps ensure compatibility between network hardware and software from different manufacturers.

✔**Objective 1.03: The TCP/IP Model** The TCP/IP model describes how data flows from one networked system to another, specifically for TCP/IP networks. Every TCP/IP protocol and application fits into one of the four layers in the model, making the TCP/IP model ideal for troubleshooting modern networks.

REVIEW QUESTIONS

1. What name is given to a network in which computers act as both clients and servers?

    A. A multitasking network

    B. A mainframe network

    C. A peer-to-peer network

    D. A LAN network

2. What standard defines the hardware technology of modern LANs?

   A. ARPANET

   B. Ethernet

   C. OSI

   D. TCP/IP

3. Which device is being used if frames are repeated down every attached Ethernet cable?

   A. Modem

   B. Switch

   C. Frame

   D. Hub

4. What device enables LANs to connect and direct packets to the correct LAN?

   A. Hub

   B. Frame

   C. Router

   D. Switch

5. A protocol operating at which layer of the OSI model is responsible for logical addressing and routing?

   A. Transport

   B. Network

   C. Session

   D. Application

6. A protocol operating at which layer of the OSI model handles the formatting of data so upper or lower layers can work with them further?

   A. Application

   B. Presentation

   C. Session

   D. Transport

7. Layer 3 is the _____ layer of the OSI model.

   A. Session

   B. Application

   C. Data Link

   D. Network

8. At which layer of the TCP/IP model are UDP datagrams created?

   A. Link/Network Interface

   B. Internet

   C. Transport

   D. Application

9. Which type of communication requires the client and server to acknowledge the transmission?

   A. ACK request

   B. Connectionless

   C. Connection-oriented

   D. Session

10. At which layer of the TCP/IP model do cables fit?

    A. Link/Network Interface

    B. Internet

    C. Transport

    D. Application

REVIEW ANSWERS

1. **C** A network with computers acting as both clients and servers is a peer-to-peer network.

2. **B** Ethernet is the standard.

3. **D** A hub repeats frames down every attached network cable.

4. **C** A router connects LANs and directs packets to the correct LAN.

5. **B** A protocol operating at the Network layer provides addressing and routing functions.

6. **B** A protocol operating at the Presentation layer handles the formatting of data (among other functions).

7. **D** Layer 3 of the OSI model is the Network layer.

8. **C** Data is divided into chunks at the Transport layer and then bundled into UDP datagrams or TCP segments, depending on which protocol is used.

9. **C** Connection-oriented communication requires the client and server to acknowledge the transmission.

10. **A** Cabling is in the Link/Network Interface layer of the TCP/IP model.

Network Media

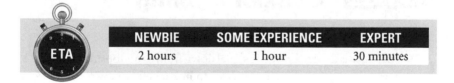

	NEWBIE	SOME EXPERIENCE	EXPERT
ETA	2 hours	1 hour	30 minutes

Techs use the term network *media* rather than *cabling* because some parts of a network's data highway can be made up of materials other than physical cable. A laser or microwave link might connect local area networks (LANs) in two buildings, for example, or a wireless device might connect laptops to your main network. Inside the building, you'll find connectors, adapters, wall ports, and other such parts.

Local Lingo

bounded media   Physical network cabling (copper and fiber).
unbounded media   Microwave, wireless, infrared, and satellite network links.

As you might imagine, a number of different network media types are available. Some are faster than others, some will work over relatively long distances, and some don't require a physical connection to the main network. This chapter covers all the major media types and their characteristics, uses, and key features.

Exam Tip

Network media and connectors and the electrical signals traveling over them are represented by standards at layer 1 (the Physical layer) of the OSI seven-layer model.

Objective 2.01   Coaxial Cabling

Coaxial cable is used to bring the signal down from a rooftop antenna to a TV set or radio receiver—or, in this case, to link together networked devices. "Coax" is the granddaddy of all mainstream network media types and is very much associated with the original designs of the popular Ethernet networking standard, developed in 1973, although today you'll only see it used with broadband Internet solutions.

Travel Advisory

Baseband vs. Broadband The coaxial cable used in early Ethernet networks carried only a single digital signal, thus *baseband.* The coaxial cable used for cable Internet and television, in contrast, carries many analog signals at once, thus *broadband.*

Coaxial cable has a central conducting core surrounded by a protective, insulating layer; an outer metal screen made of a woven copper mesh; a metal-covered plastic or foil (or both); and an overall insulating jacket (see Figure 2.1). The metal screen helps shield the data traveling down the central core from being corrupted by external signals, such as radio waves, and other sources of electromagnetic interference (EMI), such as high-current power cables, mobile phones, electric motors, fluorescent tubes, and local electrical storms. The screen also reduces the amount of data signals that can radiate from the cable to become another source of EMI and thus cause problems for other data cables and systems. The cable is referred to as *coaxial* (or simply *coax*) because both the center wire and the braided metal shield share a common axis, or centerline.

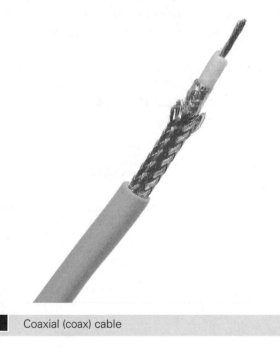

FIGURE 2.1 Coaxial (coax) cable

Coax is considered old technology and isn't used these days for new LANs, except for in fairly specialized settings such as elevator shafts. Coax will crop up when connecting a LAN to an Internet connection provided by your local cable company, as high-speed Internet through the cable lines has become a popular broadband solution.

> **Exam Tip**
>
> Coax is often preferred when connections need to run through elevator shafts because it's resistant to radio noise and is much cheaper than fiber (discussed later in this chapter.)

Coaxial Cable Types

A mind-boggling number of different types of coax are available, each one suitable for a specific purpose, such as audio, video, TV, satellite, cable, radio, and data. Each coax type has its own characteristics, closely matched to the type of signal that cable is designed to carry. These coax types are called *radio-grade (RG)*. Table 2.1 shows the RG baseband coax types used for data networking.

The nominal impedance, a measure of the wire's resistance that shows how much the cable impedes or resists the flow of electric current, is one of the factors that determines the RG type. As you can see, the nominal impedance of cable TV coax is different from that of Ethernet coax. This difference is the main reason why the cable types should not be used in conjunction with the wrong technology. The differences between Thick and Thin Ethernet are explained in the next chapter.

TABLE 2.1	Coax Cable Types for Networking		
Network Type	**Coax Type**	**Maximum Distance**	**Nominal Impedance**
Thin Ethernet baseband	RG-58	185 meters	50 ohms
Thick Ethernet baseband	RG-8 or RG-11	500 meters	50 ohms
Cable TV broadband	RG-6	Variable	75 ohms

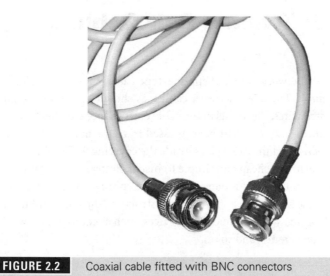

FIGURE 2.2 Coaxial cable fitted with BNC connectors

Coaxial Connectors

Coaxial cables have used many types of connectors over the years. Ancient Ethernet networks used a thin cable with a bayonet-style connector called a *BNC connector* (Figure 2.2).

The BNC refers to both the connection mechanism and the creators—Bayonet Neill-Concelman. You'll still find these connectors, but only as potential answers on CompTIA Network+ exams. Modern coaxial cables use screw-on *F connectors* (Figure 2.3)

FIGURE 2.3 Coaxial cable with the common F connectors

Objective 2.02   Twisted-Pair Cabling

Many modern networks use a telephone-type cable known as *unshielded twisted-pair (UTP)*. UTP network cables, as shown in Figure 2.4, have four pairs of twisted wires. The twists in the cable pairs reduce crosstalk and also act as a partial shield. As you might have guessed from the name, UTP has no overall metal screen—just the cable pairs inside the covering. UTP cable is popular because it is relatively cheap and simple to install. Better still, the same wiring infrastructure can be used for data and voice/telephony. That means when you install UTP cable as part of a building's infrastructure, the same cabling system can be used for many of the building's services, such as computer networks, security systems, telephones, and so on.

Local Lingo

crosstalk   An unwanted interaction, or interference, between two electrical signals.

Although UTP cable provides a low-cost solution, it supports some fairly high-tech, high-spec, high-price kits to create very sophisticated, high-performance networks.

Shielded twisted-pair (STP) cable has a screen covering the wire pairs and a ground wire running the length of the cable. STP is intended for use in electrically noisy environments. In most cases, routing network cabling away from interference is cheaper than installing shielded cabling.

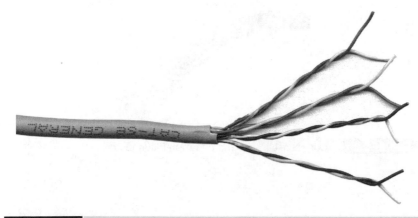

FIGURE 2.4   Four-pair UTP cable

UTP Cable Types

UTP comes in a variety of grades, called *categories,* numbered Category 1 through Category 6a, as summarized in Table 2.2. These categories define the maximum supported data speed of the cable, and they have been developed over the years to cater to faster and faster network designs.

It might have caught your eye in Table 2.2 that UTP cable is used for Ethernet networks, but a few paragraphs ago, you learned about Ethernet and *coax* cable. Well, UTP is the way forward, and Ethernet was one of the first networking standards to be reengineered to work on this media type. In addition, most new cabling installations will use Category 6 (CAT 6) or Category 6a cabling because they support all current (and planned) data speeds and standards. The category level of a piece of cable will normally be written on the cable itself, as shown in Figure 2.4, or on the box, as shown in Figure 2.5.

All cable accessories, such as the wall- or pillar-mounted data ports, must also match the category of the cable being used. Mixing CAT 5 cable with CAT 3 wall sockets, for example, could cause that part of the network (known as a *segment*) not to work properly. The post-installation network testing should pick up this type of mismatch, but it is better to get things right the first time rather than find out later you need to replace all your data outlets!

Exam Tip

For the exam, be sure to know the UTP category cable types and their associated transfer rates.

TABLE 2.2	UTP Cable Categories

Category	Maximum Rated Speed	Typical Use
Category 1	1 Mbps	Voice only—regular analog phone lines; not used for data communications
Category 3	10 Mbps	Ethernet over UTP at 10 Mbps (10BaseT)
Category 5	100 Mbps	Ethernet over UTP at 100 Mbps (100BaseT)
Category 5e	1 Gbps (1000 Mbps)	Ethernet over UTP at 1000 Mbps (1000BaseT)
Category 6	10 Gbps	10 Gigabit Ethernet (10GbE)
Category 6a	10 Gbps	10 Gigabit Ethernet (10GbE)

FIGURE 2.5 Category 5e UTP cabling

Variations in Core Wires and Sheath Materials

UTP varies in both the construction of the internal copper cores and in the material of the protective sheath on the outside of the cable. You need to use the proper variety of cable in a specific area of a building.

Most UTP cables have core strands that are single copper wires. These are called *solid-core* cables. A typical eight-wire UTP cable would have eight copper wires inside a protective sheath. You would most definitely want the strength of solid-core cables when pulling cable through building walls or between floors.

In specific spaces where cables need to make a lot of tight turns, you would use a type of UTP with the conductive core of each wire made from fine strands of copper. This type of cable is called *stranded-core* or just *stranded*. Many folks use stranded cables to connect computers to wall plates. (See also "Patch Panel" later in this chapter for the most common use of stranded cabling.) Figure 2.6 shows solid- and stranded-core cables.

The sheaths on UTP cabling come in two varieties, called riser and plenum. *Riser cable* typically has a sturdy sheath made of polyvinyl chloride (PVC) that's great for protecting the internal wires, but bad if it burns. The PVC gives off toxic fumes. You use riser cable in spaces in buildings where there's not a lot of air flow, such as trunking shafts between floors. The typical computer-to-wall plate cable is riser grade.

FIGURE 2.6   Solid- and stranded-core UTP cables

Other spaces in buildings, such as between a drop ceiling and the true ceiling, are designed to facilitate air flow. That's where air conditioning and heating returns typically run. This space is called the plenum. The sheath on *plenum cable* is made of some low-fume material, such as a fluorinated ethylene polymer (FEP), to reduce the risk of smoking out the people in the event of a fire. The sheath is often reinforced as well to facilitate pulling across long stretches. The box pictured in Figure 2.5 has "Riser" clearly marked.

Local Lingo
plenum   A fancy name for the gap between the real ceiling (or the bottom of the next floor up, if you want) and the suspended tiles.

UTP Connectors

UTP network cabling uses an eight-pin contact connector type known as an *RJ45*, as shown in Figure 2.7 (the RJ stands for *registered jack*). While network cables use an eight-pin connector, note that the telephone cable uses a four-pin connector known as the RJ11 connector.

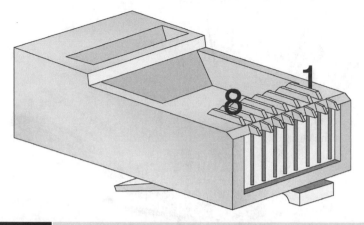

FIGURE 2.7   An RJ45 connector

Local Lingo

8P8C   Technically, the term RJ45 defines the wiring scheme and the mechanical interface of the plug. What almost every tech in the world calls an RJ45 is officially known as an 8P8C connector, for eight positions and eight contacts. So now you know.

Many UTP networking standards use only two of the four UTP cable pairs, but the best practice is always to connect all four pairs at every network connector for compatibility with other, and future, standards. That way, the wiring does not have to change when you switch to a newer networking standard that uses all four pairs of wires, such as Gigabit Ethernet.

Travel Assistance

Chapter 3 gives you the scoop on the various Ethernet standards.

UTP Wiring Standards

It probably won't come as a surprise to know that UTP connectors and wiring have associated color codes and wiring schemes. Each wire inside a UTP cable must connect to the proper pin on the connector at each end of the cable. The wires are color coded to assist in properly matching the ends; each pair of wires has a solid-colored wire and a striped wire: blue/blue-white, orange/orange-white, brown/brown-white, and green/green-white. Industry organizations, such as the Telecommunications Industry Association (TIA) and the Electronic Industries Alliance (EIA), have developed a variety of standard color codes to facilitate installation.

T568A and T568B Wiring Standards

Two major wiring standards, *T568A* and *T568B*, determine the order of the wires placed in the RJ45 connector. Using an established color-code scheme ensures that the wires match up correctly at each end of the cable. This consistency makes troubleshooting and repair easier.

Local Lingo

TIA/EIA   Most techs refer to the two popular wiring standards either without the preceding letter, such as 568B, or with the full initials of the two groups who created the standards, such as TIA/EIA568A. The CompTIA Network+ competencies use the form in this book, with just the T.

The T568A wiring standard has the wires in the order white/green, green, white/orange, blue, white/blue, orange, white/brown, and finally brown. The most common wiring standard in use today is known as the T568B standard and has the wires in the order shown in Figure 2.8.

Straight-through and Crossover Cables

When crimping a UTP cable, you can create two types of cables—a straight-through cable or a crossover cable. The typical *straight-through cable* for CAT 5/5e, for example, uses only four wires—wires 1, 2, 3, and 6. With a straight-through cable, pin 1 of the RJ45 connector on one end follows the wire to pin 1 on the other end, and as a result, pin 1 on both ends of the wire are connected.

This straight-through cable works great when connecting a workstation to a switch because the network card on the computer uses pins 1 and 2 as the

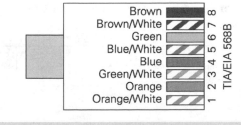

Brown	8	
Brown/White	7	
Green	6	
Blue/White	5	TIA/EIA 568B
Blue	4	
Green/White	3	
Orange	2	
Orange/White	1	

FIGURE 2.8   The T568B wiring standard

transmit pins, while pins 3 and 6 are the receive pins. On the switch, pins 1 and 2 are the receive pins, while pins 3 and 6 are the transmit pins. When using the straight-through cable, the transmit pins of the workstation will connect to the receive pins on the switch (via the straight-through cable), allowing data to be sent. Likewise, the receive pins on the workstation are connected to the transmit pins on the switch via the straight-through cable, allowing the workstation to receive data.

If you try to connect two computers directly (NIC-to-NIC) with a straight-through cable, the systems will not be able to communicate because the transmit pins (pins 1 and 2) on one system will be connected to the transmit pins on the second system, so neither system can receive data.

The transmit pins have to be connected to the receive pins at the other end, which is what the crossover cable creates. With a *crossover cable*, wires 1 and 2 (transmit) from one end of the cable are switched to the receive wire placeholders (wires 3 and 6) at the other end of the cable (shown in Figure 2.9).

When you use a crossover cable to connect two computers directly, the crossover cable will connect the transmit pins on one computer to the receive pins on the second computer using wires 1 and 2 in the cable.

Exam Tip

For the exam, know the order of wires in the T568A and T568B standards and also know which wires are switched in a crossover cable.

Rollover and Loopback

In the networking world, you will come across a number of other cable types, including rollover cables and loopback cables.

- **Rollover cable** Also known as the console cable, it's used to connect the administrator's system to the console port of a Cisco router or switch. The administrator connects the console cable to his or her

T568B   T568A

FIGURE 2.9 A crossover cable connecting two computers

Universal Serial Bus (USB) port through an adapter and then to the console port of the switch or router to administer the device and change its configuration. They call this a *rollover* cable because the wires are rolled over from one end to the other—wire 1 on one end becomes wire 8 on the other end.

- **Loopback cable** This special cable is used for self-diagnostics and typically has the wires connecting the transmit pins to the receive pins on the same system, keeping the communication local. This cable type is used only as a testing tool and is not used for network communication.

Wiring Distribution

This section outlines different cabling components and terms you will need to know for the CompTIA Network+ exam, including the patch panel and wiring distribution.

Patch Panel

Most companies have network jacks located in the walls that allow systems to connect to the network. The network jacks are connected to cables that are routed a long distance to a *patch panel* in a server room (Figure 2.10).

The patch panel has a *patch cable* that connects to the front of the patch panel and a port on a switch. When a computer connects to the network jack in the wall, the patch cable is used to map that system to the port on the switch. The concept of the patch panel allows ease of administration and flexibility in moving systems from one switch to another without visiting the workstation.

Exam Tip
Cables are typically connected from the wall jack to the patch panel by a punch-down tool. A couple of standards deal with wiring patch panels: 66 block is used for wiring the telephone system, while 110 block is used to wire the patch panel for CAT 5/6 UTP cable.

Cross-connects, MDF, and IDF

Connections from the outside world—whether network or telephone—come into a building at a location called a *demarc*, short for *demarcation point*. Demarc refers to the physical location of the connection and marks the dividing line of responsibility for the functioning of the network. You take care of the internal functioning; the person or company that supplies the upstream service to you must support connectivity and function on the far side of the demarc.

FIGURE 2.10   Typical patch panel in server room

In a private home, the digital subscriber line (DSL) or cable modem supplied by your Internet service provider (ISP) is a *network interface unit (NIU)* that serves as a demarc between your home network and your ISP (Figure 2.11). Most homes have a network interface box in addition that provides the connection for your telephone.

In an office environment, the demarc is usually more complex, given that a typical building simply has to serve a much larger number of telephones and computers. Figure 2.12 shows the demarc for a midsized building, showing both Internet and telephone connections coming in from the outside.

One challenge to companies that supply ISP/telephone services is the need to diagnose faults in the system. Most of today's NIUs come with extra "smarts" that enable the ISP or telephone company to determine if the customer has disconnected from the NIU. These special (and very common) NIUs are known as

FIGURE 2.11   Typical home network interface box

smart jacks. Smart jacks also have the very handy capability to set up a remote loopback—critical for loopback testing when you're at one end of the connection and the other connection is blocks or even miles away.

After the demarc, network and telephone cables connect to some type of box, owned by the customer, that acts as the primary distribution tool for the building. Any cabling that runs from the NIU to whatever box being used by the customer is the *demarc extension.* For telephones, the cabling might connect to a special box called a *multiplexer* and, on the LAN side, almost certainly to a powerful switch. This switch usually connects to a patch panel. This patch panel, in turn, leads to every telecommunications room in the building. This main patch panel is called a *vertical cross-connect.*

The combination of demarc, telephone cross-connects, and LAN cross-connects needs a place to live in a building. The room that stores all of this equipment is known as a *main distribution frame (MDF)* to distinguish it from the multiple *intermediate distribution frame (IDF)* rooms (aka telecommunications rooms)

FIGURE 2.12   Typical office demarc

that serve individual floors. Workstations connect to the patch panels at the IDFs through cabling runs called *horizontal cabling*. The patch panel where the horizontal cabling connects is called a *horizontal cross-connect (HCC)*. The IDFs connect to the MDF with cables called *vertical cross-connect (VCC)* cables.

Typically, the MDF connects to the cable coming from outside the building. Then a separate IDF panel may be used to represent each floor in the building, with the workstations on a particular floor connecting to the panel associated with that floor.

UTP Testing

Because UTP cable doesn't have shielding, it is much more susceptible to EMI and crosstalk than coax cabling. As a result of this vulnerability, the installation of UTP cabling must meet specific requirements. Just like coax, for example, UTP should not be routed near light fixtures in the plenum, run parallel to heavy power cables, or get run over and squashed on a regular basis by your office chair! With UTP cables, the way the wires are attached to the wall plates and the number of sharp bends in a horizontal run can adversely affect performance.

Professional installers will test every single run (segment) of UTP cabling to satisfy themselves, and their customers, that the job has been done right using a special testing kit that measures the overall length of each segment, checks various electrical characteristics, and detects possible crosstalk (with fancy names such as "near-end crosstalk" and "far-end crosstalk") between the wire pairs. Cable segments that fail to meet the required specs may not work properly at the intended (or future) data speeds and may have to be rejoined to the wall plates or, a worse case, be rerouted or replaced. Once everything has been sorted out, the printed test results are often presented to the customer as part of the network installation completion sign-off process.

> ### Exam Tip
>
> Two types of crosstalk are near-end crosstalk (NEXT) and far-end crosstalk (FEXT). NEXT occurs when a signal causes interference with a signal on an adjacent wire heading in the same direction, while FEXT occurs when a signal causes interference on an adjacent signal heading in the opposite direction.

Objective 2.03 **Optical Fiber**

Optical fiber is relatively expensive to purchase and install because it requires specialized handling and connection techniques. For this reason alone, fiber is not usually installed for desktop network connections unless a special need exists, such as locations with high levels of electromagnetic interference. In general, fiber will be used where one or more of the following apply:

- Long distances need to be covered, up to the maximum segment distance of 40 km.
- A link is needed between buildings, and other options, such as microwave and laser, are impractical (no line of sight, for example), too expensive, or electrically unworkable.
- High speeds are required (initially, 1000 Mbps Ethernet required fiber-optic cabling, but "Gigabit over copper" is readily available today).
- Security is a concern. Optical fibers don't radiate signals that can be picked up by listening equipment, and it is difficult to tap a fiber without being detected.
- The general environment is electrically unfriendly to data—that is, full of EMI, such as in a factory or in a radio/TV/radar transmitter room.
- Any potential for an electrical spark must be eliminated, such as in a laboratory using flammable gases and other volatile chemicals.

Data can be sent down an optical fiber cable as either infrared or laser light, according to the system in use and the maximum distances involved. Each type of system requires a specific type of media; infrared LED systems use *multimode fiber (MMF)*, whereas laser-diode-based systems (mainly used for high-speed, long-haul data and telecom links) use *single-mode fiber (SMF)* cable.

Travel Advisory

Infrared and laser diode light sources can cause eye damage if you stare at them directly, so never look down a fiber cable to see if it's working. Professional testing kits use optical sensors and/or cameras. If you don't have the proper equipment available, test for faults by replacing suspect fiber leads with known good ones.

An optical fiber cable has three components: the fiber itself; the cladding, which actually makes the light reflect down the fiber; and the insulating jacket. Fiber cabling is specified by its mode of operation and a two-number designator representing the core and cladding diameter in microns (μm, or millionths of a meter). The most common size used for general networking is multimode 62.5/ 125 μm, which can be used for cable runs of up to 275 meters. Almost all fiber networking standards require two fibers, and a pair is often connected together as duplex optical fiber cabling (Figure 2.13). Longer cable runs are possible with

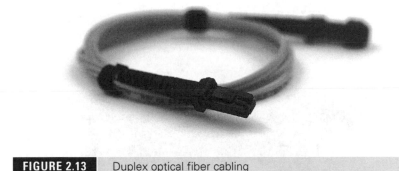

FIGURE 2.13 Duplex optical fiber cabling

other types of fiber-optic cabling (up to 80 km as of this writing, though not through an IEEE 802.3 standard).

As alluded to earlier, two types of fiber-optic cables are available:

- **Single-mode fiber** Uses a single ray of light, known as a mode, to carry the transmission over long distances (over 40+ km).

- **Multimode fiber** Uses multiple rays of light (modes) simultaneously, with each ray of light running at a different reflection angle to carry the transmission over short distances (under 2 km). MMF is cheaper than SMF and is typically used within the building due to the short distances that are required.

Exam Tip

Remember that SMF is used to reach long distances while MMF transmits over shorter distances.

Optical Fiber Connectors

Because they are optical rather than electrical, fiber cables have their own series of connector types. You cannot, for example, whack a BNC connector onto a piece of fiber (well, you probably *could*, but it won't impress anyone!).

The two most common types of fiber-optic connectors are the *ST* (stick and twist) and *SC* (stick and click) types (see Figure 2.14). ST connectors *do* look a bit BNC-ish, but be careful, because unlike a BNC connector, which can be impaled on its socket and twisted with total abandon until the locking guides engage with the fixing lugs, ST connectors have a keying mechanism to stop just this kind of youthful exuberance. If you do get carried away, you can snap the ceramic connector body—so easy does it!

FIGURE 2.14 ST and SC fiber connectors

You'll also find other fiber connectors, such as the fiber *local connector (LC)* and *mechanical-transfer registered jack (MT-RJ)*. These connectors are similar to other connector types, such as the RJ and fiber SC shape. The fiber LC is the preferred connector of the two for communications exceeding 1 Gbps due to its small form factor.

Uses for Fiber

Although science programs often delight in telling you how many times a second the entire works of Shakespeare can be transmitted down a single fiber across a transatlantic phone link, that's not the primary use for fiber cable. Most of the fiber you are likely to encounter provides interlocation links on Ethernet-based networks. Table 2.3 gives descriptions and speeds for some of the fiber-optic standards.

TABLE 2.3	Common Fiber-optic Cabling Standards			

Standard	Cabling	Cable Details	Connectors	Length
1000BaseSX	Multimode fiber	850 nm	Variable, commonly LC	220–500 m
1000BaseLX	Single-mode fiber	1300 nm	Variable, commonly LC and SC	5 km
10GBaseSR	Multimode	850 nm	LAN	26–300 m
10GBaseSW	Multimode	850 nm	SONET/WAN	26–300 m
10GBaseLR	Single-mode	1310 nm	LAN	10 km
10GBaseLW	Single-mode	1310 nm	SONET/WAN	10 km
10GBaseER	Single-mode	1550 nm	LAN	40 km
10GBaseEW	Single-mode	1550 nm	SONET/WAN	40 km

Implementing Multiple Types of Ethernet

Because Ethernet packets don't vary among the many flavors of Ethernet, network hardware manufacturers have long built devices capable of supporting more than one flavor right out of the box. Ancient hubs supported 10Base2 and 10BaseT at the same time, for example.

You can also use dedicated *media converters* to connect any type of Ethernet cabling together. Most media converters are plain-looking boxes with a port or dongle on either side. They come in all flavors:

- Single-mode fiber (SMF) to UTP/STP
- Multimode fiber (MMF) to UTP/STP
- Fiber to coaxial
- SMF to MMF

Exam Tip

The CompTIA Network+ exam competencies erroneously describe some media converters as single-mode fiber to *Ethernet* and multimode fiber to *Ethernet*. It's all Ethernet! Don't be surprised if you get one of those terms on the exam, however. Now you'll know what they mean.

The Gigabit Ethernet folks created a standard for modular ports called a *gigabit interface converter (GBIC)*. With many Gigabit Ethernet switches and other hardware, you can simply pull out a GBIC module that supports one flavor of Gigabit Ethernet and plug in another. You can replace an RJ-45 port GBIC, for example, with an SC GBIC, and it'll work just fine. Electronically, the switch or other gigabit device is just that—Gigabit Ethernet—so the physical connections don't matter. Ingenious!

The *small form-factor pluggable (SFP)*—also known as a *mini-GBIC*—and the *SFP*+ transceivers work in a similar fashion as GBICs and include connectors for the 10 Gigabit standards, among others. SFPs are smaller than GBICs so manufacturers can pack more slots onto a networking device, and they're backed by many different manufacturers.

Objective 2.04 Wireless Media Types

There have been multiple wired and wireless ways to connect computers into networks over the years, and more continue to be created all the time. The vast majority of networks use UTP cabling, with fiber to interconnect LANs and wide area networks (WANs). The CompTIA Network+ exam even expects you to know that you can link two computers together directly using a cable that plugs into a serial port with its DB-9 or RS-232 connector, something we haven't used for decades because the serial connection supports only 150 KB per second transfer rates.

Wireless connections began rolling out a few years ago and arguably are the hottest growth area in networking. This final section looks at 802.11-based networks, Bluetooth, lasers, and infrared technologies.

802.11 Wireless Networks

The Institute of Electrical and Electronics Engineers (IEEE) 802.11 committee supports four standards for wireless networking: 802.11a, 802.11b, 802.11g, and 802.11n. Each of these wireless standards uses radio links to provide network connectivity to PCs and laptop computers through a transmitter/receiver unit (transceiver), generally known as an *access point (AP)* or *wireless access point (WAP)*, which transmits and receives signals to and from the wireless network adapters (Figure 2.15). By installing a number of strategically placed transceivers, coverage over a wide area of floor space can be achieved.

FIGURE 2.15   Wireless network equipment for the office

Wireless Basics

Before we get into the wireless networking details, let's take a look at the different methods to carry radio frequency (RF) traffic that are used on a wireless network:

- **Direct Sequence Spread Spectrum (DSSS)**   DSSS is a modulation technique that transfers data using the full bandwidth of a frequency. 802.11b wireless networks use DSSS. (More on the 802.11 standards in a bit.)

- **Frequency Hopping Spread Spectrum (FHSS)**   As the name implies, with frequency hopping, FHSS transmits radio signals by switching frequencies at a high rate. The benefit of FHSS is that it is harder for someone to tap into the data as the frequency continues to change.

- **Orthogonal Frequency-Division Multiplexing (OFDM)**   With OFDM, the data is delivered by being spread across multiple parallel channels. This helps overcome some of the inherent problems in Wi-Fi networking, such as signal bounce. 802.11g and 802.11n wireless networks use OFDM transmission.

> **Travel Advisory**
>
> See Chapter 10 for a discussion of bounce problems.

802.11 networks can operate in one of two modes: ad hoc or infrastructure. In an *ad hoc mode* network, the wireless nodes communicate directly with each other; you don't need a WAP for two hosts to communicate. Although this might be handy for transferring files between two laptops in the train station, ad hoc 802.11 networking doesn't help you connect to your corporate network or the Internet.

To connect to an existing wired network, you need to use *infrastructure mode,* which uses a WAP device. The WAP is connected to the wired network and sends data between the wireless clients and systems on the wired network.

A single WAP servicing a given area is called a *Basic Service Set (BSS)*. This service area can be extended by adding more access points. This is called, appropriately, an *Extended Service Set (ESS)*.

BSSID, SSID, and ESSID

Wireless devices connected together into a network, whether ad hoc or infrastructure, require some way to identify that network. Frames bound for computers within the network need to go where they're supposed to go, even when you have more than one Wi-Fi network overlapping. The jargon gets a little crazy here, especially because marketing has come into the mix.

The *Basic Service Set Identifier (BSSID)* defines the most basic infrastructure mode network—a BSS of one WAP and one or more wireless nodes. With such a simple network, the Wi-Fi folks didn't see any reason to create some new numbering or naming scheme, so they made the BSSID the same as the Media Access Control (MAC) address for the WAP. Simple! Ah, but what do you do about ad hoc networks that don't have a WAP? The nodes that connect in an ad hoc network randomly generate a 48-bit string of numbers that looks and functions just like a MAC address, and that BSSID goes in every frame.

You could, if required, discover the MAC address for the WAP in a BSS and manually type that into the network name field when setting up a wireless computer. But that causes two problems. First, people don't want to remember strings of 48 digits, even if translated out as six hexadecimal octets, like A9–45–F2–3E–CA–12. People want names. Second, how do you connect two or more computers together into an IBSS when the BSSID has to be randomly generated?

The Wi-Fi folks created another level of naming called a *Service Set Identifier (SSID)*, a standard name applied to the BSS or IBSS to help the connection happen. The SSID—sometimes called a *network name*—is a 32-bit identification string that's inserted into the header of each frame processed by a WAP. Every Wi-Fi device must share the same SSID to communicate in a single network.

So let's take it one step further into a Wi-Fi network that has multiple WAPs, an ESS. How do you determine the network name at this level? You just use the SSID, only you apply it to the ESS as an *Extended Service Set Identifier (ESSID)*.

Unfortunately, most Wi-Fi devices just use the term *SSID*, not *ESSID*. When you configure a wireless device to connect to an ESS, you're technically using the ESSID rather than just the SSID, but the manufacturer often tries to make it simple for you by using only the term *SSID*.

Exam Tip
The CompTIA Network+ certification exam uses the two terms—*SSID* and *ESSID*—interchangeably. Concentrate on these two terms for the exam.

Wireless Standards

Like all technologies, wireless has improved over the years, and as a result, different versions of wireless networking standards exist. Let's look at each of the wireless standards—and definitely make sure you know these for the CompTIA Network+ exam!

- **802.11b**   Has a throughput of 11 Mbps and runs at the 2.4 GHz frequency. 802.11b was the first wireless standard to become the Wi-Fi standard.

- **802.11a**   Has a throughput of 54 Mbps and operates at the 5 GHz frequency. This wireless standard is incompatible with 802.11b/g, which runs at the 2.4 GHz frequency.

- **802.11g**   Improves upon the 802.11b standard by increasing the transfer rate to 54 Mbps, while staying compatible with 802.11b by running at the 2.4 GHz frequency.

- **802.11n**   Designed to run at both 2.4 GHz and 5 GHz so that it is compatible with 802.11b and 802.11g. An 802.11n-only network can take advantage of the less cluttered 5-GHz space for better coverage, and 802.11n devices are quickly becoming commonplace.

The 802.11n standard brings several improvements to Wi-Fi networking, including faster speeds and new antenna technology implementations.

The 802.11n specification requires all but handheld devices to use multiple antennas to implement a feature called *multiple in/multiple out (MIMO)*, which enables the devices to make multiple simultaneous connections. With up to four antennas, 802.11n devices can achieve amazing speeds. They also can implement *channel bonding* to increase throughput even more, where the devices use multiple radio signals simultaneously. (The official standard supports throughput of up to 600 Mbps, although practical implementation drops that down substantially.)

Many 802.11n WAPs employ *transmit beamforming*, a multiple-antenna technology that helps get rid of dead spots—or at least make them not so bad. The antennas adjust the signal once the WAP discovers a client to optimize the radio signal.

Table 2.4 summarizes the key features of the main 802.11 networking standards. Keep in mind that the distance limitations specified in the table assume perfect conditions. In the real world, walls, plumbing, and other factors will often limit your wireless network to much smaller coverage areas. Be sure to know these specs for the CompTIA Network+ exam.

Exam Tip

Make sure you know the IEEE 802.11 wireless standards and their associated characteristics for the CompTIA Network+ exam.

| **TABLE 2.4** | 802.11 Wireless Network Standards |

Standard	802.11a	802.11b	802.11g	802.11n
Maximum throughput	54 Mbps	11 Mbps	54 Mbps	Up to 600 Mbps
Maximum range	~150 feet	~300 feet	~300 feet	~300 feet
Frequency	5 GHz	2.4 GHz	2.4 GHz	2.4/5 GHz
Compatibility	802.11a	802.11 b/g/n	802.11 b/g/n	802.11 b/g/n

Wireless Frequency Ranges

I have mentioned that the different wireless standards run at either the 2.4-GHz frequency or the 5-GHz frequency. It is important to note that these frequencies are actually a *range* of frequencies, and each frequency range is known as a *channel*. If you want, you can change the channel that your wireless devices use, which will change the frequency being used by your wireless network. This is important because you may have a wireless network running on the same channel (frequency) as some of your household devices (such as a cordless phone), which will cause them to interfere with one another. In this case, you can change the channel of the wireless network to prevent the interference from occurring. Table 2.5 shows the different frequencies used by the Wi-Fi channels. You do *not* need to memorize this chart for the exam. I just included it to aid in setting up a Wi-Fi network.

Notice in Table 2.5 that the frequencies overlap from one channel to another. In fact, in the United States, only channels 1, 6, and 11 *don't* overlap! It's important that if you need to change the channel, you do so by a difference of at least two. For example, if you are running on channel 6 and you are experiencing problems, try changing all your wireless devices to channel 11.

TABLE 2.5	Wi-Fi Channels and Their Associated Frequencies
Channel	**Frequency Range**
1	2.3995 GHz–2.4245 GHz
2	2.4045 GHz–2.4295 GHz
3	2.4095 GHz–2.4345 GHz
4	2.4145 GHz–2.4395 GHz
5	2.4195 GHz–2.4445 GHz
6	2.4245 GHz–2.4495 GHz
7	2.4295 GHz–2.4545 GHz
8	2.4345 GHz–2.4595 GHz
9	2.4395 GHz–2.4645 GHz
10	2.4445 GHz–2.4695 GHz
11	2.4495 GHz–2.4745 GHz
12	2.4545 GHz–2.4795 GHz
13	2.4595 GHz–2.4845 GHz

> **Travel Advisory**
>
> **Latency**   Wireless networks experience much higher *latency*—the time delay between sending and receiving signals—than wired networks, so you might run into problems with latency-sensitive applications, such as Skype or a Google+ Hangout, which feature streaming voice and video.
>
> Although the CompTIA Network+ competencies suggest different latencies among the various Wi-Fi standards, there doesn't seem to be much variation. It's in the wired vs. wireless that you'll notice a difference.

Although wireless networks free us from the need to work with cabling and grant us mobility with our portable computers, wireless networks have three main drawbacks: cost, speed, and security. Cost is beginning to disappear as an issue—the price of wireless networking equipment has dropped dramatically as the technology has become more popular. In terms of speed, wireless networks can seem slow compared to their wired equivalents. Consider that mainstream, copper-based network solutions can give you speeds of 1000 Mbps or more for each system on a switched network, whereas a wireless network provides shared bandwidth around 300 Mbps at best.

As for security, stories abound of techno-addicts (and investigative journalists!) driving around with makeshift *Mission Impossible* antennas on their cars (often constructed from an old Pringles can), tapping into corporate wireless networks and surfing the Net for free.

> **Travel Assistance**
>
> See Chapter 10 for specifics on setting up and securing a Wi-Fi network.

Laser Links

Lasers are also an option for point-to-point links, but setup is a little trickier, and laser systems can suffer from weather-related problems (bright sun, rain, and fog) as well as loss of signal as the high-power laser emitter ages. In any case, laser (and microwave) systems require a line-of-sight path between the transmitter and receiver, so the possible effect of intermediate obstacles needs to be assessed.

Bluetooth

Bluetooth creates small wireless networks, called *Wireless Personal Area Networks (WPANs)*, between PCs and peripheral devices such as personal digital assistants

(PDAs) and printers; input devices such as keyboards and mice; and consumer electronics such as cell phones, home stereos, televisions, home security systems, and so on. Bluetooth was *not* originally designed to be a full-function networking solution, although many vendors have used it for this purpose.

Bluetooth uses the FHSS spread-spectrum broadcasting method, switching among any of the 79 frequencies available in the 2.45-GHz range. Bluetooth hops from frequency to frequency some 1600 times per second, making it highly resistant to interference. The Bluetooth specification allows for transfers of data at rates from 723 Kbps to 1 Mbps, with a maximum range of 10 meters (about 33 feet).

Bluetooth devices interoperate in a *master/slave* scheme, in which one master device controls up to seven active slave devices. These roles are designated automatically and do not require any configuration. The personal area network (PAN) created by Bluetooth is sometimes called a *piconet*. More than seven Bluetooth slave devices (up to 255) can participate in a piconet at one time, but only seven of those devices can be active at one time. Inactive slave devices are referred to as *parked* devices.

Bluetooth devices use a four-stage process to find each other and create the PAN, as detailed in Table 2.6.

The services supported by Bluetooth are called *profiles*. Here are the 13 common Bluetooth profiles:

- **Generic Access Profile** Defines how Bluetooth units discover and establish a connection with each other.
- **Service Discovery Profile** Enables the Bluetooth device's Service Discovery User Application to query other Bluetooth devices to determine what services they provide. This profile is dependent on the Generic Access Profile.
- **Cordless Telephony Profile** Defines the Bluetooth wireless phone functionality.

TABLE 2.6 Four Stages of Bluetooth

Stage	Purpose
Device discovery	The device broadcasts its MAC address and a code identifying the type of device.
Name discovery	The device identifies itself by a "friendly" name, such as *iPAQ Pocket PC*.
Association	The device joins the Bluetooth network.
Service discovery	The device announces the services that it can provide.

- **Intercom Profile**   Defines the Bluetooth wireless intercom functionality.
- **Serial Port Profile**   Enables Bluetooth devices to emulate serial port communication using RS-232 control signaling, the standard used on ordinary PC serial ports. This profile is dependent on the Generic Access Profile.
- **Headset Profile**   Defines the Bluetooth wireless telephone and PC headset functionality.
- **Dial-up Networking Profile**   Defines the Bluetooth device's capability to act as, or interact with, a modem.
- **Fax Profile**   Defines the Bluetooth device's capability to act as, or interact with, a fax device.
- **LAN Access Profile**   Defines how the Bluetooth device accesses a LAN and the Internet.
- **Generic Object Exchange Profile**   Defines how Bluetooth devices exchange data with other devices. This profile is dependent on the Serial Port Profile.
- **Object Push Profile**   Bluetooth devices use this profile to exchange small data objects, such as a PDA's vCard, with other Bluetooth devices.
- **File Transfer Profile**   Used to exchange large data objects, such as files, between Bluetooth devices. This profile is dependent on the Generic Object Exchange Profile.
- **Synchronization Profile**   Used to synchronize data between Bluetooth PDAs and PCs.

Bluetooth devices have to support identical profiles to communicate; for example, your PDA and PC both have to support the Bluetooth Synchronization Profile if you want them to sync up.

For security, Bluetooth offers proprietary 128-bit encryption and the ability to set per-user passwords to guard against unauthorized access to the Bluetooth network. Bluetooth also supports industry-standard encryption protocols such as Point-to-Point Tunneling Protocol (PPTP) and Secure Sockets Layer (SSL) (PPTP and SSL are discussed in Chapters 8 and 9) through browser-based remote access. Access to Bluetooth networks can be controlled through MAC address filtering, and Bluetooth devices can be set to nondiscovery mode to hide them effectively from other Bluetooth devices. Bluetooth specifications are shown in Table 2.7.

TABLE 2.7	Bluetooth Specifications
Standard	**Bluetooth**
Maximum throughput	1 Mbps (some devices boast 2 Mbps)
Maximum range	Typically 30 feet, but some high-powered Bluetooth devices have a maximum range of 300 feet
Frequency	2.45 GHz
Security	Proprietary 128-bit encryption, password-protected access, PPTP, SSL (through browser-based remote access client)
Compatibility	Bluetooth
Spread-spectrum method	FHSS
Communication mode	Master/slave: a single master device with up to seven active slave devices
Description	Bluetooth is designed to enable wireless communication between PCs and peripheral components, as well as consumer electronics. Bluetooth is not a full-fledged networking solution, and it is not intended to compete with or replace 802.11-based wireless networking technologies.

Infrared Wireless Networking

Wireless networking using infrared technology, although slow compared to 802.11x networks, comes standard on some laptop computers and can provide an easy way to transfer files between computers without purchasing additional hardware.

Communication through infrared devices is enabled via the *Infrared Data Association* (IrDA) protocol. The IrDA protocol stack is a widely supported industry standard and has been included in all versions of Windows since Windows 95. Apple computers also support IrDA, as do Linux boxes.

Infrared devices transmit data more slowly than most other wired or wireless networking options. Infrared devices can transfer data at up to 4 Mbps. The maximum distance between infrared devices is 1 meter, and connections must be in direct line of sight, making them susceptible to interference. An infrared link can be disrupted by anything that breaks the beam of light—a soda can, a coworker passing between desks, or even bright sunlight hitting the infrared transceiver can cause interference.

Exam Tip
Infrared devices transfer data at a maximum of 4 Mbps and have a maximum distance of 1 meter.

TABLE 2.8	IrDA Specifications
Standard	**Infrared (IrDA)**
Maximum throughput	Up to 4 Mbps
Maximum range	1 meter (39 inches)
Security	None
Compatibility	IrDA
Communication mode	Point-to-point ad hoc

Infrared is designed only to make a point-to-point connection between two devices in ad hoc mode—no equivalent to the infrastructure mode or 802.11 exists for infrared. You could, however, use an infrared access point device to enable Ethernet network communication using IrDA (although no one really does).

In terms of security, the IrDA protocol offers exactly nothing in the way of encryption or authentication. Infrared's main security feature is the fact that you have to be literally within arm's reach to establish a link. Infrared is not the best solution for a dedicated network connection, but for a quick file transfer or print job, it'll do in a pinch. Table 2.8 summarizes the key specifications for IrDA.

CHECKPOINT

✔ **Objective 2.01: Coaxial Cabling**   Coax cable is the classic example of bounded network media. Coax cable consists of an inner core and an overall metal screen, plus layers of insulation. The screen gives the cable a degree of protection against electromagnetic interference, but still, as with most copper- based media, it should be kept away from sources of interference. A wide variety of coax cable types exist, but specific types must be used for networking—not just any coax will do. Early Ethernet networks used baseband coax, the last of which sported a bayonet-style connector called a BNC.

✔ **Objective 2.02: Twisted-Pair Cabling**   The vast majority of network installations use unshielded twisted-pair (UTP) cable, a four-pair cable originally intended for telephone circuits but enhanced to carry data. Over time, various categories of UTP cable have been developed, each capable of operating at faster data rates than its predecessor. Two general types of UTP wiring can be used: patch cable uses stranded copper to make the wiring flexible, and premises cable (so-called *horizontal cable*) uses a solid core to give the wiring more strength to withstand rougher handling as it is installed in ducting and cable trays. Mixing the cable types—for example, using horizontal cable for patch leads—can lead to reliability problems.

Most UTP installations use RJ45 connectors and wall ports. RJ45 connectors have eight contacts to match the four pairs of wires in the UTP cable. The cable pairs are color-coded to make it easier to follow a standard wiring pattern when connecting media or fitting the cable to wall ports, such as T568A and T568B. Because UTP cable is not screened, it must be installed well away from other sources of electrical interference, and most installations are thoroughly tested to make sure they meet basic functional criteria. A screened version of UTP— called *STP*—is available, but it is much more expensive and rarely used unless local conditions demand a high level of screening.

✔**Objective 2.03: Optical Fiber**   Optical fiber cabling is much more expensive to install than copper alternatives, but it offers several advantages, including greater maximum distance and improved security. Two main types of optical fiber are used: single-mode fiber (SMF) and multimode fiber (MMF), the latter being the most commonly used type for general networking. Optical fiber is specified according to the core (fiber) and cladding diameter (in microns), the most common size being 62.5/125.

Optical fiber has its own set of connectors because it's an optical system, not electrical. The most common connector types are ST, SC, LC, and MTRJ. Optical fiber connectors should always be handled with care because they can be broken fairly easily.

✔**Objective 2.04: Wireless Media Types**   Wireless networking solutions exist for both point-to-point building links and general intraoffice connectivity. Today's office-based solutions are using wireless networking standards such as 802.11g or 802.11n, allowing different manufacturers to produce compatible equipment and increasing competition in the marketplace. Wireless networks operate in the office by means of one or more cells, each connecting users to the main network via an access point (AP).

Other wireless media types are Bluetooth and infrared. Bluetooth devices create personal area networks (PANs) of up to 10 meters. Infrared devices, using the IrDA protocol, can make small (1 meter) point-to-point connections.

REVIEW QUESTIONS

1. Which of the following connector types is associated with fiber-optic cable?

   A. RJ45

   B. BNC

   C. ST

   D. RG-58

2. Which of the following UTP cable categories can support data transmissions at 100 Mbps?

   A. CAT 1

   B. CAT 4

   C. CAT 5e

   D. All of the above

3. You are planning an upgrade and future proof of your current office's 10/100 network wiring. The new media must be capable of supporting up to 1000 Mbps up to 100 meters per network segment and 10 Gbps for shorter distances. Which of the following media type best satisfies your upgrade requirements?

   A. CAT 5

   B. CAT 6

   C. CAT 5e

   D. 1000BaseT

   E. 1000BaseSX

4. Which of the following connector types is associated with UTP cable and is considered a Physical-layer device?

   A. RJ45

   B. BNC

   C. SC

   D. NBC

   E. USB 3.0

5. What name is given to the problem caused when signals from adjacent cables interfere with each other?

   A. Talkback

   B. Crossover

C. Backchat

D. Crosstalk

6. Laptops seem to be losing their wireless connection when someone is talking on the cordless phone. What should you do?

   A. Reboot the wireless router

   B. Change the SSID

   C. Enable WEP

   D. Change the channel on the wireless router

7. What are the names associated with cable used to connect to a patch panel and cable used to connect an MDF to an IDF?

   A. Horizontal and vertical cross-connect

   B. Rollover and loopback

   C. 586A and 586B

   D. Crossover and crossunder

8. Which wireless standard runs at the 2.4 GHz frequency range and has a maximum transfer rate of 54 Mbps?

   A. 802.11b

   B. 802.11g

   C. 802.11a

   D. 802.11n

9. What device enables two or more Wi-Fi–enabled devices to connect to each other wirelessly and connect to a wired network?

   A. Router

   B. Switch

   C. MTRJ

   D. WAP

10. What feature of 802.11n enables devices to use multiple antennas to make multiple simultaneous connections and thus increase throughput?

    A. MIMO

    B. OFDM

    C. Transit beamforming

    D. CSMA/CD

REVIEW ANSWERS

1. **C** ST connectors are associated with fiber-optic cable.

2. **C** CAT 5e (and higher) cabling can support data transmission at 100 Mbps.

3. **B** CAT 6 UTP is the only solution mentioned capable of fulfilling the 10 Gbps requirement in the question.

4. **A** RJ45 connectors are associated with UTP cable and considered OSI Physical-layer devices.

5. **D** Crosstalk between adjacent cables causes interference.

6. **D** Because the cordless phone is running on the same frequency range as the wireless router, you are most likely getting interference from the phone when it is in use. You should try to change the channel on the router to put the wireless network on a different frequency.

7. **A** A patch cable that connects to the patch panel is called a horizontal cross-connect (HCC) cable. Cable that connects the MDF to the IDFs is called the vertical cross-connect (VCC) cable.

8. **B** 802.11g runs at the 2.4 GHz range and has a maximum transfer rate of 54 Mbps.

9. **D** A wireless access point (WAP) enables wireless nodes to connect to both wireless and wired networks.

10. **A** Multiple in/multiple out (MIMO) is the 802.11n standard for using multiple antennas simultaneously.

Network Topologies and Standards

ETA	NEWBIE	SOME EXPERIENCE	EXPERT
	4 hours	2 hours	1 hour

A network *topology* provides a general description of how the devices on the network link to each other, either physically or logically. A *physical topology* describes precisely how devices connect, such as how the wires run from machine to machine. The devices could all connect to a single central box, for example, or in a daisy chain of one computer to another. A *logical topology,* in contrast, describes how the signals used on the network travel from one computer to another. In a logical topology, for example, all the computers might physically connect to a central box, but inside the box is a ring, so the signals flow as if the computers are all in a daisy chain. This chapter looks at both physical and logical topologies to help clarify these concepts.

Topologies do not define specifics about how to implement a network installation. They provide only a very high-level look at how network nodes connect. To move from a theoretical overview to a working solution, you must implement a specific network standard. This chapter also discusses the implementation of networks and network technologies, going into detail about Ethernet, the most widely used network standard.

Particular network topologies are generally associated with specific networking standards that provide the details that define how the network sends data between devices, the type of media used, the maximum network speed, and the number of devices (nodes) that can attach to the network. Questions regarding network topologies and network standards are well represented on the CompTIA Network+ exam.

Objective 3.01 The Bus Topology and Ethernet

If you can imagine your laundry hanging on a long, straight clothesline, you have a pretty good idea of how a bus topology network is constructed. Everything hangs off one long run of cable, as shown in Figure 3.1. The bus topology has been associated with one network standard in particular—Ethernet.

FIGURE 3.1   A bus topology uses a main cable trunk.

Ethernet Overview

Ethernet, introduced by Xerox in 1973, remained a largely proprietary technology until 1979, when Xerox looked for partners to help promote Ethernet as an industry standard. Working with Digital Equipment Corporation (DEC) and Intel, the company published what became the Digital-Intel-Xerox (DIX) networking standard. The standard describes a bus topology network using coaxial cable that enables multiple computing systems and other devices to communicate with each other at 10 Mbps.

> **Local Lingo**
>
> **segment** A run of cable (media) linking one or more nodes on a network.

How Ethernet Works

Any network design must address a number of key elements: the type of media to use, how to send data across the wire, how to identify the sending and receiving computers, and how to determine which computer should use the shared cable next.

Chapter 2 discussed the physical cabling used in Ethernet. Ethernet networks can use coaxial cable, unshielded twisted-pair (UTP), shielded twisted-pair (STP), or fiber. Regardless of the physical cabling used, the data moves across the wire in essentially the same way. Any network requires a method for determining which device uses the network media at a given time.

CSMA/CD

Ethernet networks use *carrier sense, multiple access/collision detection (CSMA/CD)* to determine which computer should use the shared media at a given moment. *Carrier sense* means that each machine on the network examines the cable before sending a data frame (see Figure 3.2). If another machine is using the network, the node detects traffic and waits until the cable is free. If the node detects no traffic, the node sends its data frame.

Multiple access means that all machines have equal access to the wire. If the line is free, an Ethernet node does not have to get approval to use the wire—it just uses it. From the point of view of Ethernet, it does not matter what function the node is performing. The node could be a desktop system running Windows 7 or a high-end file server running Windows Server or Linux. In Ethernet, all nodes are created equal. But what happens when two machines listen to the cable and simultaneously determine that it is free? They both try to send.

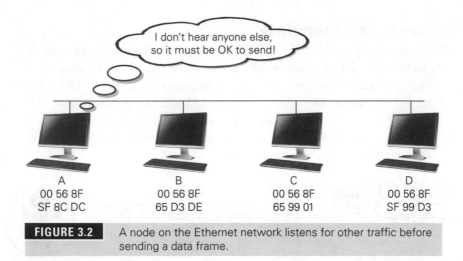

A	B	C	D
00 56 8F	00 56 8F	00 56 8F	00 56 8F
SF 8C DC	65 D3 DE	65 99 01	SF 99 D3

FIGURE 3.2   A node on the Ethernet network listens for other traffic before sending a data frame.

Collisions

When two nodes use the cable simultaneously, a *collision* occurs, and both of the transmissions are lost (see Figure 3.3). Two nodes transmitting at the same time are like two people talking simultaneously: The listener hears the mixture of the two voices and can't understand either voice.

When a collision occurs, both nodes detect the collision by listening to their own transmissions. By comparing their own transmissions with the signal they receive, they can determine whether another node has transmitted at the same time, as shown in Figure 3.4. If the nodes detect a collision, both nodes immediately stop transmitting and wait for a short, random period of time before retrying.

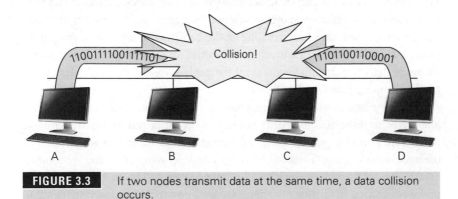

FIGURE 3.3   If two nodes transmit data at the same time, a data collision occurs.

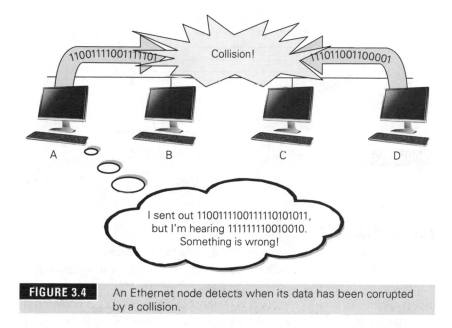

FIGURE 3.4 An Ethernet node detects when its data has been corrupted by a collision.

Because CSMA/CD is easy to implement in hardware, Ethernet network interface cards (NICs) are relatively cheap. That simplicity comes at a price: An Ethernet node will waste some amount of its time dealing with collisions instead of sending data. As you add more devices to the network and/or increase the amount of traffic—for example, by installing new, data-intensive applications on the network—the number of collisions on the network will increase as the nodes generate more frames.

Every Ethernet network wastes some amount of its available bandwidth dealing with these collisions. The typical Ethernet network advertises that it runs at either 100 Mbps or 1000 Mbps, but the advertised speed assumes that no collisions ever take place!

Termination

Ethernet networks using a physical bus topology (such as those using coax cabling) function properly only if both ends of the network bus are fitted with terminating *resistors*. Without one or more of these terminators in place, some of the energy in the electrical signals that make up the data frames bounces back up the wire, a phenomenon known as *reflection* or *signal bounce*, as shown in Figure 3.5.

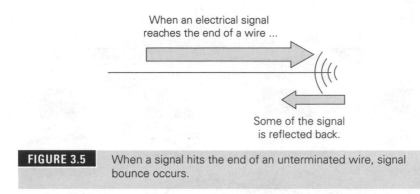

When an electrical signal
reaches the end of a wire ...

Some of the signal
is reflected back.

| FIGURE 3.5 | When a signal hits the end of an unterminated wire, signal bounce occurs. |

Cable Breaks

A cable break on a bus topology network will create two incorrectly terminated segments, causing multiple reflections in both directions. In this scenario, all stations on the network go into perpetual wait mode (see Figure 3.6). This condition disables all nodes connected to the broken cable. Because a single break can take down the entire segment and all nodes connected to it, bus-based networks are said to have a "single point of failure."

Broadcast

Broadcast traffic is destined for all hosts on the network. This is different from *unicast* traffic, which is destined only for one host on the network.

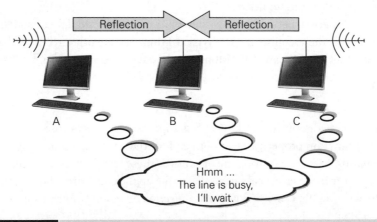

Reflection   Reflection

A   B   C

Hmm ...
The line is busy,
I'll wait.

| FIGURE 3.6 | Signal bounces (reflections) caused by a cable break disrupting the entire network |

When analyzing network traffic with a program such as Wireshark, you can easily identify broadcast traffic frames because they have a destination media access control (MAC) address of FF-FF-FF-FF-FF-FF. Broadcast traffic can be seen as wasted bandwidth because every system receives the frame.

If you determine that your network has too much broadcast traffic, you can control this by separating your network into different networks with a router. Broadcast traffic typically does not cross routers, so breaking up your network this way will minimize the amount of broadcast traffic your hosts receive.

Exam Tip

Don't confuse broadcast traffic with multicast traffic. *Multicast* traffic is traffic destined for a selected group of systems—not all systems (broadcast) and not just one system (unicast). For the CompTIA Network+ exam, be familiar with the difference between broadcast, unicast, and multicast.

Bonding

Bonding, or *port trunking,* is a network term used to describe the action of joining the bandwidth of two network cards or modems together to create more bandwidth. For example, you could bond two 100 Mbps network cards to create a 200 Mbps connection.

Ethernet Standards

In the early 1980s, the Institute of Electrical and Electronics Engineers (IEEE), an organization that defines industry-wide standards in the fields of electronics and computing, adopted the DIX Ethernet standard as a general standard for networking. The IEEE working group (or committee) responsible for general networking standards is known as the *802 committee,* and Ethernet became IEEE standard 802.3.

Exam Tip

IEEE 802.3 defines Ethernet standards.

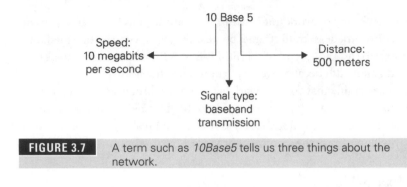

| **FIGURE 3.7** | A term such as *10Base5* tells us three things about the network. |

Ethernet on the Bus

Two main standards exist for creating a bus-based Ethernet network, with wonderfully descriptive names: *10Base5* and *10Base2*. The IEEE coined these labels, and they each describe three key features of the network, as shown in Figure 3.7:

- The *10* signifies an Ethernet network that runs at 10 Mbps.
- Base signifies that 10Base5 uses *baseband* signaling, meaning that just one channel of communication is on the cable at any time, as opposed to a *broadband* system (such as cable TV coax), which can have multiple signals on the cable.
- The *5* indicates that 10Base5 cables may not be longer than 500 meters, which is really an indication to the type of cable. The cable length that is 500 meters is called *Thicknet* cabling.
- The *2* in 10Base2 is the distance rounded up from 185 meters.

Ethernet networks using the pure bus topology have long been replaced by networks running twisted-pair or fiber-optic cable.

Objective 3.02 The Star Bus Topology

An early alternative topology to bus suggested connecting all the devices on a network into a single central box, effectively creating a star (Figure 3.8). This network design became known as a *star topology*.

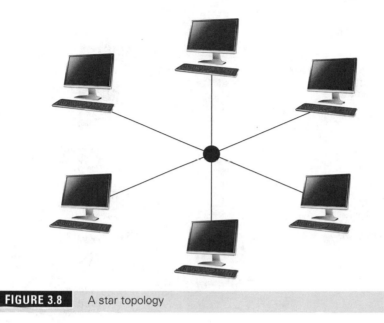

FIGURE 3.8   A star topology

The key advantage of the star topology is that a break in a cable affects only the machine connected to that cable. In Figure 3.9, machine C cannot communicate with any other node, but machines A, B, D, E, and F communicate with each other just fine.

A star topology network remained an interesting theory until some bright person got the idea to take a bus network and essentially shrink the central wire into a single box, called a *hub*. All the devices on the network would connect to the hub, creating a physical star topology network, but electronically—logically—the network would function just like a bus network. This created a hybrid topology called a *star bus*.

Exam Tip

A *hybrid topology* is a topology that mixes a bus, star, or ring topology (discussed later) together. For example, a star bus topology is a hybrid topology.

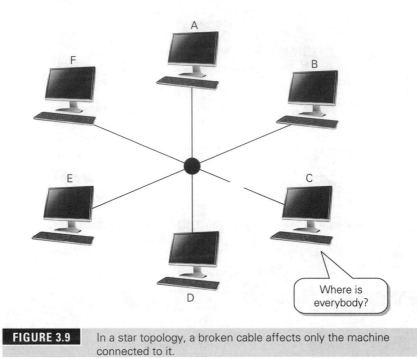

| **FIGURE 3.9** | In a star topology, a broken cable affects only the machine connected to it. |

Modern Ethernet standards use a star bus topology, with a physical star topology that provides improved fault tolerance, as well as a logical bus that maintains compatibility with older Ethernet standards. All the devices on a network connect to a central box, called a *switch* (Figure 3.10).

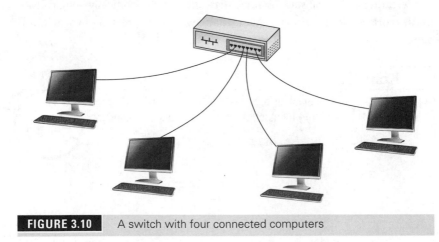

| **FIGURE 3.10** | A switch with four connected computers |

The way switches pass data between their ports represents the logical (bus) part of the star bus partnership; in effect, each switch behaves like a terminated Ethernet segment, with each port becoming a node on that segment. The nodes share the segment according to the same CSMA/CD rules used for 10Base2 and 10Base5. Using the star bus topology maintains compatibility with previous Ethernet standards but provides the stability of a star topology. If a cable gets cut, only one node drops off the network.

10BaseT and 100BaseT

The term *10BaseT* describes an Ethernet cabling system that uses a star bus topology. 10BaseT uses twisted-pair cabling rather than coax. Most of the other basic characteristics remain the same—for example, the network operates at the same speed (10 Mbps) and supports a maximum of 1024 nodes.

The name *10BaseT* doesn't quite follow the naming convention used for earlier Ethernet cabling systems. The *10* still refers to the speed: 10 Mbps. *Base* still refers to the signaling type: baseband. The *T,* however, doesn't refer to a distance limitation but to the type of cable used: twisted-pair. For the record, the maximum distance allowed between a node and a hub is 100 meters.

Once you have come to grips with 10BaseT, it is not a quantum leap to understand the key selling point of 100BaseT. *Fast Ethernet,* as 100BaseT is known, runs at 100 Mbps over twisted-pair cabling.

Most Ethernet NICs automatically switch between 10 Mbps and 100 Mbps operation to match the switch they're plugged into, and all modern switches support a mix of devices running at either speed.

Before we leave this section, you should know that there are two types of 100-megabit UTP Ethernet: 100BaseTX and 100BaseT4. 100BaseTX is, by far, the more popular version and runs over two pairs in a CAT 5 or better cable. 100BaseTX is so common that we just call it 100BaseT. 100BaseT4 is an earlier implementation that ran over CAT 3 cable, achieving the 100 Mbps speed by using all four pairs of wires.

Gigabit Ethernet

Modern developments have cranked Ethernet up to the heady speed of 1000 Mbps (1 Gbps) while retaining compatibility with the CSMA/CD standard. Various others have now been ratified by the IEEE 802.3ab and the IEEE 802.3z Gigabit Ethernet Standardization projects, as follows:

- IEEE 802.3ab
  - **1000BaseT** Gigabit Ethernet over four pairs of wires in the CAT 5e or better UTP cabling.
- IEEE 802.3z
  - **1000BaseX** Gigabit Ethernet over different cable types, which is broken down into 1000BaseSX, 1000BaseLX, and 1000BaseCX.
    - **1000BaseSX** Gigabit Ethernet over multimode fiber-optic cabling. You can remember this by the S, meaning "short distance." Multimode fiber cabling is the type of cabling that is used over short distances (less than 2 km).
    - **1000BaseLX** Gigabit Ethernet over single mode fiber-optic cabling. You can remember this by the L, meaning "long distance." Single mode fiber is the type of fiber used to cover large distances (greater than 2 km).
    - **1000BaseCX** Gigabit Ethernet over coaxial cable, supporting distances of up to 25 meters.

10/100/1000BaseT Summary

Here are the key features that distinguish 10/100/1000BaseT cabling:

- Speed of 10, 100, or 1000 Mbps according to standard
- Baseband signal type
- Distance of 100 meters from node to hub or switch

Exam Tip

Be sure to focus on Fast Ethernet (100BaseT) and Gigabit Ethernet (1000BaseT) for the CompTIA Network+ exam. Also know that the standard known as *100BaseFX* is 100 Mbps Ethernet over fiber-optic cabling.

10 Gigabit Ethernet (10 GbE)

For the highest bandwidth applications, such as interconnecting servers and connecting high-speed switches in corporate datacenters, the *10 Gigabit Ethernet* standard, also known as *10 GbE,* provides an amazingly fast Ethernet-based networking technology. The IEEE recognizes two 10 GbE standards: 802.3ae for 10 GbE over fiber-optic cabling and 802.3an for 10 GbE over copper cabling.

In addition to speed, most 10 GbE variations are designed to interoperate with Synchronous Optical Network (SONET), making it an ideal choice for connecting local networks to preexisting long-distance fiber-optic links that already use SONET. (Refer to Table 3.1, and see Chapter 8 for more information on SONET.)

TABLE 3.1   10 Gbps Ethernet Standards

Standard	Maximum Distance	Cabling	SONET Compatible
10GBaseSR	300 m	Multimode fiber	No
10GBaseSW	300 m	Multimode fiber	Yes
10GBaseLR	10 km	Single-mode fiber	No
10GBaseLW	10 km	Single-mode fiber	Yes
10GBaseER	40 km	Single-mode fiber	No
10GBaseEW	40 km	Single-mode fiber	Yes
10GBaseLX4 over single mode	300 m	Single-mode fiber	No
10GBaseLX4 over multimode	10 km	Multimode	No
10GBaseCX4	15 m	Infiniband copper cabling	No
10GBaseT	40/100 m	Category 6/6a UTP	No

> ## Exam Tip
>
> The CompTIA Network+ objectives focus on the 1 Gbps and 10 Gbps standards (10 GbE), so spend some time memorizing what standard is used with what type of cable and distance. To help you with Table 3.1, the S at the end of the standard stands for "short distance," the L stands for "long distance," and the E stands for "extended distance." The W at the end of the standard implies "WAN," which means it is used with SONET (a WAN-based technology).

Objective 3.03 Ring Topologies

In a true ring topology, every computer system is connected together in a complete loop, but the loop itself is vulnerable to a single point of failure, so two loops are often implemented in a fashion known as *counter-rotating rings* (see Figure 3.11). The goal is to ensure that if the primary ring suffers a cable failure, the two nodes on either side of the problem can detect the fault and re-route the data signals to the secondary ring (see Figure 3.12). The data flow on the secondary ring proceeds logically in the opposite direction of the primary ring, hence the counter-rotation.

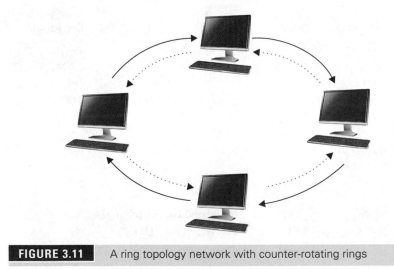

FIGURE 3.11   A ring topology network with counter-rotating rings

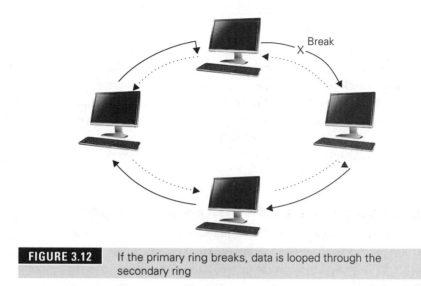

FIGURE 3.12 If the primary ring breaks, data is looped through the secondary ring

The main selling point for ring networks was the complete lack of collisions. Devices on the ring played nicely and accessed the ring when it was their turn. Regardless, Ethernet was more efficient.

Hybrid star-ring topology networks competed with Ethernet in the early days of networking. IBM's Token Ring, for example, had solid market share for a number of years. Ring and star-ring networks are long gone today.

Objective 3.04 Other Topologies

Having covered bus, star, and ring topologies, we've now considered the three main ways of stringing together network devices, but that's not the whole story. Numerous other ways and means of linking systems have been tried over the years and are also evolving as technology improves. Although these topologies are not covered in as much detail as "the big three," don't skip over the next section, because you might learn something to your advantage.

Mesh Topology

The mesh topology connects each node with multiple links, providing multiple paths between any two nodes. The mesh topology is rarely, if ever, seen in LANs because of cost: It requires so many separate links. A partial mesh, however, is used to connect networks together (see Figure 3.13). In essence, any series of interlinked networks where more than one possible data path exists between network locations can be considered to be using a mesh topology.

Because mesh topologies support multiple paths between networks, the level of fault tolerance improves as the number of paths increases.

Point-to-point and Point-to-multipoint

There are two popular layouts for topologies: point-to-point and point-to-multipoint. In a *point-to-point*, topology two systems connect directly to one another. In the past, these systems would connect directly through the serial ports with a null modem cable, but these days you can connect them using a crossover cable or a wireless connection.

A *point-to-multipoint* topology uses a central device that connects all the devices together. This topology is popular with wireless networks. With point-to-multipoint, when the central device sends data, it is received by all devices connected to the central device. But if one of the devices that are connected sends data, then it is received by only the destination system.

If you compare a star topology to a slightly rearranged point-to-multipoint topology, you might be tempted to say they're the same thing. The subtle but important difference between the two topologies is that a point-to-multipoint

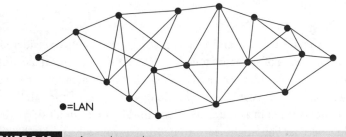

●=LAN

FIGURE 3.13   A mesh topology

topology requires an intelligent device in the center, whereas the device in the center of a star topology has little more to do than send or provide a path for a signal down all the connections.

CSMA/CA

Wi-Fi networks, whether configured in a point-to-point or point-to-multipoint topology, have some interesting obstacles to overcome so that communication happens properly. Wired Ethernet networks, as you'll recall from earlier in this chapter, negotiate use of the bus through CSMA/CD. Devices listen, send if the bus is free, and resend in the case of a collision.

Modern switched networks work even more efficiently, because devices run in full duplex and switches all but eliminate collisions. *Full duplex* means that devices can send and receive at the same time. The switches negotiate the traffic and all the devices can chatter away happily.

Travel Assistance

I go into more detail on switches in Chapter 4.

CSMA/CD won't work for wireless networking because wireless devices simply can't detect collisions for two reasons. First, radio is a *half-duplex* transmission method, which means a wireless device cannot listen and send at the same time. Second, wireless clients may not know about the existence of another client due to signal strength. This is called the *hidden node* issue.

Exam Tip

You need to know the difference between full duplex and half duplex for the CompTIA Network+ exam. Old Ethernet devices ran in half duplex, as do Wi-Fi networks. Modern switched Ethernet is full duplex.

Wireless networks need another way to deal with potential collisions. Wi-Fi networks use *carrier sense multiple access with collision avoidance (CSMA/CA)* rather than CSMA/CD. The CSMA/CA access method, as the name implies, proactively takes steps to avoid collisions, as does CSMA/CD. The difference comes in the collision avoidance.

The 802.11 standard defines two methods for collision avoidance: *Distributed Coordination Function (DCF)* and *Point Coordination Function (PCF)*. Currently, only DCF is implemented. DCF specifies rules for sending data onto the network media. For instance, if a wireless network node detects that the network is busy, DCF defines a slightly lengthy *backoff* period before a node can try to access the network again. DCF also requires that receiving nodes send an acknowledgement (ACK) for every frame that they process. The ACK also includes a value that tells other wireless nodes to wait a certain duration before trying to access the network media. This period is calculated to be the time that the data frame takes to reach its destination based on the frame's length and data rate. If the sending node doesn't receive an ACK, it retransmits the same data frame until it gets a confirmation that the frame reached its destination.

Exam Tip

Current CSMA/CA devices use the Distributed Coordination Function (DCF) method for collision avoidance.

CHECKPOINT

✔ **Objective 3.01: The Bus Topology and Ethernet** Ethernet is a very common networking standard and was first developed for use with a bus topology, where all computing devices are interconnected via a single run of coaxial cable, known as a *segment*. Although bus-based networks are relatively simple to install, their main drawback is that they have a single point of failure—one break will stop the entire segment from working. The ends of the bus must also be terminated properly for correct operation. Ethernet networks use a system called *carrier sense multiple access/collision detection (CSMA/CD)* to determine which computer should use the shared cable at a given moment. The IEEE 802.3 standard defines how Ethernet operates.

✔ **Objective 3.02: The Star Bus Topology** This topology overcomes some of the limitations of the bus topology by placing a logical bus within a hub and allowing multiple hubs to be interconnected to form a larger network. The hubs isolate cable problems to individual ports and devices so that only the device attached to a faulty cable is stopped from using the network. Classic examples of this topology include the 10BaseT and 100BaseT standards.

✔ **Objective 3.03: Ring Topologies**   True ring topologies are expensive to install because they require a large amount of interconnection between all devices on the network, but a hybrid version, known as a *star ring*, was used for Token Ring networks.

✔ **Objective 3.04: Other Topologies**   The mesh topology is commonly used to interconnect networks, not just devices on individual networks. By providing multiple pathways between networks, the mesh topology provides fault tolerance in the event of problems on one or more pathways, and this is the topology used by the Internet.

Point-to-point topologies enable two devices to connect directly, whereas point-to-multipoint uses a central intelligent device to connect all devices together. Wireless networking is defined by the various IEEE 802.11x standards. 802.11g, the most widely implemented version, uses the 2.4 GHz band to provide up to 54 Mbps of bandwidth. 802.11n, the current favorite standard, cranks the speed up to ~600 Mbps. When using infrastructure mode, one or more access points (APs) provide access to the network for wireless devices. Direct NIC-to-NIC communication (ad hoc mode) is also possible. Wireless networking solves the problem of providing network connectivity where physical cabling is not possible or not wanted, but the actual distances that can be achieved vary according to local conditions. IEEE 802.11 networks use a system called *carrier sense multiple access/collision avoidance (CSMA/CA)* to determine which computer can use the network at a given moment.

REVIEW QUESTIONS

1. Which of the following network types uses a bus topology?

   A. IEEE 802.5
   B. IEEE 802.3
   C. IEEE 802.11
   D. FDDI

2. What name is given to the access method used by Ethernet networks to determine which device can have access to the media?

   A. Token passing
   B. Collision Domain Management (CDM)
   C. CSMA/CA
   D. CSMA/CD

3. You are monitoring network traffic and notice a number of frames are destined for a MAC address of FF-FF-FF-FF-FF-FF. What type of traffic is this?

   A. Unicast

   B. Multicast

   C. Broadband

   D. Broadcast

4. To create a more efficient network in your school lab, your instructor asks you to help join the bandwidth of two 100 Mbps NIC cards to create a 200 Mbps connection and configure multiple physical ports to appear as a single uplink port on the lab router. What terms describe what you and your instructor are doing?

   A. Segmenting and preventing signal bounce

   B. Bonding and port trunking

   C. Converting multicast to unicast

   D. Multihoming and preventing broadcasts

5. Which 10 Gbps Ethernet standard uses single-mode fiber-optic cabling, supports a distance of more than 2 km, and is not SONET-compatible?

   A. 10GBaseSR

   B. 10GBaseER

   C. 10GBaseLW

   D. 10GBaseEW

6. What network topology is most fault tolerant?

   A. Bus

   B. Ring

   C. Star

   D. Mesh

7. What access method do IEEE 802.11 wireless networks use to determine which computer can use the network at a given moment?

   A. CSMA/CA

   B. CSMA/CD

   C. SSID/ESSID

   D. Point-to-point

   E. Point-to-multipoint

8. Which of the following represents the IEEE wireless network standard?

    A. IEEE 802.3

    B. IEEE 10BaseW

    C. IEEE 802.5

    D. IEEE 802.11

9. Which of the following is a Gigabit standard that uses multimode fiber-optic cabling?

    A. 1000BaseT

    B. 1000BaseCX

    C. 1000BaseLX

    D. 1000BaseSX

10. What method do Wi-Fi networks use for collision avoidance?

    A. Wi-Fi CA

    B. CA/CP

    C. DCF

    D. ACK

REVIEW ANSWERS

1. **B**   Of the possible answers, only IEEE 802.3 represents a bus standard.

2. **D**   Ethernet networks use CSMA/CD to determine which system can send data on the network.

3. **D**   A frame with the destination MAC address of FF-FF-FF-FF-FF-FF is broadcast traffic destined for every host on the network.

4. **B**   Bonding is a network term used to describe the action of joining the bandwidth of two network cards or modems. Port trunking (also sometimes referred to as bonding) allows multiple physical ports to appear as a single uplink port in switched networks.

5. **B**   10GBaseER is single-mode fiber over an extended range of up to 40 km.

6. **D**   The mesh topology is the only one that allows multiple pathways between networks.

7. **A** IEEE 802.11 wireless networks use the CSMA/CA (carrier sense multiple access/collision avoidance) access method to determine which computer can use the network at a given moment. Note that wired Ethernet networks use CSMA/CD (carrier sense multiple access/collision detection).

8. **D** IEEE 802.11 is the wireless network standard.

9. **D** 1000BaseSX is the Gigabit standard that uses multimode fiber-optic cabling, which is the type of fiber cabling used to cover short distances.

10. **C** Current CSMA/CA devices use the Distributed Coordination Function (DCF) method for collision avoidance.

Network Hardware

ETA	NEWBIE	SOME EXPERIENCE	EXPERT
	4 hours	2 hours	1 hour

Network hardware enables networking devices—nodes—to cable together into a network. That's pretty straightforward and even redundant, at least in words. The CompTIA Network+ exam expects you to know the network hardware used in Ethernet and TCP/IP networks in some detail, even the hardware no longer in use. This chapter looks at network interfaces and the magic boxes that connect devices, both wired and wirelessly.

Objective 4.01 Network Interfaces

A network interface enables a computing device to send and receive data across a network. All modern computing devices have a network interface, either wired to connect to an Ethernet network or wireless to connect to a wireless access point. Traditionally called a *network interface card (NIC)* because the interface came on a separate expansion card, today most devices have built-in NICs (though most techs still call them NICs). Figure 4.1 shows a network interface on a motherboard.

Gigabit NIC

FIGURE 4.1 Gigabit Ethernet network interface

NICs have several jobs. They provide a connection to the network media, of course, either through cables or wireless radio frequency waves. NICs also have a physical address to enable communication with other devices on the network. Finally, NICs take data from the operating system and encapsulate that data into a frame suitable for traversing the Physical-layer network.

MAC Address

Inside every NIC, burned onto some type of ROM chip, is special firmware containing a unique identifier with a 48-bit value called the *media access control address,* or *MAC address.*

No two NICs ever share the same MAC address—ever. Any company that makes NICs must contact the Institute of Electrical and Electronics Engineers (IEEE) and request a block of MAC addresses, which the company then burns into the ROMs on its NICs. Many NIC makers also print the MAC address on the surface of each NIC, as shown in Figure 4.2. Note that the NIC shown here displays the MAC address in hexadecimal notation. Count the number of hex

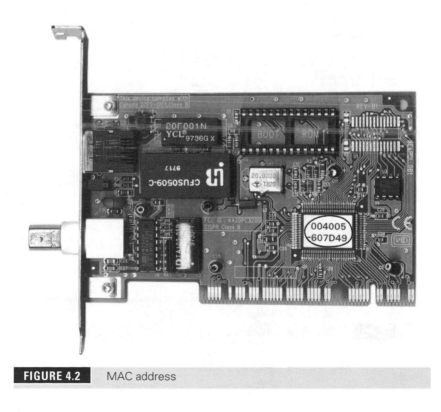

FIGURE 4.2   MAC address

characters—because each hex character represents 4 bits, it takes 12 hex characters to represent 48 bits.

The MAC address in Figure 4.2 is 004005–607D49, although in print, we represent the MAC address as 00–40–05–60–7D–49. The first six digits, in this example 00–40–05, represent the number of the NIC manufacturer. Once the IEEE issues those six hex digits to a manufacturer—often referred to as the *organizationally unique identifier (OUI)*—no other manufacturer may use them. The last six digits, in this example 60–7D–49, are the manufacturer's unique serial number for that NIC; this portion of the MAC is often referred to as the *device ID*.

Would you like to see the MAC address for your NIC? If you have a Windows system, type **ipconfig /all** from a command prompt to display the MAC address (see Figure 4.3). Note that ipconfig refers to the MAC address as the *physical address*.

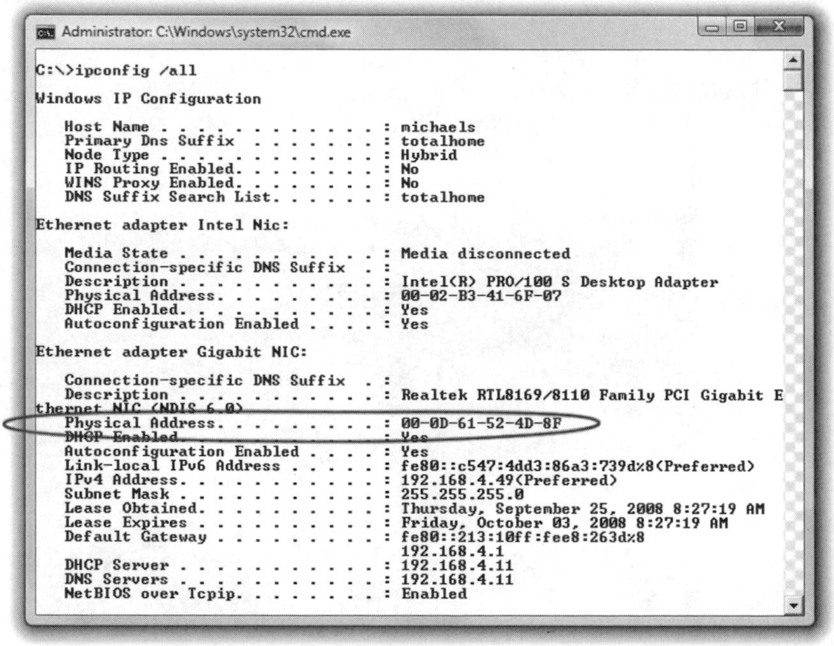

FIGURE 4.3 Output from **ipconfig /all**

Local Lingo

MAC-48 and EUI-48   IEEE forms MAC addresses from a numbering name space originally called *MAC-48,* which simply means that the MAC address will be 48 bits, with the first 24 bits defining the OUI, just as described here. The current term for this numbering name space is *EUI-48.* EUI stands for *Extended Unique Identifier.* (IEEE apparently went with the new term because they could trademark it.)

Exam Tip

Most techs just call them MAC addresses, as you should, but you might see MAC-48 or EUI-48 on the CompTIA Network+ exam.

Travel Assistance

EUI-64   Although we're not expected to exhaust the supply of 48-bit MAC addresses until the next century, IEEE has released a 64-bit successor called, appropriately, *EUI-64.* The numbering scheme is the same, but adds a couple more octets to bring it up to 64 bits. Currently, the only common uses for EUI-64 are FireWire and IPv6. (See Chapter 5 for information on the latter.)

Organizing the Data: Ethernet Frames

All network technologies break data transmitted between computers into smaller pieces called *frames,* as you'll recall from Chapter 1. Functioning at the Data Link layer (layer 2), NICs encapsulate data from the higher levels of the OSI model into frames to enable communication at the Physical layer.

Using frames addresses two networking issues. First, frames prevent any single machine from monopolizing the shared bus cable. Second, they make the process of retransmitting lost data more efficient.

Looking at the first scenario, if a sending computer sends a file as a single huge frame, the frame will monopolize the cable and prevent other machines from using it until the entire file gets to the receiving system. Using relatively small frames enables computers to share the cable easily—each computer listens on the *segment,* sending a few frames of data whenever it detects that no other computer is transmitting.

Second, in the real world, bad things can happen to good data. When errors occur during transmission, the sending system must retransmit the frames that failed to get to the receiving system in good shape. If a word processing document were transmitted as a single massive frame, the sending system would have to retransmit the entire frame—in this case, the entire document. Breaking the file up into smaller frames enables the sending computer to retransmit only the damaged frames.

Because of these benefits—shared access and more efficient retransmission—all networking technologies use frames, and Ethernet is no exception to that rule. A basic Ethernet frame contains six pieces of information: the preamble, the MAC address of the frame's recipient, the MAC address of the sending system, the type of data, the data itself, and a frame check sequence. Figure 4.4 shows these components.

Preamble

All Ethernet frames begin with a *preamble*, a 64-bit series of alternating ones and zeroes that ends with 11. The preamble gives a receiving NIC time to realize a frame is coming and to know exactly where the frame starts.

Destination and Source MAC Addresses

The second and third portions of the frame identify the destination and sending NICs, respectively. In early Ethernet networks, every node on the network

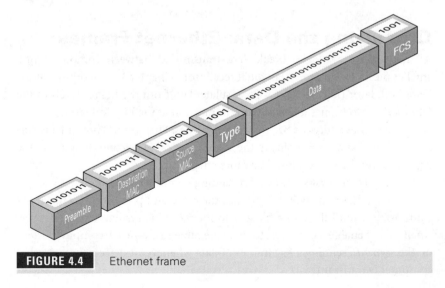

FIGURE 4.4 Ethernet frame

received every frame because they were on a shared bus cable. Nodes would use the destination MAC address to determine whether to process each frame. In today's switched Ethernet, the switch keeps a record of which node connects to which switch port and forwards data to the precise destination node. The only common traffic that goes to all nodes is broadcast traffic sent to the destination MAC of FF-FF-FF-FF-FF-FF, the *broadcast address*.

Travel Advisory

Switches Sending Multiple Frames Switches send frames to all nodes in two nonbroadcast circumstances: unknown unicasts and multicasts. If the switch doesn't recognize the MAC address, it sends the frame to every node. Additionally, some switches can't filter multicasts and instead let the NICs handle the filtering.

Type

An Ethernet frame may carry one of several types of data. The Type field helps the receiving computer interpret the frame contents at a very basic level. This way, the receiving computer can tell if the frame contains, for example, IPv4 data or IPv6 data. (See Chapter 5 for more details on IPv4 and IPv6.)

The Type field does *not* tell you if the frame carries higher-level data, such as an e-mail message or webpage. You have to dig deeper into the data section of the frame to find that information.

Data

The data part of the frame contains whatever the frame carries, what's called the *payload*. This can be an IP packet or some other type of packet used on the network. Regardless of the type of data in the payload, an Ethernet frame must have a payload of at least 46 bytes. If the payload is smaller than 46 bytes, the sending NIC will automatically add extra bytes—a *pad*—to bring the payload up to the minimum.

Frame Check Sequence

The *frame check sequence (FCS)*—Ethernet's term for the *cyclic redundancy check*—enables Ethernet nodes to recognize when bad things happen to good data. Machines on a network must be able to detect when data has been damaged in transit.

To detect errors, the computers on an Ethernet network attach a special code to each frame. When creating an Ethernet frame, the sending machine runs the data through a special mathematical formula and attaches the result, the frame check sequence, to the frame. The receiving machine opens the frame, performs the same calculation, and compares its answer with the one included with the frame. If the answers do not match, the receiving machine asks the sending machine to retransmit that frame.

Objective 4.02 Repeaters, Hubs, and Bridges

Early 10-Mbps Ethernet networks ran through various evolutionary progressions, as you'll recall from Chapter 3, and clever network designers came up with many ways to link any and all of the varieties together. They came up with devices to extend the bus topology networks from 500 m or 185 m to double or more in length. They invented devices to accommodate 10BaseT networks and sit in the center of the star bus topology.

A *repeater* takes in an electronic signal, corrects any voltage drops, and then retransmits the cleaned signals. That electronic signal with Ethernet is the frame. A repeater increases the maximum possible distance between machines by linking together two or more segments.

A *hub* enables a specific number of devices to connect to the network (one per port), and often, but not always, includes a separate port to enable hubs to be linked together to extend the network. Some hubs also include connectors for different media types—BNC, RJ-45, or fiber—but they cannot interface between networks that are based on different technologies.

Hubs are multiport repeaters, sending out every frame that one node sends to every other node connected to the hub. As a result, hubs enable multiple devices to be in the same network, but they're also all in the same collision domain and the rules of CSMA/CD apply.

Exam Tip
Repeaters and hubs are considered layer-1 (Physical-layer) devices because they work with the electrical signal.

A *bridge* acts like a repeater or hub to connect two Ethernet segments, but it goes one step beyond—filtering and forwarding traffic between those segments based on the destination MAC addresses. To *filter* traffic means to stop it from crossing from one network to the next; to *forward* traffic means to pass traffic originating on one side of the bridge to the other.

> ### Exam Tip
>
> Because bridges work with MAC addresses, they operate at layer 2, the Data Link layer, of the OSI networking model. They function in the Link/Network Interface layer of the TCP/IP model.

A newly installed Ethernet bridge initially behaves exactly like a repeater, passing frames from one segment to another. Unlike a repeater, however, a bridge monitors and records the network traffic, eventually reaching a point where it can begin to filter and forward. A bridge usually requires only a few seconds to gather enough information to start filtering and forwarding.

Although bridges offer a good solution for connecting two segments and reducing bandwidth usage, these days you'll mainly find bridges used in wireless, rather than wired, networks. (I cover those kinds of bridges at the end of this chapter.)

Objective 4.03   Switched Ethernet

While plain-vanilla 10BaseT Ethernet performed well enough for first-generation networks (which did little more than basic file and print sharing), by the early 1990s networks used more-demanding applications, such as Lotus Notes, SAP business management software, and Microsoft Exchange, which quickly saturated a 10BaseT network. Fortunately, those crazy kids over at the IEEE kept expanding the standard, giving the network tech in the trenches a new tool that provided additional bandwidth—the switch.

The Trouble with Hubs

A classic 10BaseT network with a hub can only have one message on the wire at any time. When two computers send at the same time, the hub dutifully repeats both signals. The nodes recognize the collision and, following the rules of

CSMA/CD, attempt to resend. Add in enough computers, and the number of collisions increases, lowering the effective transmission speed for the whole network. A busy network becomes a slow network because all the computers share the same collision domain.

Switches to the Rescue

An Ethernet *switch* looks like a hub because all nodes plug into it (Figure 4.5). But switches don't function like hubs inside. Switches come with extra smarts that enable them to take advantage of MAC addresses, effectively creating point-to-point connections between two conversing computers. This gives every conversation between two computers the full bandwidth of the network.

To see a switch in action, check out Figure 4.6. When you first turn on a switch, it acts exactly as though it were a hub, passing all incoming frames right back out to all the other ports. As it forwards all frames, however, the switch copies the source MAC addresses and quickly creates an electronic table of the MAC addresses of each connected computer. The table is called a *source address table (SAT)*.

> ### Exam Tip
>
> One classic difference between a hub and a switch is in the repeating of packets during normal use. Although it's true that switches initially forward all frames, they filter by MAC address in regular use. Hubs never learn and always forward all frames.

As soon as this table is created, the switch begins to do something amazing. When a computer sends a frame into the switch destined for another computer on the same switch, the switch acts like a telephone operator, creating an on-the-fly connection between the two devices. While these two devices communicate, it's as

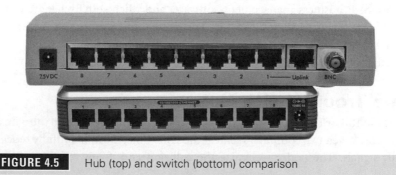

FIGURE 4.5 Hub (top) and switch (bottom) comparison

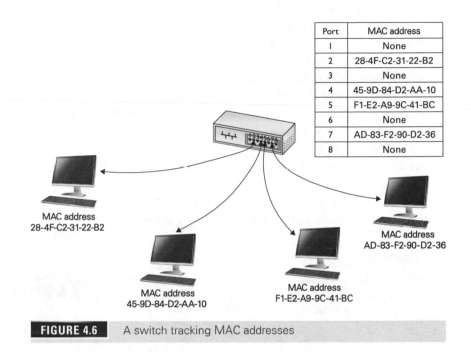

Port	MAC address
1	None
2	28-4F-C2-31-22-B2
3	None
4	45-9D-84-D2-AA-10
5	F1-E2-A9-9C-41-BC
6	None
7	AD-83-F2-90-D2-36
8	None

MAC address
28-4F-C2-31-22-B2

MAC address
AD-83-F2-90-D2-36

MAC address
45-9D-84-D2-AA-10

MAC address
F1-E2-A9-9C-41-BC

FIGURE 4.6   A switch tracking MAC addresses

though they are the only two computers on the network. Figure 4.7 shows this in action. Because the switch handles each conversation individually, each conversation runs at 10 Mbps.

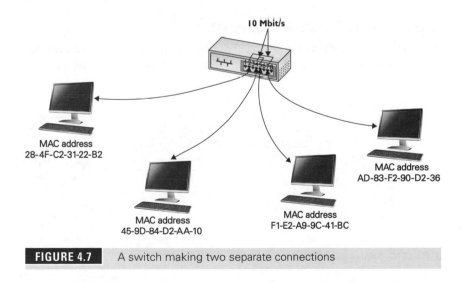

10 Mbit/s

MAC address
28-4F-C2-31-22-B2

MAC address
AD-83-F2-90-D2-36

MAC address
45-9D-84-D2-AA-10

MAC address
F1-E2-A9-9C-41-BC

FIGURE 4.7   A switch making two separate connections

Each port on a switch is in its own collision domain, plus the switch can buffer incoming frames. That means that two nodes connected to the switch can send data at the same time and the switch will handle it without any collision.

With half-duplex switches, collisions can occur and the rules of CSMA/CD apply. These collisions can only happen between the switch and a node, not between two nodes. If the switch forwards a frame to a node from any other node at the same time that the node tries to send a frame to any node through the same switchport, that's a collision.

Network developers eventually figured out how to make switches and NICs run in full-duplex mode so they could send and receive data at the same time. With full-duplex Ethernet, CSMA/CD is disabled and no collisions can occur. Each node will always get the full bandwidth of the network.

Local Lingo

Layer 2 Switch   Because a switch filters traffic on MAC addresses (and MAC addresses run at layer 2 of the OSI seven-layer model), they are sometimes called *layer 2 switches*.

Unicast messages—from one node specifically to another node—usually go only to the intended recipient when you use a switch. (The exception is when the switch does not have a MAC address in its SAT, as mentioned earlier.) The switch will send all broadcast messages to all the ports. You'll commonly hear a switched network called a *broadcast domain* to contrast it to a hub-based network with its *collision domain*.

Spanning Tree Protocol

Because you can connect switches together in any fashion, you can create redundant connections in a network. These are called *bridging loops* (Figure 4.8).

Exam Tip

The CompTIA Network+ exam refers to bridging loops as *switching loops*. The terms mean the same thing, but bridging loop is more common. Be prepared for either term on the exam.

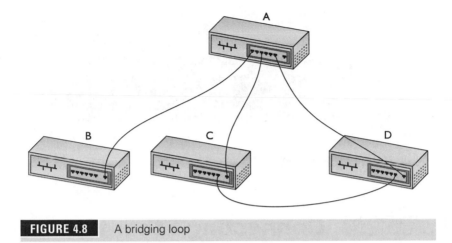

FIGURE 4.8   A bridging loop

In the early days of switches, making a bridging loop in a network setup would bring the network crashing down. A frame could get caught in the loop, so to speak, and not reach its destination.

The Ethernet standards body adopted the *Spanning Tree Protocol (STP)* to eliminate the problem of accidental bridging loops. Switches with STP enabled can detect loops, communicate with other switches, and set the looped port's state to blocking.

STP-enabled switches use a frame called a *Bridge Protocol Data Unit (BPDU)* to communicate with each other to determine things like the distances between them and to keep track of changes on the network.

Travel Assistance

Switches today all have STP enabled, and network designers create bridging loops in their networks to provide fault tolerance. Ports set as blocking still listen to the traffic on the network. If a link fails, the blocking port can become a forwarding port, thus enabling traffic to flow properly.

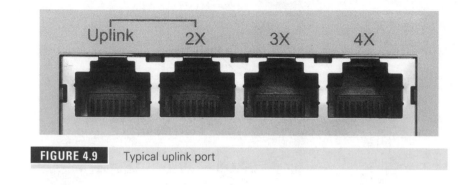

FIGURE 4.9 Typical uplink port

Objective 4.04 Connecting Ethernet Segments

You can combine multiple switches to create much bigger broadcast domains than any one switch can support. You can do this in two ways without using a bridge: via an uplink port or a crossover cable.

Uplink Ports

Uplink ports enable you to connect two switches using a *straight-through cable*. They're always clearly marked on the switch, as shown in Figure 4.9. To connect two switches, insert one end of a cable to the uplink on one switch and the other end of the cable to any one of the regular ports on the other switch. To connect more than two switches, you must daisy-chain your switches by using one uplink port and one regular port. Figure 4.10 shows properly daisy-chained switches.

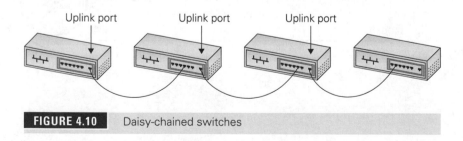

FIGURE 4.10 Daisy-chained switches

Working with uplink ports is sometimes tricky, so you need to take your time. Switch makers give their uplink ports many different names, such as crossover, MDI-X, and OUT. There are also tricks to using uplink ports. Refer to Figure 4.9. See the line connecting the uplink port and the port labeled 2X? You may use only one of those two ports, not both at the same time. Additionally, some switches place a button on one of the ports; you press this button to make it either a regular port or an uplink port (Figure 4.11). Pressing the button electronically reverses the wires inside the switch.

Exam Tip

Two terms you might see on hubs and switches and, consequently, on the exams: MDI and MDIX. A *media-dependent interface (MDI)* is a regular port on a hub or switch. A *media-dependent interface crossover (MDIX)* is an uplink port.

Crossover Cables

Switches can also connect to each other via special twisted-pair cables called crossover cables. A standard cable cannot be used to connect two switches without using an uplink port because both switches will attempt to send data on the second pair of wires (3 and 6) and will listen for data on the first pair (1 and 2). A *crossover cable* reverses the sending and receiving pairs on one end of the cable. One end of the cable is wired according to the T568A standard, whereas the other end is wired according to the T568B standard (Figure 4.12). With the sending and receiving pairs reversed, the switches can hear each other; hence, the need for two standards for connecting RJ-45 jacks to UTP cables.

A crossover cable connects to a regular port on each switch. Keep in mind that you can still daisy-chain even when you use crossover cables.

FIGURE 4.11 Pressing the Normal/Uplink button toggles the port between regular and uplink

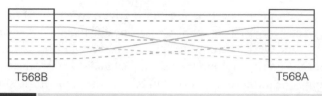

T568B   T568A

FIGURE 4.12   A crossover cable reverses the sending and receiving pairs.

In a pinch, you can use a crossover cable to connect two computers together using 10BaseT NICs with no switch between them at all. This is handy for quickie connections, such as for a nice little home network or when you absolutely, positively must chase down a friend in a computer game!

Be careful about confusing crossover cables with uplink ports. First, never connect two switches by their uplink ports with a straight-through cable. This creates two crossings, and you always need an odd amount of crossings for this to work. Take a straight-through cable; connect one end to the uplink port on one switch and the other end to any regular port on the other switch. Second, if you use a crossover cable, just plug each end into any handy regular port on each switch.

> **Travel Advisory**
>
> **Crossing Crossovers**   If you mess up your crossover connections, you won't cause any damage, but the connection will not work. Think about it. If you take a straight-through cable (that is, not a crossover cable) and try to connect two PCs directly, it won't work. Both PCs will try to use the same send and receive wires. When you plug the two PCs into a switch, the switch electronically crosses the data wires, so one NIC sends and the other can receive. If you plug a second switch to the first switch using regular ports, you essentially cross the cross and create a straight connection again between the two PCs! That won't work. Luckily, nothing gets hurt—except your reputation if one of your colleagues notes your mistake!

Objective 4.05   # Routers

Routers connect networks together. They filter and forward traffic relying on layer-3 addresses to get the traffic to the proper network. Because of the more sophisticated addressing schemes used by routers, they can support multiple routes between networks. The networks connected by the routers can be different types of networks (for example, Ethernet and DOCSIS).

Local Lingo

DOCSIS   Cable companies use the network standard called DOCSIS to enable communication via coax and cable modems. You'll learn more about this in Chapter 8.

Router technology holds together the Internet, providing multiple pathways between the hundreds of networks that make up the entire system (see Figure 4.13). Most routers, however, see much more humble service doing the same kinds of things as bridges, linking networks or sites to form a wide area network (WAN).

Exam Tip

Routers operate at layer 3 of the OSI model, also known as the Network layer.

Routers rely on layer-3 addressing, also called *network addressing*. A network address tells the router two pieces of information: the specific machine to which a packet should be delivered, and the network on which that machine resides. The IP addresses used on the Internet are examples of network addresses (see Chapter 5 for a discussion of IP addressing).

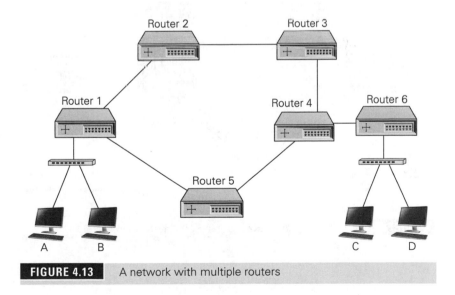

FIGURE 4.13   A network with multiple routers

Given the destination network address, a properly configured router can determine the best route to the destination machine. In Figure 4.13, router 1 needs to deliver a packet from machine A to machine D. Assuming that all the links between the routers operate at the same speed, the most efficient route for the packet should be router 1 to 5 to 4 to 6. That route requires four hops. A *hop* is the process of passing through a router en route to the final destination. Alternative routes exist, but the router ignores them because they require more hops. In the event of a break in the link between routers 1 and 5, router 1 should automatically calculate the next-best route (if one exists) and redirect traffic to the alternative route: router 1 to 2 to 3 to 4 to 6 (see Figure 4.14).

Travel Assistance

You'll find more discussion on routers and routing in Chapter 6. I can't do them justice here before giving you details about addressing in a TCP/IP network, which you'll get in Chapter 5.

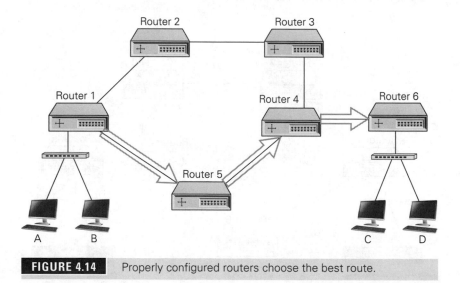

FIGURE 4.14 Properly configured routers choose the best route.

Objective 4.06 **Wireless Access Points**

A wireless access point (WAP) enables nodes with Wi-Fi NICs to connect into a LAN using radio waves. WAPs support one or more 802.11 standards and nodes that use those standards. Many WAPs support multiple standards, thus enabling a variety of Wi-Fi devices to connect and network. All 802.11n WAPs, for example, can support devices running 802.11n, 802.11g, and 802.11b; some support 802.11a devices as well.

WAPs provide a bridge between wired and wireless networks. Wired nodes using CSMA/CD can communicate seamlessly with wireless nodes using CSMA/CA, and vice versa.

WAPs designed for small office/home office (SOHO) environments generally come as part of a much larger bundle of hardware, usually called a "router," though routing is but one of the functions. The Linksys box in Figure 4.15, for example, is a combination WAP, router, and four-port switch, plus it offers excellent security features through its firmware.

FIGURE 4.15 Linksys WAP, router, and switch, all-in-one box

CHECKPOINT

✔**Objective 4.01: Network Interfaces**   A network interface card gets you on the network, but it must be the right fit for your computer system or whatever you're plugging it into. You must also make sure that it has the right connectors for the network media and that it supports the right network standard and speeds—for example, 100/1000 Mbps Ethernet. One very important task performed by a NIC is to give your computer system a unique address in the network; this is known as the *media access control (MAC)* address. This address is unique on every NIC produced, but the top 24 bits of the MAC address can be used to identify the NIC (or NIC component) manufacturer.

✔**Objective 4:02: Repeaters, Hubs, and Bridges**   Repeaters provide a simple way to extend a bus-based network over the basic 185-meter (Thinnet) or 500-meter (Thicknet), 30/100-device (Thin/Thick) segment maximums. Hubs behave like multiport repeaters to connect machines to a star bus network. Both devices have no specific understanding of the data they are passing between ports and therefore do not provide any form of traffic management.

Bridges can link together segments of a network, just like a repeater, but they also build up an internal MAC address table, identifying the computer systems on either side of their interfaces so they can determine whether a data packet actually needs to pass across the bridge; this helps with traffic management and thus improves overall network performance. Bridges pass broadcast network traffic because they break up the collision domain, but not the broadcast domain.

✔**Objective 4.03: Switched Ethernet**   Switches are layer-2 devices that act like a bridge, with each port on the switch creating a network segment. This means that each port on the switch is its own collision domain. The switch filters traffic by sending the data only to the port that has the destination MAC address connected to it. This increases overall network performance and adds to the security of the network.

✔**Objective 4.04: Connecting Ethernet Segments**   You can combine multiple switches to create bigger broadcast domains in two ways without using a bridge: via an uplink port or a crossover cable. To connect two switches, insert one end of a straight-through cable to the uplink and the other end of the cable to any one of the regular ports on the other switch. The CompTIA Network+ name for an uplink port is MDIX. To connect using a crossover cable, plug the ends of the cable into regular ports on each switch.

✔**Objective 4.05: Routers**   Routers can do all the things that bridges can do, but they also support multiple paths between networks and can link together dissimilar network types, such as Ethernet and fiber. Routers are often used for wide area networking, providing interconnectivity between networked sites. Routers do not pass broadcast traffic; instead, they manage the identification of machine locations themselves, using network addresses that contain both a machine's address and the network on which it is located.

✔**Objective 4.06: Wireless Access Points**   Wireless access points are popular network devices that allow a wireless client to connect to a wired network. Today's WAPs offer a number of capabilities such as routing and switching.

REVIEW QUESTIONS

1. What is the minimum size of an Ethernet frame?

   A. 8 bytes

   B. 64 bytes

   C. 128 bytes

   D. 256 bytes

2. Which part of the frame contains information used for checking the validity of the frame?

   A. FCS

   B. Pad

   C. Preamble

   D. Type

3. Which device enables you to connect two networks, but discards broadcast traffic?

   A. Bridge

   B. Hub

   C. Switch

   D. Router

4. At which layer of the OSI model do switches work?

   A. Layer 1

   B. Layer 2

   C. Layer 3

   D. Layer 4

5. How are the connectors wired on a crossover cable?

   A. One end is T568A; the other end is T568B.

   B. Both ends are T568A.

   C. Both ends are T568B.

   D. One end is an RJ-45; the other end is an RG-6.

6. What is the purpose of a preamble in an Ethernet frame?

   A. It gives the receiving NIC time to realize a frame is coming and to know when the frame starts.

   B. It provides the receiving NIC with the sending NIC's MAC address so communication can continue.

   C. It provides error-checking to ensure data integrity.

   D. It contains a description of the data that is to follow so the receiving NIC knows how to reassemble it.

7. Which device enables you to connect two networks that use different technologies?

   A. Hub

   B. Repeater

   C. Router

   D. Switch

8. Upon looking at the front of a switch, you notice something labeled MDI-X. What is this for?

   A. It is a special receptacle for the power cable.

   B. It is a regular port used to connect computers.

   C. It is an uplink port used to connect the switch to another switch.

   D. It is the brand name of the switch.

9. What feature of switches prevents the problem of bridging loops?

   A. STP

   B. TCP/IP

   C. IEEE 802.3

   D. UTP

10. What feature of switches keeps track of which MAC address goes to each port?

   A. FCS

   B. SAT

   C. STP

   D. UTP

REVIEW ANSWERS

1. **B**   The minimum size of an Ethernet frame is 64 bytes.

2. **A**   The frame check sequence FCS contains error-checking information.

3. **D**   Routers connect networks, but discard broadcast traffic.

4. **B**   Switches work at layer 2, the Data Link layer, because they manage traffic using MAC addresses.

5. **A**   A properly wired crossover cable is T568A on one end and T568B on the other. All T568A or all T568B defines a straight-through cable. RJ-45 is for UTP; RG-6 is for coaxial. You wouldn't find them on the same cable.

6. **A**   The preamble gives the receiving NIC time to realize a frame is coming and to know when the frame starts.

7. **C**   A router enables networks to connect even if the networks use different technologies.

8. **C**   Uplink ports are often labeled MDI-X.

9. **A**   Spanning Tree Protocol (STP) prevents bridging loops. STP also stands for shielded twisted-pair; knowing the context in which the acronym is being used is important.

10. **B**   A switch keeps track of which MAC address goes to each port with its source address table (SAT).

TCP/IP

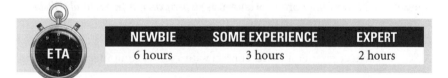

	NEWBIE	SOME EXPERIENCE	EXPERT
ETA	6 hours	3 hours	2 hours

109

In 1973, the U.S. Defense Advanced Research Projects Agency (DARPA) first proposed TCP/IP as a standard for connecting various existing networks so that they could exchange information. One aim was to develop a common standard to replace the growing number of proprietary and incompatible networks that were emerging. The work undertaken as part of the DARPA project eventually led to the development of the TCP/IP protocol suite and the Internet as we know it today. In the early days of networking, many protocols competed for market share. Microsoft networks used NetBIOS/NetBEUI, for example, and NetWare networks used IPX/SPX. Today, everybody uses TCP/IP.

Objective 5.01 The TCP/IP Protocol Suite

TCP/IP is made up of a number of protocols that work together to make it the most popular protocol in networking today. Each protocol in the *TCP/IP protocol suite* performs a specific role; this section identifies some of the popular ones.

Application Protocols

Application-level protocols are responsible for initiating some sort of request (on the client) or answering that request (on the server). When you surf the Internet, for example, you use an application (a web browser) that sends a request to a web server for a specific page. This communication happens across TCP/IP using an Application-layer protocol known as *Hypertext Transfer Protocol (HTTP)*.

Port Numbers

A TCP/IP client computer initiates contact with a server computer and uses specific values, called *port numbers,* to request a particular kind of service. Servers listen on ports that correspond to the services they offer. A web browser, for example, contacts a server at the destination port number 80; the web server listens to port 80 so it knows that the client wants a webpage.

The use of port numbers enables servers to provide more than one type of service. One of the servers in my office, for example, handles internal webpages for essential company policies. It also acts as a file server and a print server.

Finally, it handles our lunchtime gaming needs by running as a Counter-Strike or Unreal Tournament server. Clients request each of these different services using different port numbers.

Clearly defined port numbers exist for every popular, or *well-known*, TCP/IP application. A port number is a 16-bit value between 0 and 65535. Port numbers from 0 to 1023 are called *well-known port numbers* and are reserved for specific TCP/IP applications. (No TCP or UDP application can use the reserved port 0.)

Exam Tip

TCP/IP port numbers between 0 and 1023 are the well-known port numbers. You'll find them at every party.

Destination and Source Port Numbers   The client uses a *destination port number* to request a service. To communicate back and establish a session with the client, the server uses a port number specified by the client. The web client, in essence, says, "Hey, server! I'm requesting on port 80. You can reach me through my port 50002." In this example, port 50002 is the *source port number*. Port numbers that devices allocate on the fly for a source port number are also called *ephemeral ports*.

Registered and Dynamic Port Numbers   The port numbers from 1024 to 49151 are called *registered ports*. Less-common TCP/IP applications can register their ports with the Internet Assigned Numbers Authority (IANA). Unlike well-known ports, anyone can use these port numbers for their servers or for ephemeral numbers on clients. Most operating systems steer away (or are in the process of steering away) from using these port numbers for ephemeral ports, opting instead for the dynamic/private port numbers. Here's the full list of ports:

0–1023	Well-known port numbers
1024–49151	Registered ports
49152–65535	Dynamic or private ports

Sockets

Each computer on each side of a session must keep track of the status of the communication. In TCP/IP, the session information (a combination of the IP address and port number) stored in RAM is called a *socket* or *endpoint*. When discussing the information each computer stores about the connection between two computers' TCP/IP applications, the term to use is *socket pairs* or *endpoints*. A *session* or *connection* refers to the connection in general, rather than anything specific to TCP/IP. Many people still use the term *session,* however. Here's a summary of the terms used:

- Terms for the connection information stored on a single computer—*socket* or *endpoint*

- Terms for the connection information stored on two computers about the same connection—*socket pairs* or *endpoints*

- Terms for the whole interconnection—*connection* or *session*

As two computers begin to communicate, they store the information about the session—the endpoints—so they know where to send and receive data. At any given point in time, your computer probably has a large number of communications going on. If you want to know who your computer is communicating with, you need to see this list of endpoints. Windows, Linux, and Mac OS X come with *netstat,* the universal "show me the endpoint" utility. The netstat utility works at the command line, so open one up and type **netstat −n** to see something like this:

```
C:\>netstat -n
Active Connections
  Proto  Local Address          Foreign Address        State
  TCP    192.168.4.27:57913     209.29.33.25:80        ESTABLISHED
  TCP    192.168.4.27:61707     192.168.4.10:445       ESTABLISHED
C:\>
```

Travel Advisory

Even though almost all operating systems use netstat, there are subtle differences in options and output among the different versions.

When you run `netstat −n` on a typical computer, you'll see many more than just two connections! The preceding example is simplified for purposes of discussing the details. It shows two connections: My computer's IP address is 192.168.4.27. The top connection is an open webpage (port 80) on a server at 209.29.33.25. The second connection is an open Windows Network browser (port 445) on my file server (192.168.4.10). Looking on my Windows desktop, you would certainly see at least these two windows open (Figure 5.1).

Both connections require open ports on my computer. These show up under the Local Address column. Ephemeral port 57913 is open for the web browser; port 61707 is open for the network browser.

FIGURE 5.1   Two open windows

List of Application Protocols

Here are some examples of popular Application-level protocols and the port number(s) they use by default. And yes, you need to memorize the port numbers for the CompTIA Network+ exam.

Application-Layer Protocol	Ports	Transport Protocol	Description
FTP	20 and 21	TCP	*File Transfer Protocol* transfers files between clients and servers. Originally used two ports: 21 for control messages and 20 for the actual data. Only port 21 is in common use today. User names and passwords are sent in clear text, posing a potentially serious security risk.

Application-Layer Protocol	Ports	Transport Protocol	Description
Telnet	23	TCP	*Telnet* enables a user to log in remotely and execute commands on a remote host. Often used to log into UNIX/Linux hosts and managed network devices such as routers and switches. Sends user names and passwords in clear text, posing a potentially serious security risk.
SSH	22	TCP	*Secure Shell,* a secure replacement for Telnet, encrypts both login information and data sent over the connection.
SCP	22	TCP	*Secure Copy* uses the encryption provided by SSH to transfer files securely between hosts. Use SCP instead of FTP when available.
DNS	53	TCP and UDP	*Domain Name System* maps computer names to IP addresses. TCP 53 is used for DNS zone transfers, whereas UDP 53 is used for DNS queries and replies.
DHCP	67, 68	UDP	*Dynamic Host Configuration Protocol* is used to assign IP addresses automatically to clients on the network. The connectionless DHCP uses UDP port 67 for sending data to the server and UDP port 68 for sending data to the client. DHCP replaced an earlier protocol called *BOOTP* that functioned similarly.
TFTP	69	UDP	*Trivial File Transfer Protocol* transfers files between servers and clients without requiring any user login. Most commonly used for downloading operating systems and configuration files to systems with no local hard disk (for example, diskless workstations and routers).
HTTP	80	TCP	Web servers use the *Hypertext Transfer Protocol* to accept connections from and to send data to web browsers such as Google Chrome, Internet Explorer, and Mozilla Firefox.

Application-Layer Protocol	Ports	Transport Protocol	Description
SMTP	25	TCP	*Simple Mail Transfer Protocol* sends e-mail messages between mail servers. Mail clients also use SMTP to send outgoing e-mail to a mail server.
POP3	110	TCP	E-mail clients (such as Microsoft Outlook) use *Post Office Protocol version 3* to retrieve e-mail from mail servers.
IMAP4	143	TCP	E-mail clients use *Internet Message Access Protocol version 4* to access e-mail messages while leaving the messages themselves stored on the server.
NNTP	119	UDP	*Network News Transfer Protocol* transfers Usenet newsgroup messages between servers and between clients and servers.
NTP	123	UDP	*Network Time Protocol* is used to synchronize the time on TCP/IP hosts.
NetBIOS	137, 138, 139	TCP	Used to support functions such as Microsoft File and Print Sharing over TCP/IP networks.
SNMPv2/v3	161	UDP	*Simple Network Management Protocol* enables network management applications to monitor network devices remotely.
LDAP	389	TCP	Clients use the *Lightweight Directory Access Protocol* to search and update information in directories over a TCP/IP network. Directory services such as Microsoft's Active Directory can be accessed using LDAP.
Raw SMB	445	TCP	When NetBIOS support is disabled, Microsoft File and Print Sharing uses port 445.
IGMP	463	UDP	Clients use *Internet Group Multicast Protocol* to register as members of a multicast group. IGMP is popular with streaming video or gaming applications, for which the same data needs to be delivered to a group of systems at one time. This is far more efficient than sending many separate unicast messages.

Application-Layer Protocol	Ports	Transport Protocol	Description
LPR	515	TCP	The *Line Printer* protocol is used to communicate between the LPR client and the LPD (Line Printer Daemon) server. Typically used for printing using UNIX/Linux systems (and found as wrong answers in CompTIA Network+ exams).

Compound Application Protocols

Some common Application-layer protocols use multiple protocols to accomplish their tasks. HTTPS and VoIP provide good examples.

HTTP over Secure Sockets Layer (SSL) provides an encrypted connection between a web server and a web client. Most web browsers display a closed padlock to indicate a secure connection. HTTPS provides the basic fabric for e-commerce on the Internet. Although the protocol name still refers to SSL, current HTTPS implementations use *Transport Layer Security (TLS)*, an improved cryptographic protocol. HTTPS uses TCP port 443.

Exam Tip
TLS is up to version 1.2 as of this writing.

Voice over IP (VoIP) enables users to make phone calls over an IP network, such as the Internet. The user uses special VoIP boxes that support telephones that connect to the IP network instead of requiring the user to use a PC. VoIP uses a number of different protocols, two of which you must know for the CompTIA Network+ exam. The *Session Initiation Protocol (SIP)* establishes and takes down the communication channel for VoIP. The *Real-time Transport Protocol (RTP)* delivers the voice across the connection after it has been established.

SIP uses either TCP or UDP ports 5060 and/or 5061. RTP has no fixed port number, though many implementations use UDP ports 5004 and 5005.

Transport Protocols

When an application sends out a request, the request needs to be specified as either a connection-oriented request or a connectionless request, as you'll recall from Chapter 1. Two protocols handle the Transport-layer traffic in TCP/IP networks: TCP and UDP.

TCP

The *Transmission Control Protocol (TCP)* enables connection-oriented communication in networks that use the TCP/IP protocol suite. TCP is, by far, the most common type of session on a typical TCP/IP network. Figure 5.2 shows two computers. One computer (Server) runs a web server and the other (Client) runs a web browser. When you enter a computer's address in the browser running on Client, it sends a single packet with the SYN (synchronize) flag activated to the web server. If Server gets that packet, it returns a single packet with SYN, ACK (synchronize, acknowledge) flags active. Client then sends Server a single packet with an active ACK flag and immediately requests that Server begin sending the webpage. This process is called the *TCP three-way handshake*.

Once Server finishes sending the webpage, it sends a FIN, ACK (finished, acknowledge) packet. Client responds with an ACK (acknowledge) packet and then sends its own FIN, ACK packet. The server then responds with an ACK; now both parties consider the session closed (Figure 5.3).

Most TCP/IP applications use TCP because connection-oriented sessions are designed to check for errors. If a receiving computer detects a missing packet, it just asks for a repeat as needed.

Figure 5.4 shows a simplified TCP header. Notice the source port and the destination port, part of the TCP segment or UDP datagram encapsulated in the packet.

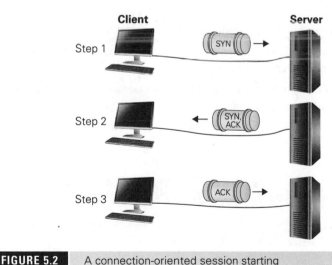

FIGURE 5.2   A connection-oriented session starting

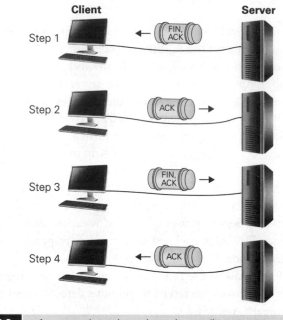

FIGURE 5.3   A connection-oriented session ending

Ports aren't the only items of interest in the TCP header. The header also contains these fields:

- **Sequence number**   This value is used to assemble/disassemble data.
- **ACK number**   This value tracks the readiness of the two communicating systems to send/receive data.
- **Flags**   These individual bits give both sides detailed information about the state of the connection.
- **Checksum**   The checksum checks the TCP header for errors.

| Source port | Destination port | Sequence number | ACK |

FIGURE 5.4   TCP header

UDP

User Datagram Protocol (UDP) runs a distant second place to TCP in terms of the number of applications that use it, but that doesn't mean UDP is not important. UDP is perfect for the types of sessions that don't require the overhead of all that connection-oriented stuff.

> **Exam Tip**
>
> Be sure that you know the difference between TCP and UDP when preparing for the CompTIA Network+ exam.

A UDP *datagram* doesn't possess any of the extras you see in TCP to make sure the data is received intact (Figure 5.5). UDP works best when you have a lot of data that doesn't need to be perfect or when the systems are so close to each other that the chances of a problem occurring are too small to bother worrying about. A few dropped frames on a Voice over IP call, for example, won't make much difference in the communication between two people. So there's a good reason to use UDP: it's smoking fast compared to TCP.

> **Exam Tip**
>
> Data gets chopped up into chunks at the Transport layer. The chunks are called *segments* with TCP and *datagrams* with UDP.

Internet Protocols

Internet-layer protocols handle addressing in a TCP/IP network. They help devices determine whether an intended recipient is local or remote.

Internet Protocol

The *Internet Protocol (IP)* is responsible for the addressing and routing of data to the remote system. *Addressing* means that IP is responsible for some sort of addressing scheme used to identify each system on the network (or Internet) and

| Source port | Destination port | Length | Checksum |

FIGURE 5.5 UDP header

for determining how to use that address to route the data to the destination. The addressing scheme that IP uses is known as an *IP address*. The IP address is a unique number assigned to your system that looks something like this: 192.168.1.10.

The full IP packet has 14 different fields. As you would expect, the destination and source IP addresses are part of the Network/Internet layer. Other fields include version, header length, and more. Dissecting the entire set of fields isn't important, but here are a few descriptions just to whet your appetite:

- **Version**   The version (Ver) field defines the IP address type: 4 for IPv4, 6 for IPv6.

- **Header Length**   The total size of the IP portion of the packet in words (32 bits) is displayed in the header length field.

- **Differentiated Services Code Point (DSCP)**   The DSCP field contains data used by bandwidth-sensitive applications like Voice over IP. (Network techs with long memories will note that this field used to be called the *Type of Service* field.)

- **Time to Live**   Routers on the Internet are not perfect and sometimes create loops. The Time to Live (TTL) field prevents an IP packet from indefinitely spinning through the Internet by using a counter that decrements by one every time a packet goes through a router. This number cannot start higher than 255; many applications start at 128.

- **Protocol**   In the vast majority of cases, the protocol field is either TCP or UDP.

Figure 5.6 shows a highly simplified IP header.

An entire section is devoted to IP addressing later in this chapter, so I will leave the rest of our discussion on IP for that section.

Internet Control Message Protocol (ICMP)

Sometimes applications are so simple that they're always connectionless and never need more than a single packet. The *Internet Control Message Protocol (ICMP)* works at layer 3 to deliver connectionless packets. ICMP handles

FIGURE 5.6   Simplified IP header

mundane issues such as disconnect messages (host unreachable) that applications use to let the other side of a session know what's happening. ICMP is used for informational and error reporting.

TCP/IP users rarely start a program that uses ICMP. For the most part, ICMP features are called automatically by applications as needed without you ever knowing. There is one very famous program that runs under ICMP, however: the venerable *Ping* utility. Run Ping from a command prompt to query if a host is reachable. Ping will show the *round trip time (RTT)*—some call this the *real transfer time*—for the ICMP packet, usually in seconds. If Ping can't find the host, the packet will time out and Ping will show you that information, too.

Objective 5.02 IPv4 Addressing

TCP/IP networks have long used the *Internet Protocol version 4 (IPv4)* protocol for addressing. (See "IPv6 Addressing" later in this chapter for a discussion about the protocol poised to replace IPv4.)

IPv4 addresses originally followed rigid blocks, called *classes*. Today's IPv4 addresses don't use classes, but are doled out under a different set of rules. Let's look at classic IPv4 addressing first, and then turn to modern IPv4 usage.

> ### Local Lingo
> **IPv4** Most writers drop the version number when discussing IP addressing. The assumption is that if there's no version number listed, it must be IPv4.

When installing TCP/IP on a system, techs need to configure three settings:

- **IP address**   A unique value that represents a node on a TCP/IP network.
- **Subnet mask**   A value used to help devices distinguish the host's network.
- **Default gateway**   The IP address of the router interface for your network. The router is responsible for sending data off your network if needed.

IP Addresses

The most common type of IP address consists of a 32-bit value. Here's an example:

11000000101010000000010000000010

Whoa! IP addresses are just strings of 32 binary digits? Yes, they are, but to make IP addresses easier for humans to use, the 32-bit binary value is broken down into four groups of eight, separated by periods, or *dots,* like this:

11000000.10101000.00000100.00000010

Each of these 8-bit values—called an *octet*—is, in turn, converted into a decimal number between 0 and 255.

If you took every possible combination of eight binary values and placed them in a spreadsheet, it would look something like the list in the left column. The right column shows the same list with a decimal value assigned to each.

Binary Value	Equivalent Decimal Value
00000000	0
00000001	1
00000010	2
00000011	3
00000100	4
00000101	5
00000110	6
00000111	7
00001000	8
(skip a bunch in the middle)	*(skip a bunch in the middle)*
11111000	248
11111001	249
11111010	250
11111011	251
11111100	252
11111101	253
11111110	254
11111111	255

Converted, the original value of 11000000.10101000.00000100.00000010 is displayed as 192.168.4.2 in IPv4's *dotted decimal notation* (also referred to as the *dotted octet numbering system*). Note that dotted decimal is simply a shorthand way for people to discuss and configure the binary IP addresses computers use.

Travel Advisory

When you type an IP address into a computer, the computer
ignores the periods and immediately converts the decimal
numbers into binary. People need dotted decimal notation,
but computers do not.

People who work on TCP/IP networks must know how to convert dotted
decimal to binary and back. You can convert easily using any operating system's
calculator. Every OS has a calculator (UNIX/Linux systems have about 100 different ones to choose from) that has a scientific or programmer mode like the
one shown in Figure 5.7.

To convert from decimal to binary, just go to decimal view, type in the value,
and then switch to binary view to get the result. To convert to decimal, just go
into binary view, enter the binary value, and switch to decimal view to get the
result.

Figure 5.8 shows the result of Windows 7's Calculator converting the decimal
value 47 into binary. Notice the result is 101111—the leading two zeroes do not
appear. When you work with IP addresses, you must always have eight digits, so
just add two more to the left to get 00101111.

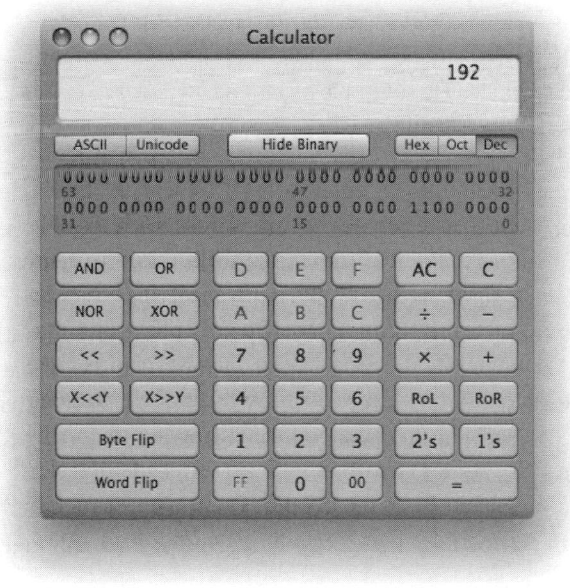

FIGURE 5.7   Mac OS X Calculator in Programmer mode

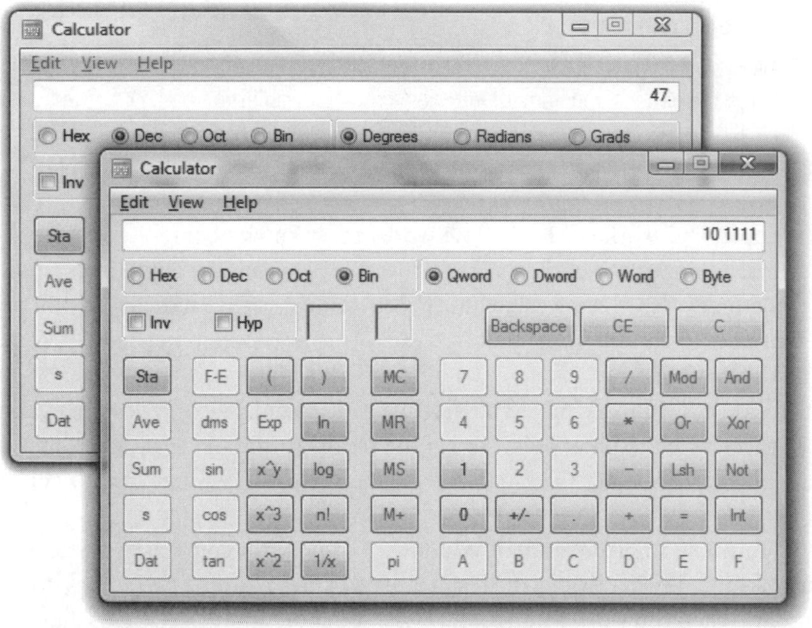

FIGURE 5.8   Converting decimal to binary with Windows 7's Calculator

Travel Advisory

Using a calculator utility to convert to and from binary/decimal is a critical skill for a network tech. Later on you'll do this again, but by hand!

Just as every MAC address must be unique on a network, every IP address must be unique as well. For logical addressing to work, no two computers on the same network may have the same IP address. In a small network running TCP/IP, every computer has both an IP address and a MAC address (Figure 5.9).

Every GUI operating system comes with graphical and command-line utilities to display a system's IP address and MAC address. Figure 5.10 shows a Mac OS X system's Network utility. Note the MAC address (00:14:51:65:84:a1) and the IP address (192.168.4.57).

You can use the command-line utility *ipconfig* to display the IP and MAC addresses. Run **ipconfig /all** to see the results shown in Figure 5.11.

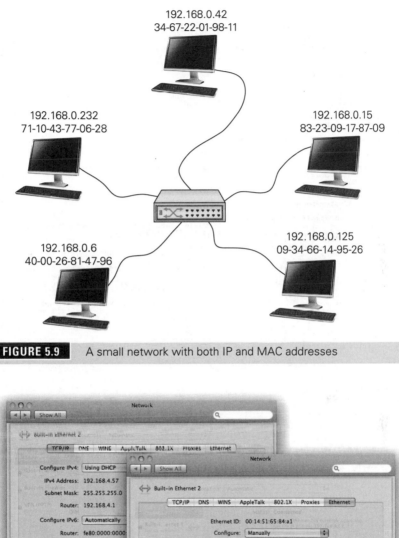

FIGURE 5.9 A small network with both IP and MAC addresses

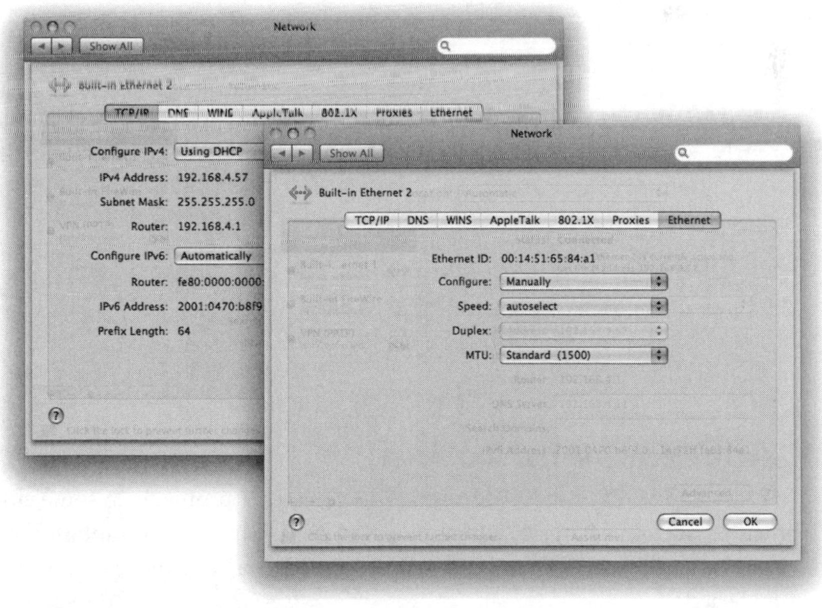

FIGURE 5.10 Macintosh OS X Network utility

```
Administrator: Command Prompt                                    ⬚ ⬚ X

Microsoft Windows [Version 6.0.6001]
Copyright (c) 2006 Microsoft Corporation.  All rights reserved.

C:\Users\scottj.TOTALHOME>ipconfig /all

Windows IP Configuration

   Host Name . . . . . . . . . . . . : scott-vista
   Primary Dns Suffix  . . . . . . . : totalhome
   Node Type . . . . . . . . . . . . : Hybrid
   IP Routing Enabled. . . . . . . . : No
   WINS Proxy Enabled. . . . . . . . : No
   DNS Suffix Search List. . . . . . : totalhome

Ethernet adapter Local Area Connection 2:

   Media State . . . . . . . . . . . : Media disconnected
   Connection-specific DNS Suffix  . :
   Description . . . . . . . . . . . : NVIDIA nForce Networking Controller #2
   Physical Address. . . . . . . . . : 00-15-F2-F4-AE-15
   DHCP Enabled. . . . . . . . . . . : Yes
   Autoconfiguration Enabled . . . . : Yes

Ethernet adapter Local Area Connection:

   Connection-specific DNS Suffix  . :
   Description . . . . . . . . . . . : NVIDIA nForce Networking Controller
   Physical Address. . . . . . . . . : 00-15-F2-F4-AE-14
   DHCP Enabled. . . . . . . . . . . : Yes
   Autoconfiguration Enabled . . . . : Yes
   IPv6 Address. . . . . . . . . . . : 2001:470:b8f9:1:1584:889a:269f:887<Deprec
ated>
   Temporary IPv6 Address. . . . . . : 2001:470:b8f9:1:4476:46b2:648c:ecdc<Depre
cated>
   Link-local IPv6 Address . . . . . : fe80::1584:889a:269f:887%8<Preferred>
   IPv4 Address. . . . . . . . . . . : 192.168.4.60<Preferred>
   Subnet Mask . . . . . . . . . . . : 255.255.255.0
   Lease Obtained. . . . . . . . . . : Monday, February 02, 2009 9:51:44 AM
   Lease Expires . . . . . . . . . . : Tuesday, February 10, 2009 9:51:13 AM
   Default Gateway . . . . . . . . . : fe80::223:4ff:fe8c:b720%8
                                       192.168.4.1
   DHCP Server . . . . . . . . . . . : 192.168.4.11
   DNS Servers . . . . . . . . . . . : 192.168.4.11
   NetBIOS over Tcpip. . . . . . . . : Enabled
```

FIGURE 5.11   The results from running `ipconfig /all`

In UNIX/Linux/Mac OS X, you can run the very similar *ifconfig* command. Figure 5.12, for example, shows the result of running **ifconfig** ("eth0" is the NIC) in Ubuntu.

Exam Tip

Make sure you know that ipconfig and ifconfig provide a tremendous amount of information regarding a system's TCP/IP settings.

IP Addresses in Action

Both LANs and WANs use IP addresses. This can create problems in some circumstances, such as when a computer needs to send data both to computers in its own network and to computers in other networks. How can this be accomplished?

```
                    vmuser@vmuser-desktop: ~
File  Edit  View  Terminal  Tabs  Help
vmuser@vmuser-desktop:~$ ifconfig
eth0      Link encap:Ethernet  HWaddr 00:0c:29:62:be:d4
          inet addr:192.168.4.43  Bcast:192.168.4.255  Mask:255.255.255.0
          inet6 addr: fe80::20c:29ff:fe62:bed4/64 Scope:Link
          UP BROADCAST RUNNING MULTICAST  MTU:1500  Metric:1
          RX packets:26569 errors:0 dropped:0 overruns:0 frame:0
          TX packets:11412 errors:0 dropped:0 overruns:0 carrier:0
          collisions:0 txqueuelen:1000
          RX bytes:29675139 (29.6 MB)  TX bytes:973598 (973.5 KB)
          Interrupt:18 Base address:0x2000

lo        Link encap:Local Loopback
          inet addr:127.0.0.1  Mask:255.0.0.0
          inet6 addr: ::1/128 Scope:Host
          UP LOOPBACK RUNNING  MTU:16436  Metric:1
          RX packets:2066 errors:0 dropped:0 overruns:0 frame:0
          TX packets:2066 errors:0 dropped:0 overruns:0 carrier:0
          collisions:0 txqueuelen:0
          RX bytes:103300 (103.3 KB)  TX bytes:103300 (103.3 KB)

vmuser@vmuser-desktop:~$ █
```

FIGURE 5.12   Results from running `ifconfig` in Ubuntu

To make all this work, IP must do three things:

- Create some way to use IP addresses so that each LAN has its own identification.
- Interconnect all of the LANs using routers and give those routers some way to use the network identification to send packets to the right network.
- Give each computer on the network some way to recognize if a packet is for the LAN or for a computer on the WAN so it knows how to handle the packet.

Network IDs

To differentiate LANs from one another, each computer on a single LAN must share a very similar IP address. Some parts of the IP address will match all the others on the LAN. Figure 5.13 shows a LAN where all of the computers share the first three numbers of the IP address, with only the last number being unique on each system.

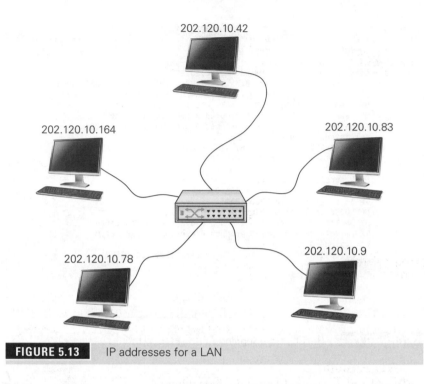

FIGURE 5.13	IP addresses for a LAN

In this example, every computer has an IP address of 202.120.10.*x*. That means the *network ID* is 202.120.10.0. The *x* part of the IP address is the *host ID*. Combine the network ID (after dropping the ending 0) with the host ID to get an individual system's IP address. No individual computer can have an IP address that matches the network ID.

Interconnecting

To organize all those individual LANs into a larger network, every TCP/IP LAN that wants to connect to another TCP/IP LAN must have a router connection. There is no exception to this critical rule. A router, therefore, needs an IP address on all the LANs that it serves (Figure 5.14) so it can correctly route packets.

That router is known as the *default gateway*. When configuring a client to access the network beyond the router, you use the IP address for the default gateway. Most network administrators give the LAN-side NIC on the default gateway the lowest host address in the network, usually the host ID of 1.

Routers use network IDs to determine network traffic. Figure 5.15 shows a diagram for a small, two-NIC router similar to the ones you see in many homes. Note that one port (202.120.10.1) connects to the LAN and the other port connects to the Internet service provider's network (14.23.54.223). Built into this

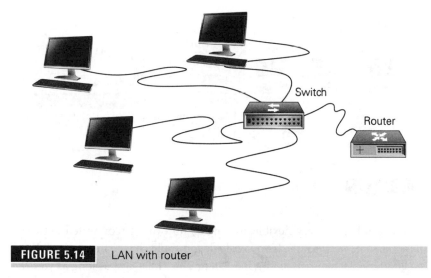

FIGURE 5.14 LAN with router

router is a *routing table,* the actual instructions that tell the router what to do with incoming packets and where to send them.

Travel Assistance

Routing tables are covered in more detail in Chapter 6.

Now let's add in the LAN and the Internet (Figure 5.16). (The LAN, of course, connects via a switch to the router.) When discussing networks in terms of network IDs, by the way, especially with illustrations in books, the common practice is to draw circles around stylized networks. Here, you should concentrate on the IDs—not the specifics of the networks.

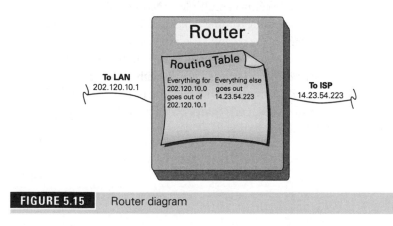

FIGURE 5.15 Router diagram

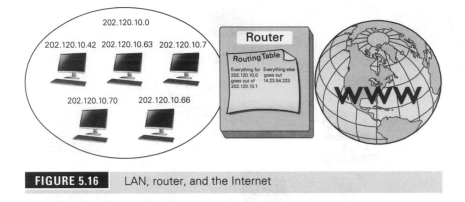

FIGURE 5.16 LAN, router, and the Internet

Network IDs are very flexible, as long as no two interconnected networks share the same network ID. If you wished, you could change the network ID of the 202.120.10.0 network to 202.155.5.0, or 202.21.8.0, just as long as you can guarantee no other LAN on the WAN shares the same network ID. On the Internet, powerful governing bodies carefully allocate network IDs to ensure no two LANs share the same network ID. I'll talk more about how this works later in the chapter.

So far you've only seen examples of network IDs where the last value is zero. This is common for small networks, but it creates a limitation. With a network ID of 202.120.10.0, for example, a network is limited to IP addresses from 202.120.10.1 to 202.120.10.254. (202.120.10.255 is a broadcast address used to talk to every computer on the LAN.) This provides only 254 IP addresses: enough for a small network, but many organizations need many more IP addresses. No worries! You can simply use a network ID with more zeroes, such as 170.45.0.0 (for a total of 65,534 hosts) or even 12.0.0.0 (for around 16.7 million hosts).

Network IDs enable you to connect multiple LANs into a WAN. Routers then connect everything together, using routing tables to keep track of which packets go where. So that takes care of the second task: interconnecting the LANs using routers and giving those routers a way to send packets to the right network.

Now that you know how IP addressing works with LANs and WANs, let's turn to how IP enables each computer on a network to recognize if a packet is going to a computer on the LAN or to a computer on the WAN. The secret to this is something called the subnet mask.

Subnet Mask

Picture this scenario. Three friends sit at their computers—Computers A, B, and C—and want to communicate with each other. Figure 5.17 illustrates the situation. You can tell from the drawing that Computers A and B are in the same LAN, whereas Computer C is on a completely different LAN. The IP addressing scheme can handle this communication, so let's see how it works.

The process to get a packet to a local computer is very different from the process to get a packet to a faraway computer. If one computer wants to send a packet to a local computer, it must send a broadcast to get the other computer's MAC address. (It's easy to forget about the MAC address, but remember that the network uses Ethernet and *must* have the MAC address to get the frame that encapsulates the packet to the other computer.) If the packet is for some computer on a faraway network, the sending computer must send the packet to the default gateway (Figure 5.18).

In the scenario illustrated in Figure 5.17, Computer A wants to send a packet to Computer B. Computer B is on the same LAN as Computer A, but that begs a question: How does Computer A know this? Every TCP/IP computer needs a tool to tell the sending computer whether the destination IP address is local or long distance. This tool is the subnet mask.

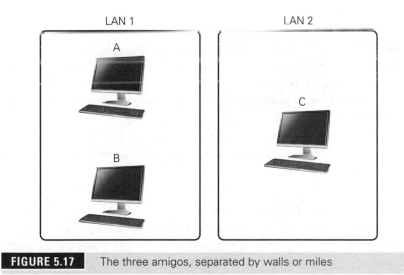

FIGURE 5.17   The three amigos, separated by walls or miles

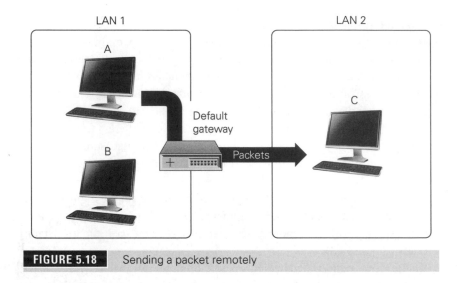

| FIGURE 5.18 | Sending a packet remotely |

A *subnet mask* is nothing more than a string of ones followed by some number of zeroes, always totaling exactly 32 bits, typed into every TCP/IP host. Here's an example of a typical subnet mask:

11111111.11111111.11111111.00000000

Convert each octet into decimal (use a calculator):

255.255.255.0

When you line up an IP address with a corresponding subnet mask in binary, the portion of the IP address that aligns with the ones of the subnet mask is the network ID portion of the IP address. The portion that aligns with the zeroes is the host ID. With simple IP addresses, you can see this with dotted decimal, but you'll want to see this in binary for a true understanding of how the computers work.

The IP address 192.168.5.23 has a subnet mask of 255.255.255.0. Convert both numbers to binary and then compare the full IP address to the ones and zeroes of the subnet mask:

	Dotted Decimal	Binary
IP address	192.168.5.23	11000000.10101000.00000101.00010111
Subnet mask	255.255.255.0	11111111.11111111.11111111.00000000
Network ID	192.168.5.0	11000000.10101000.00000101.*x*
Host ID	*x.x.x*.23	*x.x.x*.00010111

Before a computer sends out any data, it first compares the destination IP address to its own IP address using the subnet mask. If the destination IP address matches the computer's IP wherever there's a one in the subnet mask, then the sending computer knows the destination is local. *The network IDs match.*

If even one bit of the destination IP address where the ones are on the subnet mask is different, then the sending computer knows it's a long-distance call. *The network IDs do not match.*

Travel Advisory

The explanation about comparing an IP address to a subnet mask simplifies the process, leaving out how the computer uses its routing table to accomplish the goal. We'll get to routing and routing tables in Chapter 6. For now, stick with the concept of the node using the subnet mask to determine the network ID.

Exam Tip

At this point, you should memorize that 0 = 00000000 and 255 = 11111111. You'll find knowing this very helpful throughout the rest of the book.

Let's head over to Computer A and see how the subnet mask works. Computer A's IP address is 192.168.5.23. Convert that into binary:

11000000.10101000.00000101.00010111

Let's say Computer A wants to send a packet to Computer B. Computer A's subnet mask is 255.255.255.0. Computer B's IP address is 192.168.5.45. Convert this address to binary:

11000000.10101000.00000101.00101101

Computer A compares its IP address to Computer B's IP address using the subnet mask, as shown in Figure 5.19. For clarity, I've added a line to show you where the ones end and the zeroes begin in the subnet mask. Computers certainly don't need the line!

A-ha! Computer A's and Computer B's network IDs match! It's a local call. Knowing this, Computer A can now send out an ARP request, which is a broadcast, as shown in Figure 5.20, to determine Computer B's MAC address. The *Address Resolution Protocol (ARP)* is how nodes in a TCP/IP network figure out the destination MAC address based on the destination IP address.

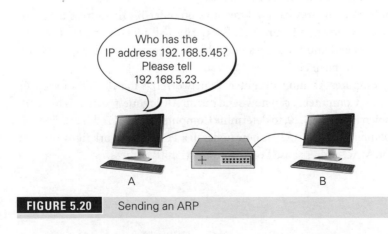

Hmm. I want to send a packet to B, but is he local or remote? Better compare IPs.

Subnet mask: 11111111111111111111111|00000000
Computer A IP: 11000000101010000000101|00010111
Computer B IP: 11000000101010000000101|00101101

He's got the same network ID as me– he's local.

A

B

FIGURE 5.19   Comparing addresses

The addressing for the ARP frame looks like Figure 5.21. Note that Computer A's IP address and MAC address are included.

Computer B responds to the ARP by sending Computer A an ARP reply (Figure 5.22). Once Computer A has Computer B's MAC address, it starts sending packets.

Who has the IP address 192.168.5.45? Please tell 192.168.5.23.

A

B

FIGURE 5.20   Sending an ARP

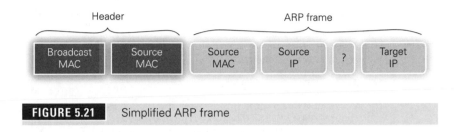

FIGURE 5.21 Simplified ARP frame

But what happens when Computer A wants to send a packet to Computer C? First, Computer A compares Computer C's IP address to its own using the subnet mask (Figure 5.23). It sees that the IP addresses do not match in the ones part of the subnet mask—meaning the network IDs don't match; therefore, this is a long-distance call.

Whenever a computer wants to send to an IP address on another LAN, it knows to send the packet to the default gateway. It still sends out an ARP, but this time to the default gateway (Figure 5.24). Once Computer A gets the default gateway's MAC address, it then begins to send packets with the destination MAC address of the default gateway in the frame, but with the destination IP address of the actual remote destination in the packet.

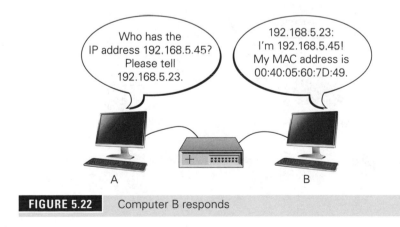

FIGURE 5.22 Computer B responds

FIGURE 5.23 Comparing addresses again

FIGURE 5.24 Sending an ARP to the gateway

Subnet masks are represented in dotted decimal like IP addresses—just remember that both are really 32-bit binary numbers. All of the following (shown in both binary and dotted decimal formats) can be subnet masks:

11111111111111111111111100000000 = 255.255.255.0
11111111111111110000000000000000 = 255.255.0.0
11111111000000000000000000000000 = 255.0.0.0

Most network folks represent subnet masks using special shorthand: a forward slash (/) character followed by a number equal to the number of ones in the subnet mask. Here are a few examples:

11111111111111111111111100000000 = /24 (24 ones)
11111111111111110000000000000000 = /16 (16 ones)
11111111000000000000000000000000 = /8 (8 ones)

An IP address followed by the / and number tells you the IP address and the subnet mask in one statement. For example, 201.23.45.123/24 is an IP address of 201.23.45.123 with a subnet mask of 255.255.255.0. Similarly, 184.222.4.36/16 is an IP address of 184.222.4.36 with a subnet mask of 255.255.0.0.

Fortunately, computers do all of this subnet filtering automatically. Network administrators need only to enter the correct IP address and subnet mask when they first set up their systems, and the rest happens without any human intervention.

> **Exam Tip**
>
> By definition, all computers on the same network have the same subnet mask and network ID.

Class IDs

To support the dispersion of IP addresses, and to make sure that no organizations used duplicate IP addresses on the Internet, IANA was formed to track and disperse IP addresses to those who need them. Initially handled by a single person (the famous Jon Postel) until 1998, IANA has grown dramatically and now oversees a number of Regional Internet Registries (RIRs) that parcel out IP addresses to large ISPs and major corporations. The RIR for North America is called the *American Registry for Internet Numbers (ARIN)*. The vast majority of end users get their IP addresses from their respective ISPs. IANA passes out IP addresses in contiguous chunks called *class licenses,* which are outlined in the following table:

	First Decimal Value	Addresses	Hosts per Network ID
Class A	1–126	1.0.0.0–126.255.255.255	16,277,214
Class B	128–191	128.0.0.0–191.255.255.255	65,534
Class C	192–223	192.0.0.0–223.255.255.255	254
Class D	224–239	224.0.0.0–239.255.255.255	Multicast
Class E	240–254	240.0.0.0–254.255.255.255	Experimental

Travel Advisory

127.0.0.0 Careful readers might have picked up on the missing range of numbers in this list: 127.0.0.0–127.255.255.255. These numbers are used for *loopback testing,* running diagnostics on a local computer. Any number in this range automatically maps to 127.0.0.1, also called the *loopback,* the *local machine,* or simply *home.*

A typical Class A license, for example, has a network ID that starts between 1 and 126; hosts on that network have only the first octet in common, with any numbers for the other three octets. Having three octets to use for hosts means you have an enormous number of possible hosts—over 16 million different number combinations. The subnet mask for Class A licenses is 255.0.0.0, which means you have 24 bits for host IDs.

Do you remember binary math? $2^{24} = 16,277,216$. Because the host can't use all zeroes or all ones (those are reserved for the network ID and broadcast IP, respectively), you subtract two from the final number to get the available host IDs.

Travel Assistance

The Internet Corporation for Assigned Names and Numbers (ICANN) manages the IANA. See www.icann.org for more details.

A Class B license, with a subnet mask of 255.255.0.0, uses the first two octets to define the network ID. This leaves two octets to define host IDs, which means each Class B network ID can have up to 65,534 different hosts.

A Class C license uses the first three octets to define only the network ID. All hosts in network 192.168.35.0, for example, would have all three first numbers in common. Only the last octet defines the host IDs, which leaves only 254 possible unique addresses. The subnet mask for Class C licenses is 255.255.255.0.

Multicast class licenses are used for one-to-many communication, such as in streaming video conferencing. There are three types of ways to send a packet: a *broadcast,* which is where every computer on the LAN hears the message; a unicast, where one computer sends a message directly to another user; and a *multicast,* where a single computer sends a packet to a group of interested computers. Multicast is often used when routers talk to each other.

Experimental addresses are reserved and never used except for occasional experimental reasons. These were originally called reserved addresses.

Exam Tip

Make sure you memorize the IP class licenses! You should be able to look at any IP address and know its class license. Here's a trick to help: The first binary octet of a Class A address always begins with a 0 (0*xxxxxxx*); for Class B, it begins with a 10 (10*xxxxxx*); for Class C, with 110 (110*xxxxx*); for Class D, with 1110 (1110*xxxx*); and for Class E, it begins with 1111 (1111*xxxx*).

Private vs Public IP Addresses

Lots of folks use TCP/IP in networks that either aren't connected to the Internet or want to hide their computers from the rest of Internet. Certain groups of IP addresses, known as *private IP addresses,* are available to help in these situations. All routers destroy private IP addresses. Those addresses can never be used on the Internet, making them a handy way to hide systems. Anyone can use these private IP addresses, but they're useless for systems that need to access the Internet—unless you use the mysterious and powerful NAT, which I'll discuss in the next chapter. (Bet you're dying to learn about NAT now!) For the moment, however, let's just look at the ranges of addresses that are designated as private IP addresses:

- 10.0.0.0 through 10.255.255.255 (1 Class A license)
- 172.16.0.0 through 172.31.255.255 (16 Class B licenses)
- 192.168.0.0 through 192.168.255.255 (256 Class C licenses)

All other Class A, B, and C IP addresses are *public IP addresses,* meaning they are routable and usable on the Internet.

Exam Tip

Make sure you can quickly tell the difference between a private and a public IP address for the CompTIA Network+ exam.

Need for Changes

IP class licenses worked well for the first few years of the Internet, but quickly ran into trouble due to the fact that they didn't quite fit for everyone. Early on, IANA gave away IP class licenses rather generously—perhaps too generously. Over time, unallocated IP addresses became scarce. In addition, the IP class licenses concept didn't scale well. If an organization needed 2,000 IP addresses, for example, it either had to take a single Class B license (wasting 63,000 addresses) or eight Class C licenses. As a result, a new method of generating blocks of IP addresses, called *Classless Inter-Domain Routing (CIDR)*, was developed.

Objective 5.03 CIDR and Subnetting

CIDR is based on a concept called *subnetting*: taking a single network ID and chopping it up into multiple smaller subnets. CIDR and subnetting are virtually the same thing. Subnetting is done by an organization—the organization is given a block of addresses and then breaks the single block of addresses into multiple subnets. CIDR is done by an ISP—the ISP is given a block of addresses, subnets the block into multiple subnets, and then passes out the smaller individual subnets to customers. Subnetting and CIDR have been around for quite a long time now and are a critical part of all but the smallest TCP/IP networks. Let's first discuss subnetting and then visit CIDR.

Subnetting

Subnetting enables a much more efficient use of IP addresses compared to class licenses. It also enables you to separate a network for security (separating a bank of public access computers from your more private computers) and for bandwidth control (separating a heavily used LAN from one that's not so heavily used).

Exam Tip

You need to know how to subnet to pass the CompTIA Network+ exam.

The cornerstone to subnetting lies in the subnet mask. You take an existing /8, /16, or /24 subnet and extend the subnet mask by adding more ones by taking away the corresponding number of zeroes. For example, let's say you have an Internet café with about 50 computers, 40 of which are for public use and 10 of which are used in the back office for accounting and such (Figure 5.25). Your network ID is 192.168.4.0/24. You want to prevent people using the public systems from accessing your private machines, so you decide to create subnets. You also have wireless Internet and want to separate wireless clients (never more than 10) on their own subnet.

You need to keep two things in mind about subnetting. First, start with the given subnet mask and add more ones to the right until you have the number of subnets you need. Second, forget the dots. They no longer define the subnets.

Never try to subnet without first converting to binary. Too many techs are what I call "victims of the dots." They are so used to working only with class licenses that they forget there's more to subnets than just /8, /16, and /24

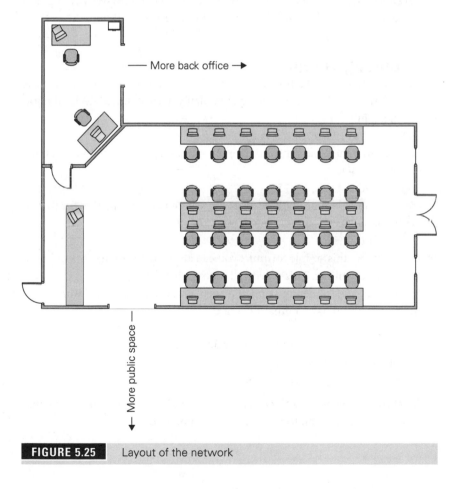

FIGURE 5.25 Layout of the network

networks. There is no reason network IDs must end on the dots. The computers, at least, think it's perfectly fine to have subnets that end at points between the periods, such as /26, /27, or even /22. The trick here is to stop thinking about network IDs and subnet masks just in their dotted decimal format and instead return to thinking of them as binary numbers.

Exam Tip

Some authors will drop the trailing zeros when using CIDR notation. I always do this when teaching because it's faster to write. So you might see a network ID like 192.168.4/24. The last octet of zero is *implied* by the /24. Either way works.

Let's begin subnetting the café's network of 192.168.4/24. Start by changing a zero to a one on the subnet mask so the /24 becomes a /25 subnet:

11111111111111111111111110000000

Calculating Hosts

Before going even one step further, you need to answer this question: On a /24 network, how many hosts can you have? Well, if you used dotted decimal notation, you might say

192.168.4.1 to 192.168.4.254 = 254 hosts

But do this from the binary instead. In a /24 network, you have eight zeroes that can be the host ID:

00000001 to 11111110 = 254

There's a simple piece of math here: $2^x - 2$, where x represents the number of zeroes in the subnet mask:

$2^8 - 2 = 254$

If you remember this simple formula, you can always determine the number of hosts for a given subnet. This is critical! Memorize this!

If you have a /26 subnet mask on your network, what is the maximum number of hosts you can have on that network?

1. Because a subnet mask always has 32 digits, a /26 subnet means you have 6 zeroes left after the 26 ones.

2. $2^6 - 2 = 62$ total hosts.

Excellent! Knowing how to determine the number of hosts for a particular subnet mask will help you tremendously in a moment.

Subnet mask   11111111111111111111111|00000000

FIGURE 5.26   Step 1 in subnetting

Your First Subnet

Let's now make a subnet. All subnetting begins with a single network ID. In this scenario, you need to convert the 192.168.4/24 network ID for the café into three network IDs: one for the public computers, one for the private computers, and one for the wireless clients.

Travel Advisory
You cannot subnet without using binary!

The primary tool for subnetting is the existing subnet mask. Write it out in binary. Place a line at the end of the ones, as shown in Figure 5.26.

Now draw a second line one digit to the right, as shown in Figure 5.27. You've now separated the subnet mask into three areas that I call (from left to right) the default subnet mask (DSM), the network ID extension (NE), and the hosts (H). These are not industry terms so you won't see them on the CompTIA Network+ exam, but they're a handy Mike Trick that makes the process of subnetting a lot easier.

You now have a /25 subnet mask. At this point, most people first learning how to subnet start to freak out. They're challenged by the idea that a subnet mask of /25 isn't going to fit into one of the three pretty subnets of 255.0.0.0, 255.255.0.0, or 255.255.255.0. They think, "That can't be right! Subnet masks are made out of only 255s and 0s." That's not correct. A subnet mask is a string of ones followed by a string of zeroes. People only convert it into dotted decimal to enter things into computers. So convert /25 into dotted decimal. First write out

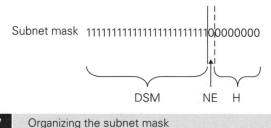

FIGURE 5.27   Organizing the subnet mask

25 ones, followed by seven zeroes. (Remember, subnet masks are *always* 32 binary digits long.)

```
1111111111111111111111110000000
```

Insert the periods in between every eight digits:

```
11111111.11111111.11111111.10000000
```

Then convert them to dotted decimal:

```
255.255.255.128
```

Get used to the idea of subnet masks that use more than 255s and 0s. Here are some examples of perfectly legitimate subnet masks. Try converting these to binary to see for yourself.

```
255.255.255.224
255.255.128.0
255.248.0.0
```

Calculating Subnets

When you subnet a network ID, you need to follow the rules and conventions dictated by the good folks who developed TCP/IP to ensure that your new subnets can interact properly with each other and with larger networks. All you need to remember for subnetting is this: start with a beginning subnet mask and extend the subnet extension until you have the number of subnets you need. The formula for determining how many subnets you create is 2^y, where y is the number of bits you add to the subnet mask.

Figure 5.28 shows a starting subnet of 255.255.255.0. If you move the network ID extension over one, it's only a single digit: 2^1.

That single digit is only a zero or a one, which gives you two subnets. You have only one problem—the café needs three subnets, not just two! So let's take the original /24 and subnet it down to /26. Extending the network ID by two digits creates four new network IDs, $2^2 = 4$. To see each of these network IDs, first convert the original network ID—192.168.4.0—into binary. Then add the four different network ID extensions to the end, as shown in Figure 5.29.

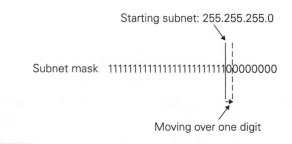

Starting subnet: 255.255.255.0

Subnet mask   11111111111111111111111100000000

Moving over one digit

FIGURE 5.28   Organizing the subnet mask

Original network ID: 192.168.4.0 /24
Translates to this in binary:
11000000.10101000.00000100.00000000

```
11000000101010000000010000000000
11000000101010000000010001000000
11000000101010000000010010000000
11000000101010000000010011000000
```

FIGURE 5.29   Creating the new network IDs

Figure 5.30 shows a sampling of the IP addresses for each of the four new network IDs.

Now convert these four network IDs back to dotted decimal:

Network ID	Host Range	Broadcast
192.168.4.0/26	(192.168.4.1–192.168.4.62)	192.168.4.63
192.168.4.64/26	(192.168.4.65–192.168.4.126)	192.168.4.127
192.168.4.128/26	(192.168.4.129–192.168.4.190)	192.168.4.191
192.168.4.192/26	(192.168.4.193–192.168.4.254)	192.168.4.255

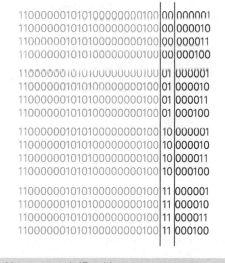

FIGURE 5.30   New network ID address ranges

The host ranges start with the first address available after the network ID. The first one is obvious, because the network ID ends with 0 in the fourth octet, so the first host would have a 1 in the fourth octet. The last number available in the host range is one number before the start of the next network ID, because the last available address on the subnet is the broadcast address.

Congratulations! You've just taken a single network ID, 192.168.4.0/24, and subnetted it into four new network IDs! Figure 5.31 shows how you can use these new network IDs in a network.

You may notice that the café only needs three subnets, but you created four—you're wasting one. Because subnets are created by powers of two, you will often create more subnets than you need—welcome to subnetting.

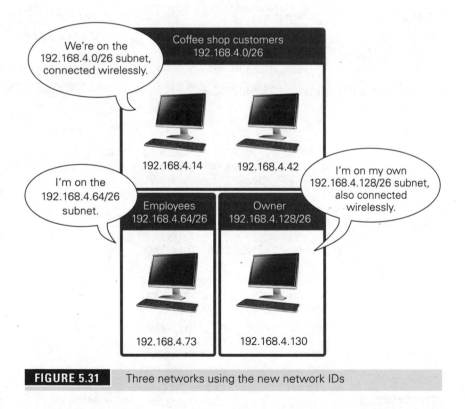

FIGURE 5.31   Three networks using the new network IDs

Travel Advisory

In terms of the café example, the unused network ID sets them up for scalability. If the café grows to need another subnet, it's already there for them to use without messing with the existing subnets.

Objective 5.04 **IPv6 Addressing**

The word is out (actually, it has been for some time)—the Internet's running out of spare 32-bit IP addresses. What is the Internet to do? Simple—use bigger addresses. But is that possible while making everything backward-compatible with the existing address scheme? Sure it is; here's IP version 6.

It sounds easy, but it has taken many years to perfect a replacement for the 32-bit IP addressing scheme.

With a 128-bit address range, IPv6 supports a mind-blowing 340,282,366, 920,938,463,463,374,607,431,768,211,456 addresses, which equates to approximately 665,570,793,348,866,943,898,599 addresses per square meter of the surface of the planet Earth.

IPv6 is in use today on parts of the Internet, but it's not having much impact on the desktop (yet). The new addressing scheme was designed to slide in place of IPv4 relatively seamlessly, and parts of the Internet infrastructure are being upgraded all the time without us noticing. IPv6 will address two major issues that plague IPv4: a shortage of addresses and the increasing complexity of routing information.

Exam Tip

For the CompTIA Network+ exam, you will need to know and identify an IPv6 address along with some basics about the IPv6 address schemes. You don't need to memorize the long numbers mentioned earlier—they're just there out of interest and to give you some sense of what "128-bit addressing" means.

IPv6 Addresses

An IPv6 address is a 128-bit address displayed in hexadecimal format and not the dotted decimal notation that is used by IPv4. The IPv6 address is divided into eight 16-bit groups that are separated by a colon (:). Many techs call these groups *hextets*, although that's not an official name. The following is an example of an IPv6 address:

```
65b3:b834:45a3:0000:0000:762e:0270:5224
```

An IPv6 address is not case-sensitive, and you do not need to place leading zeros at the beginning of the address when referencing a system that has leading zeros at the beginning. You can also replace consecutive zeros with double colons (::) when referencing an address that has a group of zeros in the address. For example, the loopback address in IPv6 is 0:0:0:0:0:0:0:1 and can be shorted to ::1, with the :: replacing all the consecutive zeros at the beginning of the address. This process is known as *compressing zeros*.

Exam Tip

You need to know that IPv6 uses a 128-bit address space. You may also be asked to identify the IPv6 loopback address: 0:0:0:0:0:0:0:1.

IPv6 uses three types of addresses: unicast, multicast, and anycast:

- **Unicast** Used for one-to-one communication.
- **Multicast** Used to send data to a group of systems.
- **Anycast** Applied to a group of systems providing a service. Clients that send data to the anycast address could have the data sent to any of the systems that are part of the anycast address.

To make life more complicated, you should be familiar with different types of unicast addresses for the CompTIA Network+ exam: global unicast, site-local unicast, and link-local unicast addresses handle different types of unicast traffic. Following is a quick breakdown of each of the different types of unicast addresses:

- **Global unicast** A public IPv6 address that is routable on the Internet. The address assigned to the host must be unique on the Internet. This address type is equivalent to a public IP address with IPv4.
- **Site-local unicast** A private address for the IPv6 protocol; the address always starts with *FEC0*. Assigning a site-local address to a system is

equivalent to using a private address in IPv4, such as 10.0.0.0. The site-local address cannot be used to communicate off the local site or network and is not reachable by other sites or systems on the Internet.

- **Link-local unicast**   An address that's automatically assigned to the system and is used to communicate only with other nodes on the link. Link-local addresses always start with *FE80*. This address type is equivalent to an APIPA address with IPv4.

Exam Tip

You should be familiar with two of the reserved addresses in IPv6: the loopback address, which is 0:0:0:0:0:0:0:1 (or ::1), and the address for a system with no address specified: 0:0:0:0:0:0:0:0 (or ::).

IPv6 Protocols

Not only has the address scheme changed with IPv6, but so have the protocols that exist in the IPv6 protocol suite. ICMPv6 provides a great example.

ICMPv6

The ICMPv6 protocol is responsible for error and status information as in IPv4, but it has been changed. ICMPv6 uses codes, while ICMPv4 used types and codes. For ICMPv6, each code indicates the type of message. Codes from 0 to 127 are used by error messages, while codes 128 to 255 are for information messages. For example, the echo request message is code 128 with ICMPv6, and the echo reply message is code 129.

ICMPv6 has expanded on its features from the ICMPv4 days. You should be familiar with the following two features of the ICMPv6 protocol:

- **Multicast Listener Discovery (MLD)**   Replaces the multicast protocol in IPv4 known as Internet Group Management Protocol (IGMP) and is used for multicast communication.

- **Neighboring Discovery (ND)**   Replaces ARP from the IPv4 days by performing the same function, but it's also responsible for neighboring router discovery, automatic address assignment, and duplicate address detection, to name a few features.

IPv6 has been totally redesigned and offers many additional new features, but for the CompTIA Network+ exam, you need to know only the basics.

Travel Advisory

Further information on IPv6 can be found at
http://technet.microsoft.com/en-ca/network/bb530961.aspx.

Objective 5.05 — Domain Name System

TCP/IP networks use *Domain Name System (DNS)* servers to translate IP addresses into names that humans can better handle and remember. DNS has
a set of rules for names and rules for name resolution that enable computers to
communicate over networks large and small.

DNS uses a hierarchical naming scheme. When a device wants to know the IP
address for a device somewhere else in a network, it queries the local DNS server.
The DNS server on a local network knows all the names and IP addresses for
local computers. If the LAN connects to other LANs, the DNS server will know
the IP address for a DNS server higher up the chain. That way, if a local computer needs to find the IP address for a remote computer, the DNS server doesn't
have to know it. It simply forwards the DNS request up to the next higher DNS
server. This continues until resolution occurs (Figure 5.32).

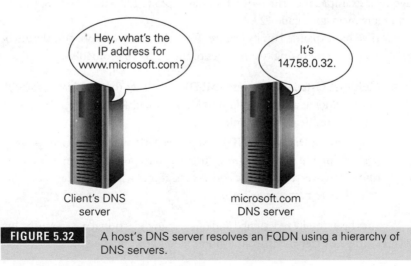

FIGURE 5.32   A host's DNS server resolves an FQDN using a hierarchy of
DNS servers.

The top-dog DNS server is actually a bunch of powerful computers dispersed around the world. They work as a team and are known collectively as the *DNS root servers* (or simply as the *DNS root*). The Internet name of this computer team is "."—that's right, just "dot." Sure, it's weird, but it's quick to type, and they had to start somewhere.

DNS root has the complete definitive name resolution table, but most name resolution work is delegated to other DNS servers. Just below the DNS root in the hierarchy is a set of DNS servers—called the *top-level domain servers*—that handle what are known as the *top-level domain (TLD) names*. These are the famous com, org, net, edu, gov, mil, and int names (although many TLDs have been added since 2001). The top-level DNS servers delegate to thousands of second-level DNS servers; these servers handle the millions of names, like totalsem.com and whitehouse.gov, that have been created within each of the top-level domains.

> ### Exam Tip
>
> The original top-level domain names were com, org, net, edu, gov, mil, and int.

A complete DNS name, including the host name and all of its domains (in order), is called a *fully qualified domain name (FQDN)*, and it's written with the root on the far right, followed by the names of the domains (in order) added to the left of the root, and the host name on the far left.

A typical DNS name for a web server, such as *www.google.com*, for example, has three components:

- .com refers to the root domain.
- .google refers to the google subdomain of the root domain.
- www refers to the specific computer (or cluster of computers, in this case).

The www.google.com FQDN maps directly to an IP address. DNS servers at the .com level certainly know the IP address for the google.com DNS server; the google.com DNS server knows the IP address for the www host.

FQDNs work at the local level too, by the way, even in networks that don't connect to the Internet. My office LAN is totalhome, with no .com or anything. So to access my file server, my employees and I type //fs7.totalhome in Network and the file server opens up. I'm using Internet FQDNs for the primary example of how DNS works because that's what most people are used to seeing.

Although this process might sound a bit complex, it works very well and provides a great deal of flexibility. Prior to the existence of DNS, every computer that wanted to use domain names had to have a local file—called a HOSTS file—that contained a table of IP addresses and their associated names. This file was stored on every system's hard disk. Because the HOSTS file changed on a daily basis, network techs had to keep downloading updates from the Internet! You can still use a HOSTS file today if you just have a small number of computers on a local network, but DNS is the way to go for bigger networks. A simple HOSTS file would look something like this:

```
109.54.94.197  scott.mikemeyersworld.com
138.125.163.17  mike.scottjernigansworld.com
127.0.0.1  localhost
```

Notice that the name localhost appears in the HOSTS file as an alias for the loopback address 127.0.0.1.

Exam Tip

Most DNS servers support a feature known as *Dynamic DNS (DDNS)*, which means that client systems can automatically register their own records in DNS upon bootup using DHCP (see the DHCP section below). This is a popular feature with Windows DNS servers. You could add a special option to the DHCP server, which is generally called the *DNS suffix*. The DNS suffix helps clients access network resources more efficiently.

DNS Records

A DNS server maintains a database of information about the domain names it knows, separating them according to type, using different *records*. For example, an A record maps a hostname to its IPv4 address. An AAAA record does the same for a hostname in an IPv6 network.

Local Lingo

MX, CNAME, PTR Other, less common DNS record types are *MX*, used by SMTP servers to determine where to send mail; *CNAME*, which maps aliases to IP addresses; and *PTR*, which is used in reverse lookups. My computer's name is mikespc.totalhome, but people in my office can ping mike.totalhome and reach the same physical computer. MX stands for Mail eXchanger; CNAME is short for canonical name; PTR is short for pointer.

DHCP

With so many settings (IP address, subnet mask, default gateway, DNS servers) to specify, the typical TCP/IP network administrator can spend days properly configuring each host manually. For troubleshooting purposes, you sometimes must put in all these settings manually, what we call *static configuration*, because the settings only change when you manually make the changes.

Fortunately, TCP/IP provides a protocol that takes much of the drudgery out of TCP/IP configuration: DHCP.

> **Travel Advisory**
>
> IPv6 uses DHCPv6 as its DHCP protocol, while the DHCP protocol that came with IPv4 is known as DHCPv4.

Dynamic Host Configuration Protocol (DHCP) servers distribute IP addresses and additional IP settings to machines on the network. Once a computer is configured to use DHCP, we call it a DHCP client. When a DHCP client boots up, it automatically sends out a special DHCP Discover packet using the broadcast address. This DHCP Discover message asks, "Are there any DHCP servers out there?" (See Figure 5.33.) What follows is a series of back-and-forth broadcasts.

The DHCP server responds to DHCP Discover requests with a DHCP Offer. The DHCP server is configured to pass out IP addresses from a range (called a *DHCP scope*) and a subnet mask (Figure 5.34). It also passes out other information, known generically as options, that cover an outrageously large number of choices, such as your default gateway, DNS server, Network Time server, and so on.

Is there a DHCP server out there? I'm wrestling with tough identity issues and need help.

FIGURE 5.33   Computer sending out a DHCP Discover message

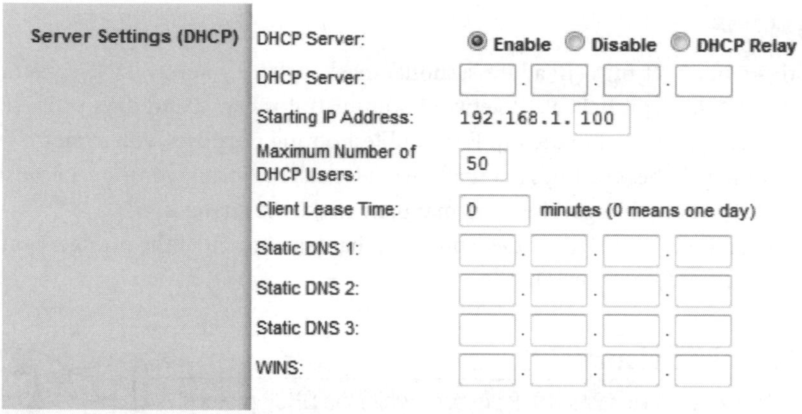

FIGURE 5.34   DHCP server main screen

> ## Exam Tip
>
> DHCP servers can be set up to reserve addresses for specific machines through what's called, appropriately, *DHCP reservations*. You use these for servers inside your network, for example, so if you had to change their IP addresses for some reason, you could do it from a central location. The other option is to use static IPs, but then you'd need to log into each server to change the IP addresses.

Figure 5.35 shows the configuration screen from the popular DHCP Server that comes with Windows Server 2008. Note the single scope. Figure 5.36 shows the same DHCP Server tool, in this case, detailing the options screen.

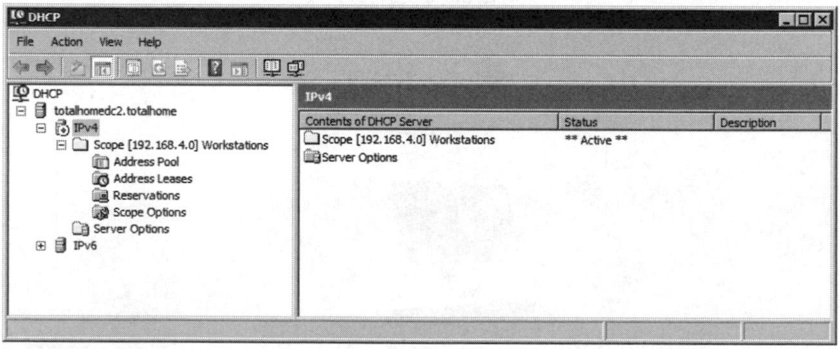

FIGURE 5.35   DHCP Server configuration screen

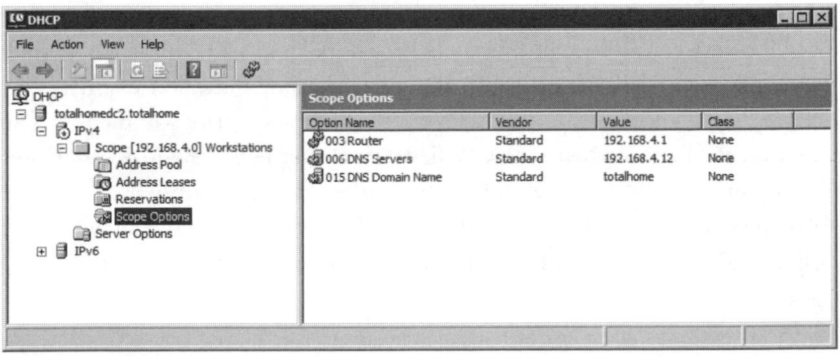

DHCP
File Action View Help
DHCP
totalhomedc2.totalhome
IPv4
Scope [192.168.4.0] Workstations
Address Pool
Address Leases
Reservations
Scope Options
Server Options
IPv6
Scope Options
Option Name
Vendor
Value
Class
003 Router
Standard
192.168.4.1
None
006 DNS Servers
Standard
192.168.4.12
None
015 DNS Domain Name
Standard
totalhome
None

FIGURE 5.36 DHCP Server options screen

The DHCP client sends out a DHCP Request—a poor name choice, as it is really accepting the offer. The DHCP server then sends a DHCP Acknowledge and lists the MAC address as well as the IP information given to the DHCP client in a database (Figure 5.37).

The acceptance from the DHCP client of the DHCP server's data is called a *DHCP lease.* A DHCP lease is set for a fixed amount of time, generally five to eight days. Near the end of the lease time, the DHCP client simply makes another DHCP Discover message. The DHCP server looks at the MAC address information and, unless another computer has taken the lease, always gives the DHCP client the same IP information, including the same IP address.

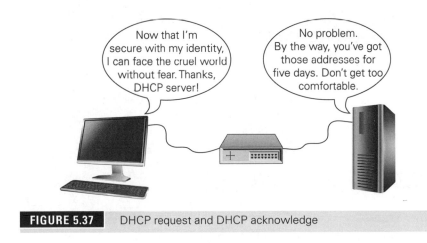

Now that I'm secure with my identity, I can face the cruel world without fear. Thanks, DHCP server!
No problem. By the way, you've got those addresses for five days. Don't get too comfortable.

FIGURE 5.37 DHCP request and DHCP acknowledge

Living with DHCP

DHCP is very convenient and, as such, very popular. It's so popular that you'll very rarely see a user's computer on any network using static addressing.

You should know how to deal with the problems that arise with DHCP. The single biggest issue is when a DHCP client tries to get a DHCP address and fails. You'll know when this happens because the operating system will post some form of error telling you there's a problem (Figure 5.38) and the DHCP client will have a rather strange address in the 169.254/16 network ID.

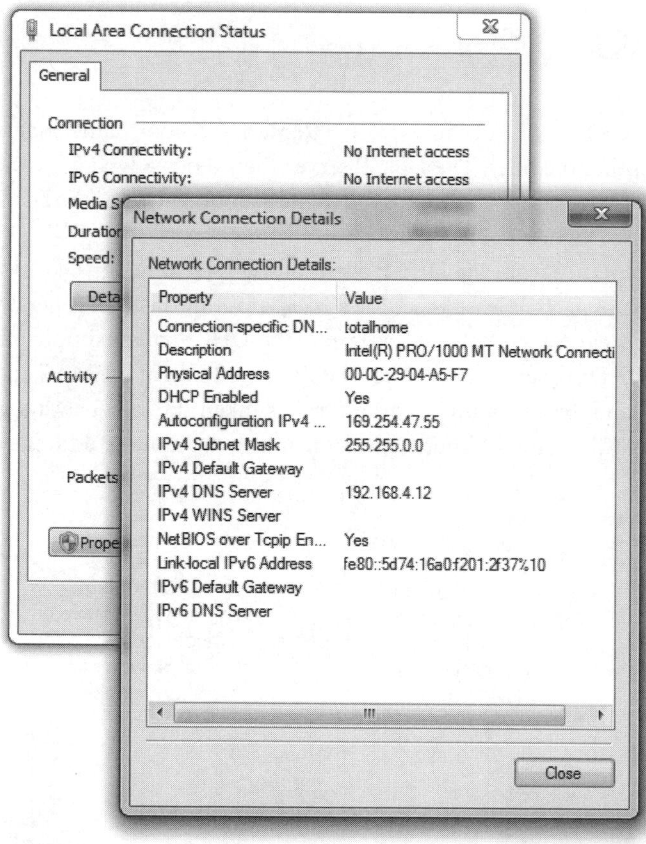

FIGURE 5.38   DHCP error in Windows 7

This special IP address is generated by *Automatic Private IP Addressing (APIPA)*. All DHCP clients are designed to generate an APIPA address automatically if they do not receive a response to a DHCP Discover message. The client only generates the last two octets of an APIPA address. This at least allows the dynamic clients on a single network to continue to communicate with each other because they are on the same network ID.

CHECKPOINT

✔**Objective 5.01: The TCP/IP Protocol Suite**   The TCP/IP suite is made up of a number of protocols that work together to make it the most popular protocol in networking today. Application-level protocols use port numbers to initiate some sort of request (on the client) and answer that request (on the server). TCP and UDP operate at the Transport layer, packaging data into segments and datagrams, and sending those to the IP for encapsulation into IP packets.

✔**Objective 5.02: IPv4 Addressing**   The original IP addressing scheme (IPv4) uses a 32-bit address to identify a host address and its network address based on a series of addressing schemes known as *IP classes*. The associated subnet mask identifies where the boundary between the network and host address lies and also allows us to change this boundary if we wish.

✔**Objective 5.03: CIDR and Subnetting**   CIDR did away with typical class IDs. Altering the default subnet mask enables you to subdivide a network ID into smaller sections, called *subnets*. Subnetting can help with general network management and also traffic management.

✔**Objective 5.04: IPv6 Addressing**   IPv6 uses a 128-bit addressing scheme to provide (in effect) a limitless supply of IP addresses, and it is needed because the 32-bit address range of IPv4 is running out of spare addresses. Parts of the Internet are already using IPv6, but it is not generally in use at the desktop yet. Be sure that you can identify an IPv6 address, and know that the loopback address is 0:0:0:0:0:0:0:1 or (::1) and that an unspecified address shows as 0:0:0:0:0:0:0:0 (or ::).

✔**Objective 5.05: Domain Name System**   Although it's easier for humans to refer to computer systems using computer names or fully qualified domain names (such as www.totalsem.com), communication between two systems can take place only if the target machine's IP address is known. TCP/IP environments use a database system called DNS (Domain Name System) to resolve IP addresses from fully qualified domain names, such as www.totalsem.com. DNS uses a hierarchical structure, with separate servers (or groups of servers) managing the resolution of various parts of a domain name. Use DHCP for automatic setup of hosts on a network, so you don't have to provide the IP address, subnet mask, and so on manually.

REVIEW QUESTIONS

1. Which of the following does not represent an IPv6 address?

    A. 2001:0db8:3c4d:0015:0000:0000:abcd:ef12

    B. 0:0:0:0:0:0:0:1

    C. 255.255.0.0

    D. ::1

2. Which of the following is a valid class B host address?

    A. 147.28.0.0

    B. 192.168.14.50

    C. 12.12.12.12

    D. 128.14.255.0

3. What is the minimum number of data bits required for subnet addressing to allow a total of five subnets to be created?

    A. 1

    B. 2

    C. 3

    D. 4

4. What port number does Telnet use?

    A. 443

    B. 23

    C. 80

    D. 43

5. Which of the following protocols provides TCP/IP name resolution?

   A. DHCP

   B. SNMP

   C. Telnet

   D. DNS

6. Which protocol provides automatic host IP address assignment?

   A. DHCP

   B. DNS

   C. NetBIOS

   D. BOOTR

7. Which protocol enables connectionless communication?

   A. DNS

   B. DHCP

   C. TCP

   D. UDP

8. What port number is used to connect to a DNS server?

   A. 20

   B. 23

   C. 53

   D. 67

9. A user calls and says his IP address is 169.154.50.12. What kind of address does he have?

   A. APIPA

   B. DHCP

   C. DNS

   D. Loopback

10. Which of the following is a valid class A address?

   A. 10.256.128.12

   B. 120.255.128.12

   C. 169.154.128.12

   D. 192.168.1.12

REVIEW ANSWERS

1. **C** 255.255.0.0 is an IPv4 class B subnet mask address. All other choices are valid IPv6 addresses.

2. **D** 128.14.255.0 is a valid class B address. Although choice A is a class B address, it is an invalid host address of all zeroes (x.x.0.0).

3. **C** Three bits allow a total of six subnets to be created, giving scope for the five we want to create. Two bits (choice B) would allow only two subnets.

4. **B** Telnet uses port 23.

5. **D** DNS provides name resolution. DHCP dynamically dishes out IP addresses and other important information to clients. SNMP is for network management, and Telnet provides terminal emulation functionality.

6. **A** DHCP, Dynamic Host Configuration Protocol, provides automatic host IP address assignment.

7. **D** UDP enables connectionless communication.

8. **C** DNS uses UDP and TCP port 53.

9. **A** The poor guy's computer can't reach a DHCP server and thus has a default APIPA address.

10. **B** Both A and B start in the right address range (first octet between 1 and 126), but the second octet in choice A contains an invalid number, because 255 is the highest number in an IPv4 octet.

Routing

	NEWBIE	SOME EXPERIENCE	EXPERT
ETA	4 hours	2 hours	1 hour

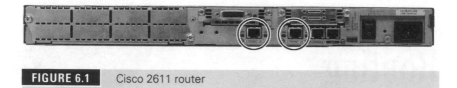

FIGURE 6.1   Cisco 2611 router

Routers interconnect networks to enable communication and resource sharing among those networks. Routers connect through physical means, such as cables or wireless radio frequency waves. Various routing protocols enable routers to exchange information and thus govern the flow of data. We touched on routers in Chapter 4 and then briefly again in Chapter 5. This chapter explores routers in more detail and looks at the process and protocols for routing.

Classically, routers are dedicated boxes that contain at least two connections, although many routers contain many more connections. In a business setting, for example, you might see a Cisco 2600 Series device, one of the most popular routers ever made. These routers are a bit on the older side, but Cisco builds their routers to last. With occasional software upgrades, a typical router will last for many years. The 2611 router shown in Figure 6.1 has two connections (the other connections are used for maintenance and configuration). The two "working" connections are circled. One port leads to one network; the other leads to another network. The router reads the IP addresses of the packets to determine where to send the packets. (I'll elaborate on how that works in a moment.)

Most techs today get their first exposure to routers with the ubiquitous home routers that enable PCs to connect to a DSL modem or a cable modem (Figure 6.2). The typical home router, however, serves multiple functions, often combining a router, a switch, and other features like a firewall (for protecting your network from intruders), a DHCP server, and much more into a single box.

FIGURE 6.2   Business end of a typical home router

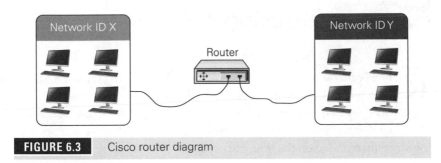

FIGURE 6.3 Cisco router diagram

Figure 6.3 shows the electronic diagram for a two-port Cisco router, whereas Figure 6.4 shows the diagram for a Linksys home router.

Note that both boxes connect two networks. The big difference is that the LAN side of the Linksys home router connects immediately to the built-in switch. That's convenient! You don't have to buy a separate switch to connect multiple computers to the cable modem or DSL receiver. Many users, and even some new techs, look at that router, though, and say, "It has five ports so it'll connect to five different networks," when in reality it can connect only two networks. The extra physical ports belong to the built-in switch.

All routers—big and small, plain or bundled with a switch—examine packets and then send the packets to the proper destination. Let's take a look at that process in more detail now.

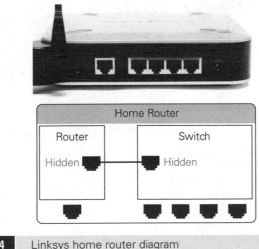

FIGURE 6.4 Linksys home router diagram

Routing Tables

Routing begins as frames come into the router for handling (Figure 6.5). The router immediately strips off the layer-2 information and drops the resulting IP packet into a queue (Figure 6.6). The important point to make here is that the router doesn't care where the packet originated. Everything is dropped into the same queue based on the time it arrived.

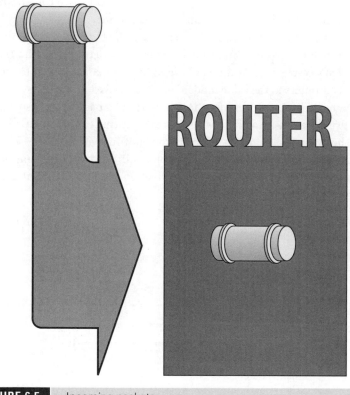

FIGURE 6.5 Incoming packets

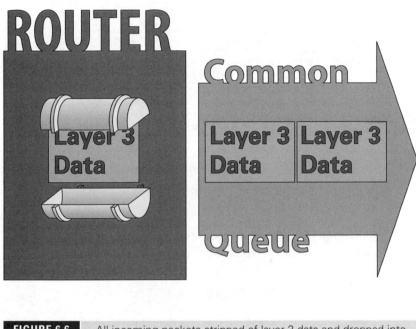

FIGURE 6.6 All incoming packets stripped of layer-2 data and dropped into a common queue

The router inspects each packet's destination IP address and then sends the IP packet out the correct port. To perform this inspection, each router comes with a *routing table* that tells the router exactly where to send the packets. Figure 6.7 shows the simple routing table for a typical home router. This router has only two ports internally: one that connects to whichever type of service provider you use to bring the Internet into your home (cable/DSL/fiber or whatever)—labeled as WAN in the Interface column of the table—and another one that connects to a built-in four-port switch—labeled LAN in the table. Figure 6.8 is a diagram for the router. Let's inspect this router's routing table; this table is the key to understanding and controlling the process of forwarding packets to their proper destination.

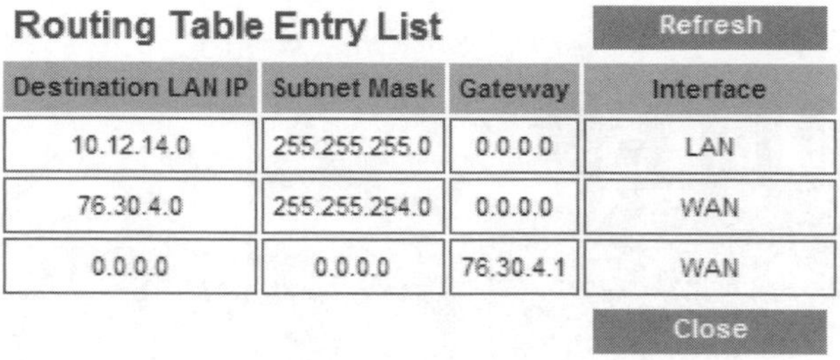

Routing Table Entry List

			Refresh
Destination LAN IP	Subnet Mask	Gateway	Interface
10.12.14.0	255.255.255.0	0.0.0.0	LAN
76.30.4.0	255.255.254.0	0.0.0.0	WAN
0.0.0.0	0.0.0.0	76.30.4.1	WAN
			Close

FIGURE 6.7   Routing table from a home router

Each row in this little router's simple routing table defines a single route. Each column identifies specific criteria. Reading Figure 6.7 from left to right shows the following:

- **Destination LAN IP** A defined network ID. Every network ID directly connected to one of the router's ports is always listed here.
- **Subnet Mask** To identify the network ID from an IP address, you need a subnet mask (described in Chapter 5).

Your router compares the destination LAN IP in the packet with the network ID and subnet mask in each route of its routing table to see if a packet matches that route. For example, if you had a packet with the destination 10.12.14.26 coming into the router, the router would use its routing table to determine that

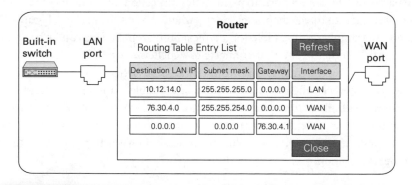

FIGURE 6.8   Electronic diagram of the router

the packet matches the first route shown in Figure 6.7. The other two columns in the routing table then tell the router what to do with the packet:

- **Gateway** The IP address for the *next hop* router; in other words, where the packet should go. If the outgoing packet is for a network ID that's not directly connected to the router, the Gateway column tells the router the IP address of a router to which to send this packet. That router then handles the packet and your router is done (you count on well-configured routers to make sure your packet will get to where it needs to go!). If the network ID is directly connected, then you don't need a gateway. Based on what's needed, this is set to 0.0.0.0, or to the IP address of the directly connected port.

- **Interface** This tells the router which of its ports to use. On this router, it uses the terms "LAN" and "WAN." Other routing tables use the port's IP address or some other type of abbreviation. Cisco routers, for example, use f0/0, f0/1, and so on.

The router compares the destination IP address on a packet to every listing in the routing table and then sends the packet out. It reads every line and then decides what to do. Some routers compare a packet to the routing table by starting from the top down, and other routers read from the bottom up. The direction the router chooses to read the routing table isn't important because the router must compare the destination IP address to every route in the routing table. The most important trick to reading a routing table is to remember that a zero (0) means "anything." For example, in Figure 6.7, the first route's destination LAN IP is 10.12.14.0. You can compare that to the subnet mask (255.255.255.0) to confirm that this is a /24 network. This tells you that any value (between 1 and 254) is acceptable for the last value in the 10.12.14/24 network ID.

Routing tables tell you a lot about the network connections. From just this single routing table, for example, the diagram in Figure 6.9 can be drawn.

So how do I know the 76.30.4.1 port connects to another network? The third line of the routing table shows the default route for this router, and almost every router has one. This line says

> (*Any destination address*) (*with any subnet mask*) (*forward it to* 76.30.4.1) (*using my* WAN port)

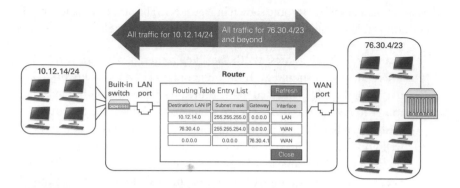

| FIGURE 6.9 | The network based on the routing table in Figure 6.7 |

Travel Advisory

Exceptions to Default Routes   There are two places where you'll find routers that do not have default routes: private (as in not on the Internet) internetworks, where every router knows about every single network, and the monstrous "Tier One" backbone, where you'll find the routers that make the main connections of the Internet. Every other router has a default route.

```
Destination LAN IP    Subnet Mask         Gateway         Interface
0.0.0.0               0.0.0.0             76.30.4.1            WAN
```

The default route is very important because this tells the router exactly what to do with every incoming packet *unless* another line in the routing table gives another route. Excellent! Interpret the other two lines of the routing table in Figure 6.7 in the same fashion:

> (*Any packet for the* 10.12.14.0) (*/24 network ID*) (*don't use a gateway*) (*just ARP on the* LAN *interface to get the MAC address and send it directly to the recipient*)

```
Destination LAN IP    Subnet Mask         Gateway         Interface
10.12.14.0            255.255.255.0       0.0.0.0             LAN
```

> (*Any packet for the* 76.30.4.0) (*/24 network ID*) (*don't use a gateway*) (*just ARP on the* WAN *interface to get the MAC address and send it directly to the recipient*)

```
Destination LAN IP    Subnet Mask         Gateway         Interface
76.30.4.0             255.255.254.0       0.0.0.0             WAN
```

I'll let you in on a little secret. Routers aren't the only devices that use routing tables. In fact, every node (computer, printer, TCP/IP-capable soda dispenser, whatever) on the network also has a routing table.

At first, this may seem silly—doesn't every computer only have a single Ethernet connection and, therefore, all data traffic has to go out that port? First of all, many computers have more than one NIC. (These are called *multihomed computers.*) But even if your computer has only a single NIC, how does it know what to do with an IP address like 127.0.01? Second, every packet sent out of your computer uses the routing table to figure out where the packet should go, whether directly to a node on your network or to your gateway. Third, the routing table tells the PC whether the communication is unicast, multicast, or broadcast.

Local Lingo

Multihoming Multihoming is using more than one NIC in a system, either as a backup or to speed up a connection. Systems that can't afford to go down (like web servers) often have two NICs that share the same IP address. If one NIC goes down, the other kicks in automatically.

Here's an example of a routing table in Windows. This machine connects to the home router described earlier, so you'll recognize the IP addresses it uses.

```
C:\>route print
===============================================================
Interface List
0x1 ........................... MS TCP Loopback interface
0x2 ...00 11 d8 30 16 c0 ...... NVIDIA nForce Networking Controller
===============================================================
===============================================================
Active Routes:
Network Destination        Netmask          Gateway       Interface  Metric
      0.0.0.0          0.0.0.0        10.12.14.1    10.12.14.201      1
   10.12.14.0      255.255.255.0     10.12.14.201  10.12.14.201      1
 10.12.14.201    255.255.255.255      127.0.0.1     127.0.0.1        1
 10.12.14.255    255.255.255.255     10.12.14.201  10.12.14.201      1
    127.0.0.0        255.0.0.0        127.0.0.1     127.0.0.1        1
  169.254.0.0      255.255.0.0       10.12.14.201  10.12.14.201     20
    224.0.0.0        240.0.0.0       10.12.14.201  10.12.14.201      1
255.255.255.255  255.255.255.255    10.12.14.201  10.12.14.201      1
Default Gateway:       10.12.14.1
===============================================================
Persistent Routes:
None
C:\>
```

Unlike the routing table for the typical home router you saw in Figure 6.7, this one seems a bit more complicated, if for no other reason than it has a lot more routes. My PC has only a single NIC, though, so it's not quite as complicated as it might seem at first glance. Take a look at the details. First note that my computer has an IP address of 10.12.14.201/24 and 10.12.14.1 as the default gateway.

Travel Advisory

Viewing Routing Tables in Linux and OS X   Every modern operating system gives you tools to view a computer's routing table. Most techs use the command line or terminal window interface—often called simply *terminal*—because it's fast. To see your routing table in Windows, Linux, or Mac OS X, for example, type this command at a terminal:
`netstat -r`
In Windows, try this command as an alternative:
`route print`

You should note two differences in the columns from what you saw in the previous routing table. First, the interface has an actual IP address—10.12.14.201, plus the loopback of 127.0.0.1—instead of the word "LAN." Second—and this is part of the magic of routing—is something called the metric.

A *metric* is just a relative value that defines the "cost" of using this route. The power of TCP/IP is that a packet can take more than one route to get to the same place. Figure 6.10 shows a networked router with two routes to the same place. The router has a route to network B with a metric of 1 using route 1, and a second route to network B using route 2 with a metric of 10.

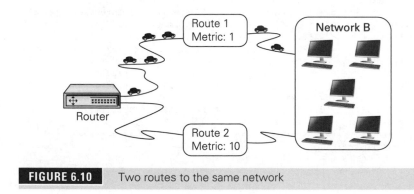

FIGURE 6.10	Two routes to the same network

Travel Advisory

When a router has more than one route to the same network, it's up to the person in charge of that router to assign a different metric for each route. With dynamic routing protocols (discussed in detail later in the chapter in "Dynamic Routing"), the routers determine the proper metric for each route.

Lowest routes always win. In this case, the router will always use the route with the metric of 1, unless that route suddenly stopped working. In that case, the router would automatically switch to the route with the 10 metric (Figure 6.11). This is the cornerstone of how the Internet works! The entire Internet is nothing more than a whole bunch of big, powerful routers connected to lots of other big, powerful routers. Connections go up and down all the time, and routers (with multiple routes) constantly talk to each other, detecting when a connection goes down and automatically switching to alternate routes.

I'll go through this routing table one line at a time. Remember, every address is compared to every line in the routing table before it goes out, so it's no big deal if the default route is at the beginning or the end. Windows machines read from bottom up, going through all local addresses before going out to the router, so that's how I'll go through it here.

The bottom line defines the default IP *flooded broadcast,* a packet with the destination address of all ones. All TCP/IP nodes that connect at the Data Link layer, regardless of network ID, will receive a packet directed to the IP broadcast of 255.255.255.255.

```
Network Destination   Netmask          Gateway        Interface      Metric
255.255.255.255       255.255.255.255  10.12.14.201   10.12.14.201       1
```

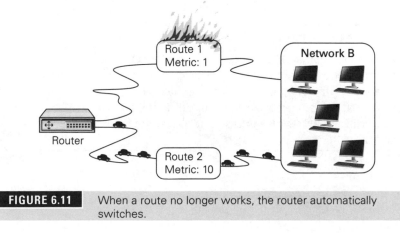

FIGURE 6.11   When a route no longer works, the router automatically switches.

The next line up is the multicast address range. Odds are good you'll never need it, but most operating systems put it in automatically.

```
Network Destination    Netmask      Gateway        Interface       Metric
224.0.0.0              240.0.0.0    10.12.14.201   10.12.14.201        1
```

The next route says that any addresses in the 169.254/16 network ID are part of the LAN (remember, whenever the gateway and interface are the same, the connection is local). If your computer uses Dynamic Host Configuration Protocol (DHCP) and can't get an IP address, this route would enable you to communicate with other computers on the network that are also having the same DHCP problem. Note the high metric.

```
Network Destination    Netmask        Gateway        Interface       Metric
169.254.0.0            255.255.0.0    10.12.14.201   10.12.14.201       20
```

This next line shows that anytime you send communications to any address starting with 127, the operating system will automatically map it to 127.0.0.1 (notice the Interface column), which *is* the official loopback address bound to the IP address and NIC. While 127.0.0.1 is the official loopback address, do appreciate that using any 128/8 address will work as the loopback. Try typing the following into a command prompt:

`Ping 127.34.32.61`

You'll see you get a successful ping—from 127.0.0.1!

```
Network Destination    Netmask        Gateway        Interface       Metric
127.0.0.0              255.0.0.0      127.0.0.1      127.0.0.1           1
```

The next line up is the *directed broadcast*. Occasionally, your computer needs to send a broadcast to the other computers on the same network ID. That's what this row signifies. The difference between a directed broadcast and a flooded broadcast is the former goes only to the targeted subnet, not the full broadcast domain.

Travel Advisory

Directed vs. Flooded Broadcasts In most networks, targeting a subnet is the same thing as targeting a broadcast domain. In a scenario where multiple subnets attach to a switched network, on the other hand, you would want to create a distinction between broadcasts that go to only the nodes on your network (a directed broadcast) or to all nodes (a flooded broadcast).

```
Network Destination    Netmask           Gateway       Interface       Metric
10.12.14.255           255.255.255.255   0.12.14.201   10.12.14.201         1
```

Okay, on to the next line. This one's easy. Anything addressed to this machine should go right back to it through the loopback (127.0.0.1). When you ping your IP address or the loopback address, nothing leaves the NIC. Traffic goes down to the NIC and then right back up to the OS.

```
Network Destination    Netmask           Gateway       Interface       Metric
10.12.14.201           255.255.255.255   127.0.0.1     127.0.0.1            1
```

The next line defines the local connection: (*Any packet for the* 10.12.14.0) (*/ 24 network ID*) (*don't use a gateway*) (*just ARP on the LAN interface to get the MAC address and send it directly to the recipient*) (*Cost of* 1 *to use this route*).

```
Network Destination    Netmask           Gateway       Interface       Metric
10.12.14.0             255.255.255.0     10.12.14.201  10.12.14.201         1
```

So, if a gateway of 10.12.14.201 here means "don't use a gateway," why put a number in at all? Local connections don't use the default gateway, although every routing table has a gateway column. The Microsoft folks had to put *something* there, thus they put the IP address of the NIC. That's why the gateway address is the same as the interface address. The NIC is the gateway between the local PC and the destination. Just pass it out the NIC and the destination will get it.

This is how Windows XP displays the gateway on this line. In Windows Vista and Windows 7, the gateway value for local connections just says "on-link"—a clear description! Part of the joy of learning routing tables is getting used to how different operating systems deal with issues like these.

The top line defines the default route: (*Any destination address*) (*with any subnet mask*) (*forward it to my default gateway*) (*using my NIC*) (*Cost of* 1 *to use this route*). Anything that's not local goes to the router and from there out to the destination (with the help of other routers).

```
Network Destination    Netmask           Gateway       Interface       Metric
0.0.0.0                0.0.0.0           10.12.14.1    10.12.14.201         1
```

In this section, you've seen two different types of routing tables from two different types of devices. Even though routing tables have different ways to list the routes and different ways to show the categories, they all perform the same job: moving IP packets to the correct interface to ensure they get to where they need to go.

Freedom from Layer 2

Routers enable you to connect different types of network technologies. You now know that routers strip off all of the layer-2 data from the incoming packets, but thus far you've only seen routers that connect to different Ethernet networks—and that's just fine with routers. But routers can connect to almost anything that stores IP packets. Not to take away from some very exciting upcoming chapters, but Ethernet is not the only networking technology out there. Once you want to start making long-distance connections, Ethernet disappears, and technologies with names like Data-Over-Cable Service Interface Specification (DOCSIS) (cable modems), Frame Relay, and Asynchronous Transfer Mode (ATM) take over. These technologies are not Ethernet, and they all work very differently than Ethernet. The only common feature of these technologies is they all carry IP packets inside their layer-2 encapsulations.

Most serious/industry-level (that is, not home) routers enable you to add interfaces. You buy the router and then snap in different types of interfaces depending on your needs. Note the Cisco router in Figure 6.12. Like most Cisco routers, it comes with removable modules.

If you're connecting Ethernet to ATM, you buy an Ethernet module and an ATM module. If you're connecting Ethernet to a DOCSIS (cable modem) network, you buy an Ethernet module and a DOCSIS module.

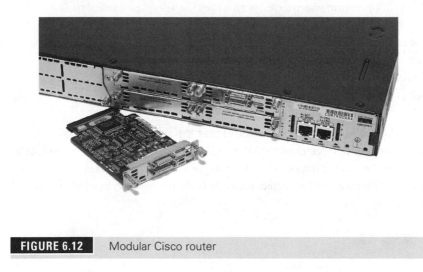

FIGURE 6.12 Modular Cisco router

Objective 6.02 # Network Address Translation

The ease of connecting computers together using TCP/IP and routers creates a rather glaring security risk. If every computer on a network must have a unique IP address, and TCP/IP applications enable you to do something on a remote computer, what's to stop a malicious programmer from writing a program that does things on your computer that you don't want done? All he or she would need is the IP address for your computer and the attacker could target you from anywhere on the network. Now expand this concept to the Internet. A computer sitting in Peoria can be attacked by a program run from Bangkok as long as both computers connect directly to the Internet. And this happens all the time.

Security is one problem. The other is a deal breaker—the IANA assigned the last of the IPv4 addresses as of February 2011. Although you can still get an IP address from an ISP, the days of easy availability are over. Routers running some form of *Network Address Translation (NAT)* hide the IP addresses of computers on the LAN but still enable those computers to communicate with the broader Internet. NAT extended the useful life of IPv4 addressing on the Internet for many years. It is extremely common and heavily in use, so learning how it works is important. Note that many routers offer NAT as a feature *in addition to* the core capability of routing. NAT is not routing, but a separate technology. With that said, you are ready to dive into how NAT works to protect computers connected by router technology and conserve IP addresses as well.

Travel Advisory

Intent Developers created NAT specifically to extend the life of IPv4. The fact that using NAT makes a network more secure is an added bonus.

The Setup

Here's the situation. You have a LAN with eight computers that need access to the Internet. With classic TCP/IP and routing, several things have to happen. First, you need to get a block of legitimate, unique, expensive IP addresses from an Internet service provider (ISP). You could call up an ISP and purchase a network ID, say 1.2.3.136/29. Second, you assign an IP address to each computer and to the LAN connection on the router. Third, you assign the IP address for the ISP's router to the WAN connection on the local router, such as 1.2.4.1. After everything is configured, the network looks like Figure 6.13. All of the clients on the network have the same default gateway (1.2.3.137). This router, called a *gateway router* (or simply a *gateway*), acts as the default gateway for a number of client computers.

This style of network mirrors how computers in LANs throughout the world connected to the Internet for the first 20 years, but the major problems of security and a finite number of IP addresses worsened as more and more computers connected.

NAT solved both of these issues for many years. NAT is a simple concept: The router replaces the source IP address of a computer with its outside interface address on outgoing packets. The simplest NAT, called *basic NAT,* does exactly that, translating the private or internal IP address to a global IP address on a one-to-one basis.

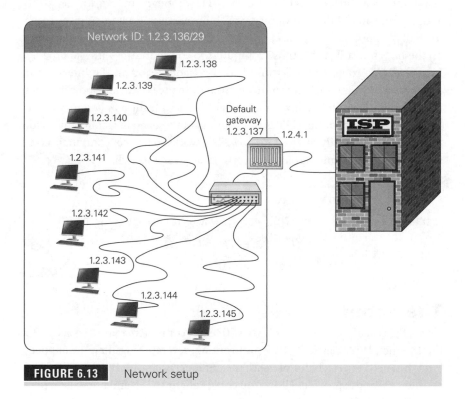

FIGURE 6.13   Network setup

> ### Exam Tip
>
> NAT replaces the source IP address of a computer with the source IP address from the outside router interface on outgoing packets. It is performed by NAT-capable routers.

Port Address Translation

Most internal networks today don't have one machine, of course. Instead, they use a block of private IP addresses for the hosts inside the network. They connect to the Internet through one or more public IP addresses.

The most common form of NAT that handles this one-to-many connection— called *Port Address Translation (PAT)*—uses port numbers to map traffic from specific machines in the network. Let's use a simple example to make the process clear. John has a network at his office that uses the private IP addressing space of 192.168.1.0/24. All the computers in the private network connect to the Internet through a single PAT router with the global IP address of 208.190.121.12/24 (see Figure 6.14).

When an internal machine initiates a session with an external machine, such as a web browser accessing a website, the source and destination IP addresses and port numbers for the TCP segment or UDP datagram are recorded in the PAT's translation table, and the private IP address is swapped for the public IP address on each packet. Plus, the port number used by the internal computer for the session is also translated into a unique port number and the router records this as well (see Figure 6.15).

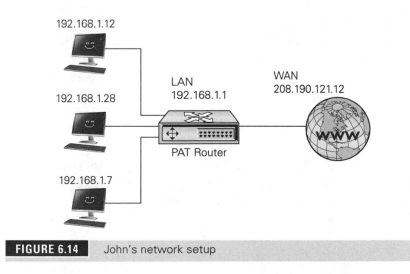

192.168.1.12

192.168.1.28

LAN
192.168.1.1

WAN
208.190.121.12

PAT Router

192.168.1.7

FIGURE 6.14   John's network setup

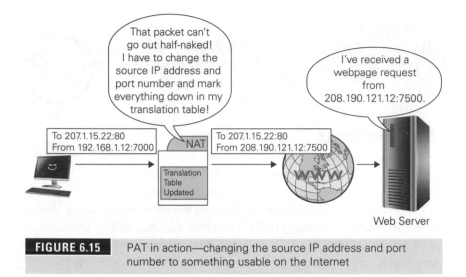

FIGURE 6.15 PAT in action—changing the source IP address and port number to something usable on the Internet

Table 6.1 shows a sample of the translation table inside the PAT router. Note that more than one computer translation has been recorded.

When the receiving system sends the packet back, it reverses the IP addresses and ports. The PAT router compares the incoming destination port and source IP address to the entry in the *NAT translation table* to determine which IP address to put back on the packet. It then sends the packet to the correct computer on the network. This works even when two computers on the inside access the same server on the outside, like in Table 6.1.

This mapping of internal IP address and port number to a translated IP address and port number enables perfect tracking of packets out and in. PAT can handle many internal computers with a single public IP address because the TCP/IP port number space is big, as you'll recall from Chapter 5, with values ranging from 0 to 65535. Some of those port numbers are used for common protocols, but many thousands are available for PAT to work its magic.

TABLE 6.1 Sample NAT Translation Table

Source	Translated Source	Destination
192.168.1.12:7000	208.190.121.12:7500	17.5.85.11:80
192.168.1.24:13245	208.190.121.12:15000	17.5.85.11:80

Local Lingo

Dynamic NAT With *dynamic NAT,* many computers can share a pool of routable IP addresses that number fewer than the computers. The NAT might have 10 routable IP addresses, for example, to serve 40 computers on the LAN. LAN traffic uses the internal, private IP addresses. When a computer requests information beyond the network, the NAT doles out a routable IP address from its pool for that communication. Dynamic NAT is also called *Pooled NAT.* This works well enough—unless you're the unlucky 11th person to try to access the Internet from behind the company NAT—but has the obvious limitation of still needing many true, expensive, routable IP addresses.

PAT takes care of all of the problems facing a network exposed to the Internet. You don't have to use legitimate Internet IP addresses on the LAN, and the IP addresses of the computers behind the routers are invisible and protected from the outside world.

Since the router is revising the packets and recording the IP address and port information already, why not enable it to handle ports more aggressively? Enter port forwarding, stage left.

Port Forwarding

The obvious drawback to relying exclusively on PAT for network address translation is that it only works for outgoing communication, not incoming communication. For traffic originating *outside* the network to access an *internal* machine, such as a web server hosted inside your network, you need to use other technologies.

Static NAT (SNAT) maps a single routable (that is, not private) IP address to a single machine, enabling you to access that machine from outside the network. The NAT keeps track of the IP address or addresses and applies them permanently on a one-to-one basis with computers on the network. You could run a web server on an internal host, for example, that has a private IP address but could still be accessed over the Internet. Because outside traffic won't know the internal IP address, you've added a layer of security from attacks on that IP address.

Exam Tip

Despite the many uses in the industry of the acronym SNAT, the CompTIA Network+ exam uses SNAT for Static NAT exclusively.

With *port forwarding*, you can designate a specific local address for various network services. Computers outside the network can request a service using the public IP address of the router and the port number of the desired service. The port-forwarding router would examine the packet, look at the list of services mapped to local addresses, and then send that packet along to the proper recipient.

You can use port forwarding to hide a service hosted inside your network by changing the default port number for that service. To hide an internal web server, for example, you could change the request port number to something other than port 80, the default for HTTP traffic. The router in Figure 6.16, for example, is configured to forward all port 8080 traffic to the internal web server at port 80.

To access that internal website from outside your local network, you would have to change the URL in the web browser by specifying the port request number. Figure 6.17 shows a browser that has :8080 appended to the URL, which tells the browser to make the HTTP request to port 8080 rather than port 80.

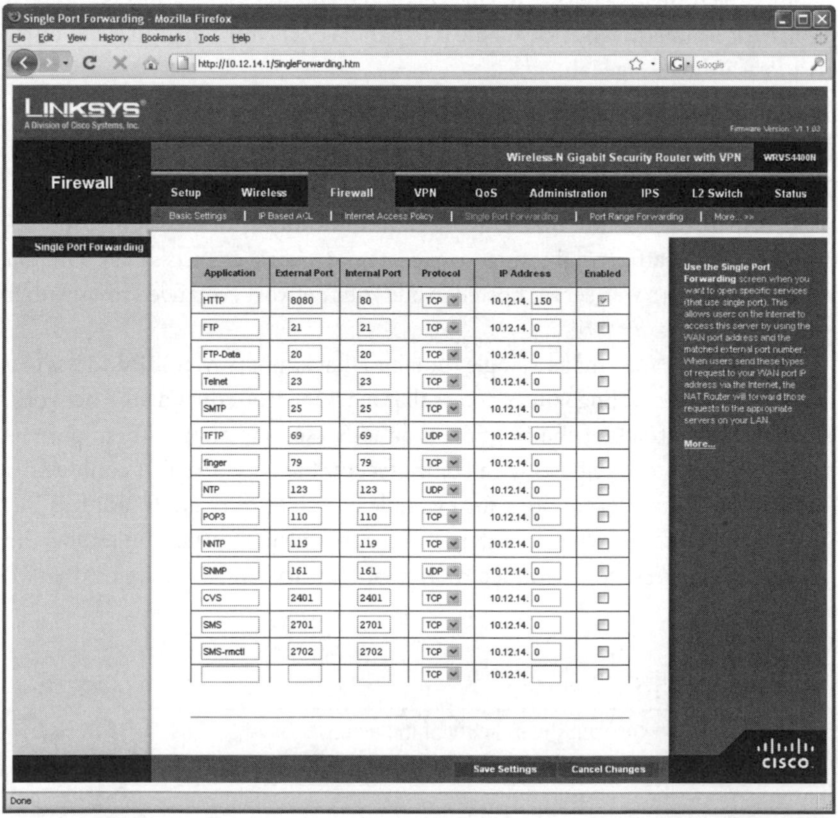

FIGURE 6.16 Setting up port forwarding on a home router

FIGURE 6.17 Changing the URL to access a website using a nondefault port number

Exam Tip

Most browsers require you to write out the full URL, including http://, when using a nondefault port number.

Configuring NAT

Configuring NAT on home routers is a no-brainer, as these boxes invariably have NAT turned on automatically. Figure 6.18 shows the screen on my home router for NAT. Note the radio buttons that say Gateway and Router.

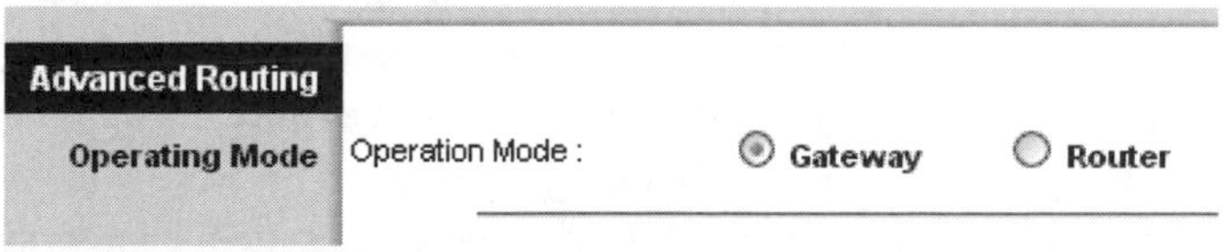

Advanced Routing

Operating Mode   Operation Mode :   ⦿ **Gateway**   ◯ **Router**

FIGURE 6.18 NAT setup on home router

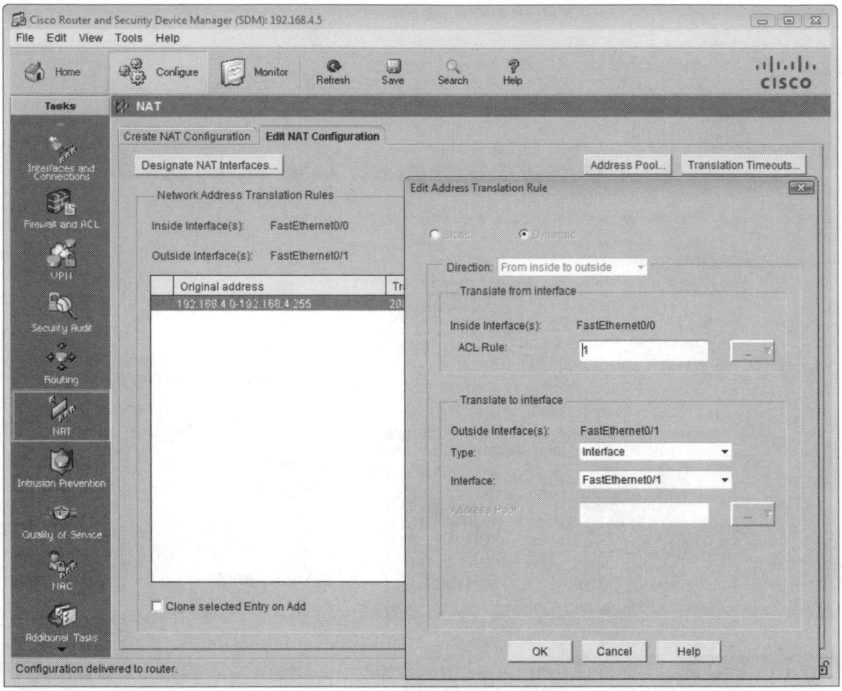

FIGURE 6.19   Configuring NAT on a commercial-grade router

By default, the router is set to Gateway, which is Linksys-speak for "NAT is turned on." If I wanted to turn off NAT, I would set the radio button to Router.

Figure 6.19 shows a router configuration screen on a Cisco router. Commercial routers enable you to do a lot more with NAT.

Objective 6.03   Dynamic Routing

Based on what you've read up to this point, it would seem that routes in your routing tables come from two sources: either they are manually entered or they are detected at setup by the router. In either case, a route seems to be a static beast, just sitting there and never changing. And based on what you've seen so far, that is absolutely true. Routers have *static routes*. But most routers also have the capability to update their routes *dynamically,* assuming they're provided with the extra smarts in the form of *dynamic routing* protocols.

Routing protocols have been around for a long time, and, like any technology, there have been a number of different choices and variants over those years. CompTIA Network+ competencies break these many types of routing protocols into three distinct groups: distance vector, link state, and hybrid. Let's start with a deeper discussion of metrics and then sort out the various dynamic routing protocols.

Routing Metrics

Earlier in the chapter, you learned that routing tables contain a factor called a *metric*. A metric is a relative value that routers use when they have more than one route to get to another network. Unlike the gateway routers in our homes, a more serious router will often have multiple connections to get to a particular network.

Dynamic routing protocols enable routers to update routing tables by communicating with other routers. If a router suddenly loses a connection, it checks alternative routes to the same network. It's the role of the metric setting for the router to decide which route to use. It always chooses the route with the lowest metric.

There is no uniform rule to set the metric value in a routing table. The various types of dynamic protocols use different criteria. Here are the most common criteria for determining a metric:

- **Maximum Transmission Unit**   Better known by the abbreviation MTU, this determines the largest frame a particular technology can handle. Most Ethernet networks use 1500-byte data fields in frames. Other technologies use smaller or larger fields. If an IP packet is too big for a particular technology, that packet is broken into pieces to fit into the network protocol in what is called *fragmentation*. Fragmentation is bad because it slows down the movement of IP packets (see the "Latency" bullet item in this list). By setting the optimal MTU size before IP packets are sent, you avoid, or at least reduce, fragmentation.

- **Bandwidth**   Some connections handle more data than others. An old dial-up connection moves, at best, 64 Kbps. A cable modem easily handles many millions of bits per second.

- **Latency**   Hundreds of issues occur that slow down network connections between routers. These issues are known collectively as *latency*. A great example is a satellite connection. The distance between the satellite and the antenna causes a delay that has nothing to do with the speed of the connection.

Different dynamic routing protocols use one or more routing metrics to calculate their own routing metric. As you learn about these protocols, you will see how each of these calculates their own metrics differently.

Distance Vector

Distance vector routing protocols use one of several algorithms to determine the best route to other routers based on the distance (*cost*) and direction (*vector*).

The simplest total cost sums the hops (the hop count) between a router and a network. A hop is defined as each time a packet goes through a router. So if you had a router one hop away from a network, the cost for that route would be 1; if it were two hops away, the cost would be 2.

All network connections are not equal. A router might have a pair of one-hop routes to a network—one using a fast connection and the other using a slow connection. The slow single-hop route, for example, might have a metric of 10 rather than the default of 1 to reflect the fact that it's slow. The total cost for this one-hop route is 10 even though it's only one hop. Don't assume a one-hop route always has a cost of 1.

Routers using a distance vector routing protocol transfer their entire routing table to other routers in the WAN. Each distance vector routing protocol has a maximum number of hops that a router will send its routing table to keep traffic down.

Assume you have four routers connected as shown in Figure 6.20. All of the routers have static routes set up between each other with the metrics shown. You add two new networks: one that connects to Router A and the other to Router D. For simplicity, call them Network ID X and Network ID Y. A computer on one network wants to send packets to a computer on the other network, but the routers in between Routers A and D don't yet know the two new network IDs. That's when distance vector routing protocols work their magic.

Because all of the routers use a distance vector routing protocol, the problem gets solved quickly. At a certain defined time interval (usually 30 seconds or

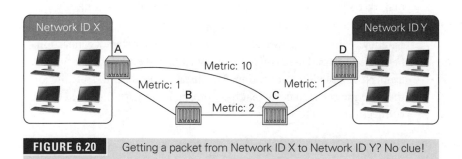

| **FIGURE 6.20** | Getting a packet from Network ID X to Network ID Y? No clue! |

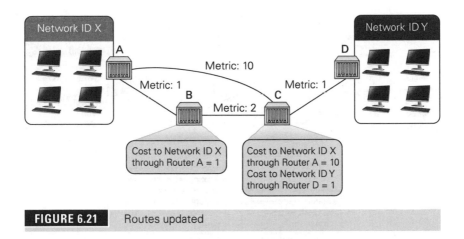

FIGURE 6.21 Routes updated

more), the routers begin sending each other their routing tables (the routers each send their entire routing table, but for simplicity, just concentrate on the two network IDs in question). On the first iteration, Router A sends its route to Network ID X to Routers B and C. Router D sends its route to Network ID Y to Router C (Figure 6.21).

This is great—Routers B and C now know how to get to Network ID X, and Router C can get to Network ID Y. There's still no complete path, however, between Network ID X and Network ID Y. That's going to take another interval. After another set amount of time, the routers again send their now updated routing tables to each other, as shown in Figure 6.22.

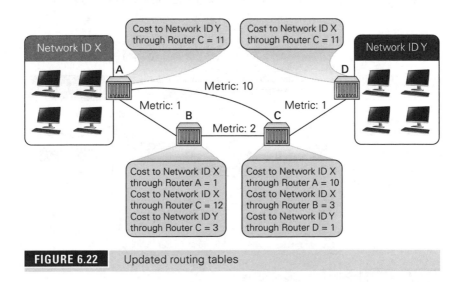

FIGURE 6.22 Updated routing tables

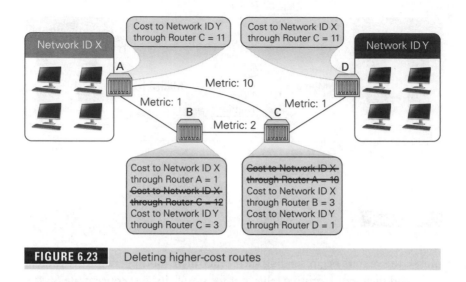

FIGURE 6.23 Deleting higher-cost routes

Router A knows a path now to Network ID Y, and Router D knows a path to Network ID X. As a side effect, Router B and Router C have two routes to Network ID X. Router B can get to Network ID X through Router A and through Router C. Similarly, Router C can get to Network ID X through Router A and through Router B. What to do? In cases where the router discovers multiple routes to the same network ID, the distance vector routing protocol deletes all but the route with the lowest total cost (Figure 6.23).

On the next iteration, Routers A and D get updated information about the lower total-cost hops to connect to Network IDs X and Y (Figure 6.24).

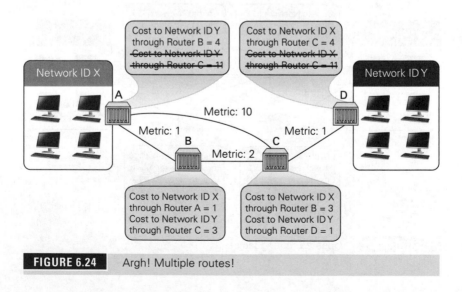

FIGURE 6.24 Argh! Multiple routes!

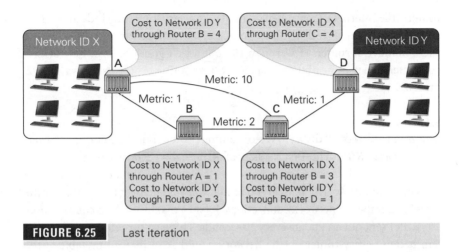

FIGURE 6.25   Last iteration

Just as Routers B and C only kept the routes with the lowest costs, Routers A and D keep only the lowest-cost routes to the networks (Figure 6.25).

Now Routers A and D have a lower-cost route to Network IDs X and Y. They've removed the higher-cost routes and begin sending data.

At this point, if routers were human they'd realize that each router has all the information about the network and stop sending each other routing tables. Routers using distance vector routing protocols, however, aren't that smart. The routers continue to send their complete routing tables to each other, but because the information is the same, the routing tables don't change.

At this point, the routers are in *convergence* (also called *steady state*), meaning the updating of the routing tables for all the routers has completed. Assuming nothing changes in terms of connections, the routing tables will not change. In this example, it takes three iterations to reach convergence.

So what happens if the route between Routers B and C breaks? The routers have deleted the higher-cost routes, only keeping the lower-cost route that goes between Routers B and C. Does this mean Router A can no longer connect to Network ID Y and Router D can no longer connect to Network ID X? Yikes! Yes, it does. At least for a while.

Routers that use distance vector routing protocols continue to send their entire routing table to each other at regular intervals. After a few iterations, Routers A and D will once again know how to reach each other, although they will connect through the once-rejected slower connection.

Distance vector routing protocols work fine in a scenario such as the previous one that has only four routers. Even if you lose a router, a few minutes later the network returns to convergence. But imagine if you had tens of thousands of routers (the Internet). Convergence could take a very long time indeed. As a result, a pure distance vector routing protocol works fine for a network with a small number of routers (fewer than 10), but it isn't good for large networks.

Routers can use one of three distance vector routing protocols: RIPv1, RIPv2, or BGP.

RIPv1

The granddaddy of all distance vector routing protocols is the *Routing Information Protocol (RIP)*. The first version of RIP—called *RIPv1*—dates from the 1980s, although its predecessors go back all the way to the beginnings of the Internet in the 1960s. RIP had several limitations that made it unsuitable for the growing number of network connections. It had a maximum hop count of only 15. RIPv1 sent out an update every 30 seconds. This also turned into a big problem because every router on the network would send its routing table at the same time, causing huge network overloads. In addition, RIPv1 routers had no authentication, leaving them open to hackers sending false routing table information. RIP needed an update.

RIPv2

RIPv2, adopted in 1994, is the current version of RIP. It works the same way as RIPv1, but fixes many of the problems. The maximum hop count of 15 continues to apply to RIPv2, but the easy configuration makes it suitable for internetworks using only a few routers. Most routers support RIPv2 (Figure 6.26).

BGP

The explosive growth of the Internet in the 1980s required a fundamental reorganization in the structure of the Internet itself, and one big part of this reorganization was the call to make the "big" routers use a standardized dynamic routing protocol. Implementing this was much harder than you might think because the entities that govern how the Internet works do so in a highly decentralized fashion. Even the organized groups, such as the Internet Society (ISOC), the Internet Assigned Numbers Authority (IANA), and the Internet Engineering

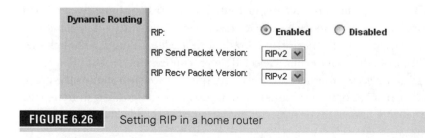

FIGURE 6.26   Setting RIP in a home router

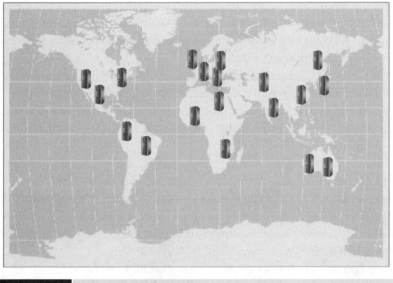

FIGURE 6.27   The Internet

Task Force (IETF), are made up of many individuals, companies, and government organizations from across the globe.

What came out of the reorganization eventually was a multitiered structure. At the top of the structure sits many Autonomous Systems. An *Autonomous System (AS)* is one or more networks, controlled by a single organization (like an ISP), whose routers are governed by a single dynamic routing policy, and often a single protocol within that AS. Figure 6.27 illustrates the central structure of the Internet.

An Autonomous System does not use IP addresses, but rather uses a special globally unique Autonomous System Number (ASN) assigned by IANA. Originally a 16-bit number, the current ASNs are 32 bits, displayed as two 16-bit numbers separated by a dot. So, 1.33457 would be a typical ASN. Just as you would assign an IP address to a router, you would configure the router to use the ASN assigned by the IANA (see Figure 6.28).

```
Router2811(config)#router bgp ?
  <1-65535>  Autonomous system number

Router2811(config)#router bgp 1902
```

FIGURE 6.28   Configuring a Cisco router to use an ASN

Autonomous Systems communicate with each other using a protocol, called generically an *Exterior Gateway Protocol (EGP)*. The network or networks within an AS communicate with protocols as well; these are called generically *Interior Gateway Protocols (IGPs)*.

Let me repeat this to make sure you understand the difference between EGP and IGP. Neither EGP nor IGP are dynamic routing protocols; rather, these are categories that represent routing protocols exchanged between routers of the same AS (IGP—further subdivided into distance vector vs. link state) or between different ASes (EGP).

The easy way to keep these terms separate is to appreciate that although many protocols are used *within* Autonomous Systems, such as RIP, the Internet has settled on one protocol for communication between each AS: the *Border Gateway Protocol (BGP-4)*. BGP is the glue of the Internet, connecting all of the Autonomous Systems. Other dynamic routing protocols, such as RIP, are, by definition, IGP. The current version of BGP is BGP-4.

The CompTIA Network+ exam objectives list BGP as a distance vector routing protocol, but it's really somewhat different. BGP doesn't have the same type of routing table as you've seen so far. Instead, BGP routers advertise information passed to them from different Autonomous Systems' *edge routers*—that's what the AS-to-AS routers are called. BGP forwards these advertisements that include the ASN and other very non-IP items.

BGP also knows how to handle a number of situations unique to the Internet. If a router advertises a new route that isn't reliable, most BGP routers will ignore it. BGP also supports policies for limiting which and how other routers may access an ISP.

BGP is an amazing and powerful dynamic routing protocol, but unless you're working deep in the router room of an AS, odds are good you'll never see it in action. Those who need to connect a few routers together usually turn to a family of dynamic routing protocols that work very differently from distance vector routing protocols.

Local Lingo

iBGP and eBGP   You can use BGP within an AS to connect networks, so you can and do run into situations where BGP is both the interior and exterior protocol for an AS. To distinguish between the two uses of the protocol, network folks refer to the BGP on the interior as the *internal BGP (iBGP)*; the exterior connection then becomes the *exterior BGP (eBGP)*.

Link State

The limitations of RIP motivated the demand for a faster protocol that took up less bandwidth on a WAN. The basic idea was to come up with a dynamic routing protocol that was more efficient than routers that simply sent out their entire routing table at regular intervals. Why not instead simply announce and forward individual route changes as they appeared? That is the basic idea of a *link state* dynamic routing protocol. There are only two link state dynamic routing protocols: OSPF and IS-IS.

OSPF

Open Shortest Path First (OSPF) is the most commonly used IGP. Most large Internet users (as opposed to ISPs) use OSPF on their internal networks. Even an AS, while still using BGP on its edge routers, will use OSPF internally, because OSPF was designed from the ground up to work within a single AS. OSPF converges dramatically faster and is much more efficient than RIP. Odds are good that if you are using dynamic routing protocols to connect your own routers, you're using OSPF.

OSPF offers a number of improvements over RIP. When you first launch OSPF-capable routers, they send out *link state advertisements (LSAs),* called *Hello packets,* looking for other OSPF routers (Figure 6.29).

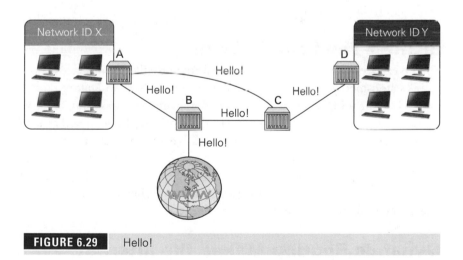

FIGURE 6.29   Hello!

A new router sends a lot of LSAs when it first starts. This is called *flooding*. Once all the routers communicate, they decide the optimal routes among them, and convergence happens almost immediately. If a route goes down, OSPF routers quickly reroute, eliminating the broken route

---

Exam Tip

OSPF corrects link failures and creates convergence almost immediately, making it the routing protocol of choice in most large enterprise networks. OSPF Version 2 is used for IPv4 networks, and OSPF Version 3 includes updates to support IPv6.

IS-IS

If you want to use a link state dynamic routing protocol and you don't want to use OSPF, your only other option is *Intermediate System to Intermediate System (IS-IS)*. IS-IS is extremely similar to OSPF. It uses the concept of areas and send-only updates to routing tables. IS-IS was developed at roughly the same time as OSPF and had the one major advantage of working with IPv6 from the start. IS-IS has some adoption with ISPs, but, for the most part, plays a distant second to the popularity of OSPF. Make sure you know that IS-IS is a link state dynamic routing protocol, and if you ever see two routers using it, call me, as I've never seen IS-IS in action.

EIGRP—The Lone Hybrid

There is exactly one protocol that doesn't really fit into either the distance vector or link state camp: Cisco's proprietary *Enhanced Interior Gateway Routing Protocol (EIGRP)*. Back in the days when RIP was dominant, there was a huge outcry for an improved RIP, but OSPF wasn't yet out. Cisco, being the dominant router company in the world (a crown it still wears to this day), came out with the Interior Gateway Routing Protocol (IGRP), which was quickly replaced with EIGRP.

EIGRP has aspects of both distance vector and link state protocols, placing it uniquely into its own "hybrid" category. EIGRP is (arguably) fading away in the face of nonproprietary IGP protocols, especially OSPF.

Dynamic Routing Makes the Internet

Without dynamic routing, the complex, self-healing Internet we all enjoy today couldn't exist. So many routes come and go so often that manually updating static routes would be impossible. Review Table 6.2 to familiarize yourself with the differences among the different types of dynamic routing protocols.

TABLE 6.2	Dynamic Routing Protocols		
Protocol	**Type**	**IGP or BGP?**	**Notes**
RIPv1	Distance vector	IGP	Old; only used on variable subnets within an AS
RIPv2	Distance vector	IGP	Supports VLSM and noncontiguous subnets
BGP-4	Distance vector	BGP	Used on the Internet; connects Autonomous Systems
OSPF	Link state	IGP	Fast, popular; uses Area IDs (Area 0/backbone)
IS-IS	Link state	IGP	Alternative to OSPF
EIGRP	Hybrid	IGP	Cisco proprietary

CHECKPOINT

✓**Objective 6.01: Routing Tables**   Routers use routing tables to determine where to send incoming packets. After stripping off the incoming frame information, a router examines the IP packet's destination address and begins comparing that address to the many routes in its routing table to determine the proper interface to use to send the packet to its destination. The router will encapsulate the packet into the appropriate frame and then send it along. You can use command-line tools to view routing tables in an OS, most commonly running `netstat -r`.

✓**Objective 6.02: Network Address Translation**   Routers running some form of *Network Address Translation (NAT)* hide the IP addresses of computers on the LAN, but still enable those computers to communicate with the broader Internet. The most common form of NAT, called Port Address Translation (PAT), uses one or more public IP addresses to enable devices on the inside of a LAN to use a block of private IP addresses. The PAT router uses port numbers to map traffic to and from specific machines in the network.

✓**Objective 6.03: Dynamic Routing**   Dynamic routing protocols enable routers to update routing tables by interacting with other routers rather than through human intervention. CompTIA expects techs to know about three categories: distance vector, link state, and hybrid. Routers using a distance vector protocol, such as RIP or BGP, send their routing tables to other routers at regular intervals. Routers using a link state protocol, such as OSPF or IS-IS, only send updates to routes, making them faster and more efficient, especially as you scale up the size of the internetwork. EIGRP doesn't quite fit either category; it's considered the only hybrid dynamic routing protocol.

REVIEW QUESTIONS

1. How many lines of a routing table does the router read when comparing the IP address and subnet mask of an incoming packet?

   A. The router reads only the first two lines to determine the proper route.

   B. The router reads the lines from the top until it reaches the proper route.

   C. The router reads the lines from the bottom until it reaches the proper route.

   D. The router reads all the lines and then determines the proper route.

2. What is the purpose of the default route in a routing table?

   A. The default route tells the router where to send every packet.

   B. The default route is used by routers solely for updating routing tables.

   C. The default route tells the router where to send every packet if not explicitly listed on another line in the routing table.

   D. The default route is used to configure the router.

3. How many IP addresses should a router have?

   A. One

   B. One or more

   C. Two

   D. Two or more

4. Which version of NAT maps a single routable IP address to a single network node?

   A. Static NAT

   B. Dynamic NAT

   C. Pooled NAT

   D. Secure NAT

5. What technology enables you to designate a specific local address for various network services?

   A. Dynamic NAT

   B. Port Address Translation

   C. Port forwarding

   D. Port filtering

6. How is the distance between routers measured?

   A. In meters

   B. In hops

   C. In routes

   D. In segments

7. Distance vector routing protocols include which of the following? (Select two.)

   A. RIP

   B. OSPF

   C. BGP

   D. ASN

8. What is one way in which Autonomous Systems differ from typical Ethernet networks?

   A. They require a minimum of 10 nodes.

   B. They cannot exceed a maximum of 255 nodes.

   C. They are not able to interact with the Internet.

   D. They do not use IP addresses.

9. Why are link state protocols more efficient than distance vector routing protocols?

   A. Entire routing tables are updated on a stricter schedule.

   B. They forward only changes to individual routes instead of forwarding entire routing tables.

   C. Packets can be sent along multiple routes at the same time.

   D. Link state can send larger packets.

10. Which of the following is a hybrid dynamic routing protocol?

    A. RIP

    B. OSPF

    C. BGP

    D. EIGRP

REVIEW ANSWERS

1. **D**   The router reads all the lines and then determines the proper route.

2. **C**   The default route tells the router where to send every packet unless another line in the routing table gives another route.

3. **D**   By definition, a router should have two or more IP addresses to connect different networks with its routing function.

4. **A**   Static NAT maps a single routable (that is, not private) IP address to a single machine.

5. **C**   Port forwarding enables you to designate a specific local address for various network services.

6. **B**   The distance between routers is measured in hops.

7. **A** and **C**   Distance vector routing protocols include RIP and BGP.

8. **D**   Autonomous Systems do not use IP addresses, but instead use a globally unique Autonomous System Number.

9. **B**   Link state protocols forward only changes to individual routes, whereas RIP forwards entire routing tables.

10. **D**   EIGRP is the sole hybrid dynamic routing protocol.

Virtualization

CHAPTER 7

ETA	NEWBIE	SOME EXPERIENCE	EXPERT
	4 hours	2 hours	1 hour

Modern networks are often hugely complex and intricate, with many different devices filling many different roles. Hungry for greater flexibility and lower hardware costs, many network techs have started using software to do jobs traditionally done by hardware. In this chapter, you will learn about *virtualization*, which means using specialized programs to act like physical devices. First, you will learn about virtual LANs, which use a single switch to create multiple broadcast domains. After that, you will read about virtual computing, or using one physical computer to run multiple virtual systems. Finally, you will learn about the place virtualization has in today's networking world.

Objective 7.01   Virtual LANs

It's rare these days to see a serious network that doesn't have remote incoming connections, public web or e-mail servers, and wireless networks, as well as the basic string of connected switches. Leaving all of these different features on a single broadcast domain creates a tremendous amount of broadcast traffic and creates a security nightmare. What if you could segment the network using the switches you already own? A *virtual local area network (VLAN)* enables you to do just that.

To create a VLAN, you take a single physical broadcast domain and chop it up into multiple virtual broadcast domains. VLANs require special switches loaded with extra programming to create the virtual networks. Imagine a single switch with a number of computers connected to it. Up to this point, a single switch is always a single broadcast domain, but that's about to change. You've decided to take this single switch and turn it into two VLANs. VLANs typically get the name "VLAN" plus a number, like VLAN1 or VLAN275. The devices usually start at 1, although there's no law or rules on the numbering. In this example, I'll configure the ports on my single switch to be in one of two VLANs—VLAN1 or VLAN2 (Figure 7.1). I promise to show you how to configure ports for different VLANs shortly, but I've got a couple of other concepts to hit first.

Figure 7.1 shows a switch configured to assign individual ports to VLANs. But there's another way to use VLANs that's supported by most VLAN-capable switches. Instead of assigning ports to a VLAN, you can assign MAC addresses to determine VLAN membership. A computer in this type of VLAN is always a member of the same VLAN no matter which port you plug the computer into on the switch.

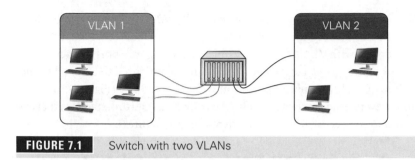

FIGURE 7.1   Switch with two VLANs

A single switch configured into two VLANs is the simplest form of VLAN possible. More serious networks usually have more than one switch. Let's say you added a switch to a simple network. You'd like to keep VLAN1 and VLAN2, but use both switches. You can configure the new switch to use VLAN1 and VLAN2, but you've got to enable data to flow between the two switches, regardless of VLAN. That's where trunking comes into play.

Trunking

Trunking is the process of transferring VLAN traffic between two or more switches. Imagine two switches, each configured with a VLAN1 and a VLAN2, as shown in Figure 7.2.

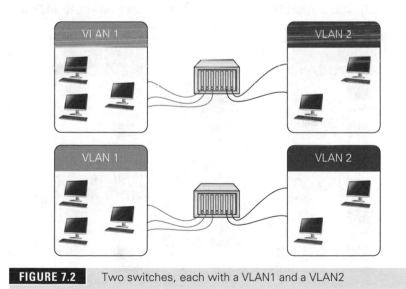

FIGURE 7.2   Two switches, each with a VLAN1 and a VLAN2

You want all of the computers connected to VLAN1 on one switch to talk to all of the computers connected to VLAN1 on the other switch. Of course, you want to do this with VLAN2 also. To do this, you configure a port on each switch as a *trunk port*. A *trunk port* is a port on a switch configured to carry all traffic, regardless of VLAN number, between all switches in a LAN (Figure 7.3).

Today, every Ethernet switch prefers the IEEE 802.1Q trunk standard that enables you to connect switches from different manufacturers.

Configuring a VLAN-capable Switch

If you want to configure a VLAN-capable switch, you need a method to perform that configuration. One method uses a serial (console) port, but the most common method is to access the switch with a web browser interface, like the one shown in Figure 7.4. Any switch that you can access and configure is called a *managed switch*.

Local Lingo
Unmanaged switch A simple switch without any configuration capability is called an *unmanaged switch*.

Though switches typically use MAC addresses, managed switches also come with an IP address for configuration. A brand-new managed switch out of the box invariably has a preset IP address similar to the preset, private IP addresses

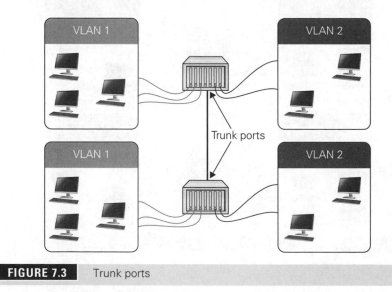

FIGURE 7.3 Trunk ports

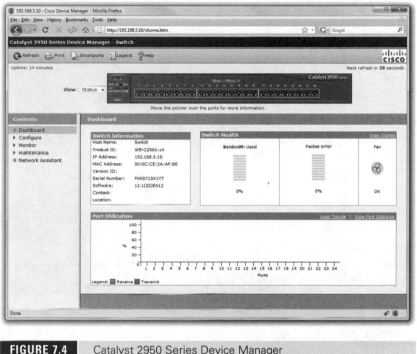

FIGURE 7.4   Catalyst 2950 Series Device Manager

you see on routers. This IP address isn't for any of the individual ports, but rather is for the whole switch. That means no matter where you physically connect to the switch, the IP address to get to the configuration screen is the same.

Every switch manufacturer has its own interface for configuring VLANs, but the interface shown in Figure 7.5 is a classic example. This is Cisco Network Assistant, a very popular tool that enables you to configure multiple devices through the same interface. Note that you first must define your VLANs.

After you create the VLANs, you usually either assign computers' MAC addresses to VLANs or assign ports to VLANs. Assigning MAC addresses means that no matter where you plug in a computer, it is always part of the same VLAN—a very handy feature for mobile users! Assigning each port to a VLAN means that whatever computer plugs into that port, it will always be a member of that port's VLAN. Figure 7.6 shows a port being assigned to a particular VLAN.

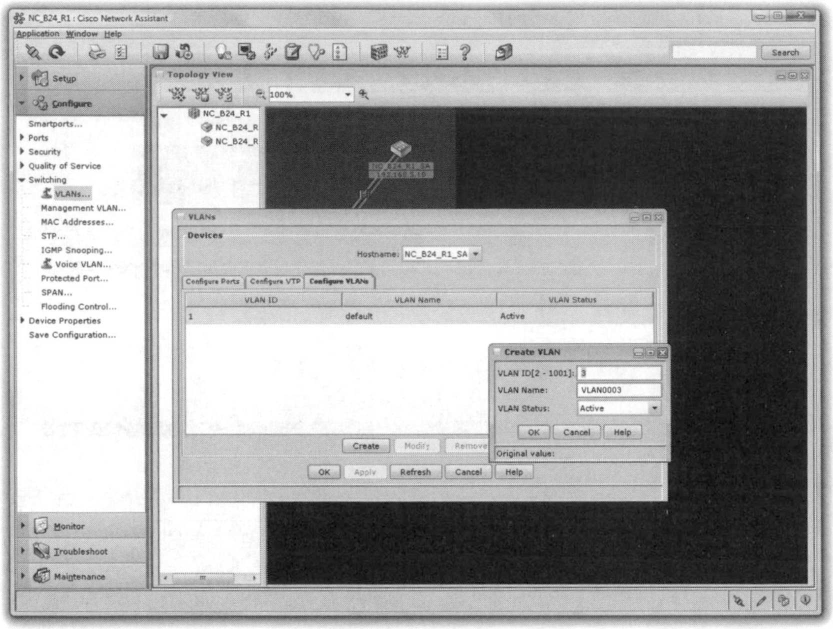

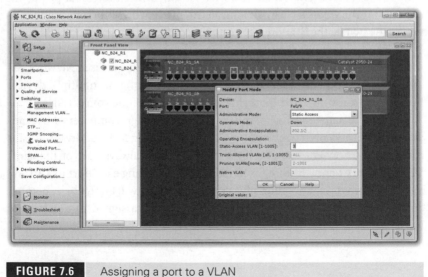

FIGURE 7.5 Defining VLANs in Cisco Network Assistant

FIGURE 7.6 Assigning a port to a VLAN

Local Lingo

Static and Dynamic VLANs based on ports are the most common type of VLAN and are commonly known as *static VLANs*. VLANs based on MAC addresses are called *dynamic VLANs*.

Travel Advisory

If you've just plugged into a VLAN, but can't seem to access the other computers on your VLAN, make sure you've plugged your computer into a port assigned to the correct VLAN. If there are no more available ports, you'll have to configure the port you're plugged into to be on the right VLAN.

VLAN Trunking Protocol

A busy network with many VLAN switches can require periods of intensive work to update. Imagine the work required to redo all the VLAN switches if you changed the VLAN configuration by adding or removing a VLAN. You'd have to access every switch individually, changing the port configuration to alter the VLAN assignment, and so on. The potential for errors is staggering.

If you misconfigure the port or assign the wrong VLAN to a set of ports, that would manifest as users who previously could access the proper resources no longer being able to access them. Or, worse, that you'd have users loose in places they should not be authorized to access. Manually tracking down and trouble-shooting these kinds of errors takes way too much time.

Travel Advisory

VTP The acronym list for the CompTIA Network+ exam refers to VTP as *Virtual Trunk Protocol,* a term that doesn't exist or at least doesn't apply to Cisco products. You'll most likely only see the initials—VTP— on the exam.

Cisco uses a proprietary protocol called *VLAN Trunking Protocol (VTP)* to automate the updating of multiple VLAN switches. With VTP, you put each switch into one of three states: server, client, or transparent. When you make changes to the VLAN configuration of the server switch, all the connected client switches and other server switches update their configurations within minutes.

When you set a VLAN switch to transparent, you tell it not to update but to hold onto its manual settings. You would use a transparent mode VLAN switch in circumstances where the overall VLAN configuration assignments did not apply.

InterVLAN Routing

Once you've configured a switch to support multiple VLANs, each VLAN is its own broadcast domain, just as if the two VLANs were on two completely separate switches and networks. There is no way for data to get from one VLAN to another unless you use a router. The process of making a router work between two VLANs is called *interVLAN routing*. Figure 7.7 shows one possible way to connect two VLANs with a single router. Note that the router has one port connected to VLAN 100 and another connected to VLAN 200. Devices on VLAN 100 may now communicate with devices on VLAN 200.

Adding a physical router like this isn't a very elegant way to connect VLANs. This forces almost all traffic to go through the router, and it's not a very flexible

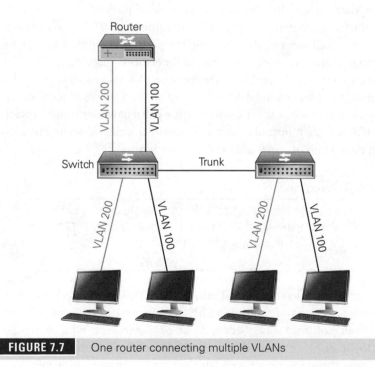

FIGURE 7.7   One router connecting multiple VLANs

FIGURE 7.8 Cisco 3550

solution if you want to add more VLANs in the future. As a result, all but the simplest VLANs have at least one very special switch that has the ability to make virtual routers. Figure 7.8 shows an older but very popular interVLAN routing–capable switch, the Cisco 3550.

The Cisco 3550 not only supports VLANs, but also enables you to create virtual routers (Switched Virtual Interfaces) or even physical routed ports to interconnect these VLANs. Figure 7.9 shows the configuration screen for the 3550's interVLAN routing between two VLANs.

Being a switch that also has the capability to create virtual routers and physical routed ports, the Cisco 3550 works at both layers 2 and 3 at the same time.

FIGURE 7.9 Setting up interVLAN routing

Objective 7.02 # Virtual Computing

In the simplest terms, *virtualization* is the process of using special software—a class of programs called *hypervisors* or *virtual machine managers*—to create a complete environment in which a guest operating system can function as though it were installed on its own computer. That guest environment is called a *virtual machine (VM)*. Figure 7.10 shows one such example: a system running Windows 7 using a program called VMware Workstation to host a virtual machine running Ubuntu Linux.

Meet the Hypervisor

A normal operating system uses programming called a *supervisor* to handle very low-level interactions among hardware and software, such as task scheduling, allotment of time and resources, and so on.

Because virtualization enables one machine—called the *host*—to run multiple operating systems simultaneously, full virtualization requires an extra layer of sophisticated programming to manage the vastly more complex interactions. One common method calls this extra programming a *hypervisor* or *virtual machine manager (VMM)*.

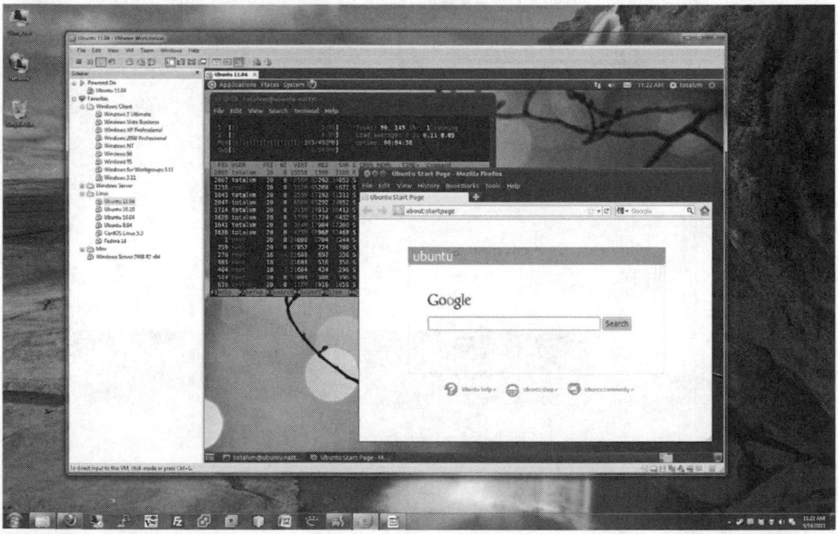

FIGURE 7.10 | VMware running Linux

A hypervisor has to handle every input and output that the operating system would request of normal hardware. With a good hypervisor like VMware Workstation, you can easily add and remove virtual hard drives, virtual network cards, virtual RAM, and so on. Figure 7.11 shows the Hardware Configuration screen from VMware Workstation.

Local Lingo

Virtual desktop   A personal computer OS running in a virtual machine is also known as a *virtual desktop.* Virtual desktops were the first type of popular virtual machines seen in the PC world, championed by VMware and quickly copied by other virtualization programs.

Virtualization even goes so far as to provide a virtualized BIOS and System Setup for every virtual machine. Figure 7.12 shows VMware Workstation displaying the System Setup, just like you'd see it on a regular computer.

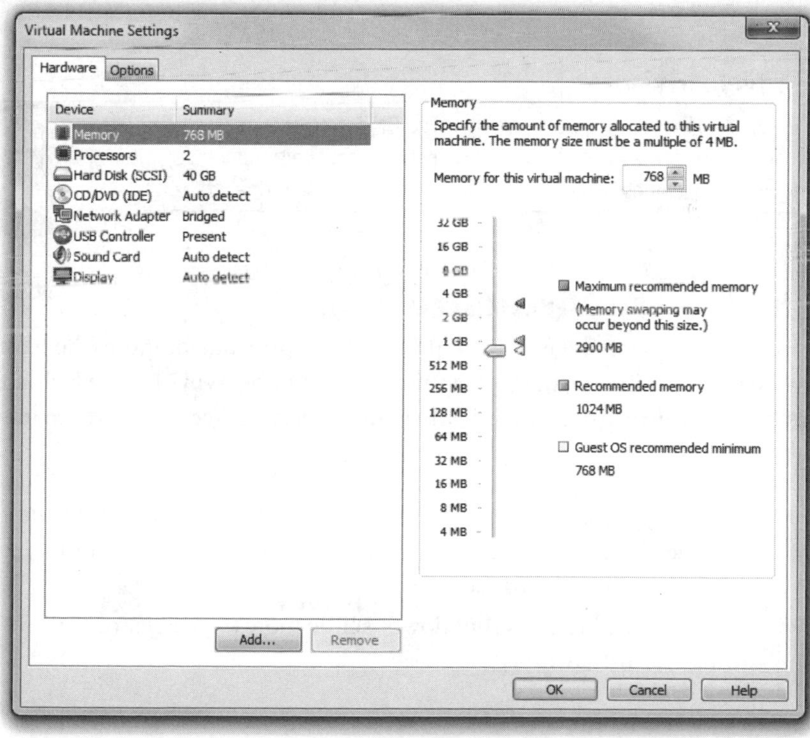

FIGURE 7.11   Configuring virtual hardware in VMware Workstation

```
                        PhoenixBIOS Setup Utility
   Main      Advanced     Security     Boot      Exit

                                               Item Specific Help
     System Time:           [14:46:17]
     System Date:           [09/19/2011]
                                               <Tab>, <Shift-Tab>, or
     Legacy Diskette A:     [1.44/1.25 MB  3½"]  <Enter> selects field.
     Legacy Diskette B:     [Disabled]

   ▶ Primary Master         [None]
   ▶ Primary Slave          [None]
   ▶ Secondary Master       [VMware Virtual ID]
   ▶ Secondary Slave        [None]

   ▶ Keyboard Features

     System Memory:         640 KB
     Extended Memory:       785408 KB
     Boot-time Diagnostic Screen:  [Disabled]


   F1   Help   ↑↓  Select Item   -/+    Change Values    F9   Setup Defaults
   Esc  Exit   ↔   Select Menu   Enter  Select ▶ Sub-Menu F10  Save and Exit
```

FIGURE 7.12   System Setup in VMware Workstation

Travel Advisory

The host machine allocates real RAM and CPU time to every running virtual machine. A host can only handle a finite number of virtual machines before experiencing degraded performance.

Why Do We Virtualize?

Virtualization has taken the networking world by storm, but for those who have never seen virtualization, the big question has got to be: Why? Let's talk about the benefits of virtualization. While you read this section, keep in mind two important things:

- A single hypervisor on a single system will happily run as many virtual machines as its RAM, CPU, and drive space allow. (RAM is almost always the main limiting factor.)
- A virtual machine that's shut down is little more than a file (or two) sitting on a hard drive.

Power Saving

Before virtualization, each server OS needed to be on a unique physical system. With virtualization, you can place multiple virtual servers on a single physical system, reducing electrical power use substantially. Rather than one machine running Windows 2008 and acting as a file server and DNS server, and a second machine running Linux for a DHCP server, for example, the same computer can handle both operating systems simultaneously. Expand this electricity savings over an enterprise network or on a data server farm, and the savings—both in terms of dollars spent and electricity used—is tremendous.

Hardware Consolidation

Similar to power saving, why buy a high-end server, complete with multiple pro-cessors, RAID arrays, redundant power supplies, and so on, and only run a single server? With virtualization, you can easily beef up the RAM and run a number of servers on a single box.

System Recovery

Possibly the most popular reason for virtualizing is to keep uptime percentage as high as possible. Let's say you have a web server installed on a single system. If that system goes down—due to hacking, malware, or so on—you need to restore the system from a backup, which may or may not be easily at hand. With virtualization, you merely need to shut down the virtual machine and reload an alternate copy of it.

> **Local Lingo**
>
> **Uptime** Uptime refers to the amount of time that a computer has been online.

Think of virtual machines like you would a word processing document. Vir-tual machines don't have a "File | Save" equivalent, but they do have something called a *snapshot* that enables you to save an extra copy of the virtual machine as it is exactly at the moment the snapshot is taken. Figure 7.13 shows VMware Workstation saving a snapshot.

System Duplication

Closely tied to system recovery, system duplication takes advantage of the fact that VMs are simply files, and like any file, they can be copied. Let's say you want to teach 20 students about Ubuntu Linux. Depending on the hypervisor you

Saving a snapshot

choose (VMware does this extremely well), you can simply install a hypervisor on 20 machines and copy a single virtual machine to all the computers. Equally, if you have a virtualized web server and need to add another web server (assuming your physical box has the hardware to support it), why not just make a copy of the server and fire it up as well?

Research

Here's a great example that happens in my own company. I sell my popular Total Tester test banks: practice questions for you to test your skills on a broad number of certification topics. As with any distributed program, I tend to get a few support calls. Running a problem through the same OS, even down to the service pack, helps me solve the problem. In the previrtualization days, I commonly had seven to ten PCs, using dual-boot, each keeping copies of a particular Windows version. Today, a single hypervisor enables me to support a huge number of Windows versions on a single machine (Figure 7.14)

Clearly there are a number of good reasons to virtualize some of the computers in a network. Let's look at implementation now.

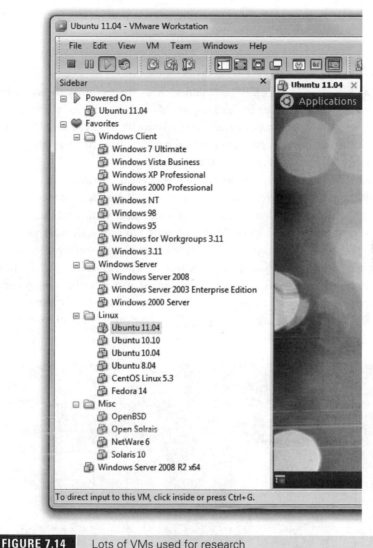

FIGURE 7.14   Lots of VMs used for research

Objective 7.03 Virtualization in Modern Networks

Virtualization manifests in many ways in modern networks. VMMs and hypervisors serve many roles in businesses, and you can choose from one of many varieties when you want to implement virtualization. In addition, virtual switches, virtual PBXes, and NaaS implementations provide solutions to very specific issues. This section examines modern virtualization.

VMMs and Hypervisors

You've already seen virtualization in action with the example shown using VMware Workstation earlier in this chapter. Many networks use a few virtual machines to augment and refine a traditional network closet. VMware Workstation is how I first performed virtualization on PCs, but the technology and power have grown dramatically over the last few years.

VMware Workstation requires an underlying operating system, so it functions essentially like a very powerful desktop application. What if you could remove the OS altogether and create a bare-metal implementation of virtualization?

VMware introduced ESX in 2001 to accomplish this goal. ESX is a hypervisor that's powerful enough to replace the host operating system on a physical box, turning the physical machine into a machine that does nothing but support virtual machines. ESX, by itself, isn't much to look at; it's a tiny operating system/hypervisor that's usually installed on something other than a hard drive. Figure 7.15 shows how I loaded my copy of ESX: via a small USB thumb drive.

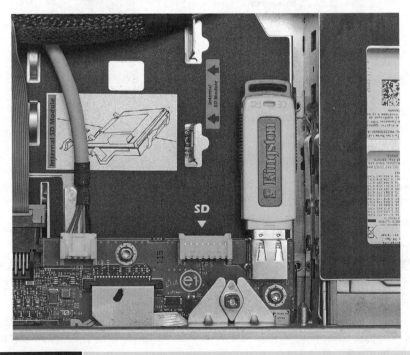

FIGURE 7.15   USB drive on server system

Power up the server; the server loads ESX off the thumb drive; and in short order, a very rudimentary interface appears where I can input essential information, such as a master password and a static IP address.

Local Lingo

ESX For all you abbreviation lovers, I have some good news and some bad news about "ESX." Officially, it means nothing. Unofficially, it stands for "Elastic Sky," which is probably why it officially means nothing.

Travel Assistance

ESXi VMware offers a free version of ESX for download. Called ESXi, it lacks a number of ESX's features, but is still quite powerful. You can get it here: http://www.vmware.com/products/vsphere-hypervisor/overview.html

---

Don't let ESX's small size fool you. It's small because it only has one job: to host virtual machines. ESX is an extremely powerful operating system/hypervisor.

Travel Advisory

Some writers will use the term *virtual machine manager* to describe virtual machine software that runs on top of a host operating system. They'll use the term *hypervisor* to describe only software that does not need a host operating system. Using this terminology, VMware Workstation is a virtual machine manager and ESX is a hypervisor. Other writers call both the hosted and bare-metal—or *native*—virtualization software products *hypervisors,* but make a distinction in other descriptive words (such as *hosted* or *native*).

Notice the built-in USB port shown in Figure 7.15. The popularity of hypervisors on dedicated servers makes these ports extremely common in a serious server box like the Dell system shown.

Powerful hypervisors like ESXi are rarely administered directly at the box. Instead you use tools such as VMware's vSphere Client, so you can create, configure, and maintain virtual machines on the hypervisor server from the comfort of a client computer running this program. Once the VM is up and running, you can close the vSphere client, but the VM will continue to run happily on the server. So you now really have two different ways to virtualize: using virtual machine managers like VMware's Workstation to manage virtual desktops and using powerful hypervisors like ESX to manage virtual servers. Granted, you could run a server like a web browser in VMware Workstation, and you also could run a copy of Windows 7 Ultimate from an ESX system. Nothing is wrong with doing either of these.

Exam Tip

For the scope of the CompTIA Network+ exam, remember that virtual servers run on hypervisors like ESX, whereas virtual desktops run on virtual machine managers.

Thus far, this chapter sounds like an advertisement for VMware. VMware really brought virtualization to the PC world and still holds a strong presence, but there are a number of alternatives to VMware products. Let's see what else is available.

Virtual Machine Managers

When it comes to the more basic virtual machine managers, you have a huge number of choices. The one you use is going to be based on features and prices.

VMware Workstation

The granddaddy and front leader for virtualization, VMware Workstation comes in both Windows and Linux versions. VMware Workstation runs on virtually (PUN!) any operating system you'll ever need and is incredibly stable and proven. Too bad it's not free.

One of the more interesting features of VMware Workstation is VMTools. VMTools adds useful features such as copy/cut and paste between the virtual desktop and the real desktop.

Virtual PC

Microsoft has offered a few different virtual machine managers over the years, and their current mainstream product is Windows Virtual PC (Figure 7.16). Windows Virtual PC is free, but has some serious limitations. First, it only works on Windows 7 Professional, Ultimate, and Enterprise. Second, it only officially supports Windows VMs, although a few intrepid souls have managed to get Linux working.

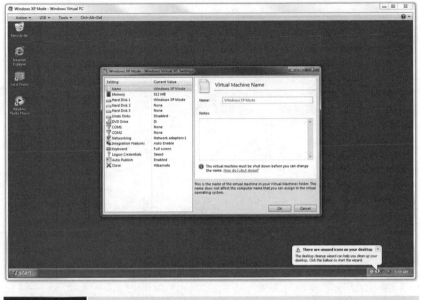

FIGURE 7.16 Windows Virtual PC

Parallels

Parallels is the most popular virtualization manager for Mac OS X, although VMware Fusion is a close second. Parallels supports all popular operating systems, and even has a fair degree of 3D graphics support; more so than even the mighty VMware. Parallels also offers Windows (Figure 7.17) and Linux versions.

KVM

Of course, the open-source world has its players, too. While picking a single product to represent the Linux/UNIX world is hard, no one who knows virtualization would disagree that KVM from Redhat is a dominant player. Unlike the other virtual machine managers discussed, KVM also supports a few non-x86 processors.

Don't think for a moment that this list is complete! There are lots of other virtual machine options for your desktop, especially if your host machine runs Linux. The most fun you'll have learning about virtualization is the playtime involved experimenting with the many options available.

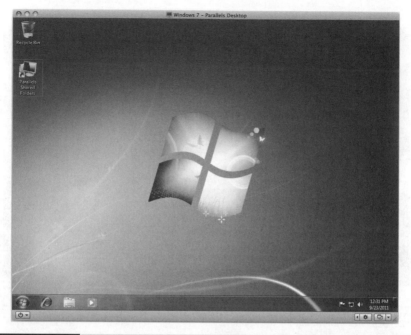

FIGURE 7.17 Parallels Desktop for Mac running a copy of Windows

Hypervisors

While you have lots of choices when it comes to virtual machine managers, your choices for real embedded hypervisors are limited to the two biggies: VMware's ESX and Microsoft's HyperV. There are others, such as Oracle's VM Server, but nothing has the market share of ESX or HyperV.

ESX

I've already discussed a few aspects of ESX, so instead I'll delve into the features that make ESX so popular. When it comes to real server virtualization, VMware truly leads the pack with a host of innovations (some of which are add-on products) that make ESX almost unstoppable. Here are a few examples:

- **Interface with large storage**   ESX virtual machines easily integrate with network attached storage (NAS) and storage area networks (SANs) to handle massive data storage.
- **Transparent fault tolerance**   ESX can monitor and automatically recover failed VMs with little or no input.

- **Transparent server transfer** You can move a *running* VM from one machine to another. How cool is that?
- **High virtual CPUs** Most hypervisors support a limited number of virtual CPUs, usually two at most. ESX can support up to 32 CPUs, depending on the vSphere product version you purchase to support it.

HyperV

Although HyperV can't stand toe-to-toe with ESX, it has a few aces up its sleeve that give it some appeal. First, it's free. This is important in that ESX, with only a few extra add-ons, can cost thousands of dollars. Second, it comes as a stand-alone product or as part of Windows Server 2008 and even on some versions of Windows 7, making it easy for those who like to play to access it. Third, its simplicity makes it easier to learn for those new to using hypervisors. Watch HyperV. If Microsoft does one thing well, it's taking market share away from arguably better, more powerful competitors, while slowly making its product better.

Virtual Switches

Imagine for a moment that you have three virtual machines running as virtual desktops. You want all of these machines to have access to the Internet. Therefore, you need to give them all legitimate IP addresses. The physical server, however, only has a single NIC. There are two ways in which virtualization gives individual VMs valid IP addresses. The oldest and simplest way is to bridge the NIC. Each virtual NIC is given a bridged connection to the real NIC (Figure 7.18). This bridge works at layer 2 of the OSI model, so each virtual NIC gets a legitimate, unique MAC address.

A subset of this type of bridging is to give every VM its own physical NIC (Figure 7.19). In this case, you're still bridging, but every virtual NIC goes straight to a dedicated physical NIC.

Your second option is to create a *virtual switch,* which is special software that enables VMs to communicate with each other without going outside of the host system. A good hypervisor (like ESX and HyperV) enables you to connect all of your virtual machines to their own virtual switch. Depending on your hypervisor, this switch can do everything you'd expect from a typical managed layer-2 switch, including VLANs (Figure 7.20).

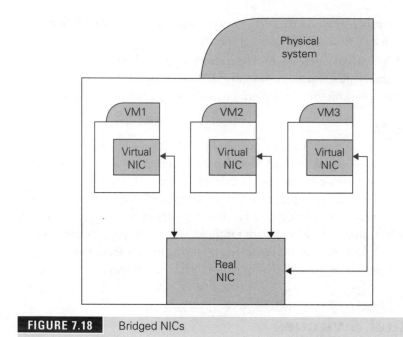

FIGURE 7.18   Bridged NICs

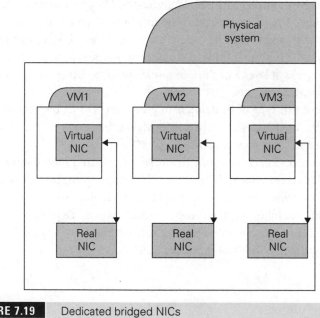

FIGURE 7.19   Dedicated bridged NICs

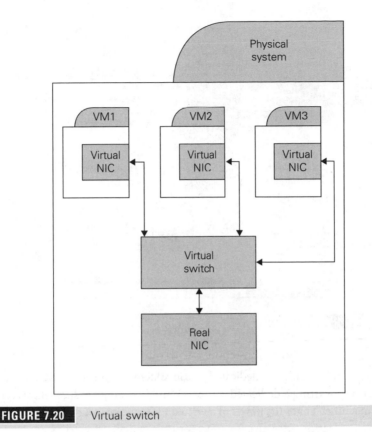

FIGURE 7.20 Virtual switch

If you really want to go crazy on virtual switches (and have lots of money), Cisco will sell you an appliance like the Cisco Nexus 1000V that offloads all of the virtual switching from the hypervisor and adds higher-layer features such as firewalls/ACLs, DHCP servers, and many other features.

Virtual PBX

The ancient PBX telephone systems used in offices since the 1970s have gone through many transformations over the last 40 years. One of the more common upgrades is to replace ancient PBX hardware with a single PC running many of the popular PBX programs like Asterisk (www.asterisk.org) or Virtual PBX (www.virtualpbx.com). Figure 7.21 shows Asterisk. These create a *virtual PBX*, software that functionally replaces a physical PBX.

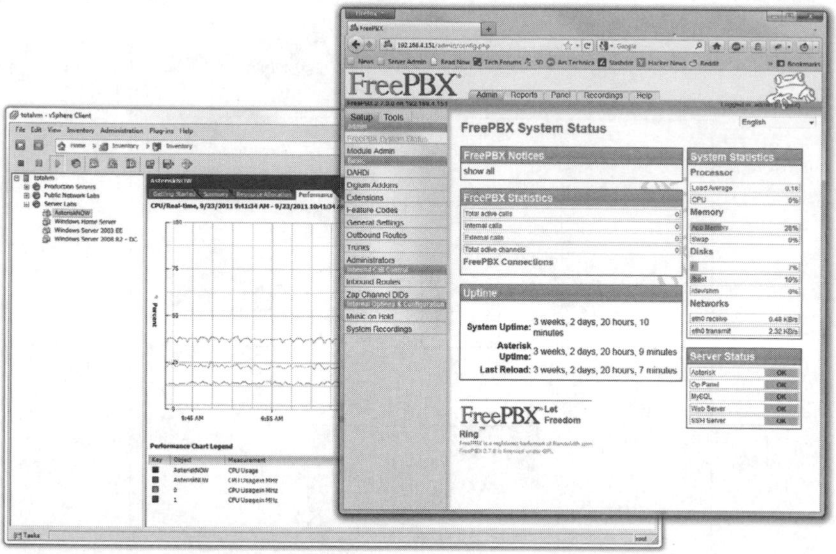

FIGURE 7.21   Asterisk running on a system

Typically this requires a dedicated single system to run the PBX software. Why not stop wasting a dedicated computer and instead just place all this on a virtual machine? That's the power of a virtual PBX system. All of the power that makes virtualization attractive is perfect for PBX systems.

Network as a Service

With hypervisor-based virtualization, you don't need to worry about where the virtualized server is physically located—you just want it to serve your data. If a virtual computer is at your location, you call it *onsite*. If a virtual server is somewhere other than at your location, you call it *offsite*. Some companies rent virtual servers to others. This is, by definition, *Network as a Service (NaaS)*, a small division of what is called *cloud computing*. Virtualization didn't invent the concept of cloud computing, but it made it cheap and practical.

Exam Tip

Other Cloud Services Cloud computing is a huge industry these days that encompasses far more than just NaaS. Another big area for cloud computing is in *application service providers (ASP)*. As the name implies, an ASP provides an application as a service. This might be a broad selection of applications, such as Google Docs, or a single application, like the payment services of PayPal. A common term for this use of the cloud is *Software as a Service (SaaS)*.

CHECKPOINT

✔**Objective 7.01: Virtual LANs** A virtual local area network (VLAN) enables you to segment a network using VLAN-capable switches. To create a VLAN, you take a single physical broadcast domain and chop it up into multiple virtual broadcast domains. VLANs help manage busy networks by reducing traffic. With interVLAN routing, you can connect the virtual networks just as if you had a physical router between them.

✔**Objective 7.02: Virtual Computing** Virtualization uses special software called hypervisors or virtual machine managers to create a complete environment in which a guest operating system can function as though it were installed on its own computer. That guest environment is called a virtual machine (VM). Going virtual offers many benefits, such as power saving, hardware consolidation, easier system recovery and duplication, and risk-free testing and research environments.

✔**Objective 7.03: Virtualization in Modern Networks** Virtualization manifests in many ways in modern networks. VMMs and hypervisors serve many roles in businesses, and you can choose from one of many varieties when you want to implement virtualization, such as Virtual PC, Parallels, ESX, and HyperV. In addition, virtual switches, virtual PBXes, and NaaS implementations provide solutions to very specific issues.

REVIEW QUESTIONS

1. What is one benefit of a VLAN?
   A. It enables remote users to connect to a local network via the Internet.
   B. It reduces broadcast traffic on a LAN.
   C. It can create a WAN from multiple disjointed LANs.
   D. It provides encryption services on networks that have no default encryption protocol.

2. The number of running virtual machines on a single host is limited by what factor?
   A. Physical RAM
   B. Virtual RAM
   C. Physical NICs
   D. Virtual NICs

3. When a virtual machine is not running, how is it stored?
   A. Firmware
   B. RAM drive
   C. Optical disc
   D. Files

4. To enable computers connected to different switches to be members of the same VLAN, what do the switches have to support?
   A. Content switching
   B. Port authentication
   C. Port mirroring
   D. Trunking

5. Which of the following operating systems would *not* run on VMware Workstation for Windows?
   A. Windows XP
   B. Apple iOS
   C. Ubuntu Linux
   D. Windows Vista

6. Which of the following virtualization programs works well with Mac OS X? (Select the best answer.)

    A. ESX

    B. KVM

    C. Parallels

    D. Virtual PC

7. The boss flies into your office yelling that the virtualized web server has been hacked and now displays only purple dinosaurs. Which of the following would be the fastest way to fix the problem?

    A. Restore from backup

    B. Run System Restore

    C. Reinstall Windows

    D. Load an earlier snapshot

8. Which of the following is *not* a good reason for virtualization?

    A. Power saving

    B. Hardware consolidation

    C. System recovery

    D. Reduced hardware costs

9. Powerful hypervisors like ESX are often booted from

    _____.

    A. Floppy diskettes

    B. USB thumb drives

    C. Firmware

    D. Windows

10. The entire hypervisor market is dominated by two players. (Select two.)

    A. ESX

    B. HyperV

    C. Parallels

    D. KVM

REVIEW ANSWERS

1. **B** VLANs reduce broadcast traffic by segmenting local networks into distinct virtual networks.

2. **A** Physical RAM imposes limits on the number of VMs you can run at the same time.

3. **D** VMs are just files, usually stored on a hard drive.

4. **D** Switches that support trunking enable each switch to be a member of multiple common VLANs.

5. **B** Apple iOS won't run on VMware for Windows.

6. **C** Parallels is the dominant virtualization program for OS X.

7. **D** The beauty of VMs is that you can load an earlier snapshot in a matter of moments.

8. **D** Switching to virtual machines may or may not save money on hardware. A good virtual machine server can cost a lot more than a series of PCs, but operating costs are reduced.

9. **B** A good hypervisor can be tiny, loading from something as small as a USB thumb drive.

10. **A** and **B** ESX and HyperV are the two big players in the native hypervisor market.

Wide Area
Networking

	NEWBIE	SOME EXPERIENCE	EXPERT
ETA	4 hours	2 hours	1 hour

Computers connect to other computers locally in a local area network (LAN)—you've read about LAN connections throughout this book—and remotely through a number of different methods. This chapter takes both a historical and a modern look at ways to interconnect a local computer or network with distant computers, what's called *remote connectivity*.

Remote connections have been around for a long time. Before the Internet, network users and developers created ways to take a single system or network and connect it to another faraway system or network. These were private interconnections of private networks. These connections were very expensive and, compared to today's options, pretty slow.

As the Internet developed, most of the same technologies used to make the earlier private remote connections became the way the Internet itself interconnects. Before the Internet was popular, many organizations used dedicated lines, called *T1 lines* (discussed in more detail later in this chapter), to connect far-flung offices. Some people still use T1 lines privately, but more often you'll see them used as an Internet connection to a company's local ISP. Private interconnections are only used today by organizations that need massive bandwidth or high security.

This chapter shows you all the ways you can make remote connections. You'll see every type of remote connection currently in popular use, from good-old telephone lines to advanced fiber-optic carriers, and even satellites. Each discussion includes details of speed, distance, and *transmission media* (the wires or wireless signals used). There are so many ways to make remote connections that this chapter is broken into three parts. The first part, "Telephony and Beyond," gives you a tour of the technologies that originally existed for long-distance voice connections that now also support data. The next part, "The Last Mile," goes into how we as individual users connect to those long-distance technologies and demonstrates how wireless technologies come into play in remote connectivity. Last, "Using Remote Access" shows you the many different ways to use these connections to connect to another, faraway computer.

Objective 8.01 Telephony and Beyond

Describing the tier 1 Internet service providers (ISPs) of the Internet is always an interesting topic. Those of us in the instruction business invariably start this description by drawing a picture of the United States and then adding lines connecting big cities, as shown in Figure 8.1.

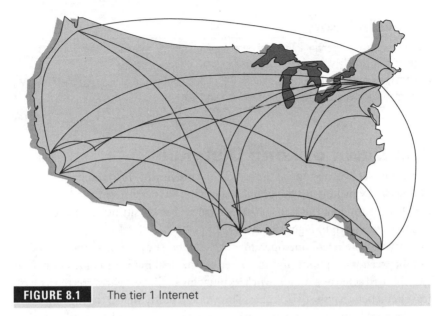

FIGURE 8.1   The tier 1 Internet

But what are these lines and where did they come from? If the Internet is just a big TCP/IP network, wouldn't these lines be Ethernet connections? Maybe copper, maybe fiber, but surely they're Ethernet? Well, traditionally they're not (with one exception; see the following Travel Advisory). The vast majority of the long-distance connections that make up the Internet use a unique type of signal called SONET. SONET was originally designed to handle special heavy-duty circuits with names like T1. Never heard of SONET or T1? Don't worry—you're about to learn quite a bit.

Travel Advisory

Even as you read this, more and more of the Internet interconnections are moving toward Gigabit and 10 Gigabit Ethernet, and 100 Gigabit is just around the corner. Cable and telephone technologies, however, continue to dominate.

Most of the connections that make up the high-speed backbone of the Internet use technologies designed at least 20 years ago to support telephone calls. We're not talking about your cool cell phone–type calls here, but rather the old-school, wire-runs-up-to-the-house, telephone-connected-to-a-phone-jack connections. (See "Public Switched Telephone Network" later in this chapter for more on this subject.) If you want to understand how the Internet connects, you have to go way back to the 1970s and 1980s, before the Internet really took off, and learn how the U.S. telephone system developed to support networks.

> **Travel Advisory**
>
> This section is just the lightest of overviews to get you through the CompTIA Network+ exam. The full history of long-distance communication is an incredible story, full of good guys, bad guys, crazy technology, and huge fortunes won and lost.

The Dawn of Long Distance

Have you ever watched one of those old-time movies in which someone makes a phone call by picking up the phone and saying, "Operator, get me Mohawk 4, 3-8-2-5!"? Suddenly, the scene changes to some person sitting at a switchboard like the one shown in Figure 8.2.

That was the telephone operator. The telephone operator made a physical link between your phone and the other phone, making your connection. The switchboard acted as a *circuit switch*, as plugging in the two wires created a physical circuit between the two phones. This worked pretty well in the first few years of telephones, but it quickly became a problem as more and more phone lines began to fill the skies overhead (Figure 8.3).

FIGURE 8.2   Old-time telephone operator (photo courtesy of the Richardson Historical and Genealogical Society)

FIGURE 8.3   Now that's a lot of telephone lines!

These first generations of long-distance telephone systems (think 1930s here) used analog signals, because that was how your telephone worked. If you graphed out a voice signal, it looked something like Figure 8.4. This type of transmission had issues, however, because analog signals over long distances, even if you amplified them, lost sound quality very quickly.

The first problem to take care of was the number of telephone wires. Individual wires were slowly replaced with special boxes called multiplexers. A *multiplexer* took a circuit and combined it with a few hundred other circuits into a single complex circuit on one wire. A *demultiplexer* (devices were both multiplexers and demultiplexers) on the other end of the connection split the individual connections back out (Figure 8.5).

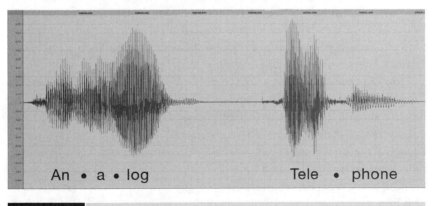

FIGURE 8.4   Another problem of early long-distance telephone systems

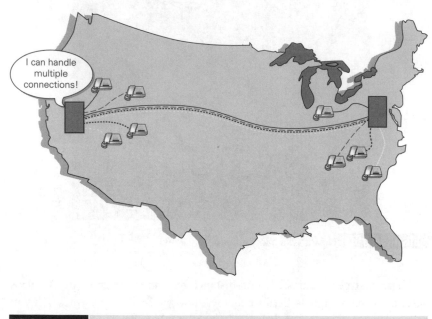

FIGURE 8.5   Multiplexers combine multiple circuits.

Over time, the entire United States was divided into hundreds, eventually thousands, of local exchanges. *Local exchanges* were a defined grouping of individual phone circuits served by a single multiplexer (calls within the exchange were handled first by human operators, who were replaced, eventually, with dial tones and special switches that interpreted your pulses or tones for a number). One or more exchanges were (and still are) housed in a physical building called a *central office* (Figure 8.6) where individual voice circuits all came together. Local calls were still manually connected (although dial-up began to appear in earnest by the 1950s, after which many operators lost their jobs), but any connection between exchanges was carried over these special multiplexed trunk lines. Figure 8.7 shows a very stylized example of how this worked.

How did they put a bunch of voice calls on a single piece of cable, yet still somehow keep them separate? To understand the trick, you need to appreciate a little bit about frequency. A typical telephone only detects a fairly limited frequency range—from around 350 Hz to around 4,000 Hz. This range covers enough of the human speech range to make a decent phone call. As the individual calls came into the multiplexer, it added a certain frequency multiplier to each call, keeping every separate call in its own unique frequency range (Figure 8.8). This process is called *frequency division multiplexing (FDM)*.

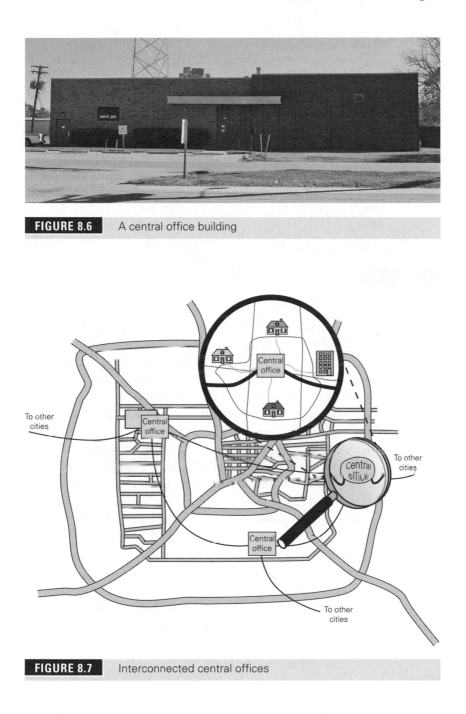

FIGURE 8.6   A central office building

FIGURE 8.7   Interconnected central offices

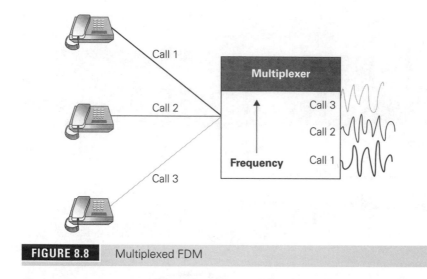

| FIGURE 8.8 | Multiplexed FDM |

This analog network still required a physical connection from one phone to the other, even if those phones were on opposite sides of the country. Long distance used a series of trunk lines, and at each intersection of those lines an operator had to connect the calls. When you physically connect two phones together on one circuit, you are using something called *circuit switching*. As you might imagine, circuit switching isn't that great for long distance, but it's your only option when you use analog.

This analog system worked pretty well from the 1930s through the 1950s, but telephones became so common and demand so heavy that the United States needed a new system to handle the load. The folks developing this new system realized that they had to dump analog and replace it with a digital system—sowing the seeds for the remote connections that eventually became the Internet.

Digital data transmits much easier over long distances than analog data does because you can use repeaters. (You cannot use repeaters on analog signals.) If you remember from earlier chapters, a repeater is not an amplifier. An amplifier just increases the voltage and includes all the pops and hisses created by all kinds of interference. A repeater takes the entire digital signal and re-creates it out the other end (Figure 8.9).

The downside to adopting a digital system was that the entire telephone system was analog: every telephone, every switch, every multiplexer. The task of converting the entire analog voice system to digital was a massive undertaking. Luckily, much of the U.S. phone system at that time was a monopoly run by a company called AT&T. A single company could make all of its own decisions

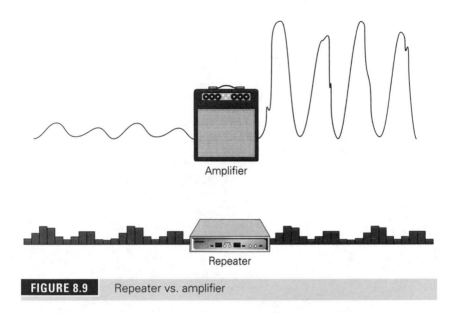

Amplifier

Repeater

FIGURE 8.9   Repeater vs. amplifier

and its own standards—one of the few times in history where a monopoly was probably a good thing. The AT&T folks had a choice here: completely revamp the entire U.S. phone system, including replacing every single telephone in the United States, or just make the trunk lines digital and let the central offices convert from analog to digital. They chose the latter.

Even today, a classic telephone line in your home or small office uses analog signals—the rest of the entire telephone system is digital. The telecommunications industry calls the connection from a central office to individual users the *last mile*. The telephone company's decision to keep the last mile analog has had serious repercussions that still challenge us even in the 21st century (Figure 8.10)

Travel Assistance
Attempts were made to convert the entire telephone system, including your telephones, to digital, but these technologies never took off (except in a few niches). See "ISDN" later in this chapter.

Digital Telephony

When you learned about networks in the first few chapters of this book, you learned about cabling, frame types, speeds, switching, and so on. All of these are important for computer networks. Well, let's do it again (in a much simpler format) to

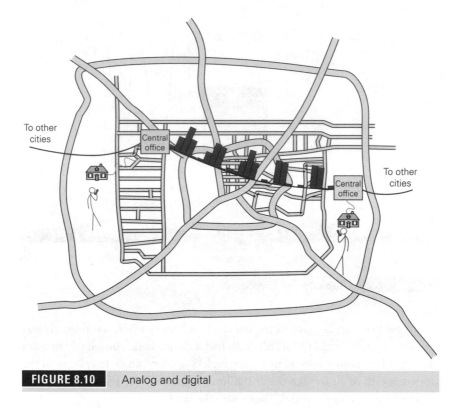

FIGURE 8.10 Analog and digital

see the cabling, frame types, speed, and switching used in telephone systems. Don't worry—unlike computer networks, in which a certain type of cable might run different types of frames at different speeds, most of the remote connections used in the telephony world tend to have one type of cable that only runs one type of frame at one speed.

Let's begin with the most basic data chunk you get in the telephone world: DS0.

It All Starts with DS0

When AT&T decided to go digital, it knew all phone calls had to be broken into a digital sample. AT&T decided (some people say "guessed" or "compromised") that if it took an analog signal of a human voice and converted it into eight-bit chunks 8,000 times a second, it would be good enough to re-create the sound later. Figure 8.11 shows an example of the analog human voice seen earlier being converted into a digital sample.

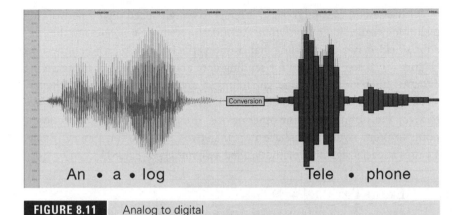

An • a • log   Tele • phone

FIGURE 8.11   Analog to digital

Local Lingo

Modem   A modulator takes a digital signal and converts it into an analog signal. A demodulator takes an analog signal and converts it into a digital signal. The typical modulator/demodulator device in computers is a *modem.*

Converting analog sound into eight-bit chunks 8,000 times a second creates a data stream (called a *digital signal*) of 8 × 8,000 = 64 kilobits per second (Kbps). This digital signal rate, known as *DS0,* makes up the simplest data stream (and the slowest rate) of the digital part of the telephone system. Each analog voice call gets converted into a DS0 signal at the telephone company's central office. From there they are multiplexed into larger circuits.

Now that we have our voice calls converted to digital data, we need to get them to the right telephone. First, we need network technologies to handle the cabling, frames, and speed. Second, we need to come up with a method to switch the digital voice calls across a network. To handle the former, we need to define the types of interconnections, with names like T1 and OC3. To handle the latter, we no longer connect via multiplexed circuit switching, as we did back with analog, but rather are now using packet switching. I'll show you what I mean as I discuss the digital lines in use today.

Copper Carriers: T1 and T3

The first (and still popular) digital trunk carriers used by the telephone industry are called *T-carriers.* There are a number of different versions of T-carriers, and the CompTIA Network+ exam expects you to know something about them. Let's begin with the most common and most basic, the venerable T-carrier level 1 (T1).

T1 has several meanings. First, it refers to a high-speed digital networking technology called a *T1 connection.* Second, the term *T1 line* refers to the specific, shielded, two-pair cabling that connects the two ends of a T1 connection (Figure 8.12). Two wires are for sending data and two wires are for receiving data. At either end of a T1 line, you'll find an unassuming box called a *channel service unit/digital service unit (CSU/DSU).* The CSU/DSU provides an interface between the T1 line and some other device, often a router. A T1 connection is point-to-point—you cannot have more than two CSU/DSUs on a single T1 line. T1 uses a special signaling method called a *digital signal 1 (DS1).*

Exam Tip

You can connect two CSU/DSU boxes together directly by using a *T1 crossover cable.* Like the UTP crossover cables you've seen previously in the book, the T1 crossover cable simply reverses the send/receive pairs on one end of the cable. You'll only see this in use to connect older routers together. The CSU/DSU connections provide convenient link points.

DS1 uses a relatively primitive frame—the frame doesn't need to be complex because with point-to-point no addressing is necessary. Each DS1 frame has 25 pieces: a framing bit and 24 channels. Each DS1 channel holds a single eight-bit DS0 data sample. The framing bit and data channels combine to make 193 bits per DS1 frame. These frames are transmitted 8,000 times/sec, making a total throughput of 1.544 Mbps (Figure 8.13). DS1 defines, therefore, a data transfer speed of 1.544 Mbps, split into twenty-five 64 Kbps DS0 channels. The process of having frames that carry a portion of every channel in every frame sent on a regular interval is called *time division multiplexing (TDM).*

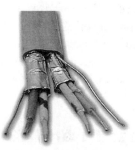

FIGURE 8.12   T1 line

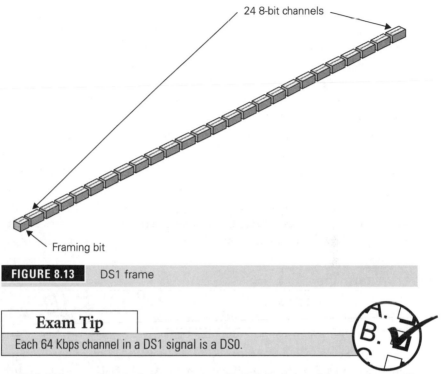

24 8-bit channels

Framing bit

| FIGURE 8.13 | DS1 frame |

Exam Tip

Each 64 Kbps channel in a DS1 signal is a DS0.

With Ethernet, the whole frame encapsulates a single set of data, such as an IP packet that, in turn, encapsulates a single type of TCP segment or UDP datagram. It generally takes multiple frames to get the data to the recipient, where the frames are removed, the IP packet is removed, and the segment or datagram gets put together to make the data transfer complete.

The cool thing about the DS1 frame, though, is that you don't have to use the whole frame for a single set of data. With the right CSU/DSU at either end, you can specify which channels go with a specific thread of data. The frame continues down the line even if some of the channels contain no data at all. The CSU/DSU at the other end collects the data streams and keeps them separate. To paraphrase the immortal words of Professor Egon, "Never cross the streams." (You have seen *Ghostbusters,* right?) Otherwise, you'd lose data.

Travel Advisory

People rarely use the term "DS1." Because T1 lines only carry DS1 signals, you usually just say T1 when describing the signal, even though the term DS1 is more accurate.

A T1 line is a dedicated phone connection that you lease, usually on a monthly basis, from the telephone company. It has no telephone number, and it's always connected. An entire T1 bundle is expensive, so many telephone companies let you buy just some of these individual channels, a practice known as *fractional T1 access*.

A *T3 line* supports a data rate of about 45 Mbps on a dedicated telephone connection. It consists of 672 individual DS0 channels. T3 lines (sometimes referred to as *DS3 lines*) are mainly used by regional telephone companies and ISPs connecting to the Internet.

Similar to the North American T1 line, E-carrier level 1 (*E1*) is the European format for digital transmission. An E1 line carries signals at 2.048 Mbps (32 channels at 64 Kbps), compared to the T1's 1.544 Mbps (24 channels at 64 Kbps). E1 and T1 lines can interconnect for international use. There are also E3 lines, which carry 16 E1 lines, with a bandwidth of about 34 Mbps.

> ## Exam Tip
>
> E1 and SONET use a derivative of the *High-Level Data Link Control (HDLC)* protocol as the control channel.

A CSU/DSU, as mentioned earlier, connects a leased T1 or T3 line from the telephone company to a customer's equipment. A CSU/DSU has (at least) two connectors: one that goes to the T1/T3 line running out of your demarc and another connection that goes to your router. It performs line encoding and conditioning functions and often has a loopback function for testing. Many newer routers have CSU/DSUs built into them. Figure 8.14 shows the front of a Juniper Networks router with two T1 interfaces.

Many routers feature two interfaces on one router, with the dual links providing redundancy if one link goes down. The CSU part of a CSU/DSU protects the T1 or T3 line and the user equipment from lightning strikes and other types of electrical interference. It also stores statistics and has capabilities for loopback testing. The DSU part supplies timing to each user port, taking the incoming user's data signals and converting the input signal into the specified line code and then framing the format for transmission over the provided line.

Make sure you know the four T-carriers shown in Table 8.1.

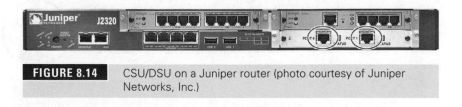

FIGURE 8.14   CSU/DSU on a Juniper router (photo courtesy of Juniper Networks, Inc.)

TABLE 8.1	T-carriers	
Carrier	**Channels**	**Speed**
T1	24	1.544 Mbps
T3	672	44.736 Mbps
E1	32	2.048 Mbps
E3	512	34.368 Mbps

Fiber Carriers: SONET/SDH and OC

T-carriers were a great start into the digital world, but in the mid-1980s, fiber-optic cabling became the primary tool for long-distance communication all over the world. By then, AT&T's monopoly was gone, replaced by a number of competing carriers. Competition was strong and everyone was making their own fiber transmission standards. In an incredible moment of corporate cooperation, in 1987, all of the primary fiber-optic carriers decided to drop their own standards and move to a new international standard called *Synchronous Optical Network (SONET)* in the United States and *Synchronous Digital Hierarchy (SDH)* in Europe.

All of these carriers adopting the same standard created a world of simple interconnections between competing voice and data carriers. This adoption defined the moment that truly made the Internet a universal network. Before SONET, interconnections happened, but they were outlandishly expensive, preventing the Internet from reaching many areas of the world.

SONET remains the primary standard for long-distance, high-speed, fiber-optic transmission systems. SONET, like Ethernet, defines interface standards at the Physical and Data Link layers of the OSI seven-layer model. The physical aspect of SONET is partially covered by the Optical Carrier standards, but it also defines a ring-based topology that most SONET adopters now use. SONET does not require a ring, but a SONET ring has fault tolerance in case of line loss. As a result, most of the big long-distance optical pipes for the world's telecommunications networks are SONET rings.

> **Exam Tip**
>
> SONET is one of the most important standards for making all WAN interconnections—and it's also the least likely standard you'll ever see because it's hidden away from all but the biggest networks.

The real beauty of SONET lies in its multiplexing capabilities. A single SONET ring can combine multiple DS1, DS3, and even European E1 signals and package them into single, huge SONET frames for transmission. Clearly, SONET needs high-capacity fiber optics to handle such large data rates. That's where the Optical Carrier standards come into play!

The *Optical Carrier (OC)* standards denote the optical data-carrying capacity (in bps) of fiber-optic cables in networks conforming to the SONET standard. The OC standard describes an escalating series of speeds, designed to meet the needs of medium-to-large corporations. SONET establishes OC speeds from 51.8 Mbps (OC-1) to 39.8 Gbps (OC-768).

Still want more throughput? Many fiber devices now use a very clever feature called *Wavelength Division Multiplexing (WDM)* or its newer and more popular version, *Dense WDM (DWDM)*. DWDM enables an individual single-mode fiber to carry multiple signals by giving each signal a different wavelength. The result varies, but a single DWDM fiber can support around 150 signals, enabling, for example, a 51.8 Mbps OC-1 line to run at 51.8 Mbps × 150 signals = 7.77 *gigabytes per second!* DWDM has become very popular for long-distance lines, as it's usually less expensive to replace older SONET/OC-*x* equipment with DWDM than it is to add more fiber lines.

Exam Tip	
DWDM isn't just upgrading SONET lines; DWDM works just as well on long-distance fiber Ethernet.	

SONET uses the *Synchronous Transport Signal (STS)* signal method. The STS consists of two parts: the *STS payload* (which carries data) and the *STS overhead* (which carries the signaling and protocol information). When folks talk about STS, they add a number to the end of "STS" to designate the speed of the signal. For example, STS-1 runs a 51.85 Mbps signal on an OC-1 line. STS-3 runs at 155.52 Mbps on OC-3 lines, and so on. Table 8.2 describes the most common optical carriers.

Packet Switching

All of these impressive connections that start with *T*s and *O*s are powerful, but they are not in and of themselves a complete WAN solution. These WAN connections with their unique packets (DS0, STS, and so on) make up the entire mesh of long-range connections called the Internet, carrying both packetized voice data and TCP/IP data packets. All of these connections are point-to-point, so you need to add another level of devices to enable you to connect multiple T1s,

TABLE 8.2	Common Optical Carriers	
SONET Optical Level	**Line Speed**	**Signal Method**
OC-1	51.85 Mbps	STS-1
OC-3	155.52 Mbps	STS-3
OC-12	622.08 Mbps	STS-12
OC-24	1.244 Gbps	STS-24
OC-48	2.488 Gbps	STS-48
OC-192	9.955 Gbps	STS-192
OC-256	13.22 Gbps	STS-256
OC-768	39.82 Gbps	STS-768

T3s, or OC connections together to make that mesh. That's where packet switching comes into play.

Exam Tip

The first generation of packet-switching technology was called *X.25.* It enabled remote devices to communicate with each other across high-speed digital links without the expense of individual leased lines. CompTIA also refers to X.25 as the *CCITT Packet Switching Protocol.*

Packets, as you know, need some form of addressing scheme to get from one location to another. The telephone industry came up with its own types of packets that run on T-carrier and OC lines to get data from one central office to another. These packet-switching protocols are functionally identical to routable network protocols like TCP/IP. Today's WAN connections predominantly use two different forms of packet switching: Frame Relay and ATM.

Local Lingo

Packet switches   Machines that store and forward packets using any type of packet-switching protocol are called *packet switches.*

Frame Relay

Frame Relay is an extremely efficient packet-switching standard, designed for and used primarily with T-carrier lines. It works especially well for the off-again/on-again traffic typical of most LAN applications. Frame Relay switches packets quickly, but without any guarantee of data integrity at all. You can't even count on it to deliver all the frames, because it will discard frames whenever there is network congestion. At first this might sound problematic—what happens if you have a data problem? In practice, however, a Frame Relay network delivers data quite reliably because T-carrier digital lines that use Frame Relay have very low error rates. It's up to the higher-level protocols to error-check as needed. Frame Relay was extremely popular in its day, but newer technologies such as ATM and especially MPLS are beginning to replace it. If you decide to go with a T1 line in the United States, you'll probably get a T1 line running Frame Relay, although many companies use the newer ATM standard as their packet-switching solution with T-carrier lines.

ATM

Don't think automatic teller machine here! *Asynchronous Transfer Mode (ATM)* is a network technology originally designed for high-speed LANs in the early 1990s. ATM only saw limited success in the LAN world but became extremely popular in the WAN world. In fact, until the recent advent of MPLS (see "MPLS" next), most of the SONET rings that moved voice and data all over the world used ATM for packet switching. ATM integrated voice, video, and data on one connection, using short and fixed-length packets called *cells* to transfer information. Every cell sent with the same source and destination traveled over the same route.

ATM existed because data and audio/video transmissions have different transfer requirements. Data tolerates a delay in transfer, but not signal loss (if it takes a moment for a webpage to appear, you don't care). Audio and video transmissions, on the other hand, tolerate signal loss but not delay (delay makes phone calls sound choppy and clipped). Because ATM transferred information in cells of one set size (53 bytes long), it handled both types of transfers well. ATM transfer speeds ranged from 155.52 to 622.08 Mbps and beyond. If your location was big enough to order an OC line from your ISP, odds were good that OC line connected to an ATM switch.

> ### Travel Advisory
>
> Referring to ATM in the past tense might seem a bit premature. Plenty of ISPs still use ATM, but it's definitely on the way out due to MPLS.

MPLS

Frame Relay and ATM were both fantastic packet-switching technologies, but they were designed to support any type of traffic that might come over the

FIGURE 8.15   MPLS header

network. Today, TCP/IP, the predominant data technology, has a number of issues that neither Frame Relay nor ATM address. For example, ATM uses a very small frame, only 53 bytes, which adds quite a bit of overhead to 1,500-byte Ethernet frames. To address this and other issues, many ISPs (and large ISP clients) use an improved technology called *Multiprotocol Label Switching (MPLS)* as a replacement for Frame Relay and ATM switching.

MPLS adds an MPLS label that sits between the layer-2 header and the layer-3 information. Layer 3 is always IP, so MPLS labels sit between layer 2 and the IP headers. Figure 8.15 shows the structure of an MPLS header.

The MPLS header consists of four parts:

- **Label**   A unique identifier, used by MPLS-capable routers to determine how to move data.
- **Cost of Service (CoS)**   A relative value used to determine the importance of the labeled packet. (This is also often labeled Exp, for *experimental.*)
- **S**   In certain situations, a single packet may have multiple MPLS labels. This single bit value is set to 1 for the initial label.
- **Time to Live (TTL)**   The TTL determines the number of hops the label can make before it's eliminated.

Figure 8.16 shows the location of the MPLS header.

The original idea for MPLS was to give individual ISPs a way to move traffic through their morass of different interconnections and switches more quickly and efficiently by providing network-wide *Quality of Service (QoS)*. QoS is a means of sorting IP packets to provide priority based on header information. MPLS-capable routers avoid running IP packets through their full routing

FIGURE 8.16   MPLS header inserted in a frame

tables and instead use the header information to route packets quickly. Where "regular" routers use QoS on an individual basis, MPLS routers use their existing dynamic routing protocols to send each other messages about their overhead, enabling QoS to span an entire group of routers (Figure 8.17). This creates an *MPLS-topology* network.

Let's see how the MPLS-labeled packets, combined with MPLS-capable routers, create improved throughput. To see this happen, I need to introduce a few MPLS terms:

- **Forwarding Equivalence Class (FEC)**   FEC is a group of devices (usually computers) that tend to send packets to the same place, such as a single broadcast domain of computers connected to a router.
- **Label switching router (LSR)**   An LSR looks for and forwards packets based on their MPLS label. These are the "MPLS routers" mentioned previously.
- **Label edge router (LER)**   An LER is an MPLS router that has the job of adding MPLS labels to incoming packets that do not yet have a label.
- **Label Distribution Protocol (LDP)**   LSRs and LERs use the LDP to communicate dynamic information about their state. Figure 8.17 shows an example of LDP in action.

Figure 8.18 shows a highly simplified MPLS network. Note the position of the LERs and LSRs.

FIGURE 8.17   MPLS routers talk to each other about their overhead.

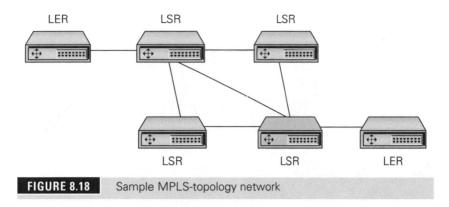

FIGURE 8.18   Sample MPLS-topology network

When an MPLS network comes online, administrators will configure initial routing information, primarily setting metrics to routes (Figure 8.19).

LERs have the real power in determining routes. Because LERs are the entrances and exits for an MPLS network, they talk to each other to determine the best possible routes. As data moves from one FEC, the LERs add an MPLS label to every packet. LSRs strip away incoming labels and add their own. This progresses until the packets exit out the opposing LER (Figure 8.20).

Although MPLS was originally used just to move data quickly between LERs, MPLS's label-stacking ability makes it a perfect candidate for end-user VPNs. Instead of having to set up your own VPN, an ISP using MPLS can set up and lease you a fully functional connection to your network. The ISP makes the VPN for you; you just insert an RJ-45 plug into the switch in your office and it works. This feature of MPLS is called a *permanent virtual circuit (PVC)* and is a popular product sold by ISPs to connect two customer locations.

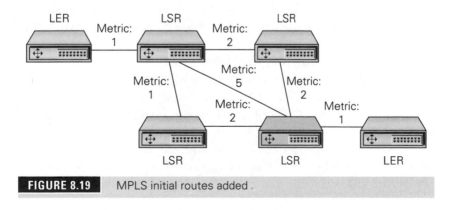

FIGURE 8.19   MPLS initial routes added .

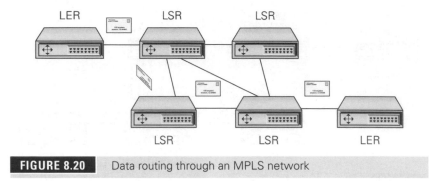

FIGURE 8.20 Data routing through an MPLS network

Real-World WAN

There are two reasons to use a telephony WAN connection: to get your LAN on the Internet or to make a private connection between two or more of your private LANs. How you go about getting one of these lines changes a bit depending on which you want to do. Let's start with connecting to the Internet.

Traditionally, getting a WAN Internet connection was a two-step process: you talked to the telephone company to get the line physically installed and then talked to an ISP to provide you with Internet access. Today, almost every telephone company is also an ISP, so this process is usually simple. Just go online and do a web search of ISPs in your area and give them a call. You'll get a price quote, and, if you sign up, the ISP will do the installation.

You can use a few tricks to reduce the price, however. If you're in an office building, odds are good that a T1 or better line is already installed and that an ISP is already serving people in your building. Talk to the building supervisor. If there isn't a T1 or better line, you have to pay for a new line. If an interconnect is nearby, this option might be inexpensive. If you want the telephone company to run an OC line to your house, however, brace for a quote of thousands of dollars just to get the line.

The telephone company runs your T-carrier (or better) line to a demarc. This demarc is important because this is where the phone company's responsibility ends! Everything on "your" side of the demarc is your responsibility. From there, you or your ISP installs a CSU/DSU (for T-carriers) and that device connects to your router.

Depending on who does this for you, you may encounter a tremendous amount of variance here. The classic example (sticking with T-carrier) consists of a demarc, CSU/DSU, and router setup, as shown in Figure 8.21.

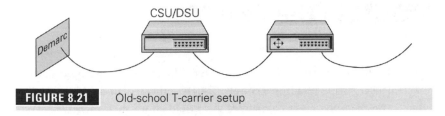

Old-school T-carrier setup

T-carriers have been around so long that many of these parts are combined. You'll often see a single box that combines the CSU/DSU and the router in one handy device, such as the Juniper router shown earlier in Figure 8.14.

WAN telephony carriers are incredibly dependable—far more dependable than inexpensive alternatives (like cable modems)—and that's one of the main reasons people still use them. But you should definitely know how to test your end of the connection if you ever suspect a problem. The single most important test is called the *Bit Error Rate Test (BERT)*. A BERT test verifies the T-carrier connection from end to end. Every CSU/DSU has a different way to BERT test. Just make sure you know how to perform the test on yours!

Alternative to Telephony WAN

Over the last few years, many ISPs started replacing their T1, T3, and OC*x* equipment with good-old Ethernet. Well, not "good-old" Ethernet—rather, superfast 10 Gbps Ethernet running on single-mode fiber and connected to DWDM-capable switches. As a result, in many areas—especially metropolitan areas—you can get native Ethernet right to your office. Anyone want 10 Gbps to their router? If you've got the money and you're in a larger city, you can get it now.

These Ethernet connections also work great for dedicated connections. A good friend of mine leases a dedicated 10 Gbps Ethernet connection from his company's data center in Houston, Texas, to his office in London, England. It costs roughly $15,000/month. DSL and cable have been around for quite a while and deserve some serious discussion. You can't install your own DSL or cable modem connection, however, as you can with telephony WAN carriers. For example, you can't have your own private cable modem connection between two of your offices. DSL and cable modems are only for Internet connections and, as a result, are really more of a last-mile issue—let's discuss DSL and cable in the next section.

Objective 8.02   The Last Mile

Speed is the key to the Internet, but historically there's always been one big challenge: getting data from central offices to individual users. Although this wasn't a problem for larger companies that could afford their own WAN connections, what about individuals and small companies that couldn't or wouldn't pay hundreds of dollars a month for a T1? This area, the infamous last mile, was a serious challenge early on for both Internet connections and private connections because the only common medium was standard telephone lines. A number of last-mile solutions have appeared over the years, and the CompTIA Network+ exam tests you on the most popular ones—and a few obscure ones as well. Here's the list:

- Dial-up
- DSL
- Cable
- Satellite
- Fiber
- BPL

Dial-up

Many different types of telephone lines are available, but all the choices break down into two groups: dedicated and dial-up. *Dedicated lines* are always off the hook (that is, they never hang up on each other). They are always on.

A dedicated line (like a T1) does not have a phone number. In essence, the telephone company creates a permanent, hard-wired connection between the two locations, rendering a phone number superfluous. *Dial-up lines,* by contrast, have phone numbers; they must dial each other up to make a connection. When they're finished communicating, they hang up. Two technologies make up the overwhelming majority of dial-up connections: PSTN and ISDN.

Public Switched Telephone Network

The oldest, slowest, and most common original phone connection is the *public switched telephone network (PSTN)*. PSTN is also known as *plain old telephone service (POTS)*. PSTN is just a regular phone line, the same line that used to run into everybody's home RJ-11 telephone jacks from the central office of your *Local Exchange Carrier (LEC)*. The LEC is the telephone company (telco) that provides local connections and usually the one that owns your local central office.

Because PSTN was designed long before computers were common, it was designed to work with only one type of data: sound. Here's how it works. The telephone's microphone takes the sound of your voice and translates it into an electrical analog waveform. The telephone then sends that signal through the PSTN line to the phone on the other end of the connection. That phone translates the signal into sound on the other end using its speaker. Note the word *analog*. The telephone microphone converts the sounds into electrical waveforms that cycle 2,400 times a second. An individual cycle is known as a *baud*. The number of bauds per second is called the *baud rate*. Pretty much all phone companies' PSTN lines have a baud rate of 2,400. PSTN connections use a connector called RJ-11. It's the classic connector you see on all telephones (Figure 8.22).

When you connect your modem to a phone jack, the line then runs to your *network interface unit (NIU)*, or demarc. The term "network interface unit" is more commonly used to describe the small box on the side of a home that accepts the incoming lines from the telephone company and then splits them to the different wall outlets. "Demarc" more commonly describes large connections used in businesses. The terms are interchangeable and always describe the interface between the lines the telephone company is responsible for and the lines for which you are responsible (Figure 8.23).

Computers, as you know, don't speak analog—only digital/binary (0 or 1) will do. In addition, the people who invented the way PCs communicate decided to divide any digital signal going in and out of your computer into eight bits at a time. To connect over phone lines, PCs need two devices: one that converts this eight-bit-wide (parallel) digital signal from the computer into serial (one-bit-wide) digital data and then another device to convert (modulate) the

FIGURE 8.22   RJ-11 connectors (top and side views)

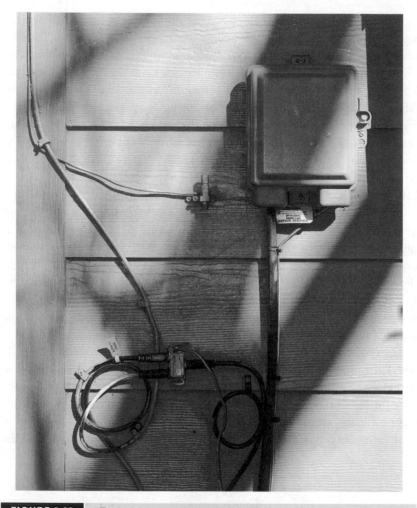

FIGURE 8.23 Typical home demarc

data into analog waveforms that can travel across PSTN lines. You already know that the device that converts the digital data to analog and back is called a *modulator-demodulator (modem)*. The modem also contains a device called a *Universal Asynchronous Receiver/Transmitter (UART)*. The UART takes the eight-bit-wide digital data and converts it into one-bit-wide digital data and hands it to the modem for conversion to analog. The process is reversed for incoming data. Even though internal modems are actually both a UART and a modem, we just say the word "modem" (Figure 8.24).

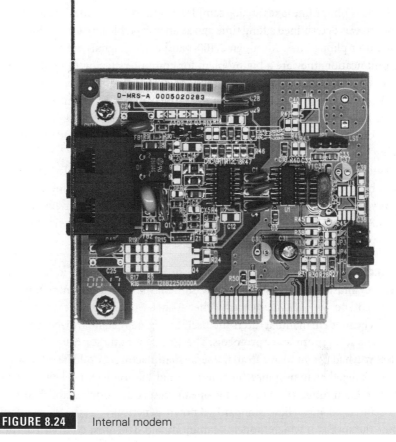

FIGURE 8.24 Internal modem

Exam Tip

Internal modems are both a UART and a modem. External modems use a serial or USB port. The serial or USB port contains the UART, so the external modem truly is just a modem.

Baud vs. Bits per Second   Modems use phone lines to transmit data at various speeds. These speeds cause a world of confusion and problems for computer people. This is where a little bit of knowledge becomes dangerous. Standard modems you can buy for your home computer normally transmit data at speeds up to 56 Kbps. That's 56 kilobits per second, *not* 56 kilobaud! Many people confuse the terms *baud* and *bits per second*. This confusion arises because the baud rate and bits per second are the same for modems until the data transfer rate surpasses 2,400 bps.

A PSTN phone line takes analog samples of sound 2,400 times a second. This standard was determined a long time ago as an acceptable rate for sending voice traffic over phone lines. Although 2,400-baud analog signals are fine for voice communication, they are a big problem for computers trying to send data because computers only work with digital signals. The job of the modem is to take the digital signals it receives from the computer and send them out over the phone line in an analog form, using the baud cycles from the phone system. A 2,400 bps modem—often erroneously called a 2,400-baud modem—uses 1 analog baud to send 1 bit of data.

As technology progressed, modems became faster and faster. To get past the 2,400-baud limit, modems modulated the 2,400-baud signal multiple times in each cycle. A 4,800 bps modem modulated two bits per baud, thereby transmitting 4,800 bps. All PSTN modem speeds are a multiple of 2,400, with the latest (and last) generation of modems achieving $2,400 \times 24 = 57,600$ bps (56 Kbps).

V Standards For two modems to communicate with each other at their fastest rate, they must modulate signals in the same fashion. The two modems must also negotiate with, or *query,* each other to determine the fastest speed they share. The modem manufacturers themselves originally standardized these processes as a set of proprietary protocols. The downside to these protocols was that unless you had two modems from the same manufacturer, modems often would not work together. In response, the International Telegraph and Telephone Consultative Committee (*CCITT*), a European standards body, established standards for modems. These standards, known generically as the *V standards,* define the speeds at which modems can modulate. The most common of these speed standards are as follows:

- **V.22** 1,200 bps
- **V.22bis** 2,400 bps
- **V.32** 9,600 bps
- **V.32bis** 14,400 bps
- **V.34** 28,000 bps
- **V.90** 57,600 bps
- **V.92** 57,600 bps

Local Lingo

ITU-T The CCITT was renamed the International Telecommunication Union Telecommunication Standardization Sector (ITU-T) way back in 1993.

The current modem standard now on the market is the *V.92 standard.* V.92 has the same download speed as the V.90, but upstream rates increase to as much as 48 Kbps.

Point-to-Point Protocol Modems use a protocol for making a secure connection to an ISP, called *Point-to-Point Protocol (PPP).* PPP enables two devices to connect directly, authenticate with user name and password, and negotiate a network protocol. That protocol today, of course, is TCP/IP.

ISDN

PSTN lines traditionally just aren't that good. While the digital equipment that connects to a PSTN supports a full 64 Kbps DS0 channel, the combination of the lines themselves and the conversion from analog to digital means that most PSTN lines rarely go faster than 33 Kbps—and, yes, that includes the 56 Kbps connections.

The phone companies were motivated to come up with a way to generate higher capacities. Their answer was fairly straightforward: make the last mile digital. Since everything but the last mile was already digital, by adding special equipment at the central office and the user's location, phone companies felt they could achieve a true, steady, dependable throughput of 64 Kbps per line over the same copper wires already used by PSTN lines. This process of sending telephone transmission across fully digital lines end-to-end is called *Integrated Services Digital Network (ISDN)* service.

Exam Tip

ISDN also supports voice but requires special ISDN telephones.

ISDN service consists of two types of channels: *Bearer channels (B channels)* carry data and voice information using standard DS0 channels (64 Kbps), whereas *Delta channels (D channels)* carry setup and configuration information at 16 Kbps. Most ISDN providers let the customer choose either one or two B channels. The more common setup is two B/one D, called a *Basic Rate Interface (BRI)* setup. A BRI setup uses only one physical line, but each B channel sends 64 Kbps, doubling the throughput total to 128 Kbps.

Another type of ISDN is called *Primary Rate Interface (PRI)*. ISDN PRI is actually just a full T1 line, carrying 23 B channels.

The physical connections for ISDN bear some similarity to PSTN modems. An ISDN wall socket is usually something that looks like a standard RJ-45 network jack. This line runs to your demarc. In home installations, many telephone companies install a second demarc separate from your PSTN demarc. The most common interface for your computer is a device called a *terminal adapter (TA)*. TAs look like regular modems and, like modems, come in external and internal variants. You can even get TAs that also function as hubs, enabling your system to support a direct LAN connection (Figure 8.25).

Exam Tip

Remember, a B channel is a DS0 channel.

You generally need to be within approximately 18,000 feet of a central office to use ISDN. When you install an ISDN TA, you must configure the other ISDN telephone number you want to call, as well as a special number called the *Service Profile ID (SPID)*. Your ISP provides the telephone number, and the telephone company gives you the SPID. (In many cases, the telephone company is also the ISP.) Figure 8.26 shows a typical installation screen for an internal ISDN TA in an old version of Windows. Note that each channel has a phone number in this case.

| **FIGURE 8.25** | A TeleWell ISDN terminal adapter |

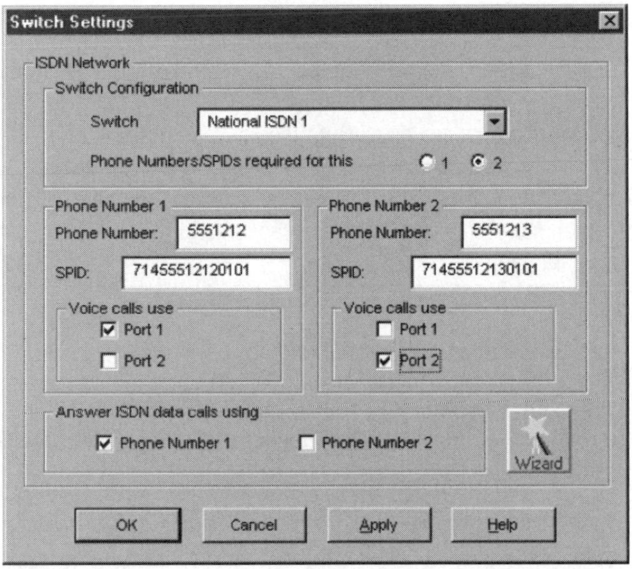

FIGURE 8.26   ISDN settings in an old version of Windows

DSL

Many telephone companies offer a *digital subscriber line (DSL)* connection, an almost fully digital, dedicated (no phone number) connection. DSL represented the next great leap forward past ISDN for telephone lines. A physical DSL connection manifests as just another PSTN connection, using the same telephone lines and RJ-11 jacks as any regular phone line.

DSL comes in a number of versions, but the three most important to know for the CompTIA Network+ exam are *Symmetric DSL (SDSL)*, *Asymmetric DSL (ADSL)*, and the newer *Very High Bitrate DSL (VDSL)*. SDSL lines provide the same upload and download speeds, making them excellent for those who send as much data as they receive, although SDSL is relatively expensive (VDSL is a new form of SDSL—see "VDSL" later in this section). ADSL uses different upload and download speeds. ADSL download speeds are much faster than the upload speeds. Most small office and home office (SOHO) users are primarily concerned with fast *downloads* for things like webpages and can tolerate slower upload speeds. ADSL is always much less expensive than SDSL, and VDSL is usually the most expensive.

Travel Advisory

To use DSL, you must be within 18,000 feet of a central office. The closer you are, the faster your connection will be. Several companies offer a service called *Extended DSL (XDSL)* that can go much farther away from the central office, but that's not a standard. Depending on the implementation, Extended DSL is a rebranded T1 or partial T1 line or something completely proprietary to the telecommunications company offering the service. Buyer beware!

SDSL

SDSL provides equal upload and download speed and, in theory, provides speeds up to 15 Mbps, although the vast majority of ISPs provide packages ranging from 192 Kbps to 9 Mbps.

ADSL

ADSL provides theoretical maximum download speeds up to 15 Mbps and upload speeds up to 1 Mbps. All ADSL suppliers "throttle" their ADSL speeds, however, and provide different levels of service. Real-world ADSL download speeds vary from 384 Kbps to 15 Mbps, and upload speeds go from as low as 128 Kbps to around 768 Kbps.

VDSL

VDSL is the latest version of DSL to appear. Although not as many people use it as regular DSL (at least in the United States), its ability to provide speeds of 100+ Mbps in both directions makes it an attractive option. VDSL achieves these speeds by adding very advanced methods to encode the data. Don't get too excited about these great speed increases. They are very distance dependent: you won't get 100 Mbps unless you're around 300 meters from the DSLAM (see "DSL Features"). VDSL is designed to run on copper phone lines, but many VDSL suppliers use fiber-optic cabling to increase distances. In the United States, these fiber VDSL services are fiber-to-the-home solutions. The two most popular carriers are AT&T's U-verse and Verizon's Fiber Optic Service (FiOS).

Exam Tip

The CompTIA Network+ objectives offer *Variable* Digital Subscriber Line as the words that match the VDSL initials. No such DSL variant exists. VDSL stands for *Very High Bitrate* DSL. You'll probably only see the initials on the exam, so no worries on that score.

DSL Features

One nice aspect of DSL is that you don't have to run new phone lines. The same DSL lines you use for data can simultaneously transmit your voice calls.

All versions of DSL have the same central office–to–end user distance restrictions as ISDN—around 18,000 feet from your demarc to the central office. At the central office, your DSL provider has a device called a *DSL Access Multiplexer (DSLAM)* that connects multiple customers to the Internet.

> **Travel Advisory**
>
> No DSL provider guarantees any particular transmission speed and will only provide service as a "best efforts" contract—a nice way to say that DSL lines are notorious for substantial variations in throughput.

Installing DSL

DSL operates using your preexisting telephone lines (assuming they are up to specification). This is wonderful but also presents a technical challenge. For DSL and your run-of-the-mill POTS line to coexist, you need to filter out the DSL signal on the POTS line. A DSL line has three information channels: a high-speed downstream channel, a medium-speed duplex channel, and a POTS channel. Segregating the two DSL channels from the POTS channel guarantees that your POTS line will continue to operate even if the DSL fails. You accomplish this by inserting a filter on each POTS line, or a splitter mechanism that enable all three channels to flow to the DSL modem but sends only the POTS channel down the POTS line. The DSL company should provide you with a few POTS filters for your telephones. If you need more, most computer/electronics stores stock DSL POTS filters.

The most common DSL installation consists of a *DSL modem* connected to a telephone wall jack and to a standard NIC in your computer (Figure 8.27). A DSL modem is not an actual modem—it's more like an ISDN terminal adapter—but the term stuck, and even the manufacturers of the devices now call them DSL modems.

Many offices use DSL. In my office, we use a special DSL line (we use a digital phone system, so the DSL must be separate) that runs directly into our equipment room (Figure 8.28).

This DSL line runs into our DSL modem via a standard phone line with RJ-11 connectors. The DSL modem connects to our gateway router with a CAT 5e patch cable, which, in turn, connects to the company's switch. Figure 8.29 shows an ADSL modem and a router, giving you an idea of the configuration in our office.

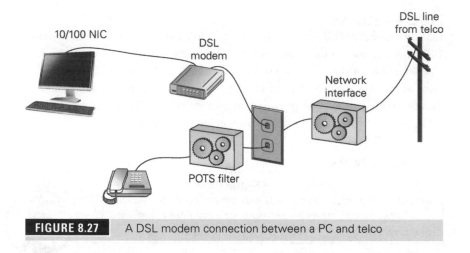

| FIGURE 8.27 | A DSL modem connection between a PC and telco |

Home users often connect the DSL modem directly to their PC's NIC. Either way, you have nothing to do in terms of installing DSL equipment on an individual system—just make sure you have a NIC. The person who installs your DSL will test the DSL line, install the DSL modem, connect it to your system, and verify that it all works. With DSL, be aware that you might run into an issue with something called *Point-to-Point Protocol over Ethernet (PPPoE)*.

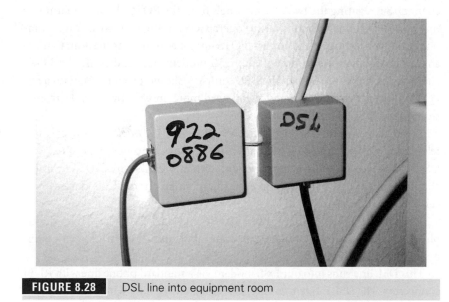

| FIGURE 8.28 | DSL line into equipment room |

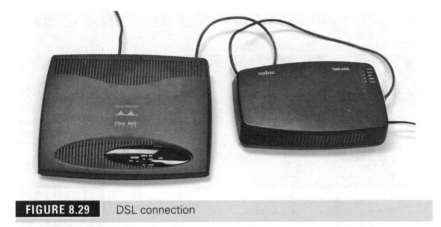

FIGURE 8.29 DSL connection

The first generation of DSL providers used a *bridged connection;* once the DSL line was running, it was as if you had snapped an Ethernet cable into your NIC. You were on the network. Those were good days for DSL. You just plugged your DSL modem into your NIC and, assuming your IP settings were whatever the DSL folks told you to use, you were running.

The DSL providers didn't like that too much. There was no control—no way to monitor who was using the DSL modem. As a result, the DSL folks started to use PPPoE, a protocol that was originally designed to encapsulate PPP frames into Ethernet frames. The DSL people adopted it to make stronger controls over your DSL connection. In particular, you could no longer simply connect; you now had to log on with an account and a password to make the DSL connection. PPPoE is now predominant on DSL. If you get a DSL line, your operating system has software to enable you to log onto your DSL network. Most SOHO routers come with built-in PPPoE support, enabling you to enter your user name and password into the router itself (Figure 8.30).

Cable Modems

The first big competition for ADSL came from the cable companies. Cable modems have the impressive benefit of phenomenal top speeds. These speeds vary from cable company to cable company, but most advertise speeds in the (are you sitting down?) *5 to 100 megabits per second* range. Many cable modems provide a throughput speed of 5 to 30 Mbps for downloading and 2 Mbps to 10 Mbps for uploading—there is tremendous variance among different providers.

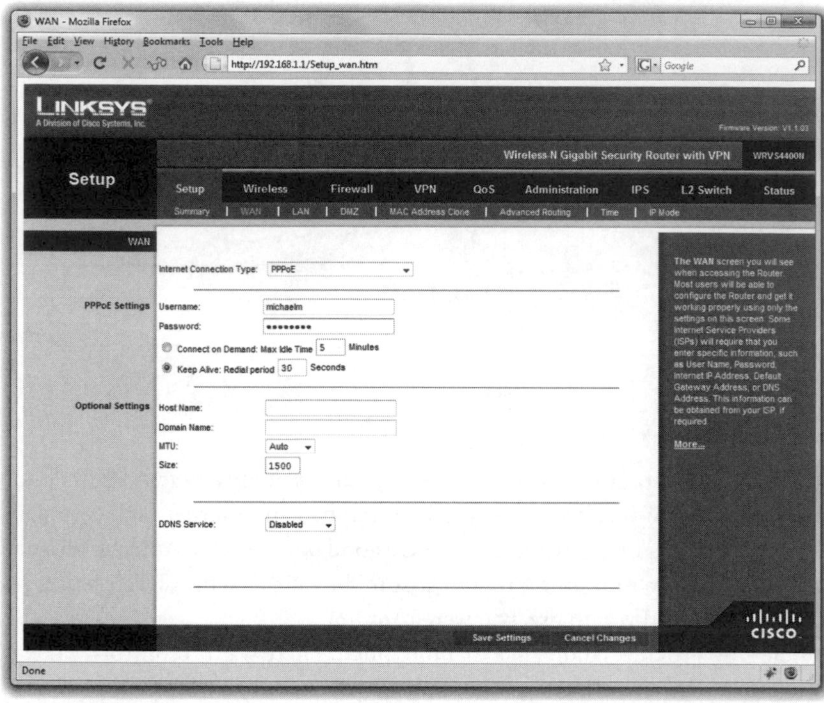

FIGURE 8.30 PPPoE settings in SOHO router

A cable modem installation consists of a cable modem connected to a cable. The cable modem gets its own cable connection, separate from the one that goes to the television. It's the same cable line, just split from the main line as if you were adding a second cable outlet for another television. As with ADSL, cable modems connect to PCs using a standard NIC (Figure 8.31).

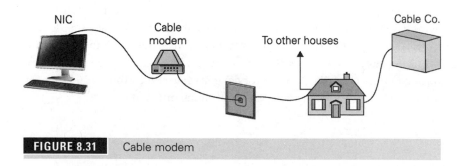

FIGURE 8.31 Cable modem

Cable modems connect using coax cable to a head end, similar to a telephone company's central office. Head ends, in turn, connect to the cable company's network. This network uses a unique protocol called *Data Over Cable Service Interface Specification (DOCSIS)*. Most recently, the specification was revised (DOCSIS 3.0) to increase transmission speeds significantly (this time both upstream and downstream) and introduce support for Internet Protocol version 6 (IPv6).

Exam Tip
Many companies sell routers with a built-in cable or DSL modem.

You'll have a hard time telling a cable modem from a DSL modem. The only difference, other than the fact that one will have "cable modem" printed on it whereas the other will say "DSL modem," is that the cable modem has a coax BNC connector and an RJ-45 port; the DSL modem has an RJ-11 port and an RJ-45 port.

Cable modems have proven themselves to be reliable and fast and have surpassed DSL as the broadband connection of choice in homes. Cable companies are also aggressively marketing to business customers with high-speed packages, making cable a viable option for businesses.

Satellite

Living in the countryside may have its charms, but you'll have a hard time getting high-speed Internet out on the farm. For those too far away to get anything else, satellite may be your only option. Satellite access comes in two types: one-way and two-way. *One-way* means that you download via satellite but you must use a PSTN/dial-up modem connection for uploads. *Two-way* means the satellite service handles both the uploading and downloading.

Satellite isn't as fast as DSL or cable modems, but it's still faster than PSTN. Both one-way and two-way satellite connections provide around 500 Kbps download and 50 Kbps upload.

Travel Advisory
Companies that design satellite communications equipment haven't given up on their technology. At the time of this writing, at least one company, HughesNet, offered speeds up to 2 Mbps download. You can surf with that kind of speed!

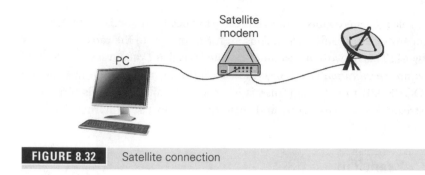

FIGURE 8.32   Satellite connection

Satellite requires a small satellite antenna, identical to the ones used for satellite television. This antenna connects to a satellite modem, which, in turn, connects to your PC or your network (Figure 8.32).

Exam Tip
Neither cable modems nor satellites use PPP, PPPoE, or anything else that begins with three Ps.

Cellular WAN

Anyone with a smart phone these days appreciates the convenience of using wireless cellular technology on the road. Who doesn't love firing up an Android phone and cruising the Internet from anywhere? The CompTIA Network+ exam expects you to know a few abbreviations. I'll divide these into three groups: mobile data services, 802.16 (WiMAX), and LTE.

Mobile Data Services

Mobile data services have names like GSM, GRPS, EDGE, and HSPDA (there are many more standards). These services use the cellular telephone network to provide access. Mostly used with cell phones and smart phones, most mobile data services also sell wireless NICs that you can plug into laptops and desktop computers (Figure 8.33).

802.16

Products that use the *802.16* wireless standard—often called *WiMAX*—are appearing in select markets everywhere. Although speed for 802.16-compliant devices is about the same as 802.11b, manufacturers claim a range of up to

30 miles. This kind of range makes 802.16 perfect for so-called metropolitan area networks (MANs). Before you get too excited, though, keep in mind that the speed of the network will almost certainly decrease the farther away from the base station (the WAP) the nodes are. Effective range could be as little as three miles, but that still beats 300 feet in my book.

If you want WiMAX access right now, you'll probably end up going to CLEAR or Sprint (currently the biggest WiMAX ISPs in America) for a WiMAX home router that plugs directly into your own router (Figure 8.34). They even sell WiMAX/802.11 wireless hot spots, although they limit the number of concurrent connections you can have.

LTE

WiMAX has only one serious competitor—*Long Term Evolution (LTE)*. LTE marks the latest evolution of the popular High-Speed Packet Access (HSPA), better known to the cellular world as GSM or 3G technology. LTE has some

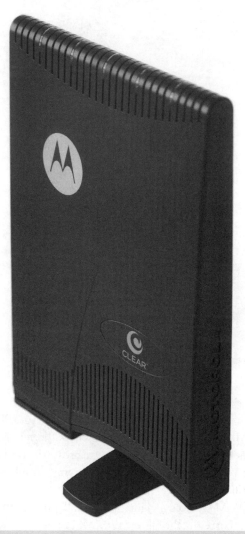

FIGURE 8.34   CLEAR home modem (photo courtesy of CLEAR)

heavy-hitter companies behind it, such as AT&T, Verizon, and Sprint. LTE has become quite popular for portable Internet access (see Figure 8.33 for an example), but changes in the landscape in late 2011 and 2012 should see the end of WiMAX altogether. Sprint and CLEAR, the early WiMAX champions, are moving (or have moved, depending on when you're reading this) to LTE in 2012.

Local Lingo

Evolved High-Speed Packet Access   Many companies have adopted a standard called *HSPA+* that provides wireless speeds of up to 84 Mbps down and 22 Mbps up. This standard competes with LTE.

Fiber

DSL was the first popular last-mile WAN option, but over the years cable modems have taken the lead. In an attempt to regain market share, telephone providers are now rolling out fiber-to-the-home/fiber-to-the-premises options that are giving the cable companies a scare. In the United States, two companies, AT&T (U-verse) and Verizon (FiOS), are offering very attractive ISP, television, and phone services at speeds that will eventually increase above 100 Mbps. These services are quickly gaining in popularity and giving cable companies a run for their money.

To make rollouts affordable, most fiber-to-the-home technologies employ a version of *passive optical network (PON)* architecture that uses a single fiber to the neighborhood switch and then individual fiber runs to each final destination. PON uses WDM to enable multiple signals to travel on the same fiber and then passively splits the signal at the switch to send traffic to its proper recipient.

BPL

With the exception of fiber, most wired networks use electrical signaling to enable systems to interconnect. Rather than running all new wiring dedicated to networks, why not use the vast infrastructure of wiring already in place in just about every home and office in the developed world? Enterprising engineers have been working to provide networking over electrical power lines for many years now with varying degrees of success. The overall field is called *powerline communications (PLC)* and encompasses everything from voice transmission to home automation to high-speed Internet access.

Local Lingo

HomePlug   The most successful PLC technology is HomePlug, a collection of standards for creating LANs in houses, running smart meters for more efficient electrical use, and home automation. The HomePlug Powerline Alliance, with a membership of over 60 companies, actively promotes the various HomePlug standards and devices.

Broadband over Power Line (BPL) is one specific field of technologies that tries to bring usable Internet access to homes and businesses through the electrical power grid. The various companies that have rolled this out, such as Ambient Corporation, Current Technologies, and Motorola, have had some success, though the electrical grid poses serious challenges to networking because of noise and interference from other devices. Most BPL rollouts to date have failed, but companies continue to explore the possibilities.

Which Connection?

With so many connection options for homes and small offices, making a decision is often a challenge. Your first question is availability: Which services are available in your area? The second question is, How much bandwidth do you need? The latter is a question of great debate. Most services are more than happy to increase service levels if you find that a certain level is too slow. I usually advise clients to start with a relatively slow level and then increase if necessary. After all, once you've tasted the higher speeds, going slower is hard, but the transition to faster is relatively painless!

Going Connection Shopping

You've already checked the availability of DSL and ISDN in your neighborhood, but now you have more choices! Do you have cable or satellite available? A great website to start your search is www.dslreports.com. It has a handy search feature that helps you determine the types of service and the costs for DSL, cable, and other services. Which one makes sense for you?

Objective 8.03 Using Remote Access

Because most businesses are no longer limited to a simple little shop like you would find in a Dickens novel, many people need to be able to access files and resources over a great distance. Enter remote access. *Remote access* uses WAN and LAN connections to enable a computer user to log onto a network from the other side of a city, a state, or even the globe. As people travel, information has to remain accessible. Remote access enables users to connect a server at the business location and log into the network as if they were in the same building as the company. The only problem with remote access is that there are so many ways to do it! I've listed the six most common forms of remote access here:

- **Dial-up to the Internet**   Using a dial-up connection to connect to your ISP
- **Private dial-up**   Using a dial-up connection to connect to your private network
- **Virtual private network**   Using an Internet connection to connect to a private network (discussed in Chapter 9)
- **Dedicated connection**   Using a non-dial-up connection to another private network or the Internet
- **Remote terminal**   Using a terminal emulation program to connect to another computer
- **VoIP**   Voice over IP

In this section, I discuss the issues related to configuring these six types of connections. After seeing how to configure these types of remote connections, I move into observing some security issues common to every type of remote connection.

Local Lingo

Extranet   You'll see the term *extranet* more in books than in the day-to-day workings of networks and network techs. So what is an extranet? Whenever you allow authorized remote users to access some part of your private network, you have created an extranet.

Dial-up to the Internet

Dial-up is the oldest and least expensive method to connect to the Internet and is still somewhat common. Even with broadband and wireless so prevalent, every self-respecting network tech (or maybe just old network techs like me) keeps a dial-up account as a backup. You buy a dial-up account from an ISP (many wireless and broadband ISPs give free dial-up—just ask). All operating systems come with dial-up support programs, but you'll need to provide the following:

- A modem (most operating systems check for a modem before setting up a dial-up connection)
- The telephone number to dial (provided to you by the ISP)

- User name and password (provided to you by the ISP)
- Type of connection (dial-up always uses PPP)
- IP information (provided to you by the ISP—usually just DHCP)

Every operating system comes with the software to help you set up a dial-up connection. In Windows Vista or Windows 7, for example, select the "Set up a dial-up connection" option in the Network and Sharing Center (Figure 8.35). Whatever the name, this tool is what you use to create dial-up connections.

Private Dial-Up

A private dial-up connection connects a remote system to a private network via a dial-up connection. Private dial-up does not use the Internet! Private dial-up requires two systems. One system acts as a *remote access server (RAS)*. The other system, the client, runs a connection tool (usually the same tool you just read about in the previous section).

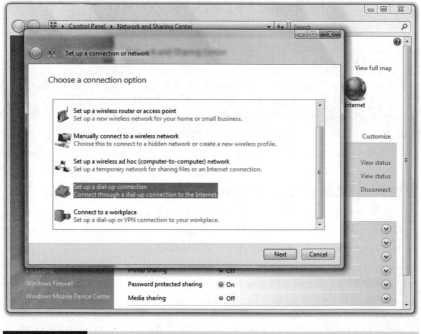

FIGURE 8.35   Dial-up on Windows 7

In Windows, a RAS is a server running Remote Access Service (RAS), dedicated to handling users who are not directly connected to a LAN but who need to access file and print services on the LAN from a remote location. For example, when a user dials into a network from home using an analog modem connection, she is dialing into a RAS. Once the user authenticates, she can access shared drives and printers as if her computer were physically connected to the office LAN.

You must set up a server in your LAN as a RAS server. That RAS server, which must have at least one modem, accepts incoming calls and handles password authentication. RAS servers use all the standard authentication methods (PAP, CHAP, EAP, 802.1X, and so on, which Chapter 9 covers in detail) and have separate sets of permissions for dial-in users and local users. You must also configure the RAS to set the rights and permissions for all of the dial-in users. Configuring a RAS system is outside the scope of this book, however, because each one is different (Figure 8.36).

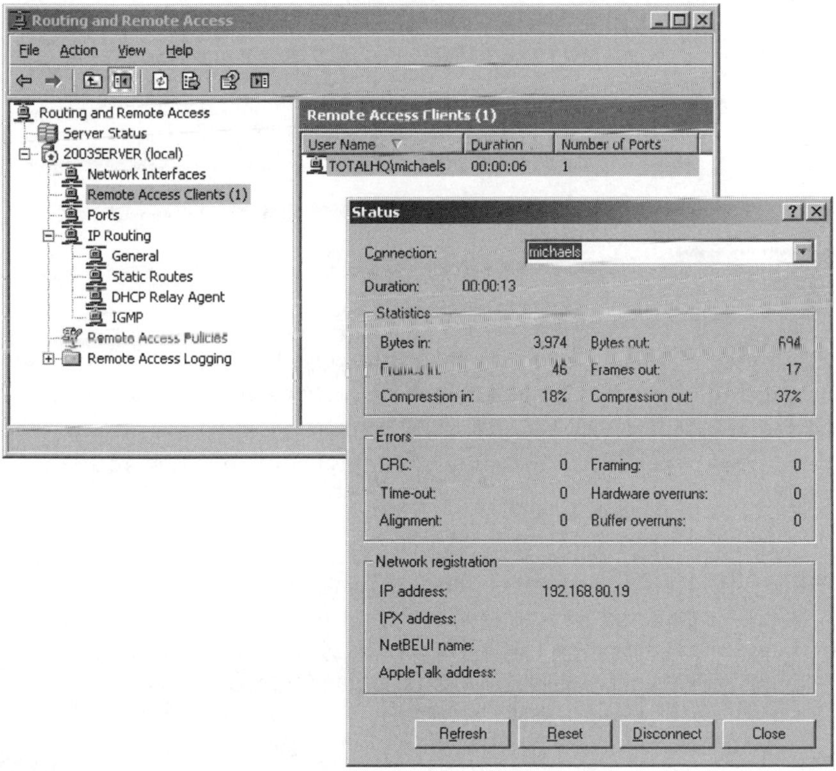

FIGURE 8.36   Windows RAS in action

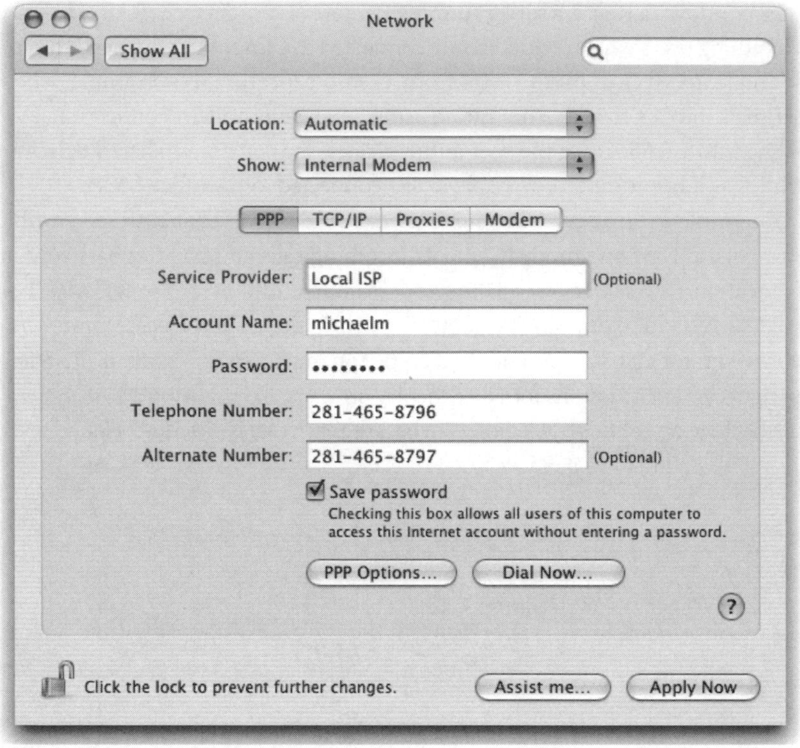

FIGURE 8.37 Dial-up on Macintosh OS X

Creating the client side of a private dial-up connection is identical to setting up a dial-up connection to the Internet. The only difference is that instead of having an ISP tell you what IP settings, account name, and password to use, the person who sets up the RAS server tells you this information (Figure 8.37).

Local Lingo

RAS *Remote access server* refers to both the hardware component (servers built to handle the unique stresses of a large number of clients calling in) and the software service component of a remote access solution. You might call it a catchall phrase. When you run Microsoft's Remote Access Service on a server, you turn that server into a remote access server.

Most techs call RAS "razz," rather than using the initials "R-A-S." This creates a seemingly redundant phrase used to describe a system running RAS: "RAS server." This helps distinguish servers from clients and makes geeks happier.

Dedicated Connection

Dedicated connections are remote connections that are never disconnected. Dedicated connections can be broken into two groups: dedicated private connections between two locations and dedicated connections to the Internet. Dedicated private connections manifest themselves as two locations interconnected by a (usually high-speed) connection such as a T1 line (Figure 8.38).

Each end of the T1 line goes into a router (after going through a CSU/DSU, of course). Note that this connection does not use the Internet in any way—it is not a VPN connection. Private dedicated connections of this type are expensive

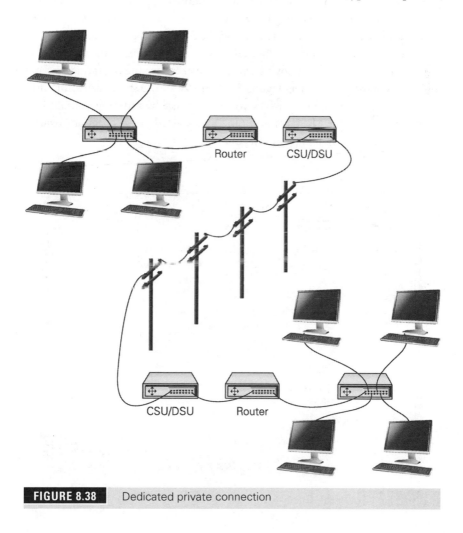

FIGURE 8.38   Dedicated private connection

and are only used by organizations that need the high bandwidth and high security these connections provide. These connections are invisible to the individual computers on each network. There is no special remote connection configuration of the individual systems, although you may have to configure DHCP, DNS, and WINS servers to ensure that the network runs optimally.

DSL and Cable

Dedicated connections to the Internet are common today. Cable modems and DSL have made dedicated connections to the Internet inexpensive and very popular. In most cases, you don't have to configure anything in these dedicated connections. Many cable and DSL providers give you a CD-ROM that installs different items, such as testing software, PPPoE login support, and little extras like e-mail clients and software firewalls. Personally, I prefer not to use these (they add a lot of stuff you don't need) and instead use the operating system's tools or a hardware router. Figure 8.39 shows the DSL wizard built into Windows 7. This program enables you to connect by entering your PPPoE information for your ADSL connection. Once started, these programs usually stay running in the system tray until your next reboot.

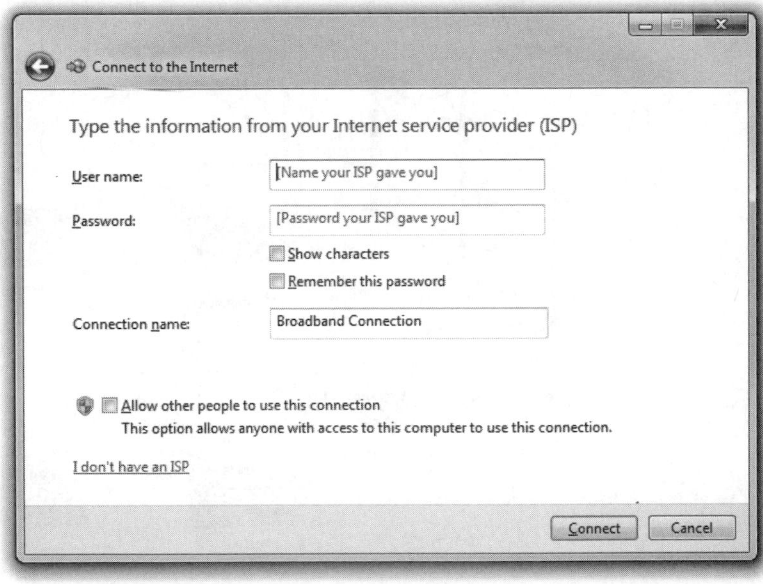

FIGURE 8.39   PPPoE connection

Cable Issues

Dedicated cable connections add a little complexity to the installation options because most cable networks bring television and often voice communication into the same line. This complicates things in one simple way: *splitters.*

If you have a cable connection coming to your house and you have a television set in two rooms, how do you get cable in both rooms? Easy, right? Just grab a two-way splitter from Radio Shack and run an extra pair of cables, one to each room. The problem comes from the fact that every time you split a cable signal, the signal degrades by half. This is called, logically, a *split cable* problem.

The quality of a signal can be measured in *decibels (dB),* a unit that describes a ratio between an ideal point—a reference point—and the current state of the signal. When discussing signal strength, a solid signal is 0 dB. When that signal degrades, it's described as a *dB loss* and a negative number. An increase in signal is *gain* and gets a positive number. Decibels are logarithmic units that, if you've forgotten the high school math, means that going up or down the scale in a simple number translates into a huge number in a percentage scale.

For example, when you split a cable signal into two, you get half the signal strength into each new cable. That's described as a –3 dB signal. Split it again and you've got a –6 dB signal. Although 6 isn't a big number in standard units, it's horribly huge in networking. You might have a 20 Mbps cable connection into your house, but split it twice and you're left with a 5 Mbps connection. Ouch!

The standard procedure with cable connections is to split them once: one cable goes to the cable modem and the other to the television. You can then split the television cable into as many connections as you need or can tolerate as far as reception quality

Remote Terminal

You can use a terminal emulation program to create a *remote terminal,* a connection on a faraway computer that enables you to control that computer as if you were sitting in front of it, logged in. Terminal emulation has been a part of TCP/IP from its earliest days, in the form of good-old Telnet. Because it dates from pre-GUI days, Telnet is a text-based utility; all modern operating systems are graphical, so there was a strong desire to come up with graphical remote terminal tools. Citrix Corporation made the first popular terminal emulation products—the *WinFrame/MetaFrame* products (Figure 8.40).

Remote terminal programs all require a server and a client. The server is the computer to be controlled. The client is the computer from which you do the

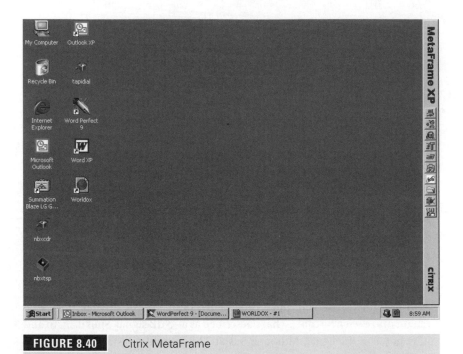

FIGURE 8.40	Citrix MetaFrame

controlling. Citrix created a standard called *Independent Computing Architecture (ICA)* that defined how terminal information was passed between the server and the client. Citrix made a breakthrough product—so powerful that Microsoft licensed the Citrix code and created its own product called Windows Terminal Services. Not wanting to pay Citrix any more money, Microsoft then created its own standard called *Remote Desktop Protocol (RDP)* and unveiled a new remote terminal called *Remote Desktop Connection (RDC)* starting with Windows XP. Figure 8.41 shows Windows Remote Desktop Connection running on a Windows 7 system, connecting to a Windows 2008 Server.

Exam Tip
All RDP applications run on port 3389 by default.

Unfortunately, Terminal Services only works in the Windows environment; however, a number of third parties make absolutely amazing terminal emulation programs that run on any operating system. The best of these, *VNC* (VNC stands for Virtual Network Computing) doesn't let you share folders or printers because it is only a terminal emulator (Figure 8.42), but it runs on every operating

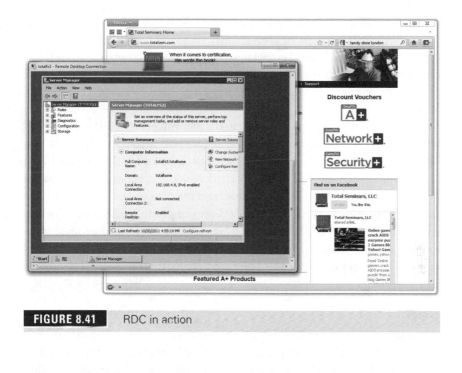

RDC in action

VNC in action

system, is solid as a rock, and even runs from a web browser. It works nicely in Secure Shell (SSH) tunnels for great security, plus it comes by default with every copy of Mac OS X and almost every Linux distribution. Why bother sharing if you can literally be at the screen? Oh, and did I mention that VNC is completely free?

VoIP

Voice over IP (VoIP) uses an IP network to transfer voice calls. VoIP works so well because it uses an existing network you're already paying for (your Internet connection) to replace another network you're also paying for (PSTN lines). The technology needed for VoIP isn't very challenging, but making a VoIP system that's standardized so everyone can use it (and still contact those who choose to use PSTN) requires international standards, making it quite a bit harder. VoIP is still a very fractured world, but it's getting closer to universally adopted standards—one day everyone will be able to contact everyone else, no matter what brand of VoIP they use. To do this, you need to know three important standards: RTP, SIP, and H.323.

RTP

The *Real-time Transport Protocol (RTP),* the heavily adopted bedrock of VoIP standards, defines the type of packets used on the Internet to move voice or data from a server to clients. The vast majority of VoIP solutions available today use RTP.

Exam Tip

The CompTIA Network+ objectives inexplicably drop the word "Transport" from this protocol and call it the *Real Time Protocol.* There's no such thing. It's the Real-time *Transport* Protocol.

SIP and H.323

Session Initiation Protocol (SIP) and *H.323* handle the initiation, setup, and delivery of VoIP sessions. VoIP requires a lot of special features that are not very common in many other Internet protocols. The biggest one is multicasting. You don't ever really use multicasting unless you want to show a number of people a video or want to make a conference call. SIP and H.323 both have methods for handling multicasting.

Exam Tip

SIP and H.323 both run on top of RTP. Most VoIP solutions are either SIP/RTP or H.323/RTP

Skype

Almost every VoIP solution available today uses SIP or H.323 running on top of RTP, with one huge exception: the very famous and incredibly popular Skype. Skype was unveiled in 2003 by Niklas Zennström, a Swedish computer guy famous for inventing the Kazaa peer-to-peer file-sharing system. Skype is completely different from and completely incompatible with any other type of VoIP solution: Skype doesn't use servers, but instead uses a peer-to-peer topology that is identical to the old Kazaa network. Skype calls are also encrypted using a proprietary encryption method. No one has a standard method for VoIP encryption at this time, although many smart people are working hard on the issue.

Streaming Media with RSTP

VoIP isn't the only thing that takes advantage of protocols such as RTP. Streaming video is now mainstream, and many streaming video servers (Windows Media Player, QuickTime, and many others) use a popular protocol called Real Time Streaming Protocol (RTSP). Like SIP and H.323, RSTP runs on top of RTP. RSTP has a number of features that are perfect for video streaming, such as the ability to run, pause, and stop videos. RSTP runs on TCP port 554.

CHECKPOINT

✔ **Objective 8.01: Telephony and Beyond**   The Internet backbone uses technologies designed more than 20 years ago to support telephone calls. There are two reasons to use a telephony WAN connection: to get your LAN on the Internet or to make a private connection between two or more of your private LANs. T1, T3, E1, and E3 are all popular methods of high-speed communication. SONET is the primary standard for long-distance, high-speed, fiber-optic transmission in the United States. WANs use packet switching technologies like ATM and Frame Relay to transmit data over multiple connection types.

✔ **Objective 8.02: The Last Mile**   The last mile represents the challenge of increasing connection speeds between the user and the central office. Many technologies exist to facilitate this connection, including dial-up, ISDN, DSL, cable, satellite, fiber, and broadband over powerline (BPL). You can also use cellular WAN technologies, including WiMAX and LTE.

✔**Objective 8.03: Using Remote Access**   Remote access allows users to log onto networks remotely, making files and network resources available to users across the city, state, or globe. There are six common forms of remote access. You can make a dial-up connection to the Internet. You can connect to another computer using a private dial-up connection. Virtual private networks enable you to tunnel from a local computer to a remote network. Dedicated connections use non-dial-up methods to connect to a private network or the Internet. A remote terminal uses a terminal emulation program to connect to another computer. VoIP (voice over IP) uses an IP network to make voice calls.

REVIEW QUESTIONS

1. Which standard supports a throughput of up to 39.8 Gbps?

   A. ISDN

   B. VDSL

   C. SONET

   D. MPLS

2. If you purchase a T1 line in the United States, how will packets be switched? (Select two.)

   A. OC

   B. Frame Relay

   C. ATM

   D. BERT

3. What describes the problem with "the last mile"?

   A. The connection from a central office to a user's home is analog, whereas the rest of the network is digital.

   B. Users must live within a mile of a central office in order to guarantee Quality of Service (QoS).

   C. SONET connections are limited to a maximum distance of one mile, and connecting central offices via multiplexers is expensive and difficult to maintain.

   D. Copper wires that carry analog telephone signals are limited to a maximum distance of one mile.

4. What terms describe a common telephone connection? (Select two.)

   A. ISDN

   B. POTS

   C. Fractional T1

   D. PSTN

5. What marks where the telephone company's responsibility ends and yours begins?

   A. Multiplexer

   B. Demarc

   C. Primary Rate Interface

   D. Bridges connection

6. The CCITT established which set of standards?

   A. Optical Carrier (OC)

   B. DSL (ADSL, SDSL, VDSL)

   C. Data Over Cable Service Interface Specification (DOCSIS)

   D. V standards

7. Which is the fastest ISDN connection?

   A. BERT

   B. BRI

   C. PRI

   D. ATM

8. Sinjay is 200 meters from his ISP's DSLAM. Which DSL version will provide him with, theoretically, up to 100 Mbps of both download and upload speed?

   A. DS3

   B. ADSL

   C. SDSL

   D. VDSL

9. Which protocol is used by cable companies?

   A. MPLS

   B. DOCSIS

   C. PSTN

   D. SIP

10. What is the benefit to using a satellite connection?

    A. It offers speeds faster than both DSL and cable.

    B. The upload and download speeds are always equal.

    C. It is often available in remote locations where DSL and cable are not.

    D. It offers better security than both DSL and cable.

REVIEW ANSWERS

1. **C**   SONET supports throughput up to 39.8 Gbps as defined in the OC-768 standard.

2. **B** and **C**   Frame Relay and ATM are packet-switching technologies used on T1 lines.

3. **A**   The last mile describes the analog run from the central office to a user's location.

4. **B** and **D**   POTS and PSTN are interchangeable terms for common telephone networks.

5. **B**   The telephone company's responsibility ends at the demarc. All wires and equipment on the other side are the responsibility of the customer.

6. **D**   The CCITT developed the V standards for modems.

7. **C**   A Primary Rate Interface combines 23 B channels for a total throughput of about 1.5 Mbps.

8. **D**   Because he is within 300 meters of his ISP's DSLAM, VDSL is a viable option, and it supports 100 Mbps in both directions.

9. **B**   Cable companies use Data Over Cable Service Interface Specification (DOCSIS).

10. **C**   Satellite connections are often the only option for users in remote locations.

Network Security

ETA	NEWBIE	SOME EXPERIENCE	EXPERT
	4 hours	2 hours	1 hour

The very nature of networking makes networks vulnerable to many threats. By definition, a network must allow multiple users to access serving systems, but at the same time, you must protect the network from harm.

The news may be full of tales about *hackers* and other malicious people with nothing better to do than lurk around the Internet and trash the peace-loving systems of good folks like us, but in reality, hackers are only one of many serious network threats. The average network faces many more threats from the folks who are authorized to use it than from those who are not authorized.

Local Lingo

Hacker   In some circles, the term "hacker" describes folks who love the challenge of overcoming obstacles and perceived limitations—and that's a positive thing! At least for this chapter, I define a "hacker" as an unauthorized person who intentionally tries to access resources on your network. That's the way the term is generally used today.

In addition, don't think all network threats are people. Let's not forget natural disasters like floods and hurricanes. Even third parties can unintentionally wreak havoc—what will you do if your building suddenly lacks electricity? A *network threat* can be any number of factors or elements that share one essential feature: the potential to damage network data, machines, or users.

To protect your network, you need to implement proper *network access control (NAC),* which means control over information, people, access, machines, and everything in between.

This chapter begins with a discussion of common threats and then continues with securing user accounts. The third part talks about securing a network against unwanted action from the outside. The final part examines securing desired connections from outside the network. Let's jump in.

Objective 9.01   Common Threats

The threats to your network are real and widespread. Here's a list of some of the more common potential threats to your network. The sections that follow give details on these threats and explain how to deal with them.

- System crashes and other hardware failures
- Administrative access control weaknesses

- Malware, such as viruses and worms
- Social engineering
- Man-in-the-middle attacks
- Denial of Service (DoS) attacks
- Physical intrusion
- Attacks on wireless connections

System Crash/Hardware Failure

Like any technology, computers can and will fail—usually when you can least afford for it to happen. Hard drives crash, servers lock up, the power fails—it's all part of the joy of working in the networking business. Because of this, you need to create redundancy in areas prone to failure (like installing backup power in case of electrical failure) and performing those all-important data backups. Beyond that, the idea is to deploy redundant hardware to provide *fault tolerance*. Take advantage of technologies like Redundant Array of Inexpensive Disks (RAID) to spread data across multiple drives. Buy a server case with multiple power supplies, or add a second NIC.

Administrative Access Control

All operating systems and many TCP applications come with some form of access control list (ACL) that defines what users can do with the server's shared resources. An access control might be a file server giving a user read-only permission to a particular folder or an FTP server only allowing certain user IDs to use certain folders. Every operating system—and many Internet applications are packed with administrative tools and functionality. You need these tools to get all kinds of work done, but by the same token, you need to work hard to keep these capabilities out of the reach of those who don't need them.

> ### Exam Tip
>
> The CompTIA Network+ exam does not test you on the details of file system access controls. In other words, don't bother memorizing details like NTFS permissions, but do appreciate that fine-grained controls are available.

Make sure you know the "super" accounts native to Windows (administrator), Linux (root), and Mac OS X (root). You must carefully control these accounts.

Travel Assistance
Administering your super accounts is only part of what's called *user account control*. See "Securing User Accounts" later in this chapter for more details.

Malware

The term *malware* defines any program or code (macro, script, and so on) designed to do something on a system or network that you don't want to have happen. Malware comes in quite a variety of guises, such as viruses, worms, macros, Trojans, rootkits, adware, and spyware. Let's examine all these malware flavors and then finish with how to deal with them.

Virus

A *virus* is a program that has two jobs: to replicate and to activate. *Replication* means it makes copies of itself, often as code stored in boot sectors or as extra code added to the end of executable programs. *Activation* is when a virus does something like erase the boot sector of a drive. A virus only replicates to other drives, such as thumb drives or optical media. It does not replicate across networks. Plus, a virus needs human action to spread and a host file to infect.

Worm

A *worm* functions similarly to a virus, though it replicates exclusively through networks. A worm, unlike a virus, doesn't have to wait for someone to use a removable drive to replicate, nor does it need a host file. If the infected computer is on a network, a worm will immediately start sending copies of itself to any other computers on the network it can locate. Worms can exploit inherent flaws in program code like *buffer overflows,* where a buffer cannot hold all the data sent to it. Finally, a worm doesn't need to be inherently malicious; it could be an innocent file used to attack a computer repeatedly.

Macro Virus

Many applications include tools that enable you to create *macros,* a group of commands that you can run at once. Macros help users automate repetitive tasks, so they're useful. Malicious programmers can take advantage of the macros available, however, to attack a computer. These are called *macro viruses.* You can embed a macro virus—since it's just a macro, after all—in the affiliated program file. When that file is opened, the macro virus runs automatically and does its nefarious work.

Trojan

A *Trojan* is a piece of malware that looks or pretends to do one thing while, at the same time, doing something evil. A Trojan may be a game, like poker, or a free screensaver. The sky is the limit. The more "popular" Trojans turn an infected computer into a server and then open TCP or UDP ports so a remote user can control the infected computer. They can be used to capture keystrokes, passwords, files, credit card information, and more. This type of Trojan is called a *remote administration tool (RAT)*, although you don't need to know that for the CompTIA Network+ exam. Trojans do not replicate.

Local Lingo

Trojan horse   A Trojan is often called a *Trojan horse,* after the giant wooden horse created by the Greeks during the Trojan War. The Greeks sailed away from the city of Troy, but left the horse behind, so the Trojans wheeled the horse into the city. Unbeknownst to the Trojans, Greek soldiers were hidden in the horse. When the Greeks sailed back under the cover of darkness, the hidden soldiers had opened the city gates and thus opened the city to the loving arms of their comrades.

Rootkit

For a virus or Trojan to succeed, it needs to come up with some method to hide itself. As awareness of malware has grown, antimalware programs make it harder to find new locations on a computer to hide. A *rootkit* is usually a Trojan that takes advantage of very low-level operating system functions to hide itself from all but the most aggressive of antimalware tools. Worse, a rootkit, by definition, gains privileged access to the computer. Rootkits can strike operating systems, hypervisors, and even firmware.

Adware/Spyware

There are two types of programs that are similar to malware in that they try to hide themselves to an extent. *Adware* is a program that monitors the types of websites you frequent and uses that information to generate targeted advertisements, usually pop-up windows. Many of these programs use Adobe Flash. Adware isn't, by definition, evil, but many adware makers use sneaky methods to get you to use adware, such as using deceptive-looking webpages ("Your computer is infected with a virus—click here to scan NOW!"). As a result, adware is often considered malware. Some of the computer-infected ads actually install a virus when you click them, so avoid these things like the plague.

Spyware is a function of any program that sends information about your system or your actions over the Internet. The type of information sent depends on the program. A spyware program will include your browsing history. A more aggressive form of spyware may send keystrokes or all of the contacts in your e-mail. Some spyware makers bundle their product with ads to make them look innocuous. Adware, therefore, can contain spyware.

Dealing with Malware

You can deal with malware in several ways: antimalware programs, training and awareness, policies and procedures, patch management, and incident response.

At the very least, every computer should run an antimalware program. If possible, add an appliance that runs antimalware programs against incoming data from your network. Many such appliances exist, but they are most common in proxy servers (see Chapter 10). Also, an antimalware program is only as good as its updates—keep everyone's definition file up to date with, literally, nightly updates. Users must be trained to look for suspicious ads, programs, and pop-ups, and understand that they must not click these things. Your organization should have policies and procedures in place so everyone knows what to do if they encounter malware. Finally, a good network administrator maintains proper incident response records to see if any pattern to attacks emerges. He or she can then adjust policies and procedures to mitigate these attacks.

Exam Tip

One of the most important malware mitigation procedures is to keep systems under your control patched and up to date through proper *patch management*. Microsoft does a very good job of putting out bug fixes and patches as soon as problems occur. If your systems aren't set up to update automatically, then perform manual updates regularly.

Antimalware Programs

You can download many excellent antimalware programs for free, either for extended trial periods or for indefinite use. Download one or more antimalware programs, such as these:

- **Malwarebytes Anti-Malware (www.malwarebytes.org)** Malwarebytes' Anti-Malware program rocks the house in terms of dealing with malicious software. They offer both a free version that scans your computer for malware and quarantines it and a PRO version that actively protects against any incoming malware. Anti-Malware is my first choice in dealing with malware on a client's computer.

- SUPERAntiSpyware (www.superantispyware.com)   Many techs absolutely love SUPERAntiSpyware, another antispyware program that tackles all sorts of unpleasant malware. Like Anti-Malware, SUPERAntiSpyware has both free and professional editions.

Social Engineering

A nice percentage of attacks against your network come under the heading of *social engineering*—the process of using or manipulating people inside the networking environment to gain access to that network from the outside. The term "social engineering" covers the many ways humans can use other humans to gain unauthorized information. This unauthorized information may be a network login, a credit card number, company customer data—almost anything you might imagine that one person or organization may not want a person outside of that organization to access.

Social engineering attacks aren't hacking—at least in the classic sense of the word—although the goals are the same. Social engineering is where people attack an organization through the people in it or physically access the organization to get the information they need.

The most classic form of social engineering is the telephone scam in which someone calls a person and tries to get him or her to reveal his or her user name/password combination. In the same vein, someone may physically enter your building under the guise of having a legitimate reason for being there, such as a cleaning person, repair technician, or messenger. The attacker then snoops around desks, looking for whatever he or she has come to find (one of many good reasons not to put passwords on your desk or monitor). The attacker might talk with people inside the organization, gathering names, office numbers, or department names—little things in and of themselves, but powerful tools when combined later with other social engineering attacks.

These old-school social engineering tactics are taking a backseat to a far more nefarious form of social engineering: phishing.

> **Travel Advisory**
>
> All these attacks are commonly used together, so if you discover one of them being used against your organization, it's a good idea to look for others.

Phishing

In a *phishing* attack, the attacker poses as some sort of trusted site, like an online version of your bank or credit card company, and solicits you to update your financial information, such as a credit card number. You might get an e-mail message, for example, that purports to be from PayPal telling you that your account needs to be updated and provides a link that looks like it goes to http://www.paypal.com. Clicking the link, however, opens a site that resembles the PayPal login but is actually http://100.16.49.21/2s82ds.php, a phishing site.

Man in the Middle

In a *man-in-the-middle* attack, a person inserts him- or herself into a conversation between two others, covertly intercepting traffic thought to be only between those other people. The man in the middle might gather those conversations to gain access to passwords or other sensitive data or to the shared keys in an encrypted conversation. The attacker might then use a rogue access point to get into the network or social engineering techniques to gain access to a wired network.

Denial of Service

Denial of Service (DoS) attacks are the work of hackers whose only interest is in bringing a network to its knees. They accomplish this by flooding the network with so many requests that it becomes overwhelmed and ceases functioning. These attacks are most commonly performed on web and e-mail servers, but virtually any part of a network can be attacked via some DoS method.

The secret to a successful DoS attack is to send as many packets as possible to the victim. Not only do you want to send a lot of packets—you also want the packets to contain some kind of request that the victim must process as long as possible to force the victim to deal with each attacking packet for as long as possible.

You can employ one of several methods to get a good DoS going, but the CompTIA Network+ objectives expressly mention a *smurf* attack. A *smurf* attack is when an attacker floods a network with ICMP Echo Request packets sent to the broadcast address. The trick that makes this attack special is that the return address of the pings is spoofed to that of the intended victim. When all the computers on the network respond to the initial ping, they send their response to the intended victim. The attacker can then amplify the effect of the attack by the number of responding machines on the network. Due to modern network management procedures and controls built into modern operating systems, the danger of the smurf attack has been largely mitigated.

Far more menacing than a simple DoS attack are *distributed denial of service (DDoS)* attacks. A DDoS uses multiple (as in hundreds or up to hundreds of thousands of) computers under the control of a single operator to launch a devastating attack. DDoS operators don't own these computers, but instead use malware to take control of them. A single computer under the control of an operator is called a *zombie*. A group of computers under the control of one operator is called a *botnet*.

Exam Tip

Zombified computers aren't obvious. DDoS operators often wait weeks or months after a computer's been infected to take control of it.

To take control of your network's computers, someone has to install malware on the computer. Again, antimalware, training, and procedures will keep you safe from zombification (but feel free to make some joke about eating human brains).

Physical Intrusion

You can't consider a network secure unless you provide some physical protection to your network. I separate physical protection into two different areas: protection of servers and protection of clients.

Server protection is easy. Lock up your servers to prevent physical access by any unauthorized person. Large organizations have special server rooms, complete with card-key locks and tracking of anyone who enters or exits. Smaller organizations should at least have a locked closet. While you're locking up your servers, don't forget about any network switches! Hackers can access networks by plugging into a switch, so don't leave any switches available to them.

Physical server protection doesn't stop with a locked door. One of the most common mistakes made by techs is walking away from a server while still logged in. Always log off your server when it's not in use.

Locking up all of your client systems is difficult, but your users should be required to perform some physical security. First, all users should lock their computers when they step away from their desks. Instruct them to press the WINDOWS KEY-L combination to perform the lock. Hackers take advantage of unattended systems to get access to networks.

Second, make users aware of the potential for Dumpster diving and make paper shredders available. Dumpster diving means going through a company's trash to find information, such as names, e-mail addresses, and so on. Last, tell users to mind their work areas. It's amazing how many users leave passwords readily available. I can go into any office, open a few desk drawers, and will invariably find little yellow sticky notes with user names and passwords. If users must write down passwords, tell them to put them in locked drawers!

Attacks on Wireless Connections

With more and more wireless networks coming online every day, it shouldn't be much of a surprise that they've drawn the attention of the bad guys. Attacks on wireless connections come in several forms, such as leeching, cracking wireless encryption, rogue access points, and evil twin attacks.

Leeching

Leeching is using another person's wireless network without that person's permission. Leeching takes some of the bandwidth the other person has paid for, so it's simply theft with another name.

In the heady early days of Wi-Fi networks, people would seek out unprotected networks by using sniffer hardware and cruising neighborhoods. This process, called *war driving*, often resulted in marks or symbols stenciled onto a nearby fence, gate, door, wall, or whatever, marking the open Wi-Fi signal. The marking was called *war chalking*. Neither practice is common today, but you might see the terms on the CompTIA Network+ exam.

> ### Travel Advisory
> Many people concatenate the terms, so *wardriving* and *warchalking*. Be prepared to see them with or without the space.

Cracking Wireless Encryption

Most Wi-Fi networks today use some form of encryption to stop casual leeching, but that doesn't necessarily stop the sophisticated thief. Wi-Fi networks use one of three types of encryption: WEP, WPA, and WPA2. All three are crackable, though WPA2 offers more security than WEP or WPA.

> ### Local Lingo
> **Encryption**   *Encryption* is a method of securing messages by scrambling and encoding each packet as it is sent across an unsecured medium, such as the Internet. Each encryption level provides multiple standards and options.

The techniques for *WEP cracking* and *WPA cracking* are simple: run a sniffer program, capture packets in the air with a *packet sniffing* program, and then run a program to sniff out the password or preshared key. WEP networks can be cracked in under a minute; WPA, with a very strong key using letters, numbers, and symbols, will take hours or longer to crack, depending on the computing power of the machine running the hacking software.

Travel Assistance
Chapter 10 discusses the differences among the Wi-Fi encryption standards.

Rogue Access Points

A *rogue access point* is an unauthorized wireless access point (WAP) installed in a computer network. Rogue access points are a huge problem today. Anyone can easily purchase an inexpensive WAP and just plug it into a network. To make the issue even worse, almost all WAPs are designed to work using the preinstalled configuration, giving bad guys easy access to your network from a location physically outside your network.

The biggest reason rogue access points exist is that members of an organization install them for convenience. Users like their own wireless networks and, due to lack of training, don't appreciate the danger unsecured access points pose. Bad guys getting into your physical location and installing rogue access points is less common.

Evil Twin

Hackers can use an *evil twin* attack to fool people into logging into a rogue access point that looks very similar to a legitimate access point. The evil twin access point might have an SSID that matches a legitimate SSID, for example, only it's off by a letter or a character. People who log into the evil twin will have their keystrokes recorded in the hopes of stealing passwords and other valuable information. An evil twin is basically a *wireless phishing* attack.

Objective 9.02 Securing User Accounts

Even the smallest network will have a number of user accounts and groups scattered about with different levels of permissions. Every time you give a user access to a resource, you create potential loopholes that can leave your network vulnerable to unauthorized access, data destruction, and other administrative nightmares. You can categorize all of these potential dangers as *internal threats*. To protect your network from these threats, you need to implement the right controls over passwords, user accounts, groups, and permissions. The whole process begins with authentication.

Authentication

Authentication is the process of identifying yourself to the network or to a system and then having your identification criteria verified. The most popular example of authentication is when you log on to the network first thing in the morning. You are typically presented with a dialog box asking for your user name and password. Once you type your user name and password and click the logon button, the information is verified against a database of user names and passwords that are allowed access to the network.

Authentication Principles

You can categorize ways to authenticate into three broad areas: ownership factors, knowledge factors, and inherent factors. A *knowledge factor* is something the user knows, like a password or personal identification number (PIN). An *ownership factor* is something the user has, like an ID card or security token. An *inherent factor* is something that is part of the user, like a fingerprint or retinal pattern.

Multifactor authentication provides the best authentication, where a user must use two or more factors to prove his or her identity. Note that multifactor means more than one factor, not just more than one *thing*. Logging in with a user name and password is two things, for example, but because both fall into the category of what a user knows, it's not multifactor authentication.

Many organizations use *two-factor authentication*, typically some sort of physical token that, when inserted, prompts for a password. That way, the user authenticates with both what she has and what she knows.

Authentication Protocols

An authentication protocol determines how your user name and password are sent from your workstation to the authentication server, such as Microsoft Active Directory. Each authentication protocol is unique in how it sends the user name and password to the authentication server, with some protocols being more secure than others.

PAP   *Password Authentication Protocol (PAP)* is a simple authentication protocol that sends the user name and password to the authentication server in clear text. PAP is typically used in remote access situations in which the client is dialing in to the network. After a PPP link has been established, a user name/password pair is repeatedly sent (in plain text) until authentication is acknowledged or until the connection is terminated (see Figure 9.1).

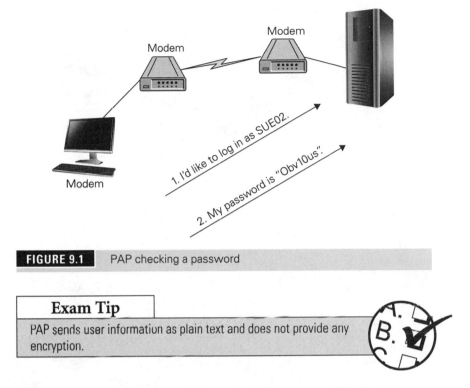

FIGURE 9.1   PAP checking a password

Exam Tip

PAP sends user information as plain text and does not provide any encryption.

CHAP   *The Challenge Handshake Authentication Protocol (CHAP)* is more secure than PAP. After a remote connection is established, the server sends a *challenge message* to the client system (the requestor) for confirmation of the user's password. The requestor generates a response using a one-way hash function—using a hashing protocol such as MD5—and the server compares the response to its expected hash value (see Figure 9.2). If the values match, the connection is acknowledged; otherwise, it is terminated.

In this way, a server can ask you if you know what your password is without your actually having to send it to the server for comparison. The server can generate a new challenge message at any time, which makes CHAP very secure because the authentication can be refreshed at any time. Instead of using MD5, CHAP can also encrypt its messages using the Data Encryption Standard (DES) algorithm—a very popular way of encrypting information using a long binary key—but it's not as secure as MD5.

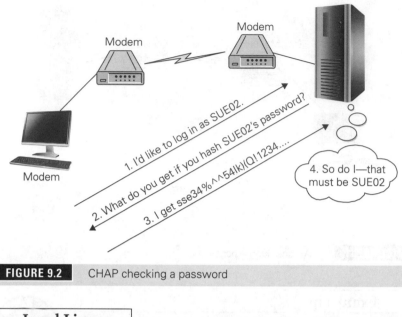

Modem

Modem

Modem

1. I'd like to log in as SUE02.

2. What do you get if you hash SUE02's password?

3. I get sse34%^^54Ik\/Q!1234....

4. So do I—that must be SUE02

FIGURE 9.2   CHAP checking a password

Local Lingo

One-way hash function   A computing function that takes a variable-length string as the input and produces a fixed-length binary value (hash) as the output. The process is irreversible—it is extremely difficult to find a string that produces a given hash value (hence, it's a one-way function). Message Digest 5 (MD5) is a common hash algorithm.

MS-CHAP   *MS-CHAP* is the Microsoft implementation of CHAP and has had a couple versions created over the years—MS-CHAPv1 and MS-CHAPv2. MS-CHAPv2 improved on some of the cryptography weaknesses of MS-CHAPv1 and is the only MS-CHAP version supported by Windows 7.

EAP   A newer authentication protocol called the *Extensible Authentication Protocol (EAP)* is popular in wireless security, but can also be used for remote access solutions. EAP is a framework that incorporates many facets of security such as authentication and encryption services.

802.1X   Another method of implementing authentication on a network is through network access control using the IEEE 802.1X standard. The *IEEE 802.1X* standard is popular in wireless solutions that require the client to authenticate before a connection is made.

The 802.1x standard involves three main systems:

- **Supplicant** The term used for the client that is authenticating to the network or that desires to have network access.
- **Authenticator** The device to which the client is trying to connect. This device has been configured to require authentication before the client is allowed to connect. Popular examples of authenticators are a wireless access point and a network switch.
- **Authentication server** The server to which the authentication request is sent. When the client connects to the authenticator, it then sends an authentication request to the authentication server, which then checks its authentication database to verify that the supplicant is allowed access to the network.

Local Lingo

Posture assessment Some devices use posture assessment as part of the authentication or authorization process. They check to see if the machine that wants to connect meets specific requirements in terms of patches installed or whether an antivirus software is active. Routers configured for the Cisco-proprietary Network Admission Control (NAC) are a good example of devices that use posture assessment.

PKI *Private Key Infrastructure (PKI)* is a cryptography system that can be used for authentication and encryption services. The PKI structure starts by having a certificate authority installed that is responsible for issuing digital certificates used for authentication or encryption services.

AAA *Authentication, Authorization, and Accounting (AAA)* are three core services offered by popular AAA protocols such as RADIUS and TACACS+. The following list outlines the three services provided by AAA:

- **Authentication** Occurs when a user identifies herself to the system and the identity is verified against an authentication database.
- **Authorization** After the user is authenticated, she is then granted access to resources or services on the network.
- **Accounting** The tracking of network and resource usage on the network.

Examples of popular AAA protocols include:

- **RADIUS** *Remote Authentication Dial-In User Service* is a popular service for remote access, which you'll read more about in Chapter 10. Many vendors offer RADIUS server solutions, such as Microsoft Windows Server.

- **TACACS+** *Terminal Access Controller Access-Control System Plus* is an AAA protocol that provides AAA services for access to routers, network access points, and other networking equipment. TACACS+ is Cisco proprietary.

Kerberos *Kerberos* is an authentication protocol for TCP/IP networks with many clients all connected to a single authenticating server—no point-to-point here! Kerberos works nicely in a network, so nicely that Microsoft adopted it as the authentication protocol for all Windows networks using a domain controller.

Exam Tip

Kerberos uses UDP or TCP port 88 by default

The cornerstone of Kerberos is the *Key Distribution Center (KDC)*, which has two processes: the *Authentication Server (AS)* and the *Ticket-Granting Service (TGS)*. In Windows server environments, the KDC is installed on the domain controller (Figure 9.3).

When your client logs onto the domain, it sends a request that includes a hash of the user name and password to the AS. The AS compares the results of that hash to its own hash (as it also stores the user name and password) and, if they match, sends a *Ticket-Granting Ticket (TGT)* and a timestamp (Figure 9.4).

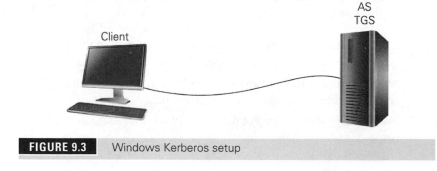

FIGURE 9.3 Windows Kerberos setup

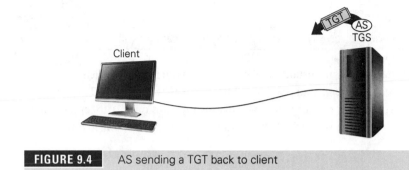

FIGURE 9.4 AS sending a TGT back to client

The ticket has a default lifespan in Windows of ten hours. The client is now authenticated but not yet authorized.

> **Exam Tip**
>
> The TGT is sometimes referred to as *Ticket to Get Ticket*.

The client then sends the timestamped TGT to the TGS for authorization. The TGS sends a timestamped service ticket (also called a *token* or *access token*) back to the client (Figure 9.5).

The token authorizes the user to access specific resources without reauthenticating. Any time the client attempts to access a folder, printer, or service anywhere in the domain, the server sharing that resource uses the token to see exactly what access the client may have to that resource. If you try to access some other feature under Windows, you won't need to log in again because the TGT is still valid. The TGS will authorize access with a new token.

FIGURE 9.5 TGS sending token to client

Exam Tip
In Windows, the security token is called a Security Identifier (SID).

Timestamping is important for Kerberos because it forces the client to request a new token every eight hours or for different or new resources. This prevents third parties from intercepting the tokens and attempting to crack them. Kerberos tokens can be cracked, but it's doubtful this can be done in under eight hours.

Authorization

Once a user has been authenticated to the system, he or she is then authorized, or not authorized, to access different network resources. Following are some examples of authorization in Windows networks:

- **Permissions**   Depending on your user account, you may be given permission to access files, folders, and printers.
- **Rights**   A right is your privilege to perform an operating system task. Examples of rights are changing the system time or backing up files.

Logon and Access Security

Basic security issues that are common to all networks include the level of security, the proper use of passwords, and the centralization of control. Most decent computer systems won't let you get very far unless you have been authenticated and authorized to access the resource. Windows networks use two types of access control: share-level access control and user-level access control.

Implementing Share-Level Security

Older Windows operating systems use *share-level access control,* where a network administrator assigns each shared resource a password. These *resources* are generally either shared folders where data or programs are stored or shared printers. All users attempting to access the resource must supply the same password. Network administrators usually consider share-level control to be weak and difficult to manage.

With share-level security options, you can choose to have a password (or not), and it can be for read-only or full access to the resource—and that's it!

Implementing User-Level Security

With *user-level access control,* a network administrator creates an account for each user, usually on a central server that can itself manage the access to resources on other systems. Most administrators prefer to have a single place to go when adding, changing, or deleting a user account. A *user account* defines the rights and privileges of a specific person when that person accesses a computer system or network. When a user sits down at the computer, he supplies an account name and password, which the computer checks against its security database. If the password specified matches the one listed for that user account in the database, the computer assumes from that point forward that the user is valid and grants him all the rights and permissions that have been assigned to that user account. The user doesn't need to remember a share-level password for each resource he wants to access.

To avoid the excessive workload of assigning specific permissions to each user individually, network administrators organize users with similar needs into *groups* (see Figure 9.6). It *would* be possible to manage each user individually,

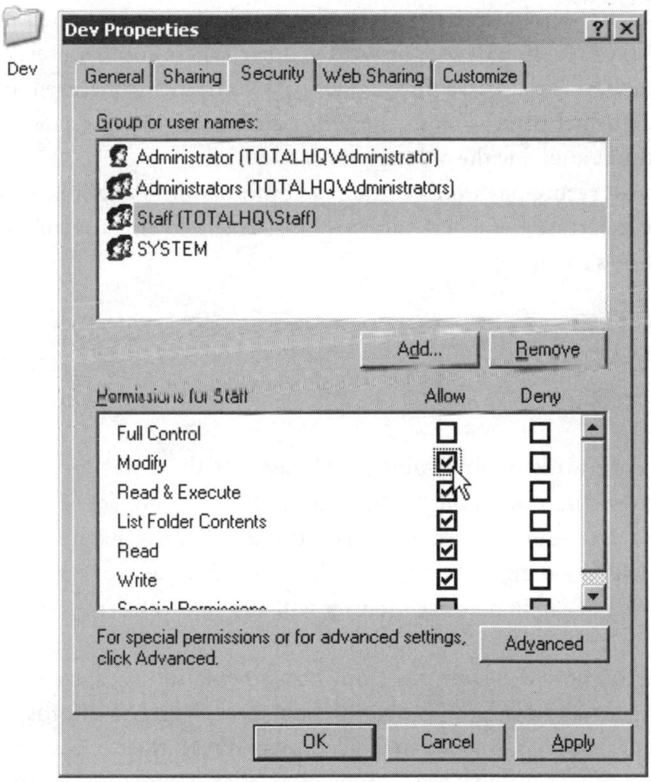

FIGURE 9.6   Assigning permissions to the sales group

but suppose 30 users need access to both the DEV shared resource and the STAFFPRINT printer—which would be easier?

- To create a group called STAFF, add the 30 users to the group and give STAFF access permission to the two resources (by virtue of their membership in that group, the 30 users can now access both resources).
- Or, give 30 user accounts permission to access DEV and then repeat the same exercise for STAFFPRINT.

Clearly the former would be a bit less work initially. Over time, groups make things a lot easier. If you put a new resource online, say a shared media server called BREAKTIME, you could give access to all 30 users by making only one change—adding permission to the STAFF group to access BREAKTIME.

Using Passwords

Of course, user-level security works well only when users keep their passwords secure. Passwords should never be written down where another user might find them, and users should never reveal their passwords to anyone, even the administrator of the network. In most cases, the administrator can reset a user's password without knowing the old password.

The most secure passwords contain a combination of eight or more letters (some in uppercase), numbers, and symbols. The following list contains examples of strong passwords:

- Jar56o$imum
- RhjP!!op11
- 100bobot&w

A good network administrator should assume that, over time, some users' passwords will become public knowledge. To limit the impact of these exposed passwords, a careful network administrator sets passwords to expire periodically, usually once every 30 days or less. Should a password become public knowledge, the gap in network security will automatically close when the user changes the password.

No matter how well your password implementation goes, using passwords always creates administrative problems. First, users forget passwords and someone (usually you) has to access their account and reset their passwords. Second, users will write down passwords, giving hackers an easy way into the network if those bits of paper fall into the wrong hands. If you've got the cash, you have two alternatives to passwords: smart devices and biometrics.

Smart devices are cards with magnetic stripes, USB keys, or other small devices that you insert into your PC in lieu of entering a password. They work extremely well and are incredibly difficult to bypass. The downside is that they might be lost or stolen.

Exam Tip

Many companies use smart devices for *single sign-on,* a method of authentication that, in one shot, both authenticates the user and gives the user access (authorization) to all the resources he or she has permission to access. That way the user only has to do the sign-on stuff once.

If you want to go seriously space age, then biometrics are the way to go (Figure 9.7). *Biometric devices* scan fingerprints, retinas, or even the sound of the user's voice to provide a foolproof replacement for both passwords and smart devices. Biometrics have been around for quite a while, but were relegated to extremely high-security networks due to their high cost (thousands of dollars per device). That price has dropped substantially, making biometrics worthy of consideration for some networks.

FIGURE 9.7 A biometric fingerprint reader

Objective 9.03 **Firewalls**

Firewalls protect networks from *external threats*—potential attacks from out-side your network—by filtering packets using a number of methods, such as hiding IP addresses using NAT, selectively blocking TCP/UDP ports, or even fil-tering traffic based on MAC addresses. From there, things get much more com-plex, so for now, let's define a firewall as a device that filters IP traffic to protect networks and computers. But a firewall doesn't have to be a dedicated device.

You run into firewalls in two very different places. The first place is a device at the edge of your network. Given that there's already a router at the edge of your network, you'd be hard pressed to find a router today that does not also act as a firewall. Because the firewall is in a box on the network, these are called *network-based* firewalls (also called *hardware firewalls,* although many use software too). The second place is software installed on your computer that does the same job but only firewalls packets coming in and out of your system. These are called *host-based* firewalls (also called *software firewalls*). In a perfect world, your net-work has a network-based firewall at the edge of your network and all of your systems run a host-based firewall.

Hiding the IPs

The first and most common technique for protecting a network is to hide the real IP addresses of the internal network systems from the Internet. If a hacker gets a real IP address, he or she can begin to probe that system, looking for vulnerabilities. If you can prevent a hacker from getting an IP address to probe, you've stopped most hacking techniques cold. You already know how to hide IP addresses using *Network Address Translation (NAT).* That's why most routers have built-in NAT ca-pability. Not only does NAT reduce the need for true public IP addresses, but it also does a great job protecting networks from hackers because it is difficult to access a network using private IP addresses hidden behind a NAT-enabled router.

> **Travel Advisory**
>
> Because NAT was not designed as a security feature, it leaves a few glaring holes for bad guys to exploit. NAT does not stop inbound traffic that users inside the network request, for example, so malicious code could make its way into the network. NAT offers no packet inspection either. It just tracks port numbers. In a real-world network, you cannot rely on NAT for security. You *must* use some kind of firewall that offers port filtering, packet filtering, or some other kind of security. These are discussed in the sections that follow.

Port Filtering

The second most common firewall tool is assuring port security through *port filtering,* also called *port blocking.* Hackers often try less commonly used port numbers to get into a network. Port filtering simply means preventing the passage of any TCP or UDP segments or datagrams through any ports other than the ones prescribed by the system administrator. Port filtering is effective, but it requires some serious configuration to work properly. The question is always, "Which ports do I allow into the network?"

When you open your browser and access a webpage, your web browser sends out TCP segments to the web server with the destination port of 80. Web servers require this, and it's how TCP/IP works. No one has problems with the well-known ports like 80 (HTTP), 21 (FTP), 25 (SMTP), and 110 (POP3), but there are a large number of lesser-known ports that networks often want opened.

Exam Tip

One early exploit of open ports came in the form of an *FTP bounce attack,* where a malicious user could run the port command on an FTP server to discover any open ports. Modern FTP servers block this kind of attack, but you get the idea. Open ports can be dangerous.

I recently installed port filtering on my personal firewall and everything worked great –until I decided to play the popular game *World of Warcraft* on the Internet. (Note to WoW nerds: On the Blackwater Raiders server, I'm "Pelape.") I simply could not connect to the Internet servers until I discovered that *World of Warcraft* requires TCP port 3724 open to work over the Internet. After reconfiguring my port filter (I reopened port 3724), I was able to play WoW, but when I tried to help one of my friends using Microsoft Remote Desktop, I couldn't access his system! Want to guess where the problem was? Yup, I needed to open port 3389. How did I figure these out? I didn't know which ports to open, but I suspected that my problem was in the port arena so I fired up my web browser (thank goodness that worked!) and went to the World of Warcraft and Microsoft websites, which told me which ports I needed to open. This constant opening and closing of ports is one of the prices you pay for the protection of port filtering, but it sure stops hackers if they can't use certain ports to gain access.

Most routers that provide port blocking manifest it in one of two ways. The first way is to have port filtering close *all* ports until you open them explicitly. The other port filtering method is to leave all ports open unless you explicitly close them. The gotcha here is that most types of IP sessions require *dynamic port* usage. For example, when my system makes a query for a webpage on HTTP port 80, the web server and my system establish a session using a *different* port to send the webpages to my system. Figure 9.8 shows the results of running the netstat -n switch while I have a number of webpages open—note the TCP ports used for the incoming webpages (the Local Address column). Dynamic ports can cause some problems for older (much older) port filtering systems, but almost all of today's port filtering systems are aware of this issue and handle it automatically.

Packet Filtering

Port filtering deals only with port numbers; it completely disregards IP addresses. If an IP packet comes in with a filtered port number, the packet is blocked, regardless of the IP address. *Packet filtering* or *IP filtering* works in the same way, except it blocks packets based on IP addresses. *Packet filters,* also known as *IP filters,* will block any incoming or outgoing packet from a particular IP address or range of IP addresses. These addresses are stored in an access control list (ACL) of some kind.

Packet filters are far better at blocking outgoing IP addresses because the network administrator knows and can specify the IP addresses of the internal systems. Blocking outgoing packets is a good way to prevent users on certain systems from accessing the Internet. Figure 9.9 shows a configuration page from a router designed to block different ranges of IP addresses and port numbers.

```
Administrator: C:\Windows\system32\cmd.exe

C:\>netstat -n

Active Connections

  Proto  Local Address          Foreign Address         State
  TCP    192.168.4.81:5357      192.168.4.60:62390      ESTABLISHED
  TCP    192.168.4.81:49184     207.46.107.21:1863      ESTABLISHED
  TCP    192.168.4.81:49185     205.188.7.198:5190      ESTABLISHED
  TCP    192.168.4.81:49187     205.188.248.161:5190    ESTABLISHED
  TCP    192.168.4.81:49189     64.12.104.181:5190      ESTABLISHED
  TCP    192.168.4.81:51866     192.168.4.9:445         ESTABLISHED
  TCP    192.168.4.81:54496     205.188.13.16:5190      ESTABLISHED
  TCP    192.168.4.81:57156     205.188.234.1:80        ESTABLISHED
  TCP    192.168.4.81:58024     216.239.51.125:5222     ESTABLISHED
  TCP    192.168.4.81:65440     192.168.4.10:445        ESTABLISHED
  TCP    192.168.4.81:65518     66.163.181.180:5050     ESTABLISHED

C:\>
```

FIGURE 9.8   The netstat –n command showing HTTP connections

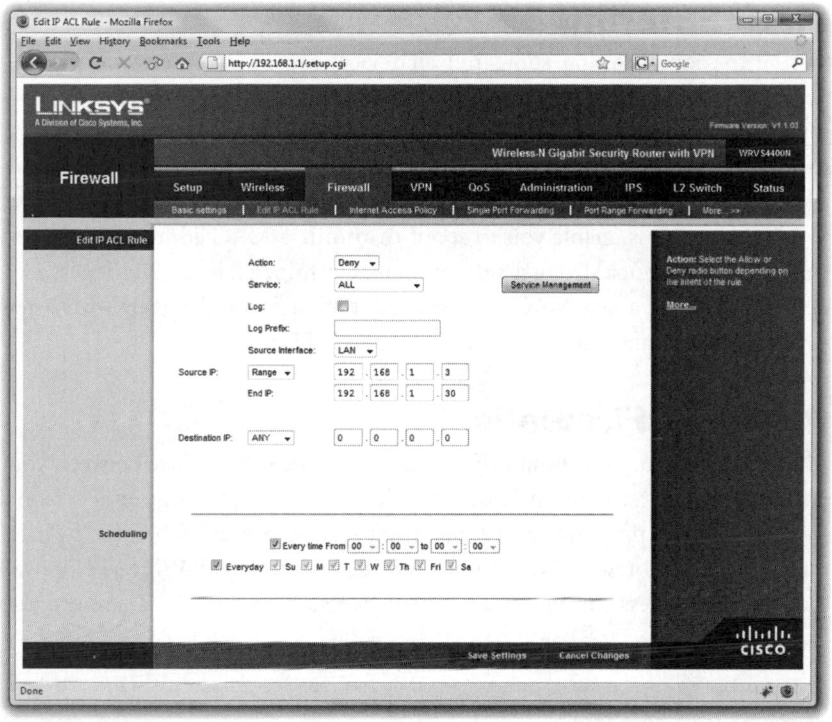

FIGURE 9.9 Blocking IP addresses

This type of filtering is called *stateless filtering* because the device that does the filtering just checks the packet for IP addresses and port numbers and blocks or allows accordingly. Each packet is judged as an individual entity to determine whether it should be allowed into the network. Stateless filtering works at layer 3 of the OSI seven-layer model. Stateless filtering is inexpensive and easy to implement, but has one issue: once you've opened a particular path into your network, that path is open. Someone spoofing IP information could get in.

A more secure method of filtering is to use devices that do *stateful filtering,* or *stateful inspection,* where all packets are examined as a stream. Stateful devices can do more than allow or block; they can track when a stream is disrupted or packets get corrupted and act accordingly. The best of the stateful filtering devices are application proxies, working at layer 7 of the OSI seven-layer model. The only real problems with application proxies are that they tend to be slower than stateless filters and more expensive.

MAC Filtering

Similar to packet filtering, some firewall devices can allow or deny access to the network based on the MAC address of the client; what's called *MAC filtering*. Because every network device has a unique 48-bit MAC address, MAC filtering should make for a very secure network. It's often one of the implemented security measures in wireless networks, for example, because setting it up is quick.

Many programs enable you to spoof or mimic a MAC address, though, so MAC filtering is not a strong deterrent for a determined hacker. Plus it gets a little tedious to add a new MAC address every time a friend drops by with a new smart phone or tablet and wants to use your Wi-Fi.

Personal Firewalls

Although you can (and should) buy a hardware firewall to place between your system and the Internet, a single user should, at the very least, employ a personal software firewall program. Every operating system comes with some form of built-in personal firewall. Every copy of Windows comes with Windows Firewall that you can access through the Control Panel (Figure 9.10). There are also

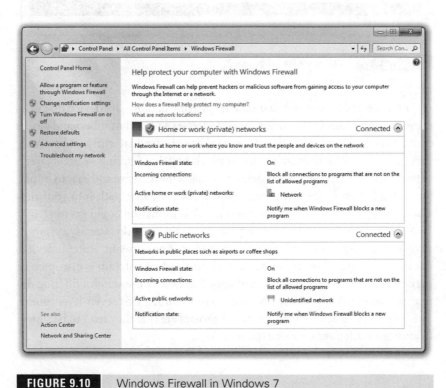

FIGURE 9.10   Windows Firewall in Windows 7

third-party software firewalls like ZoneAlarm Pro (Figure 9.11). These personal firewall programs are quite powerful and have the added benefit of being easy to use. These days, an individual Internet user has no excuse not to use a personal firewall.

By default, Windows Firewall *blocks* all incoming IP packets that attempt to initiate a session. This is great for networks that only use the Internet to browse the Web or grab e-mail, but will cause problems in circumstances where you want to provide any type of Internet server on your network. You can, however, manually open ports through the firewall (Figure 9.12).

Exam Tip

The settings on firewalls are called *rules.* Many firewalls use the term *implicit deny any* to describe a rule like Windows Firewall's block setting for inbound traffic.

Windows Firewall is set to *allow* all outgoing traffic by default, though you can change this behavior.

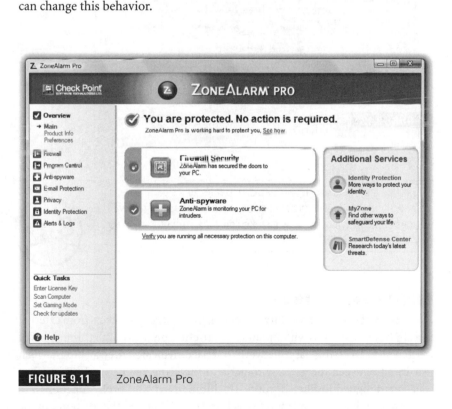

FIGURE 9.11   ZoneAlarm Pro

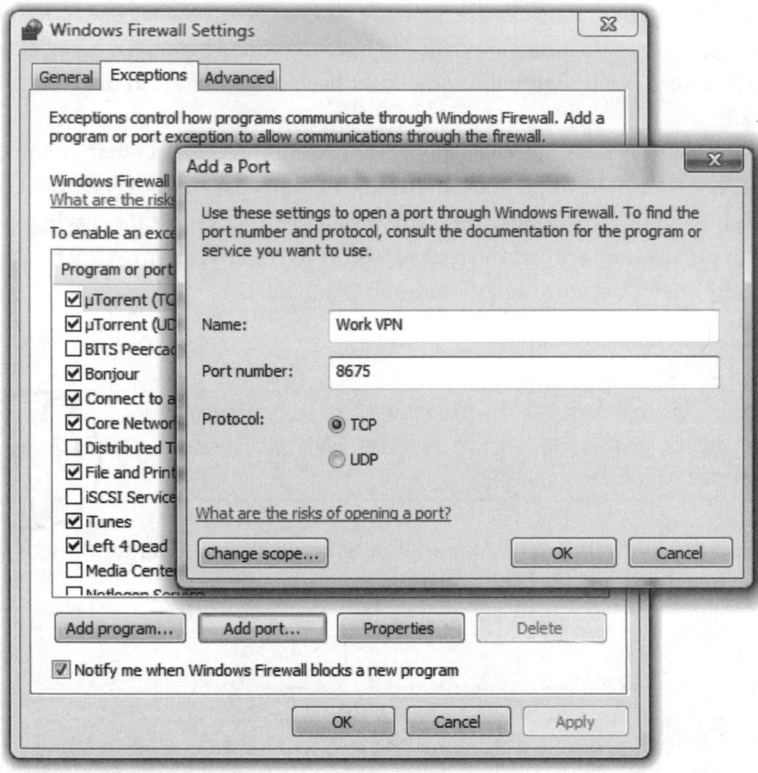

FIGURE 9.12   Opening TCP/IP ports in Windows Firewall

Exam Tip

Look for the CompTIA Network+ exam to refer to network setups where the firewall resides in a dedicated box as a *network-based firewall*. The exam calls firewall programs installed on your computer, such as Windows Firewall, *host-based firewalls*.

Network Zones

Large networks need heavy-duty protection that not only protects from external threats, but also does so without undue restriction on the overall throughput of the network. To do this, large networks often use dedicated firewall boxes, which usually sit between the gateway router and the protected network. These firewalls are designed to filter IP traffic (including NAT and proxy functions), as well as to provide high-end tools to track and stop incoming threats. Some of the firewall systems even contain a rather interesting feature called a honeypot. A *honeypot* is a device (or a set of functions within a firewall) that creates a fake network called a *honeynet,* which seems attackable to a hacker. Instead of trying to access the real network, hackers are attracted to the honeypot, which records their actions and keeps them away from the true network. Plus, you can study the hackers' methods to help shore up your vulnerabilities.

Once you start to add publicly accessible servers to your network, like web and e-mail servers, you're going to have to step up to a more serious network protection configuration. Because web and e-mail servers must have exposure to the Internet, you will need to create what's called a *demilitarized zone (DMZ),* a lightly protected network positioned between your firewall and the Internet. You can configure a DMZ in a number of ways. Figure 9.13 shows one classic example using an external and an internal router.

Local Lingo
Intranet   A private, protected network is called an *intranet.*

Vulnerability Scanners

A number of fine utility programs can scan a network to determine things like open ports, passive applications, and more. *Nmap,* for example, has been around since 1997, is updated regularly, and has been made available as

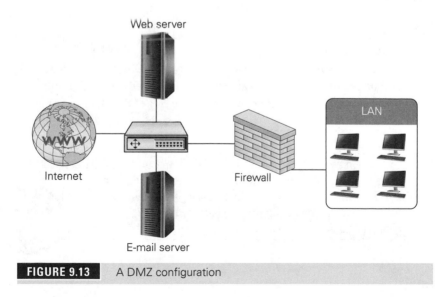

| FIGURE 9.13 | A DMZ configuration |

open-source software. It was designed initially to do what its name would suggest—map a network so a system administrator doesn't have to walk from room to room, creating a physical map of all the computers. In numerous updates, features have been added, and Nmap is now used heavily as a *vulnerability scanner.* You can find Nmap at http://nmap.org/.

Another excellent tool is *Nessus,* also free for noncommercial use. Tenable Network Security maintains and updates the Nessus products. You can download Nessus from www.nessus.org.

Objective 9.04 Securing Remote Connections

The mad proliferation of high-speed Internet connections to most households in the United States has enabled a lot of workers to work partly from home. Although this provides one cost-effective solution to the rising price of gasoline and of physical commuting, from a network security standpoint, it opens up a potential can of worms. Network techs and administrators must strike a fine balance between making resources readily available over the Internet and making certain that only authorized users get access to those resources.

IPsec

Every authentication and encryption protocol and standard you've learned about so far works *above* the Network layer of the OSI seven-layer model. *Internet Protocol Security (IPsec)* is an authentication and encryption protocol suite that works at the Internet/Network layer (layer 3 of the OSI model).

Local Lingo
IPsec   The *Internet Engineering Task Force (IETF)* specifies the IPsec protocol suite, managing updates and revisions. One of those specifications regards the acronym for the protocol suite, calling it *IPsec* with a lowercase "s" rather than IPS or IPSec, which you might imagine to be the initials or acronym. Go figure.

IPsec works in two different modes: Transport mode and Tunnel mode. In Transport mode, only the actual payload of the IP packet is encrypted: the destination and source IP addresses and other IP header information are still readable. In Tunnel mode, the entire IP packet is encrypted and then placed into an IPsec endpoint where it is encapsulated inside another IP packet. The mode you use depends on the application (Figure 9.14).

The IPsec protocol suite uses many open-source protocols to provide both tight authentication and robust encryption. You do not need to know how each of the protocols works for the CompTIA Network+ exam, but you should recognize which protocols function within IPsec. Here are the main protocols:

- *Authentication Header (AH)* for authentication
- *Encapsulating Security Payload (ESP)* for implementing authentication and encryption
- *Internet Security Association and Key Management Protocol (ISAKMP)* for establishing security associations (SAs) that define things like the protocol used for exchanging keys
- *Internet Key Exchange (IKE* and *IKEv2)* and *Kerberized Internet Negotiation of Keys (KINK),* two widely used key exchanging protocols

In addition, IPsec can encrypt data using any number of encryption algorithms, such as MD5, which you read about earlier in this chapter.

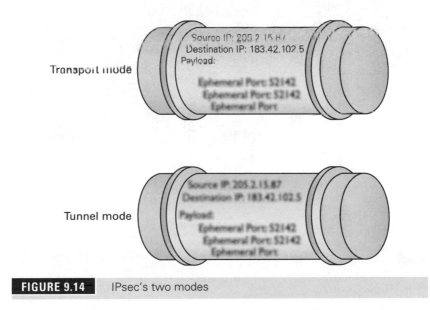

FIGURE 9.14   IPsec's two modes

Virtual Private Networks

Several standards use encrypted tunnels between a computer or a remote network and a private network through the Internet (Figure 9.15), resulting in what is called a *virtual private network (VPN)*.

An encrypted tunnel requires *endpoints*—the ends of the tunnel where the data is encrypted and decrypted. In the tunnels you've seen thus far, the client for the application sits on one end and the server sits on the other. VPNs do exactly the same thing. Either some software running on a computer or, in some cases, a dedicated box must act as an endpoint for a VPN (Figure 9.16).

Exam Tip

CompTIA calls devices that handle encrypted tunnels *encryption devices*.

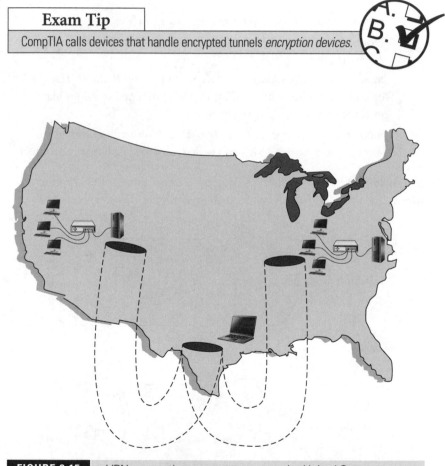

FIGURE 9.15   VPN connecting computers across the United States

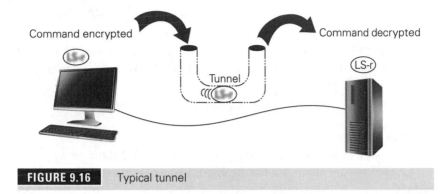

FIGURE 9.16   Typical tunnel

The key with the VPN is that all of the computers should be on the same network—and that means they must all have the same network ID. For example, you would want the laptop that you are using in an airport lounge to have the same network ID as all of the computers in your LAN back at the office. But there's no simple way to do this. If it's a single client trying to access a network, that client is going to take on the IP address from its local DHCP server. In the case of your laptop in the airport, your network ID and IP address come from the DHCP server in the airport, not the DHCP server back at the office.

To make the VPN work, you need a VPN client program protocol that uses one of the many tunneling protocols available. This remote client connects to the local LAN via its Internet connection, querying for an IP address from the local DHCP server. In this way, the VPN client will be on the same network ID as the local LAN. The remote computer now has two IP addresses. First, it has its Internet connection's IP address, obtained from the remote computer's ISP. Second, the VPN client creates a tunnel endpoint that acts like a NIC (Figure 9.17). This virtual NIC has an IP address that connects it to the local LAN.

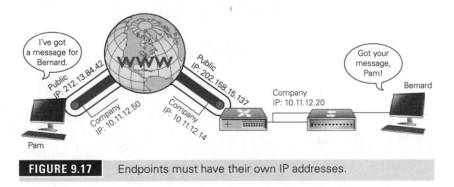

FIGURE 9.17   Endpoints must have their own IP addresses.

Clever network engineers have come up with many ways to make this work, and those implementations function at different layers of the TCP/IP model. PPTP and L2TP, for example, work at the Link layer. Many VPNs use IPsec at the Internet layer to handle encryption needs. SSL VPNs work at the Application layer.

SSL and TLS are Application-layer protocols, not Transport layer.

PPTP VPNs

So how do you make IP addresses appear out of thin air? What tunneling protocol have you learned about that has the smarts to query for an IP address? That's right! Good old PPP! Microsoft got the ball rolling with the *Point-to-Point Tunneling Protocol (PPTP)*, an advanced version of PPP that handles this right out of the box. The only trick is the endpoints. In Microsoft's view, a VPN is intended for individual clients to connect to a private network, so Microsoft places the PPTP endpoints on the client and the server. The server endpoint is a special remote access server program, originally only available on Windows Server, called *Routing and Remote Access Service (RRAS)* on the server—see Figure 9.18.

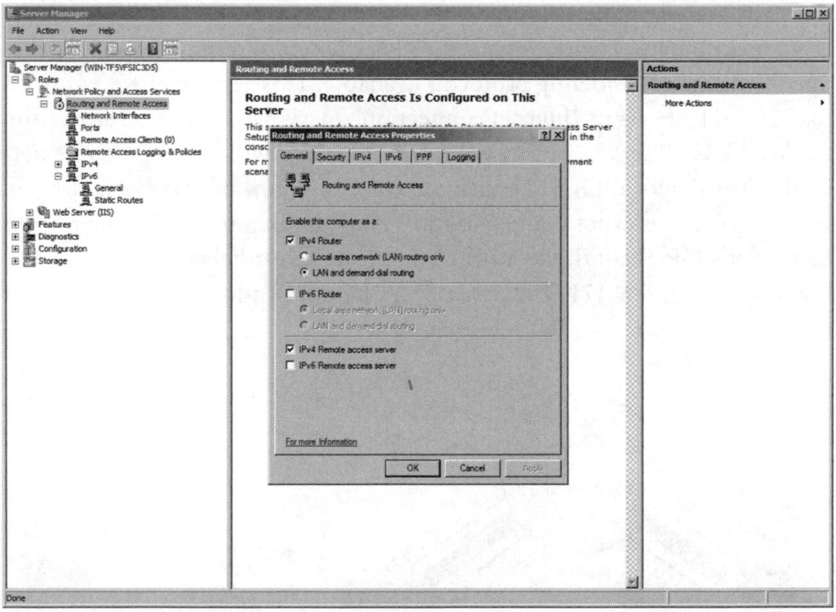

FIGURE 9.18   RRAS in action

On the Windows client side, you run Create a New Connection. This creates a virtual NIC that, like any other NIC, does a DHCP query and gets an IP address from the DHCP server on the private network (Figure 9.19).

Exam Tip

A system connected to a VPN looks as though it's on the local network, but performs much slower than if the system was connected directly back at the office because it's not local at all.

When your computer connects to the RRAS server on the private network, PPTP creates a secure tunnel through the Internet back to the private LAN. Your client takes on an IP address of that network as if your computer is directly connected to the LAN back at the office, even down to the default gateway. If you open your web browser, your client will go across the Internet to the local LAN and then use the LAN's default gateway to get to the Internet! Using a web browser will be much slower when you are on a VPN. Every operating system comes with some type of built-in VPN client that supports PPTP (among others). Figure 9.20 shows Network, the Mac OS X VPN connection tool.

This type of VPN connection, where a single computer logs into a remote network and becomes, for all intents and purposes, a member of that network, is commonly called a *client-to-site* connection.

FIGURE 9.19 VPN connection in Windows

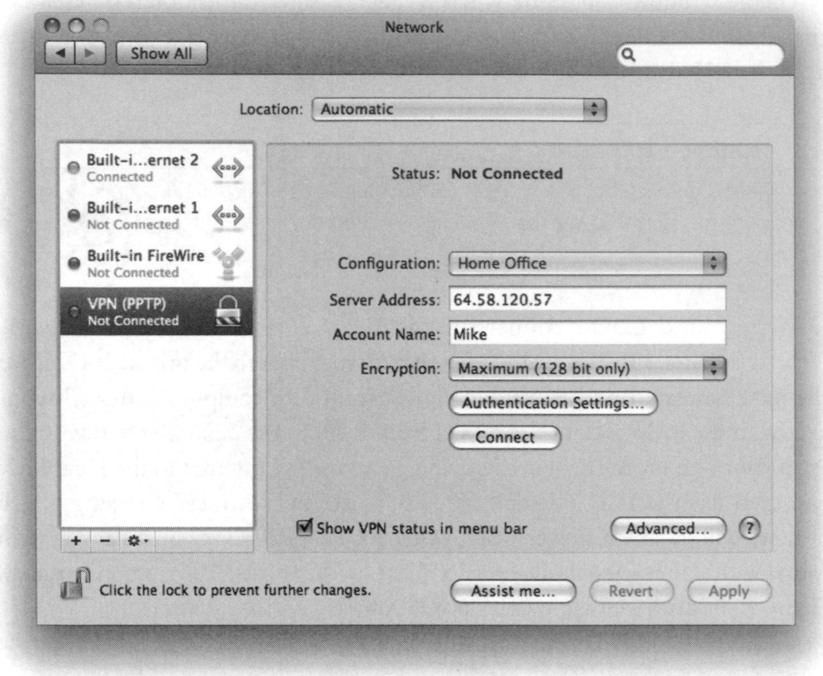

FIGURE 9.20 VPN on a Macintosh OS X system

L2TP VPNs

Microsoft pushed the idea of a single client tunneling into a private LAN using software. Cisco, being the router king that it is, came up with its own VPN protocol called *Layer 2 Tunneling Protocol (L2TP)*. L2TP took all the good features of PPTP and L2F and added support to run on almost any type of connection possible, from telephones to Ethernet to ultra-high-speed optical connections. Cisco also moved the endpoint on the local LAN from a server program to a VPN-capable router, called a *VPN concentrator*, such as the Cisco 2811 Integrated Services Router shown in Figure 9.21.

FIGURE 9.21 Cisco 2811 Integrated Services Router

> **Exam Tip**
>
> Cisco made hardware that supported PPP traffic using a proprietary protocol called *Layer 2 Forwarding (L2F)*. L2F did not come with encryption capabilities, so it was replaced by L2TP a long time ago. You'll sometimes see the term on the CompTIA Network+ exam as an incorrect answer.

Cisco provides free client software to connect a single faraway PC to a Cisco VPN. This creates a typical client-to-site connection. Network people often directly connect two Cisco VPN concentrators to connect two separate LANs permanently. It's slow, but inexpensive, compared to a dedicated high-speed connection between two faraway LANs. This kind of connection enables two separate LANs to function as a single network, sharing files and services as if in the same building. This is called a *site-to-site* VPN connection.

L2TP differs from PPTP in that it has no authentication or encryption. L2TP generally uses IPsec for all security needs. Technically, you should call an L2TP VPN an "L2TP/IPsec" VPN. L2TP works perfectly well in the single-client-connecting-to-a-LAN world, too. Every operating system's VPN client fully supports L2TP/IPsec VPNs.

> **Travel Advisory**
>
> The years have seen plenty of crossover between Microsoft and Cisco. Microsoft RRAS supports L2TP, and Cisco routers support PPTP.

SSL VPNs

Cisco has made a big push for companies to adopt VPN hardware that enables VPNs using Secure Sockets Layer (SSL). These types of VPNs work at the Application layer and offer an advantage over Link- or Internet-based VPNs because they don't require any special client software. Clients connect to the VPN server using a standard web browser, with the traffic secured using SSL. The two most common types of *SSL VPNs* are SSL portal VPNs and SSL tunnel VPNs.

> **Travel Advisory**
>
> Many VPN connections use the terms *client* and *server* to denote the functions of the devices that make the connection. You'll also see the terms *host* and *gateway* to refer to the connections, such as a *host-to-gateway tunnel*.

With SSL portal VPNs, a client accesses the VPN and is presented with a secure webpage. The client gains access to anything linked on that page, be it e-mail, data, links to other pages, and so on.

With tunnel VPNs, in contrast, the client web browser runs some kind of active control, such as Java or Flash, and gains much greater access to the VPN-connected network. SSL tunnel VPNs create a more typical client-to-site connection than SSL portal VPNs, but the user must have sufficient permissions to run the active browser controls.

Travel Advisory

There are other VPN options besides PPTP, L2TP, and SSL, and some of them are quite popular. First is OpenVPN, which, like the rest of what I call "OpenXXX" applications, uses Secure Shell (SSH) for the VPN tunnel. Second is IPsec. The tech world is now seeing some pure (no L2TP) IPsec solutions that use IPsec tunneling for VPNs, such as Cisco Easy VPN.

CHECKPOINT

✔**Objective 9.01: Common Threats**   Attackers use many different means to hack into systems and compromise networks. Be familiar with social engineering attacks as well as the different types of network attacks! Remember that spoofing is the altering of the source address, a buffer overflow is sending too much data to a program, and a Denial of Service prevents the system from performing its job.

✔**Objective 9.02: Securing User Accounts**   Authentication occurs when users identify themselves to the network and that identity is verified against a database and either allowed or denied access to the network. Once the users are authenticated, they are then authorized to access network resources or not allowed access to those resources. Even the smallest network will have a number of user accounts and groups scattered about with different levels of permissions. Every time you give a user access to a resource, you create potential loopholes that can leave your network vulnerable to unauthorized access, data destruction, and other administrative nightmares. To protect your network from these threats, you need to implement the right controls over passwords, user accounts, groups, and permissions.

✔**Objective 9.03: Firewalls**   Firewalls   protect   networks   from   *external threats*—potential attacks from outside your network—by filtering packets using a number of methods, such as hiding IP addresses using NAT, selectively blocking TCP/UDP ports, or even filtering traffic based on MAC addresses. A firewall doesn't have to be a dedicated device; it can be a program as well.

✔**Objective 9.04: Securing Remote Connections**   Several standards use encrypted tunnels to create a virtual private network that enables users outside the network to connect securely inside the network. To make a VPN work, you need a VPN client and a VPN server. Some of the methods used are PPTP, L2TP, and SSL VPNs.

REVIEW QUESTIONS

1. What aspect of protecting your network involves theft of equipment?

   A. Packet filtering

   B. Physical security

   C. Policies

   D. Port filtering

2. What is another name for port filtering?

   A. Port blocking

   B. Port filing

   C. Port folders

   D. Port segments

3. Where would a DMZ more commonly be found?

   A. On a single PC

   B. On a server

   C. On a SOHO

   D. On a larger network

4. Just after opening a Microsoft Excel spreadsheet, Rowan notices that some of his filenames have changed and that his network connection no longer works. What type of malware has most likely infected his computer?

   A. Worm

   B. Macro

   C. Trojan

   D. Rootkit

5. What problem does a rogue access point introduce?

A. Unauthorized physical access to a server

B. Unauthorized access to a wired network

C. Unauthorized access to a wireless network

D. Unauthorized physical access to a router or gateway

6. Which statements about passwords are true? (Select two.)

A. You should change your password regularly.

B. You should use familiar terms, like your pet's name or your birthday, as your password because it will be easy for you to remember.

C. Writing your password on a piece of paper in case you forget it is okay as long as you keep the paper in a locked drawer.

D. You may not use spaces in a password.

7. Which statement is true?

A. A DoS uses a zombie, whereas a DDoS uses a botnet to attack a single system.

B. A DoS uses a botnet, whereas a DDoS uses a zombie to attack a single system.

C. A DoS attacks a single system, whereas a DDoS attacks multiple systems.

D. A DoS attacks systems on the Internet, whereas a DDoS attacks systems in a DMZ.

8. What is a honeypot?

A. It acts as a fake network, luring potential hackers away from the actual network.

B. It is a security measure that slows unauthorized network access to a crawl (as if running in honey), making your network undesirable to hackers.

C. It is what hackers call an easily hacked network.

D. It is a specialized padlock manufactured for the sole purpose of securing computer systems.

9. You receive an e-mail from your credit card company informing you that your card number has been stolen. You click a link in the e-mail and are taken to what looks like your credit card company's website, where you are asked to enter your credit card number to determine if it is among those that were recently stolen. What should you do?

A. Enter your credit card number immediately to determine if it is among those stolen because this is the only way to protect against unauthorized charges to your account.

B. Call the toll-free number listed on the website to verify it is legitimate before entering your card number.

C. Call the toll-free number listed on the website and read your card number over the phone to the customer service representative.

D. Close your browser without entering your card number because it is likely a phishing scam, and then call the toll-free number listed on the back of your actual credit card to verify that is the case.

10. Which authentication protocol is time sensitive and is the default authentication protocol on Windows domains?

A. PPP

B. MS-CHAP

C. IPsec

D. Kerberos

REVIEW ANSWERS

1. **B**   The theft of equipment can be prevented with adequate physical security.

2. **A**   Another name for port filtering is port blocking.

3. **D**   A demilitarized zone (DMZ) would normally be found protecting a larger network with web and e-mail servers.

4. **B**   Because the problems occurred after opening a file in its associated program, a malicious macro is likely embedded in the spreadsheet.

5. **C**   A rogue access point provides unauthorized access to a wireless network.

6. **A** and **C**   Change your password regularly. If you must write it down to help you remember it, keep it locked in a drawer.

7. **A**   A DoS attack uses a single infected computer (zombie), whereas a DDoS attack uses multiple infected computers (botnet) to attack a single system.

8. **A** A honeypot acts as a fake network, diverting would-be hackers away from your real network.

9. **D** This is likely a phishing scam. Call the number listed on the back of your physical card to verify.

10. **D** Kerberos is the time-sensitive authentication protocol used on Windows domains.

The Complete
Network

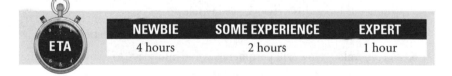
	NEWBIE	SOME EXPERIENCE	EXPERT
ETA	4 hours	2 hours	1 hour

This chapter begins by discussing the features of the mainstream network operating systems and clients, and then discusses the administrative side of networking, including one essential job that everyone hates—paperwork! Don't ignore this stuff—it's important information for the CompTIA Network+ exam and may help you back at the office, too!

Objective 10.01 Designing and Implementing a SOHO Network

The CompTIA Network+ exam doesn't define a list titled "The *x* Steps to Design and Build a Network." As you've read this book, however, you've probably discovered what needs to happen. For this objective, I'll use the following list because I've built hundreds of networks using these steps.

1. **List of requirements**   Define the network's needs. Why are you installing this network? What primary features do you need?

2. **Network design**   What equipment do you need to build this network? How should you organize the network?

3. **Compatibility issues**   Are you using existing equipment, applications, or cabling that has compatibility issues?

4. **Internal connections**   What type and length of structured cabling do you need? Does this network need wireless?

5. **External connections**   How do you connect to the Internet?

6. **Peripherals**   How will peripherals come into play? Are you connecting any printers, fax machines, or scanners?

7. **Security**   How will you deal with computer, data, and network security?

Although I've numbered them here, these steps might come in any order. Even though network security is in the seventh position, for example, you might make a decision concerning the firewall as early as Step 2. Don't be afraid to jump around a bit as needed to construct the network. Let's start building a network using this list. For each point on the list, I'll use a scenario or two to consider some of the pitfalls and issues that might pop up.

Designing a SOHO network isn't too terribly challenging. There simply aren't enough computers, switches, routers, printers, or servers to overwhelm the design process. The challenge comes in the actual implementation of the network. Here, the "gotchas" come hot and heavy, no matter how well you think you've planned ahead. The secret is to stick with your checklist and, above all, be patient!

Define the Network Needs

This step works just how it sounds like it should. First, you think about what you want your network to *do*. Do you need to run a small office? Do you want to be able to share your media among your household computers? How many devices will be accessing your network? Do you want the network to be wireless or wired? Write down the answers to these questions, since they will guide the rest of your network setup.

Once you know what your network will do, think about all the things your network will *need*—routers, software, cables, workstations, etc. It's also a good idea at this point to run a wireless site survey if you want to set up a wireless network—some office environments aren't very friendly to wireless signals, and you'll need to be aware of that. Don't get too carried away with this step—you don't need to know the precise model of router you need yet, but you should have a general idea of what you should be looking for.

Defining network needs never actually ends. All networks are highly evolving entities and new ideas, applications, and equipment appear on an ongoing basis.

Network Design

Now you need to work on the finer details. This is the shopping list step. Network design quantifies the equipment, operating systems, and applications used by the network. This step ties closely with Step 3, compatibility issues.

You need to address the following equipment:

- Workstations
  - Decide the exact type of workstation you need. Do you want machines running Windows 7 or Linux? What kind of processor do you want? How much hard drive space do you need? What applications will you need to use?
- Servers
  - Just like with workstations, you need to determine the type of servers, if any, you'll need for your office.

- Equipment room
  - Decide the size and location of your equipment room. Do you need racks for your servers? Remember not to put the equipment room too close to, for example, a bathroom or other area where water damage might occur. Also determine how you'll cool the equipment room. It can get hot in there!
- Peripherals
  - Figure out what type of printer or scanner your network will need. You might not need a lot of peripherals, but most offices have at least one networked printer.
- Cabling
  - Get some measurements of your office to determine the length of each run of cable you'll install. Also decide on the type of cable you want to install for your needs. Lower-grade cable might cost you less, but it will limit the transfer speeds of your network, so you may want to spring for the good stuff.

Compatibility Issues

If you are building a new home network from scratch, which of your existing parts could work in the new network? Do you have older equipment that might have compatibility issues, like an old 100BaseT switch or router?

If you needed to use all of your old equipment, visualize your new network connecting to it and how you might get around some of these issues. Does your old printer have a way to connect to the network directly? Where would you connect your Xbox 360? What if you have older TVs? Will they work with a powerful, HDMI-equipped video card?

Create an inventory of your old equipment and jot down any compatibility issues you might imagine taking place.

Internal Connections

Now that you have an idea of your equipment and what you want to do with it, you need to get everything properly connected using structured cabling. Once you connect all your equipment, configure any internal VLANs, IP addressing schemes, DHCP/DNS servers, gateways, and so on.

External Connections

No network is an island anymore. At the very least, you need an ISP so you can Google and update your Facebook page—err, I mean, get work done online. In a

SOHO network, you don't have to deal with many of the issues you'd see in larger networks. A typical home-type ISP (DSL or cable) should be more than enough for them in terms of bandwidth. On the other hand, you will probably need to be connected to the Internet all the time (or pay the price in lost business), so you may want to consider a second ISP as a fallback plan in case the primary ISP fails.

Peripherals

Since you already know what kinds of peripherals you'll need, all you have to do is buy and install them. It's always a good idea to test a network printer from every workstation in the office, just in case.

Security

Thinking about network security is like thinking about network electricity: security is not really a single step but an integral part of all the steps. When you set up your wireless network, make sure to set up encryption of some sort. When you install your equipment room, make sure the door locks. Make sure all the users of your network have appropriate permissions and strong passwords. Good security will not only offer you peace of mind, but it could save your business, too.

Objective 10.02 Implementing a Wireless Network

In Chapter 2, you learned about wireless concepts and theories, such as the different wireless standards and the frequencies assigned to different channels. Be sure to refer to the sections in Chapter 2 where we discussed each wireless setting. This section will tell you how to change these settings.

Installing the Access Point

When you purchase a wireless access point (WAP), you simply need to plug the power in and then connect the cable from your Internet service provider (ISP) to the WAN port (see Figure 10.1) on the WAP. This will typically leave four more ports available, which are the local ports for the network switch.

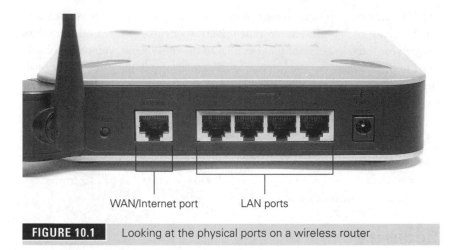

WAN/Internet port   LAN ports

FIGURE 10.1   Looking at the physical ports on a wireless router

Once you have connected the Internet to the WAN port, you are up and running. By default, the wireless functions of the wireless router are preconfigured and enable anyone to connect to the wireless network and surf the Internet! But that is not really a good thing, security-wise, so you need to make sure that you take some basic steps to secure your wireless network.

Local Lingo

Power over Ethernet   Wireless access points need electrical power, but they're invariably placed in strange locations (like ceilings or high up on walls) where providing electrical power is not convenient. Better WAPs support a standard called *Power over Ethernet (PoE)* that enables them to receive their power from the same Ethernet cables that transfer their data. The switch that connects the WAPs must support PoE, but as long as both the WAP and the switch support PoE, you don't have to do anything other than just plug in Ethernet cables. As you might imagine, it costs extra to get WAPs and switches that support PoE, but the convenience of PoE for wireless networks makes it a popular option.

Set the Admin Password

Your first task is to change the administrator password so that no one else can administer your router. To change this password on your wireless router, you go to a web browser and type the address **192.168.0.1** or **192.168.1.1** (depending on the manufacturer and software) into the address/URL bar. Then check the router's manual for the user name and password to log in as an administrator. Once you've logged in, you will need to find the page that enables you to set the admin password. For example, on my D-Link DIR-615 Wireless N router, I chose the Tools link (at the top) and then the Admin link on the left (shown in Figure 10.2).

Change Wireless Settings

After you change the admin password, you need to change the SSID (network name) of the wireless router. You'll remember from Chapter 2 that for clients to connect to the wireless network, they need to know the SSID. Figure 10.3 shows how to change the network name (the SSID).

Notice in Figure 10.3 that you can disable wireless entirely by unchecking the Enable Wireless option. You can also perform the following functions to control your wireless network environment:

- **Wireless Mode** On this router, you can set the wireless mode to determine the compatibility with different wireless standards. As you can see in Figure 10.3, my router is set to support 802.11n, 802.11g, and 802.11b clients.

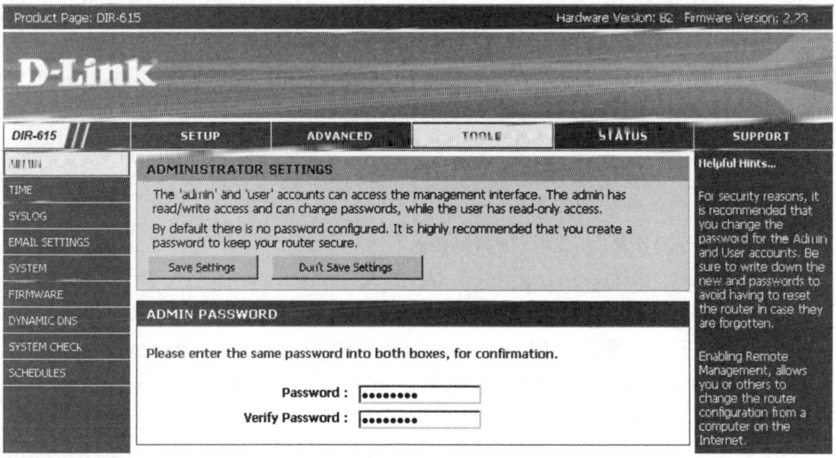

FIGURE 10.2 Changing the admin password on a D-Link router

```
WIRELESS NETWORK SETTINGS

              Enable Wireless :  ☑  [Always ▼]  [ Add New ]
        Wireless Network Name :  [dlink            ]  (Also called the SSID)
                  802.11 Mode :  [Mixed 802.11n, 802.11g and 802.11b ▼]
      Enable Auto Channel Scan :  ☑
             Wireless Channel :  [2.437 GHz - CH 6  ▼]
            Transmission Rate :  [Best (automatic)  ▼]  (Mbit/s)
                Channel Width :  [20 MHz            ▼]
             Visibility Status :  ⊙ Visible  ○ Invisible
```

FIGURE 10.3	Changing the wireless network settings such as the SSID channel and visibility (SSID broadcasting)

- **Wireless Channel** In Figure 10.3, the router is configured to auto-select a channel. In this case, it's using channel 6—the default channel used by wireless networks. If you find that devices such as cordless phones interfere with your wireless network, you can try changing the channel of the router to something different by turning off Auto Channel Scan and then choosing the channel from the drop-down list.

- **Visibility Status** On most routers, this setting is typically known as "SSID Broadcasting." SSID broadcasting advertises the router's name to clients so that they can connect. On this router, you disable SSID broadcasting by setting the Visibility Status to Invisible. Clients will not see the wireless network unless they have been configured manually to do so.

Implement MAC Filtering

Once you have set the basic wireless settings, you will configure MAC filtering, which is used to permit or deny MAC addresses that can connect to your wireless network. To configure MAC filtering on the D-Link router, you'd go to the Advanced link at the top and then choose Network Filter on the left, as shown in Figure 10.4.

On this router, you would choose to Turn MAC Filtering On from the drop-down list and then specify the MAC addresses by typing them in or choosing them from a list of DHCP clients in the drop-down list.

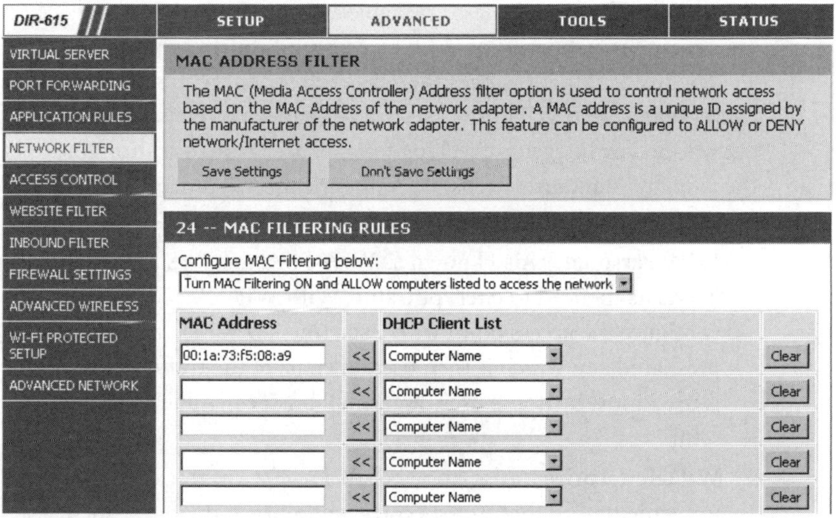

FIGURE 10.4 Filtering which system can connect to the wireless network with MAC filtering

Implement Encryption

To provide real security for your wireless network, you must encrypt your data. Turning off the SSID broadcast and creating MAC address reservations will not stop a truly determined intruder. With *encryption,* data packets are digitally encoded (using an encryption key) before being transmitted onto the wireless network. The receiving network device has to possess the encryption key to unscramble the packet and process the data. Therefore, any data packets surreptitiously grabbed by an intruder out of the air are useless without the encryption key. A number of encryption protocols can be used to secure your wireless network; you can use Wired Equivalent Privacy (WEP), Wi-Fi Protected Access (WPA), or Wi-Fi Protected Access 2 (WPA2).

- **WEP** Encrypts using a 64-bit or 128-bit encryption key to scramble data packets. WEP is a flawed standard that can be cracked using well-known hacker tools such as AirSnort. If your WAPs and NICs provide no other option, WEP does increase the security of your network by keeping out casual intruders, but a hacker can crack WEP with relative ease. You need something better to protect yourself from a motivated intruder.

- **WPA**   Provides a better, less crackable encryption standard that addresses the weaknesses of WEP by using 128-bit encryption and TKIP, a protocol that changes the keys used for encryption for every packet that is sent. WPA offers security enhancements such as an encryption key integrity-checking feature, user authentication through the industry-standard Extensible Authentication Protocol (EAP), and other advanced features that WEP lacks. WPA runs in one of two modes:

  - **WPA-Personal**   Also known as WPA-PSK, this uses a preshared key as its method to encrypt traffic. With WPA-Personal you will configure the access point with a starting key value, known as the preshared key, which is then used to encrypt the traffic. This mode is used most by home users and small businesses due to its simple setup.

  - **WPA-Enterprise**   Also known as WPA-802.1X, this is a WPA implementation that uses a central authentication server such as a RADIUS server for authentication, authorization, and accounting features. WPA-Enterprise is used by larger companies so that they can use their existing authentication server to control who has access to the wireless network and to log network access.

- **WPA2**   Improves upon the security of WPA and should be used instead of WPA if you have the choice. WPA2 uses the Advanced Encryption Standard (AES) protocol instead of TKIP and also supports a number of additional features such as added protection for ad hoc networks and key caching. Because WPA2 uses AES as its encryption protocol, it supports 128-bit, 192-bit, and 256-bit encryption.

Upgrade the Antenna

Depending on the placement of your WAP and the distance to your client machines, you may want to install a better antenna on your WAP. This will increase your WAP's signal strength, enabling you to get faster connections at a longer distance. You have several choices for the type of antenna you use, depending on your requirements.

For a typical network, you want blanket coverage and would place a WAP with an omnidirectional antenna in the center of the area (Figure 10.5). With an omnidirectional antenna, the radio wave flows outward from the WAP. Most wireless networks use this combination, especially in the consumer space. The standard straight-wire antennas that provide the most omnidirectional function are called dipole antennas.

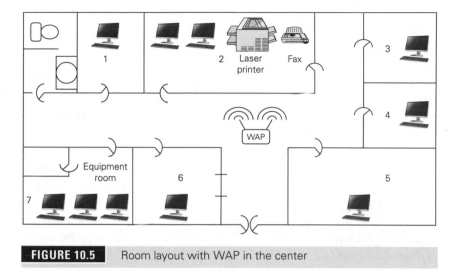

FIGURE 10.5   Room layout with WAP in the center

When you don't necessarily want to broadcast to the world, you can use one or more directional antennas to create a nicely focused network. A directional antenna, as the name implies, focuses a radio wave into a beam of sorts. Directional antennas come in a variety of flavors, such as parabolic, dish, and Yagi, to name just a few. A parabolic antenna looks like a satellite dish. A Yagi antenna (named for one of its Japanese inventors) is often called a *beam antenna* and can enable a focused radio wave to travel a long way, even miles!

Security Concerns with Signaling

The placement and signal strength of your WAP can have an effect on the security of the wireless network overall. Try to get the proper antennas and signal strength that match your space and needs. If you're installing in a typical small office, for example, try not to let the signal bleed into adjacent offices. Why present a tempting target to the person next door who wants to perfect his hacking skills?

Installing the Client

After you have configured the router, you'll need to connect the clients to the wireless network. To do this, you can view a list of wireless clients by right-clicking the wireless network icon in the taskbar and then choosing View Available Wireless Networks.

From the list of wireless networks, choose which wireless network you want to connect to, as shown in Figure 10.6.

If SSID broadcasting has been disabled, you will not see the wireless network in the list of available wireless networks, so you will need to configure the connection manually through the Change Advanced Settings option, shown in Figure 10.6.

When you choose to specify a manual setting, you will need to type the name of the SSID you want to connect to and then specify the data encryption mode, as shown in Figure 10.7.

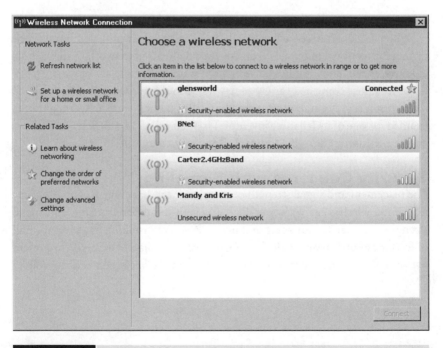

FIGURE 10.6   Viewing a list of available wireless networks

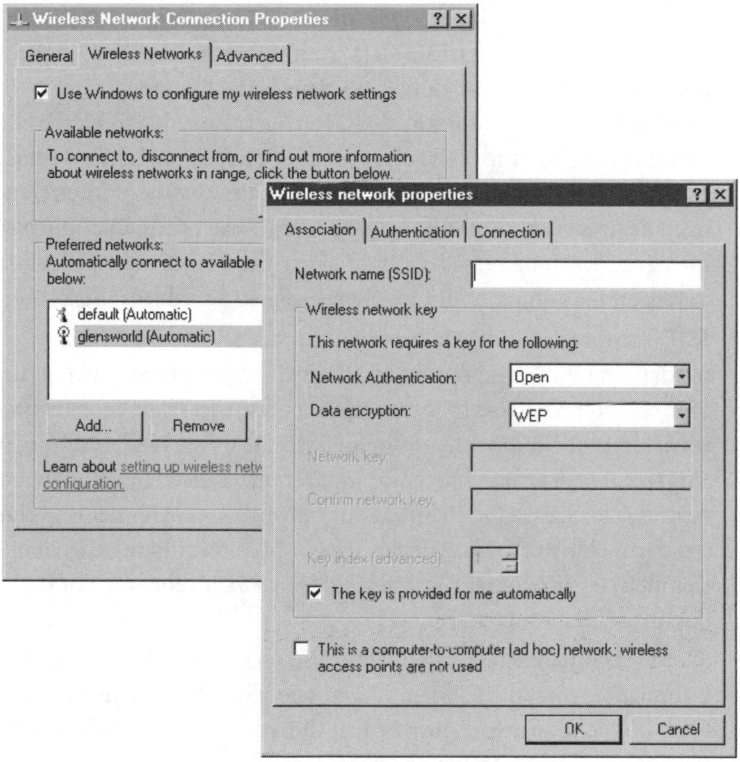

FIGURE 10.7 Adding a wireless network manually

Troubleshooting Wireless Networking

When working with wireless networks, you may not be able to connect to the network for a number of reasons, such as the following:

- **Interference** You may have trouble keeping a connection with your wireless network because of interference with other electronic equipment, such as cordless phones or microwaves. Try changing the channel on your wireless network. Wireless signals also have a tendency to "bounce" off of solid objects, so sometimes making small adjustments to furniture placement can help.

- **Incorrect encryption** You may be trying to use the wrong encryption method or specifying the wrong encryption key. You will need to verify these settings before trying to connect.

- **Incorrect channel or incorrect frequency** Your wireless client may be trying to use a channel that differs from the channel the wireless router is using. Changing the channel will change the frequency used by the wireless network. In addition, 802.11n routers are able to transmit on both the 2.4 GHz and 5 GHz frequencies. The 5 GHz range is much less crowded than the 2.4 GHz range, reducing the chance of interference from devices such as telephones and microwave ovens. Too much signal interference can increase latency, making the network sluggish and slow to respond. Running in the 5 GHz range greatly reduces this problem.

- **SSID mismatch** Another problem can occur when you have overlapping WAP signals sent by WAPs that aren't broadcasting their SSIDs. If you have one of these wireless networks saved in your system, your computer could attempt to log into the other WAP, resulting in an *SSID mismatch error*. One fix for interference caused by other wireless devices is to change the channel your network uses. Another is to change the channel the offending device uses, if possible. If you can't change channels, try moving the interfering device to another area or replacing it with a different device.

- **Standards mismatch** A standards mismatch means that your computer is configured for 802.11n when you are actually trying to connect to an old 802.11a wireless network. Be sure that the cards are compatible with the standard used by the wireless router.

- **Distance** Wireless networks are typically limited to 120 feet inside and 300 feet outside. Your system may experience shorter networking distances due to interference. You can use a wireless repeater or build a long-range antenna to extend the range of your wireless network.

- **Incorrect WAP placement** Wireless routers use a vertical antenna that sends a signal in all directions. This creates a signal "hole" in the middle, so if wireless clients are trying to connect to the wireless network and are below the antenna (potentially in the hole of the circle area), you may need to move the client or move the antenna.

Exam Tip

The CompTIA Network+ exam might use the phrase "incorrect switch placement" even though, technically, the WAP function in a typical Wi-Fi box is not a switch.

Objective 10.03 Specialized Network Devices

For the CompTIA Network+ exam, you need to be familiar with the networking devices discussed earlier in the book such as switches, routers, and firewalls. You need to be familiar with the following terms:

- **Multilayer switch** A switch that runs at different layers of the OSI model. For example, you can have a single switch that can perform layer-2 functions such as MAC filtering, virtual LANs, and spanning tree, in addition to layer-3 functions, acting as a router that supports routing protocols such as Routing Information Protocol (RIP) and Enhanced Interior Gateway Routing Protocol (EIGRP).

- **Content switch** A switch that can implement performance features on different types of traffic. Examples of the performance features may be data caching or load-balancing services.

- **Intrusion detection system (IDS)** An application (often running on a dedicated IDS box) that inspects incoming packets, looking for active intrusions. A good IDS knows how to find attacks that no firewall can find, such as viruses, illegal logon attempts, and other well-known attacks. An IDS always has some way to let the network administrators know if an attack is taking place: at the very least the attack is logged, but some IDSs offer a pop-up message, an e-mail, or even a text message to your phone. Third-party IDS tools, on the other hand, tend to act in a much more complex and powerful way. You have two choices with a real IDS: network based or host based.

  - **Network-based IDS (NIDS)** Consists of multiple sensors placed around the network, often on one or both sides of the gateway router. These sensors report to a central application that, in turn, reads a signature file to detect anything out of the ordinary (Figure 10.8).

  - **host-based IDS (HIDS)** Software running on individual systems that monitors for events such as system file modification or registry changes (Figure 10.9). More expensive third-party system IDSs do all this and add the ability to provide a single reporting source—very handy when one person is in charge of anything that goes on throughout a network.

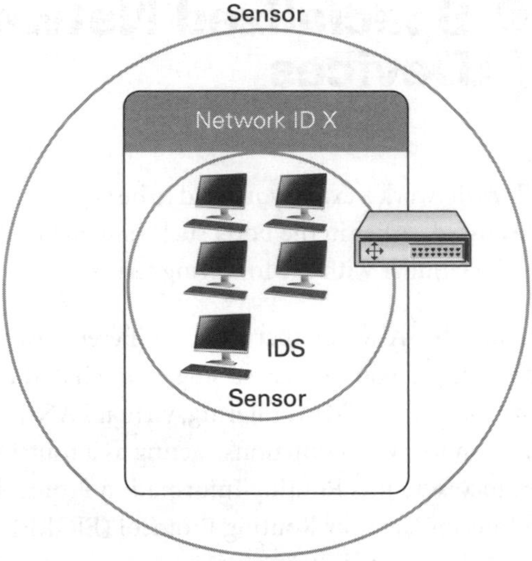

FIGURE 10.8 Diagram of network-based IDS

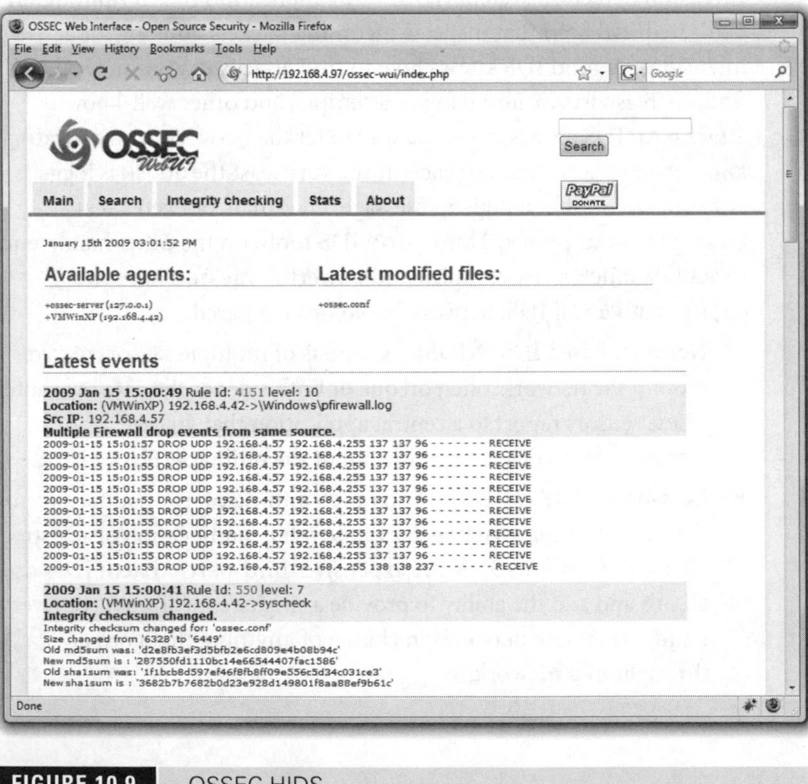

FIGURE 10.9 OSSEC HIDS

A well-protected network uses both a NIDS and a HIDS. A NIDS monitors the incoming and outgoing traffic from the Internet, whereas the HIDS monitors the individual computers.

Exam Tip

The CompTIA Network+ exam can refer to an IDS system by either its location on the network—thus NIDS or HIDS—or by what the IDS system does in each location. The network-based IDS scans using signature files, thus it is a *signature-based IDS*. A host-based IDS watches for suspicious behavior on systems, thus it is a *behavior-based IDS*.

- **Intrusion prevention system (IPS)**   Very similar to an IDS, but an IPS adds the capability to react to an attack. Depending on what IPS product you choose, an IPS can block incoming packets on the fly based on IP address, port number, or application type. An IPS might go even further, literally fixing certain packets on the fly. As you might suspect, you can roll out an IPS on a network and it gets a new name: a *network intrusion prevention system (NIPS)*.

Exam Tip

The CompTIA Network+ exam refers to intrusion detection and prevention systems collectively by their initials, *IDS/IPS*.

Local Lingo

Port mirroring   IDS/IPS often takes advantage of something called *port mirroring*. Many advanced switches have the capability to mirror data from any or all physical ports on a switch to a single physical port. It's as though you make a customized, fully configurable promiscuous port. Port mirroring is incredibly useful for any type of situation where an administrator needs to inspect packets coming to or from certain computers. You implement port mirroring in the managed switch's configuration screens.

- **Load balancer**   Hardware or software that provides load-balancing services and is designed to divide the network activity between multiple hosts. Load balancers offer a number of other features such as data caching.

- **Multifunction network device**   A device that has features of many different devices built in. A great example would be the typical home router that you purchased for your network—this device is a firewall, NAT, DHCP server, DNS server, switch, and wireless access point.
- **DNS server**   A server on the network that converts the FQDN to an IP address.
- **Bandwidth shaper**   Performs bandwidth shaping, also known as traffic shaping, where traffic is purposely held back, or delayed, based on its type. Traffic shaping conserves bandwidth at different times for specific applications.
- **Proxy server**   A device that requests resources, such as webpages, for the client system and then returns the page to the client system instead of the client system retrieving the content itself.
- **CSU/DSU**   The channel service unit/data service unit is the device that connects to your router, which connects your network to the digital link, such as a T1 or T3 link.
- **VPN concentrator**   A specific device designed to offer a highly secure VPN solution to an organization using the highest level of security technologies such as encryption and authentication services.

Objective 10.04   Network Configuration Management

The more complicated a network becomes, the more vulnerable it becomes in terms of security, efficiency, duplication or unnecessary redundancy, and unnecessary cost. Chapter 9 covered many of the security issues, but left a major component for coverage here, configuration management. *Configuration management* is a set of documents, policies, and procedures designed to help you maintain and update your network in a logical, orderly fashion so you may lessen the risks of these vulnerabilities. Your network should standardize on types of NICs, cabling, network operating systems, and network applications to make certain that when upgrades need to happen, they do so with the utmost efficiency.

> **Local Lingo**
>
> **Asset management**   Managing each aspect of a network, from documentation to performance to hardware, falls into a broad category called *asset management*.

If you want to upgrade your users from Windows XP to Windows 7, for example, you neither want to create a huge security risk for your network, nor waste a lot of money, time, and effort by realizing *after the fact* that an important application wasn't compatible with the new OS. That's not the way to do it in the real world!

Configuration Management Documentation

The *configuration management documentation* enables you to see many things about your network quickly. Good documentation helps you to troubleshoot a network efficiently. You can also determine as quickly as possible both how to upgrade components of that network and what effects such an upgrade might have. Configuration management documentation covers everything, from the wires used to how the people using the network should be trained. You can think about the configuration management documentation in four broad categories:

* Network connectivity
* Baselines
* Policies, procedures, and configurations
* Regulations

Network Connectivity

Documentation on network connectivity describes the many details about both the machines on the network and how they connect. The documentation can be hard copy or electronic and falls into three categories:

* Wiring schemes
* Network diagrams
* Network maps

Wiring Schemes   A *wiring scheme* describes the cabling and connectors used in the network. In this documentation you find the specific types of UTP used, such as CAT 5e or CAT 6, and the TIA/EIA standard used in the RJ-45 crimps (Figure 10.10). You'll discover multimode or single-mode fiber (or both,

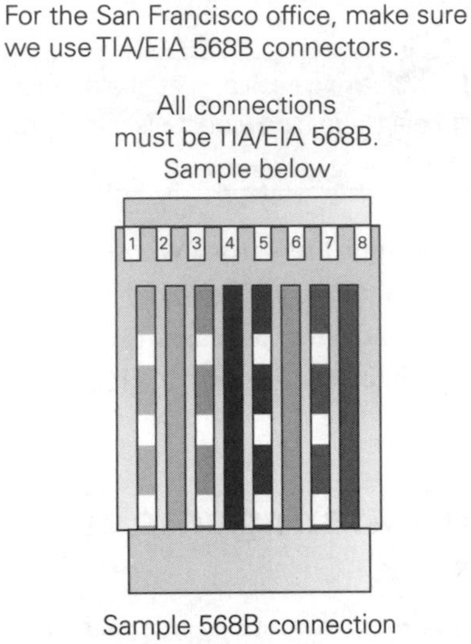

For the San Francisco office, make sure
we use TIA/EIA 568B connectors.

All connections
must be TIA/EIA 568B.
Sample below

Sample 568B connection

FIGURE 10.10 Wiring scheme detail on the TIA/EIA standard used throughout the network

depending on the run) and which connectors plug into the PCs, switches, and routers. CompTIA shortens the category name for this type of documentation to *wire schemes*.

Exam Tip

CompTIA Network+ refers to a *wiring scheme* as a *wire scheme* in the current exam objectives and the *wiring schematics* in the previous objectives. Expect to see any of the three terms on the exam.

Network Diagrams A *network diagram* shows devices on the network and how they connect. It shows the physical runs and defines the type of connection, such as Gigabit Ethernet, T1, and so on. A network diagram includes every router, switch, server, CSU/DSU, cable modem, and wireless access point, including the make and model and firmware upgrade. Figure 10.11 shows a typical network diagram.

The network administrator creates the network diagram. Lucky for you, two critical tools make your job easier. First are standardized icons. As you look at Figure 10.11, you might notice the icons are somewhat cryptic. That's because many years ago Cisco developed this shorthand to represent any type of networking device you might imagine.

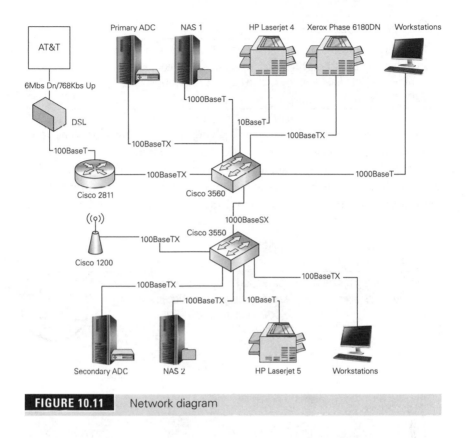

Network diagram

Cisco generally calls these "network topology icons," and they are the accepted standard to use whenever you're drawing a network. Figure 10.12 shows some examples of the more common topology icons.

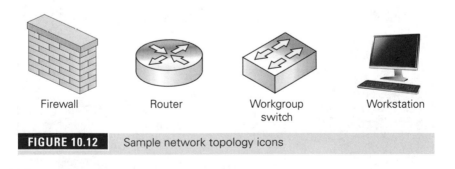

Sample network topology icons

Travel Assistance

New network devices show up all the time, so there's no single place to see every network topology icon available. That said, Cisco keeps a fairly complete list here: www.cisco.com/web/about/ac50/ac47/2.html.

Your second tool is one of the many drawing programs that support network topology icons. You can use a presentation tool like Microsoft PowerPoint, but Microsoft Visio is the most famous tool for drawing any type of network diagram. Visio adds a number of extras that make putting together any type of diagram a snap. Figure 10.13 shows how I made Figures 10.11 and 10.14: with Visio!

Exam Tip

Having cabling runs and devices properly documented is all part of a broader category called *cable management*. Good documentation helps you troubleshoot and fix problems quickly.

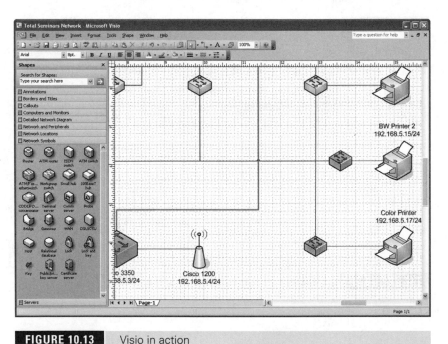

FIGURE 10.13   Visio in action

Network Maps   A *network map* goes deeper into the individual components of the network, documenting IP addresses, ports, protocols, and more. You can create a network map manually using tools like Visio. Figure 10.14 shows such a network map.

Exam Tip

Most techs and companies use the terms *network diagram* and *network map* interchangeably or have strict definitions that reverse what you read here. Don't sweat the differences for the exam. Just know that part of your configuration management documentation involves mapping out the nodes and including IP address, connection speed, and so forth.

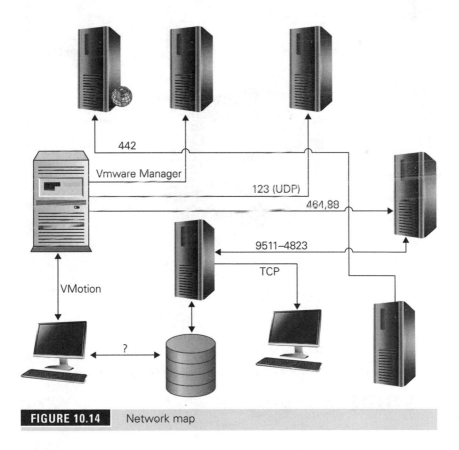

FIGURE 10.14   Network map

Alternatively, you can create a network map with powerful programs such as Nmap. You know about Nmap from Chapter 9, where you saw it scanning for unusual open ports. It offers many configuration features, including telling you whether an open port is using TCP or UDP, for example. Plus this sort of application can create stunning graphical representations of your network.

Figure 10.15 shows a graphic of my office network. Figure 10.16 has zeroed in on a single router, examining open protocols and TCP/IP applications in use. Both screens are from Zenmap, a graphical interface for Nmap.

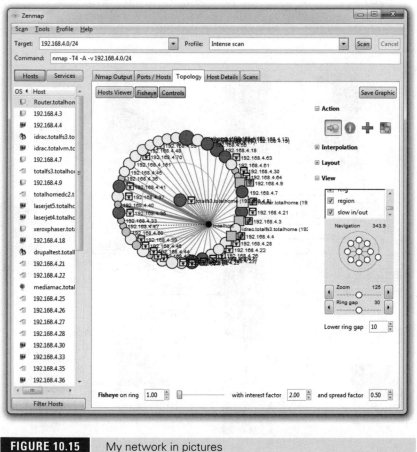

FIGURE 10.15   My network in pictures

Zenmap

Scan Tools Profile Help

Target: 192.168.4.0/24 ▾   Profile: Intense scan ▾   Scan   Cancel

Command: nmap -T4 -A -v 192.168.4.0/24

| Hosts | Services |

Nmap Output | Ports / Hosts | Topology | Host Details | Scans

OS ◄	Host
	Router.totalhon
	192.168.4.3
	192.168.4.4
	idrac.totalfs3.to
	idrac.totalvm.tc
	192.168.4.7
	totalfs3.totalho
	192.168.4.9
	totalhomedc2.t
	laserjet5.totalhc
	laserjet4.totalhc
	xeroxphaser.tot
	192.168.4.18
	drupaltest.totall
	192.168.4.21
	192.168.4.22
	mediamac.total
	192.168.4.25
	192.168.4.26
	192.168.4.27
	192.168.4.28
	192.168.4.30
	192.168.4.33
	192.168.4.35
	192.168.4.36

Filter Hosts

Router.totalhome (192.168.4.1)

⊞ **Comments**

⊟ **Host Status**
State: up
Open ports: 5
Filtered ports: 0
Closed ports: 995
Scanned ports: 1000
Up time: Not available
Last boot: Not available

⊟ **Addresses**
IPv4:   192.168.4.1
IPv6:   Not available
MAC: 00:23:04:8C:B7:20

⊟ **Hostnames**
Name - Type: Router.totalhome - PTR

⊟ **Operating System**
Name: Cisco Aironet 1200-series WAP or 2610XM router (IOS

Accuracy: 99%

⊟ **Ports used**
Port-Protocol-State: 22 - tcp - open
Port-Protocol-State: 1 - tcp - closed

⊟ **OS Class**

Type	Vendor	OS Family	OS Generation	Accuracy
router	Cisco	IOS	12.X	99
WAP	Cisco	IOS	12.X	99

FIGURE 10.16   Router close up

Exam Tip

Make updating your network documentation the last step of any changes you make to the network.

Baselines

The best way to know when a problem is brewing is to know how things perform when all's well with the system. Part of any proper configuration management documentation is a *baseline*: a log of performance indicators such as CPU usage, network utilization, and other values to give you a picture of your network and servers when they are working correctly. A major change in these values can point to problems on a server or the network as a whole.

All operating systems come with some form of baseline tools. A common tool used to create a baseline on Windows systems is the Performance Monitor utility that comes with all versions of Windows. You'll see Performance Monitor at work in Chapter 12.

Policies, Procedures, and Configurations

Network security, costs, time, and employee and management frustration—all of these things matter when managing a complex network. As part of any good documentation, therefore, you'll find policies about what people can and cannot do with network hardware and software. You'll see procedures outlined for what to do when upgrading components or adding new user accounts. You'll also get down-to-the-user-interface-level information about how software and hardware should be configured.

Much of this should be familiar from a CompTIA A+ certification level. For example, what's a great way to keep a Windows PC from becoming vulnerable to a new piece of malware floating around the Internet? C'mon, one guess! Keep it patched and up to date with Windows Update, right? Exactly.

Properly created configuration management documentation will inform network folks what to do with user training. Who gets it? Which departments? What level of access should you give new employees versus seasoned and trusted veterans?

Many of the policies and procedures help protect your network from harm. In CompTIA terms, they *mitigate security risks* like those outlined in gory detail in Chapter 9! Two policies affect most users: acceptable use and security. After explaining these polices, I'll also give you a configuration example.

Acceptable Use Policy   An *acceptable use policy* defines exactly what you can and cannot do with your computers and network. Some classic areas defined by an acceptable use policy include personal computer use and adding personal software. Can a user access Facebook on a work computer, for example, or install a game?

Security Policy An organization's *security policy* defines procedures employees should perform to protect the network's security. Security policies cover a wide gamut. They define password complexity, explain to users how to deal with social engineering, and clarify how to deal with virus attacks. Security policies almost always define action plans to deal with serious events that might threaten your network.

Configuration *Configurations* are the results of the procedures. Documenting configurations for critical systems is important. Imagine if a carefully configured gateway router suddenly lost all of its settings and no one had made a backup! Every configurable device in today's networking world comes with some tool to document its configuration. Figure 10.17 shows a part of one of the most common of all network configuration files, Cisco's IOS startup configuration. It can be displayed by running `show startup-config` on all of Cisco's IOS-based routers and switches.

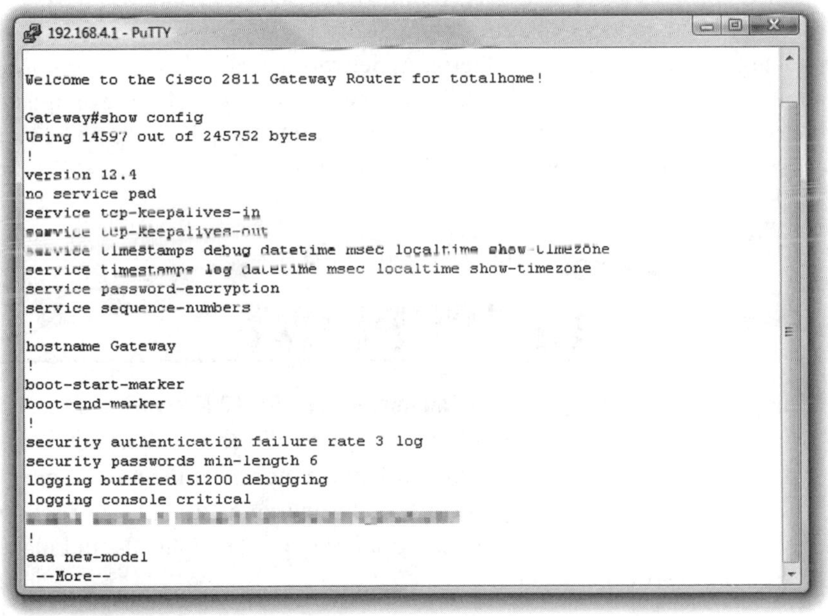

```
192.168.4.1 - PuTTY

Welcome to the Cisco 2811 Gateway Router for totalhome!

Gateway#show config
Using 14597 out of 245752 bytes
!
version 12.4
no service pad
service tcp-keepalives-in
service tcp-keepalives-out
service timestamps debug datetime msec localtime show-timezone
service timestamps log datetime msec localtime show-timezone
service password-encryption
service sequence-numbers
!
hostname Gateway
!
boot-start-marker
boot-end-marker
!
security authentication failure rate 3 log
security passwords min-length 6
logging buffered 51200 debugging
logging console critical
!
aaa new-model
 --More--
```

FIGURE 10.17 Section of `show startup-config`

Regulations

Very few people profess to like *regulations,* the rules that govern behavior in the workplace. Nevertheless, regulations help keep networks and people safe and productive. Every decent configuration management documentation talks about regulations, such as what to do when you have a safety violation or some sort of potentially bad accident.

Change Management Documentation

Although CompTIA seems to separate the detailed overview of the network from how to upgrade it, most networking professionals use the term *change management documentation* to describe this single body of knowledge. An example will make this clear. Let's say you want to change your network by adding a demilitarized zone (DMZ) because you want to add a server that people outside the network can access easily.

The change management documentation shows you network diagrams so you can verify where to place the DMZ and what other machines are potentially affected by the change. Plus, it gives you the detailed information on what to do to get approval from supervisors, get through the budgeting office, and so on.

Change management documentation details the procedures and policies to update the documentation so after each network change, your master documents are accurate. This information is extremely important! Failure to update the correct document will eventually result in you looking really bad when an otherwise minor troubleshoot turns into a nightmare.

CHECKPOINT

✔**Objective 10.01: Designing and Implementing a SOHO Network**   Every good tech should be comfortable designing a small network. Start out by defining your network's needs, which will make the rest of the process much simpler. After that, design your network, fix any compatibility issues, set up your internal and external connections, install your peripherals, and make sure your network is secure.

✔**Objective 10.02: Implementing a Wireless Network** You will need to be very familiar with wireless networking for the CompTIA Network+ exam, so be sure to read over the theory that was presented in Chapter 2 and also know the basic steps to implement and troubleshoot a wireless network. Know that different wireless standards such as 802.11b, 802.11g, and 802.11n use a number of methods to help secure the wireless network, such as MAC filtering and data encryption, via WPA or WPA2.

✔**Objective 10.03: Specialized Network Devices** For the exam, you need to be familiar with a wealth of different types of devices starting with switches, routers, and NAT devices. Also be familiar with multifunctioning devices such as wireless routers and proxy servers.

✔**Objective 10.04: Network Configuration Management** The more compli-cated a network is, the more vulnerable it is in terms of security, efficiency, and other aspects. Configuration management helps you maintain and up-date your network in a logical and orderly fashion to lessen these vulnerabili-ties. Networks should be standardized on the types of NICs, cabling, network operating systems, and network applications to make upgrades to the network as efficient as possible. Configuration management documen-tation includes network connectivity, baselines, policies, procedures, configurations, and regulations.

REVIEW QUESTIONS

1. The first step in designing a new SOHO network is to
   A. Define a list of requirements.
   B. Determine the type of ISP you will use.
   C. Check the existing cable.
   D. Determine what security you need.

2. With what technology can you avoid finding an AC outlet for a WAP?
   A. AES
   B. PoE
   C. Powered Wi-Fi
   D. TKIP

3. What should you use when you want to limit access to your wireless network based on the physical, hard-coded address of each wireless network device?

    A. Bus scheduling

    B. Encoding

    C. Encryption

    D. MAC address filtering

4. Which of the following is the wireless network encryption method that is most secure?

    A. MAC address filtering

    B. WEP

    C. WPA

    D. WPA2

5. Where should you place a WAP to get optimal coverage of a room?

    A. In the center of the room.

    B. On the north wall, halfway up.

    C. On the wall opposite any potential interference devices.

    D. It doesn't matter. Replace the default antenna with a more powerful one.

6. What is true of a multilayer switch?

    A. It can work at multiple OSI layers at the same time.

    B. It can work with one of several OSI layers at a time, depending on its configuration mode. Working at a different layer requires making a configuration change and resetting the switch.

    C. It can communicate with other switches that work at different OSI layers.

    D. It has twice the ports of a standard switch because it contains two regular switches, one stacked on top of the other.

7. How does an IPS compare to an IDS?

    A. An IPS is more secure because it uses IPsec.

    B. An IDS is more secure because it uses L2TP.

    C. An IPS is more robust because it can react to attacks.

    D. An IDS is more robust because it can react to attacks.

8. Which feature of advanced switches enables an administrator to inspect packets coming to or from specific computers?

   A. Bandwidth shaping

   B. Load balancing

   C. IPS

   D. Port mirroring

9. Your boss asks you for a diagram showing every server on the network. What do you provide to her?

   A. Logical RAID

   B. Network diagram

   C. Wiring scheme

   D. Baseline

10. What is defined in a security policy? (Select two.)

    A. What users can and cannot do with their computers

    B. How complex user passwords should be

    C. How to deal with social engineering hacking attempts

    D. How users should install their own software

REVIEW ANSWERS

1. **A**   Defining requirements is the first step in designing a SOHO network.

2. **B**   Power over Ethernet (PoE) provides power through the network cable, thus eliminating the need to plug a WAP into an AC outlet.

3. **D**   MAC address filtering should be used when you want to limit access to your wireless network based on the hard-wired address of each wireless network device.

4. **D**   WPA2 is a wireless encryption method that improves on the security features of WPA. MAC address filtering can be easily spoofed and bypassed. Wired Equivalent Privacy (WEP) is not secure anymore.

5. **A**   Placing the WAP in the center of the room will give the most coverage.

6. **A**   A multilayer switch can work at multiple OSI layers at the same time.

7. **C**   An IPS is more robust because it can react to attacks.

8. **D** Port mirroring enables an administrator to inspect packets coming to or from certain computers.

9. **B** A network diagram shows every router, switch, server, CSU/DSU, cable modem, and wireless access point on the network.

10. **B** and **C** A security policy describes how to deal with hacking attempts and password complexity. What users can and cannot do with their computers and what software they can install is covered under the acceptable use policy.

Troubleshooting
Networks

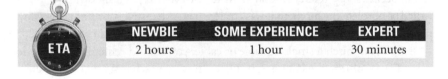

ETA	NEWBIE	SOME EXPERIENCE	EXPERT
	2 hours	1 hour	30 minutes

355

Did you ever watch the television show *ER*? It was a medical drama centering on a group of attractive doctors and nurses working in an emergency room. They spent much of their time casually checking up on patients and having witty conversations. But, at some point during every episode, something terrible happens and the ambulances pull up. People come crashing through the doors with a patient. Everyone starts shouting and the music gets very dramatic. It's an actual emergency and there is a life that needs saving!

A network tech is a little bit like an ER doctor, except you'll probably be fixing things by yourself and all that shouting will be in your head. You won't always have a lot to do to keep a network running, but when something goes wrong and you see the server being wheeled through the doors on a gurney (if you happen to have a gurney, of course), you need to know how to troubleshoot a network. You'll also need to know the symptoms of hardware malfunctions and which tools to use to fix them. The dramatic music is optional.

Objective 11.01 The Troubleshooting Process

Troubleshooting is a dynamic, fluid process that requires you to make snap judgments and act on them to try and make the network go. Any attempt to cover every possible scenario would be futile and probably not in your best interest, because any reference that tried to list every troubleshooting problem would be obsolete the moment it was created. If an exhaustive listing of all network problems is impossible, then how do you decide what to do and in what order?

Before you touch a single console or cable, you should remember two basic rules: To paraphrase the Hippocratic Oath, "First, do no harm." If at all possible, don't make a network problem bigger than it was originally. This is a rule I've broken thousands of times, and you will too. But if I change the good doctor's phrase a bit, it's possible to formulate a rule you can actually live with: "First, do not trash the data!" My gosh, if I had a dollar for every megabyte of irreplaceable data I've destroyed, I'd be rich! I've learned my lesson, and you should learn from my mistakes. The second rule is: Always make good backups! Computers can be replaced; data that is not backed up is, at best, expensive to recover and, at worst, gone forever.

No matter how complex and fancy, any troubleshooting process can be broken down into simple steps. Having a sequence of steps to follow makes the entire troubleshooting process simpler and easier, because you have a clear set of goals to achieve in a specific sequence.

The CompTIA Network+ objectives contain a detailed troubleshooting methodology that provides a good starting point for our discussion. Here are the basic steps in the troubleshooting process:

1. Identify the problem.
   a. Gather information.
   b. Identify symptoms.
   c. Question users.
   d. Determine if anything has changed.

2. Establish a theory of probable cause.
   a. Question the obvious.

3. Test the theory to determine cause.
   a. Once theory is confirmed, determine next steps to resolve the problem.
   b. If theory is not confirmed, reestablish new theory or escalate.

4. Establish a plan of action to resolve the problem and identify potential effects.

5. Implement and test the solution or escalate as necessary.

6. Verify full system functionality and, if applicable, implement preventative measures.

7. Document findings, actions, and outcomes.

Identify the Problem

First, identify the problem. That means grasping the true problem, rather than what someone tells you. A user might call in and complain that he can't access the Internet from his workstation, for example, which could be the only problem. But the problem could also be that the entire wing of the office just went down and you've got a much bigger problem on your hands. You need to gather information, identify symptoms, question users, and determine if anything has changed on the network. Doing this will help you get to the root of the problem.

Gather Information, Identify Symptoms, and Question Users

If you are working directly on the affected system and not relying on somebody on the other end of a telephone to guide you, you will establish the symptoms through your observation of what is (or isn't) happening. If you're trouble-shooting over the telephone (always a *joy*, in my experience), you will need to ask questions based on what the user is telling you. These questions can be *close-ended,* which is to say there can only be a yes-or-no-type answer, such as, "Can you load a webpage?" You can also ask *open-ended* questions, such as, "Tell me what you see on the screen."

The type of question you use at any given moment depends on what informa-tion you need and on the user's knowledge level. If, for example, the user seems to be technically oriented, you will probably be able to ask more close-ended ques-tions because they will know what you are talking about. If, on the other hand, the user seems to be confused about what's happening, open-ended questions will al-low him or her to explain in his or her own words what is going on.

One of the first steps in trying to determine the cause of a problem is to under-stand the extent of the problem—is it specific to one user or is it network-wide? Sometimes this entails trying the task yourself, both from the user's machine and from your own or another machine.

For example, if a user is experiencing problems logging into the network, you might need to go to that user's machine and try to use his or her user name to log in. Doing this tells you whether the problem is a user error of some kind, as well as enables you to see the symptoms of the problem yourself. Next, you probably want to try logging in with your own user name from that machine, or have the user try to log in from another machine. In some cases, you can ask other users in the area if they are experiencing the same problem to see if the issue is affect-ing more than one user. Depending on the size of your network, you should find out whether the problem is occurring in only one part of your company or across the entire network.

What does all of this tell you? Essentially, it tells you how big the problem is. If nobody in an entire remote office can log in, you may be able to assume that the problem is the network link or router connecting that office to the server. If no-body in any office can log in, you may be able to assume the server is down or not accepting logins. If only that one user in that one location can't log in, the prob-lem may be with that user, that machine, or that user's account.

Exam Tip

Eliminating variables is one of the first tools in your arsenal of diagnostic techniques.

Determine If Anything Has Changed

The goal of this step is to identify if anything has changed that might have caused the problem. You may not have to ask many questions before the person using the problem system can tell you what has changed, but, in some cases, establishing if anything has changed can take quite a bit of time and involve further work behind the scenes. Here are some examples of questions to ask:

- "Tell me exactly what was happening when the problem occurred."
- "Has anything been changed on the system recently?"
- "Has the system been moved recently?"

Notice the way I've tactfully avoided the word *you,* as in "Have *you* changed anything on the system recently?" This is a deliberate tactic to avoid any implied blame on the part of the user. Being nice never hurts, and it makes the whole troubleshooting process more friendly.

You should also *internally* ask yourself some isolating questions, such as, "Was that machine involved in the software push last night?" or "Didn't a tech visit that machine this morning?" Note you will only be able to answer these questions if *your* documentation is up to date. Sometimes, isolating a problem may require you to check system and hardware logs (such as those stored by some routers and other network devices), so make sure you know how to do this.

Travel Advisory

Avoid aggressive or accusatory questions.

Establish a Theory of Probable Cause

This step comes down to experience—or good use of the support tools at your disposal, such as your knowledge base. You need to select the most *probable* cause from all the *possible* causes, so the solution you choose fixes the problem the first time. This may not always happen, but whenever possible, you want to avoid spending a whole day stabbing in the dark while the problem snores softly to itself in some cozy, neglected corner of your network.

Don't forget to question the obvious. If Bob can't print to the networked printer, check to see that the printer is plugged in and turned on, for example.

Test the Theory to Determine Cause

With the third step, you need to test the theory, but do so without changing anything or risking any repercussions. If you have determined that the probable cause for Bob not being able to print is that the printer is turned off, go look. If that's the case, then you should plan out your next step to resolve the problem. Do not act yet! That comes next.

If the probable cause doesn't pan out, you need to go back to step 2 and determine a new probable cause. Once you have another idea, test it.

The reason you should hesitate to act at this third step is that you might not have permission to make the fix or the fix might cause repercussions you don't fully understand yet. For example, if you walk over to the print server room to see if the printer is powered up and online and find the door padlocked, that's a whole different level of problem. Sure, the printer is turned off, but management has done it for a reason. In this sort of situation, you need to escalate the problem.

To *escalate* has two meanings: either to inform other parties about a problem for guidance or to pass the job off to another authority who has control over the device/issue that's most probably causing the problem. Let's say you have a server with a bad NIC. This server is used heavily by the accounting department, and taking it down may cause problems you don't even know about. You need to inform the accounting manager to consult with them. Alternatively, you'll come across problems over which you have no control or authority. A badly acting server across the country (hopefully) has another person in charge to whom you need to hand over the job.

Establish a Plan of Action and Identify Potential Effects

By this point, you should have some ideas as to what the problem might be. It's time to "look before you leap." An action plan defines how you are going to fix this problem. Most problems are simple, but if the problem is complex, you need to write down the steps. As you do this, think about what else might happen as you go about the repair. If you take out a switch without a replacement switch at hand, the users might experience excessive downtime while you hunt for a new switch and move them over. If you replace a router, can you restore all the old router's settings to the new one or will you have to rebuild from scratch?

Implement and Test the Solution or Escalate as Necessary

Once you think you have isolated the cause of the problem, you should decide what you think is the best way to fix it and then try your solution, whether that's giving advice over the phone to a user, installing a replacement part, or adding a software patch. All the way through this step, try only one likely solution at a time.

As you try each possibility, always *document* what you do and what results you get. This isn't just for a future problem either—during a lengthy troubleshooting process, it's easy to forget exactly what you tried two hours before or which thing you tried produced a particular result. Although being methodical may take longer, it will save time the next time—and it may enable you to pinpoint what needs to be done to stop the problem from recurring at all, thereby reducing future call volume to your support team—and as any support person will tell you, that's definitely worth the effort!

Then you need to test the solution. This is the part everybody hates. Once you think you've fixed a problem, you should try to make it happen again. If you can't, great! But sometimes you will be able to re-create the problem, and then you know you haven't finished the job at hand. Many techs want to slide away quietly as soon as everything seems to be fine, but trust me on this, it won't impress your customer when her problem flares up again 30 seconds after you've left the building—not to mention that you get the joy of another two-hour car trip the next day to fix the same problem, for an even more unhappy client! In the scenario where you are providing support to someone else rather than working directly on the problem, you should make *her* try to re-create the problem. This tells you whether she understands what you have been telling her and educates her at the same time, lessening the chance that she'll call you back later and ask, "Can we just go through that one more time?"

Exam Tip	
Always test a solution before you walk away from the job!	

Verify Full System Functionality and Implement Preventative Measures

Okay, now that you have changed something on the system in the process of solving one problem, you must think about the wider repercussions of what you have done. If you've replaced a faulty NIC in a server, for instance, will the fact that the MAC address has changed (remember, it's built into the NIC) affect anything else, such as the login security controls or your network management and inventory software? If you've installed a patch on a client PC, will this change the default protocol or any other default settings that may affect other functionality? If you've changed a user's security settings, will this affect his or her ability to access other network resources? This is part of testing your solution to make sure it works properly, but it also makes you think about the impact of your work on the system as a whole.

Make sure you test the full system so you don't have to have a second tech call to resolve an outstanding issue. This saves time and money and helps your customer do his or her job better. Everybody wins.

Also at this time, if applicable, implement measures to avoid a repeat of the problem. If that means you need to educate the user to do or not do something, teach him or her tactfully. If you need to install software or patch a system, do it now.

Document Findings, Actions, and Outcomes

It is *vital* that you document the problem, symptoms, and solutions of all support calls, for two reasons: First, you're creating a support database to serve as a knowledge base for future reference, enabling everyone on the support team to identify new problems as they arise and know how to deal with them quickly, without having to duplicate someone else's research efforts. Second, documentation enables you to track problem trends and anticipate future workloads, or even to identify a particular brand or model of an item, such as a printer or a NIC, that seems to be less reliable or that creates more work for you than others. Don't skip this step—it *really* is essential!

Exam Tip

Memorize these problem analysis steps:

1. Identify the problem.
   a. Gather information.
   b. Identify symptoms.
   c. Question users.
   d. Determine if anything has changed.
2. Establish a theory of probable cause.
   a. Question the obvious.
3. Test the theory to determine cause.
   a. Once theory is confirmed, determine next steps to resolve problem.
   b. If theory is not confirmed, reestablish new theory or escalate.
4. Establish a plan of action to resolve the problem and identify potential effects.
5. Implement and test the solution or escalate as necessary.
6. Verify full system functionality and, if applicable, implement preventative measures.
7. Document findings, actions, and outcomes.

Objective 11.02 Troubleshooting Network Hardware

Once you know the troubleshooting process, you can start searching for signs of trouble on your network. Because there are so many places for a network to act up or outright fail, I'll cover the top network hardware faults first. I'll discuss logical network issues in Chapter 12.

Power Issues

Power issues generally fall into two categories: complete loss of power and dying power supplies. Power failure stops computing devices cold, and the symptoms are pretty obvious—no sound, no lights, and not working. If a single device is affected but the rest of the network is not, then try switching out for a known good component. If network power is off, check circuit breakers.

A dying power supply can create all kinds of havoc with components, ranging from "kind of working" to "the lights come on but nobody's home" sorts of scenarios. Often the most telling symptom is a series of seemingly random errors that don't point to any one thing. Test by swapping with a known good power supply or by using a multimeter (see the section "Multimeters" later in this chapter).

Finally, every network should have an uninterruptible power supply (UPS) as a backup for each server or rack of servers. The batteries in UPSs go out, so be certain to check them periodically and replace as necessary.

Network Media

Symptoms of network media faults can range from the inability of a single client to connect to the network to the failure of an entire system. The topology of your network determines the extent of a problem caused by a single failure and how you troubleshoot media-related problems. On a bus-based network, for example, a single cable break will shut down the entire segment, but with a UTP-based star-bus topology, a cable fault may affect only one client, unless it's the cable between two switches or a switch and a server. Also, with a star topology, you may have a single point of failure if the switch breaks down.

Media faults can generally be categorized as follows:

- Cable breaks
- Cable shorts
- Incorrect wiring to connectors
- Badly fitted or damaged connectors
- Incorrect or overlong cables or segments
- Cables located near sources of interference
- Environmental effects (heat, cold, water, and so on)

Most network cable installers carry an arsenal of tools to help them install and test new structured cabling systems. These tools range from inexpensive *crimpers* (the tools that put the connectors on the ends of the cables) and *punch-down tools* (the tools that push UTP wiring into the connectors on wall plates or into punch-down connectors on patch panels like those shown in Figure 11.1) to multi-thousand-dollar *cable testers* that plug into two ends of a cable (which I'll discuss further later in the chapter). The higher-end testers provide acres of detailed information to ensure that the electrical properties of a cable pass a battery of TIA/EIA standards. These tools are indispensable to the folks who install cable, and most of them require that techs undergo significant training before they can use and understand them.

FIGURE 11.1 Punch-down connectors on the back of a patch panel

Visual Indications of Problems

Apart from the obvious—a completely severed cable, for instance—look for help from link lights on NICs and switches. Broken UTP cables tend to cause link lights on NICs and switches to turn off. Using these visual indicators is important; inspecting connectors on cables for signs of damage is not always easy because the fault may be internal to the connector, and testing by substitution is an easier option.

> ### Travel Advisory
>
> Some network techs tie a knot at one end of a known faulty cable as close to the connector as possible. This ensures that the cable doesn't get placed back with good cable stock. Even if it does, it will be easy to see that the cable shouldn't be used.

Check the NIC

A bad NIC can also cause problems. Use the utility provided by your OS to verify that the NIC works. If you've got an NIC with diagnostic software, run it—this software will check the NIC's circuitry. The NIC's female connector is a common failure point, so NICs that come with diagnostic software often include a special test called a *loopback test*. A loopback test sends data out of the NIC and checks to see if it comes back. Some NICs perform only an internal loopback, which tests the circuitry that sends and receives, but not the actual connecting pins. A true external loopback requires a *loopback plug* inserted into the NIC's port. If an NIC is bad, replace it.

Bad Modules

Most good routers and switches come with interchangeable components, enabling manufacturers to make a base model device and then offer components to address each customer's individual needs. These components come in a number of different shapes and sizes, such as the gigabit interface converter (GBIC) that gives customers the ability to match their router and switch connections to whatever type of fiber already exists in their location. You'll recall from Chapter 2 the small form-factor pluggable (SFP) connector used in many Cisco and other brand switches.

You can easily install these modules. Turn off the router or switch, remove a protective plate (if one exists), plug in the module, and turn the switch/router back on.

If you install a module that doesn't work, use the same tests that you'd perform on any port on a switch or router. The fact that these are modules doesn't change the troubleshooting tools you've learned about in this book.

Troubleshooting Other Physical Network Issues

A number of different network communication issues could arise when you're troubleshooting network issues; as a result, the Network+ exam is heavy on troubleshooting. Following are popular issues that deal with the physical network:

- **Crosstalk (near end and far end)**   This term refers to interference from adjacent wires. If you experience a lot of signal degradation, it could be due to crosstalk. To fix the problem, try using another cable type that has more shielding.

- **Attenuation** This refers to the degradation of the signal as it travels great distances. If you cannot communicate with a system that is too far away, you might have exceeded the maximum cable length for that type of cable. To fix the problem, you add a repeater to the middle of the connection to boost the signal or use a different cable type.

- **Shorts** A short in the network cable could cause network downtime. When experiencing connectivity issues, use a cable analyzer or try a replacement cable to identify whether there is a short in the cable.

- **Open impedance** High impedance can cause signal bounce, which can cause communication issues. This signal bounce could be due to an incorrectly wired cable or an incorrect connector. You can use a cable tester or analyzer to determine whether connectivity exists between the two ends of the cable. If it doesn't, you will need to recrimp the cable.

Exam Tip

The CompTIA Network+ objectives use the term *open short* at the time of this writing. There should be a comma after "open," however, so you know you're looking at two different types of broken cable issues.

- **TX/RX reversed** When making your own cables, make sure you insert the wires according to the same standard (TIA/EIA 568A or TIA/EIA 568B) on both ends of the cable. If you don't, you might end up swapping the sending and receiving wires (known as *TX/RX reversed*) and inadvertently creating a crossover cable.

- **Interference** You may receive radio or electromagnetic interference (EMI) from external components. Be sure to route network cables away from power cables and other interference sources. Cable placement is very important!

- **Temperature** The temperature in the telecommunications room should be maintained and monitored properly. If you lose the air conditioning, for example, and leave systems running, the equipment will overheat and shut down—sometimes with serious damage. To prevent this, all serious telecommunications rooms should have *temperature monitors*.

- **Environment** Likewise, you need to control the level of humidity in a telecommunications room. You can install *environmental monitors* that keep a constant watch on humidity, temperature, and more, for just a few hundred dollars. The devices cost little in comparison to the equipment in the telecommunications room that you're protecting.

Issues That Need To Be Escalated

Loops on the network can cause problems with communication. Loops created between your switches can cause the network to go down due to confusion in the MAC address table, or routing loops can occur where each router is sending the data back to the other router:

- **Switching loops**   Loops on the network will typically bring the network down. This is why Cisco switches use Spanning Tree Protocol (STP). It prevents loops by placing one of the ports in the loop in a blocking state. If you have intermittent problems with the network where systems seem to lose connections randomly, it could be a loop issue. Check how you have everything wired and remove the cable that creates a loop.

- **Routing problems**   If all clients on the network cannot communicate with systems on another network, you most likely have a routing problem. Check the routing table on the router and ensure that a route exists to the network you are trying to reach. Verify the routes on each router on the network to ensure that the routers are not simply sending the data back and forth.

Objective 11.03 Testing Equipment

Network techs use various tools to test for faults, such as wiring that's out of spec. These types of faults do not generate any physical symptoms, and they can be found only by performing a range of tests. The most common types of test equipment are described here.

Multimeters

A multimeter, shown in Figure 11.2, can be used to test a cable or bus segment for open or short circuits by testing an electrical characteristic called *resistance*, which is measured in *ohms*. A good cable will have close to zero resistance (0 ohms) between its ends (pin 1 to pin 1 on a UTP cable). A faulty or broken cable will show a higher-than-normal resistance—anything above a few ohms to infinity.

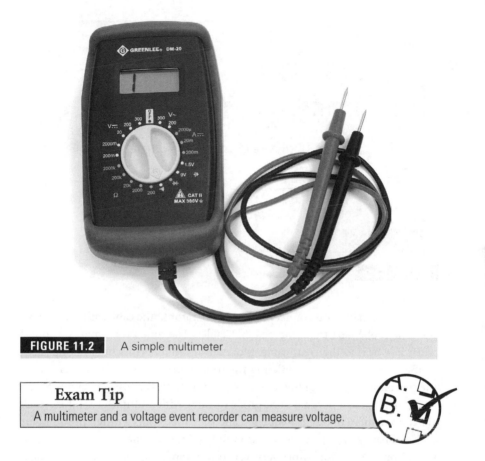

FIGURE 11.2 A simple multimeter

Exam Tip

A multimeter and a voltage event recorder can measure voltage.

Tone Locators and Toner Probes

Even in the best of networks, labels fall off ports and outlets, mystery cables disappear behind walls, and new cable runs are added without documentation. To help you figure out which end belongs to a cable when you are working with a stack of cables, you can use tone locators. A *toner* is a generic term for two separate devices that are used together: a tone generator and a tone probe. These two devices are often referred to as *Fox and Hound,* the brand name of a popular toner made by Triplett Corporation. The tone generator connects to a cable with alligator clips, tiny hooks, or a network jack, and it sends an electrical signal along the wire at a certain frequency. A tone probe emits a sound if it comes close to the cable to which the tone generator is connected (see Figure 11.3).

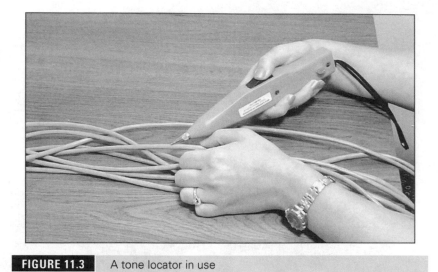

FIGURE 11.3   A tone locator in use

To trace a cable, you connect the tone generator to the cable, and then move the tone probe next to all the possible cables. The tone probe makes a sound when it is next to the right cable. More advanced toners include phone jacks, enabling the person manipulating the tone generator to communicate with the person manipulating the tone probe: "Jim, move the tone generator to the next port!" Some toners have one probe working with multiple generators. Each generator emits a different frequency, and the probe emits a different sound for each frequency. Good toners cost around US$75. Bad toners can cost less than US$25, but usually don't work very well. If you want to support a network, you'll need to own a toner.

Together, a good, medium-priced cable tester and a good toner are the most important tools used by folks who support, but don't install, networks. Be sure to add a few extra batteries—avoid the frustration of sitting on the top of a ladder holding a cable tester or toner that has just run out of juice!

Cable Testers

As the name implies, cable testers test cables. But before we can talk about cable testers, we have to determine what makes a cable bad. When troubleshooting cables, ask the following questions:

- How long is this cable?
- Is it over its rated length?

- Are any of the wires broken?

- If there is a break, where is it?

- Are any of the wires shorted together?

- Are any of the wires not in the correct order?

- Is there too much electrical or radio interference from external components?

Cable testers are designed to answer some or all of these questions, depending on the amount of money you are willing to pay. The low end of the cable-tester market consists of devices that test only for broken wires; these testers are often called *continuity testers*. Some cheap testers will also test for improperly wired cables, such as having the wires in a different order at either end, or they may test for shorts in the cable (see Figure 11.4).

Exam Tip

A *certifier* is a normal cable tester that will also report on characteristics such as speed and duplex settings. You might see this on the CompTIA Network+ exam as a *cable certifier.*

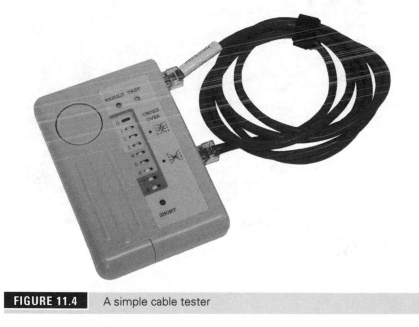

FIGURE 11.4   A simple cable tester

These cheap testers usually require you to insert both ends of the cable into the tester. That can be a little bit tough if the cable is already installed in the wall! A number of testers come in two parts so that you can connect the tester to a cable in the wiring room while taking the other part of the tester to the wall jack (located elsewhere) for that cable.

Medium-priced testers add the ability to tell you the length of the cables by switching the mode of the tester to what is usually known as the "length" mode. They also tell you where a break or short is located in a cable. These are generically called *Time-Domain Reflectometers,* or *TDRs* (see Figure 11.5). *Optical Time-Domain Reflectors* (OTDRs) serve the same purpose as TDRs, but are used for fiber-optic cabling.

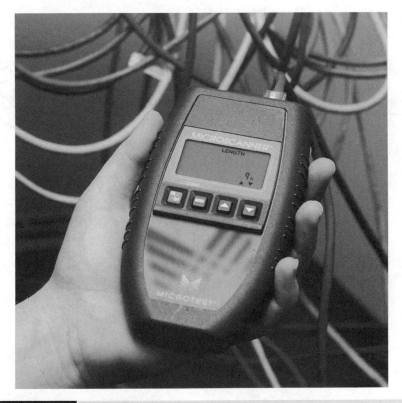

FIGURE 11.5 Time-Domain Reflectometer

The medium-priced testers have a small loopback device that gets inserted into the far end of the cable, enabling the tester to work with installed cables. This is the type of tester that you want. With a basic unit, you can plug in both ends of a patch lead, and the tester will check for correct wiring and open or short circuits. If you are testing a wall port, you generally fit a loopback plug into the socket at the other end to complete the circuit and enable testing.

A combination of troubleshooting methodology and test equipment will enable you to determine whether a particular cable is bad. In most troubleshooting situations, you will use other clues to determine whether you have a hardware or software problem. In the "I can't log in" scenario, for example, if you have determined that everyone else in the area can log in and that this user can log on from another location, you have narrowed the problem either to a configuration or hardware issue. If all network activity is broken (that is, if nothing is available on the network, or you can't ping the default gateway), you may choose to test cables by connecting the PC to the server. This is not the only option, but it is one variable that can be tested and eliminated.

Travel Advisory

When troubleshooting network problems, don't forget to check the simple stuff first—you can save yourself a lot of time. For example, make sure that cables are physically connected, or verify that the printer is online before trying more complicated solutions.

Exam Tip

Here are a few more tools you should be familiar with for the Network+ exam:
Butt set   Used to test telephone lines.
Cable stripper   Used to strip the covering off the cable. These are popular functions of cable crimpers that are used to cut and seal the connector on the end of the cable.

CHECKPOINT

✔ **Objective 11.01: The Troubleshooting Process** Follow the troubleshooting process to find solutions for your network's issues. Begin by identifying the problem. Establish a theory of probable cause, and then test that theory to determine if you were right. Once you've found the cause, establish a plan of action and identify potential effects. Test your solution or escalate the issue to someone else, if needed. Before leaving your client, verify full system functionality, implement preventative measures, and document the outcome.

✔ **Objective 11.02: Troubleshooting Network Hardware** Look for symptoms in your network hardware to track down potential issues. Watch out for cable issues, such as breaks, shorts, and incorrect cable wiring. Check the link lights on each piece of network hardware. Also look for crosstalk, high temperatures, interference, and other physical network issues.

✔ **Objective 11.03: Testing Equipment** Use the proper tools and equipment to test your network hardware. A multimeter checks for short circuits by measuring the resistance on the wires. A tone locator and toner probe, or Fox and Hound, helps you track down both ends of a network cable. A cable tester can tell you a lot about what is happening with your cables.

REVIEW QUESTIONS

1. Which of the following is the final step of the troubleshooting model?

   A. Establish a theory of probable cause.

   B. Test the solution.

   C. Document your findings.

   D. Establish a plan of action.

2. Susan cannot log in to the network. Which of the following would be the best question to ask first?

   A. "Tell me exactly what happens when you try to log in."

   B. "What did you do?"

   C. "What protocols are installed?"

   D. "Which operating system are you using?"

3. Which of the following are open-ended questions? (Select all that apply.)

   A. "Has anything been changed on the system recently?"

   B. "Can you see a power light on the monitor?"

   C. "What lights can you see on the monitor?"

   D. "Tell me what happens when you move the mouse."

4. Which of the following are physical network issues associated with network media? (Select all that apply.)

   A. Attenuation

   B. Crosstalk

   C. Wrong subnet mask

   D. Shorts

5. Which of the following steps should be first in a troubleshooting model?

   A. Document your findings.

   B. Test your theory.

   C. Identify the problem.

   D. Implement the solution.

6. Which of the following tools can identify a cabling fault due to an overlong segment?

   A. Multimeter

   B. TDR

   C. Tone locator

   D. Punch-down tool

7. Isabel suspects that electrical interference is affecting a segment of network cabling. What is one of the first things she should do to test her diagnosis?

   A. Use a TDR.

   B. Use a protocol analyzer.

   C. Install a length of optical fiber.

   D. Move the media.

8. Which of the following is used to test fiber-optic cabling?

   A. Multimeter

   B. Butt set

   C. OTDR

   D. TDR

9. Stella complains that her computer can't connect to the network. You theorize that her NIC might be faulty. What step should you follow next?

    A. Try replacing the NIC.

    B. Ask Stella what is wrong.

    C. Replace the cable with CAT 6.

    D. Verify her system works.

10. Abigail receives several reports that users are experiencing server connection issues. She walks to the server closet to investigate the issue and finds that it is incredibly humid inside. What should she have installed to avoid this problem?

    A. Cable tester

    B. Environmental monitor

    C. Temperature monitor

    D. Fox and Hound

REVIEW ANSWERS

1. **C**   Once you have solved the problem, always document your findings so that you or someone else may more quickly come to a solution next time.

2. **A**   Identify the problem by asking the user what happens when she attempts to log in.

3. **C**, **D**   Any question that cannot be answered with a "yes" or "no" is an open-ended question.

4. **A**, **B**, **D**   Using the wrong subnet mask would be a logical network issue, not a network media issue.

5. **C**   The troubleshooting theory begins by identifying the problem.

6. **B**   A TDR can accurately measure segment length. A multimeter cannot.

7. **D**   Try moving the affected media first before moving on to more complicated solutions.

8. **D**   An Optical Time Domain Reflectometer (OTDR) tests fiber-optic cabling.

9. **A**   Test your theory by replacing the NIC. If it works, verify full system functionality and document your findings.

10. **B**   An environmental monitor can track humidity; a temperature monitor does not.

Network Utilities
and Optimization

	NEWBIE	SOME EXPERIENCE	EXPERT
ETA	3 hours	2 hours	1 hour

You've seen the numerous problems that can crop up in network hardware and learned how to combat them. But how do you fix problems you can't see? In most cases, you'll have to do some extra digging to track down logical network problems. Many software tools can help you diagnose and repair network errors. You can also use many of these tools to increase and optimize a network's performance. A third category of tools helps you monitor a network's performance. This chapter provides an in-depth discussion of all of these tools.

Objective 12.01 TCP/IP Utilities

TCP/IP offers powerful troubleshooting utilities that all network techs should know. The CompTIA Network+ certification exam tests your knowledge of when to use each of the utilities discussed in this section, so be sure that you are familiar with these commands!

> **Travel Advisory**
>
> **Case matters** With command-line commands such as the ones you're about to study, make note of the case for each command. With few exceptions, learn all commands in lowercase. Windows doesn't care that much, but every other operating system cares a lot, and running a command with the improper case will result in a failed command.

ipconfig and ifconfig

When troubleshooting a system connected to the network, the first thing you will most likely want to find out is whether the system has an IP address. The following commands can be used to determine the IP settings on the system.

ipconfig

The *ipconfig* command is used in Windows to display the IP address information of the system. The following is a list of popular ipconfig commands:

- **ipconfig**   Displays the IP address, subnet mask, and default gateway
- **ipconfig /all**   Displays all TCP/IP settings and the MAC address
- **ipconfig /displaydns**   Displays the DNS resolver cache

- ipconfig /flushdns   Clears out the DNS resolver cache
- ipconfig /registerdns   Renews client DNS registration information

ifconfig

The *ifconfig* command displays or sets settings on a network card on a UNIX/ Linux/OS X system. The following is a list of popular ifconfig commands:

- **ifconfig**   Displays the network card and IP settings
- **ifconfig eth0 up**   Enables the first Ethernet card
- **ifconfig eth0 down**   Disables the Ethernet card

The *ping* utility (all operating systems) tests connections between two nodes. To test the connection between two nodes, sit at one of the systems and type in ping followed by the hostname or IP address of the other node. Ping uses the Internet Control Message Protocol (ICMP) to send an ICMP Echo Request to determine whether the other machine can receive the test packet and reply to it. A node that can be reached will respond, and the ping command will report success. Ping can also test for the availability of Internet-based services using fully qualified domain names (FQDNs), but note that some sites block ICMP Echo Requests to dissuade their sites from being used for testing—and some corporate Internet security systems also block ICMP Echo Requests to external sites. The output of the ping command looks like this:

```
C:\>ping 192.168.2.1
Pinging 192.168.2.1 with 32 bytes of data:
Reply from 192.168.2.1: bytes=32 time<10ms TTL=255
Reply from 192.168.2.1: bytes=32 time<10ms TTL=255
Reply from 192.168.2.1: bytes=32 time<10ms TTL=255
Reply from 192.168.2.1: bytes=32 time<10ms TTL=255
Ping statistics for 192.168.2.1:
    Packets: Sent = 4, Received = 4, Lost = 0 (0% loss),
Approximate round trip times in milli-seconds:
    Minimum = 0ms, Maximum =  0ms, Average =  0ms

C:\PING www.google.com
Pinging www.google.com [216.239.33.100] with 32 bytes of data:
Reply from 216.239.33.100: bytes=32 time=270ms TTL=49
Reply from 216.239.33.100: bytes=32 time=271ms TTL=49
Reply from 216.239.33.100: bytes=32 time=270ms TTL=49
Reply from 216.239.33.100: bytes=32 time=271ms TTL=49
Ping statistics for 216.239.33.100:

    Packets: Sent = 4, Received = 4, Lost = 0 (0% loss),
Approximate round trip times in milli-seconds:
    Minimum = 270ms, Maximum =  271ms, Average =  270ms

C:\ping www.madethisup.com
Unknown host www.madethisup.com.
```

You should read the messages ping reports back when it cannot reach another machine. They can contain important clues about the source of the problem.

If ping cannot turn a name into an IP address, for example, it will report back, "Unknown host" or some similar message. (The exact message returned by the ping command varies depending on the operating system.) If ping resolves an IP address but cannot reach the specified address, ping will display a different message, such as "Destination host unreachable." Keep the following points in mind when you receive such a message:

- **Unknown host**   This message means, "I don't know the IP address!" You probably specified an invalid/unused DNS name.

- **Destination host unreachable**   This message means, "I can't get to that IP address." In this case, you should check for possible routing problems—for example, have you specified a default gateway?

If a seemingly valid host is specified but that host doesn't appear to be responding, you will see a sequence similar to the following:

```
C:\> ping 192.168.2.223
Pinging 192.168.2.223 with 32 bytes of data:
Request timed out.
Request timed out.
Request timed out.
Request timed out.
Ping statistics for 192.168.2.223:
    Packets: Sent = 4, Received = 0, Lost = 4 (100% loss),
Approximate round trip times in milli-seconds:
    Minimum = 0ms, Maximum =  0ms, Average =  0ms
```

tracert

The *tracert* (or *traceroute* on UNIX/Linux/OS X systems) command traces the route between two hosts. The tracert command will send back a response with each router it hits. This enables you to determine if communication is slow because a link has gone down between your computer and the destination. If you know that three routers are normally between you and the destination, and the tracert returns six responses, you know that your packets are taking an indirect pathway (due to a link being down). The following listing shows a trace to the Total Seminars' web server from a machine in the UK (the –d switch tells tracert to display IP addresses without the corresponding domain names):

```
C:\> tracert -d www.totalsem.com
Tracing route to www.totalsem.com [64.226.214.168]
over a maximum of 30 hops:
```

```
 1  <10 ms   <10 ms   <10 ms   192.168.2.1
 2   80 ms    70 ms    80 ms   194.159.254.93
 3   80 ms    90 ms    90 ms   194.159.254.100
 4   90 ms    91 ms    90 ms   194.159.252.54
 5   90 ms   100 ms    90 ms   194.159.36.234
 6   90 ms    90 ms    90 ms   213.206.130.81
 7   81 ms    90 ms    90 ms   213.206.128.41
 8  130 ms   131 ms   120 ms   213.206.129.38
 9  130 ms   120 ms   121 ms   80.77.64.33
10  200 ms   200 ms   201 ms   144.232.19.29
11  210 ms   210 ms   211 ms   144.232.19.98
12  210 ms   200 ms   211 ms   144.232.7.253
13  220 ms   211 ms   220 ms   144.232.9.198
14  220 ms   221 ms   220 ms   144.232.12.18
15  220 ms   221 ms   220 ms   160.81.204.10
16  220 ms   221 ms   220 ms   64.224.0.99
17  230 ms   221 ms   240 ms   totalsem.com [64.226.214.168]
Trace complete.
```

Exam Tip

The ping and traceroute commands are excellent examples of *connectivity software,* utilities that enable you to determine if a connection can be made between two computers.

---

arp

The *arp* utility (Windows) helps diagnose problems associated with the Address Resolution Protocol (ARP). TCP/IP hosts use arp to determine the physical (MAC) address that corresponds with a specific logical (IP) address. The arp utility, when used with the –a option, displays any IP addresses that have been resolved to MAC addresses recently. Here's an example:

```
C:\>arp -a
Interface: 192.168.43.5 on Interface 0x1000002
  Internet Address   Physical Address   Type
  192.168.43.2       00-40-05-60-7f-64  dynamic
  192.168.43.3       00-40-05-5b-71-51  dynamic
  192.168.43.4       00-a0-c9-98-97-7f  dynamic
```

netstat

The *netstat* command (all operating systems) enables a network tech to examine network statistics about a system. These statistics include information such as the ports listening on the system and any connections that have been established. The following is some output from the netstat command:

```
C:\>netstat
Active Connections
```

```
Proto  Local Address  Foreign Address  State
TCP    brian:1030     BRIAN:1274  ESTABLISHED
TCP    brian:2666     totalsem.com:pop3  TIME_WAIT
TCP    brian:2670     totalsem.com:pop3  TIME_WAIT
TCP    brian:2672     www.cnn.com:80  TIME_WAIT
TCP    brian:2674     www.nytimes.com:80  ESTABLISHED
TCP    brian:2460     MARSPDC:nbsession  ESTABLISHED
TCP    brian:1273     NOTES01:2986  TIME_WAIT
TCP    brian:1274     BRIAN:1030  ESTABLISHED
```

The netstat command can provide a wide range of information depending on the command-line switches used. Type `netstat /?` at a command prompt to list the optional command-line switches:

```
NETSTAT [-a] [-e] [-n] [-o] [-s] [-p proto] [-r] [interval]
  -a        Displays all connections and listening ports.
  -e        Displays Ethernet statistics. This may be
            combined with the -s option.
  -n        Displays addresses and port numbers in numerical
            form.
  -o        Displays the owning process ID associated with
            each connection.
  -p proto  Shows connections for the protocol specified by
            proto; proto may be any of: TCP, UDP, TCPv6, or
            UDPv6.  If used with the -s option to display
            per-protocol statistics, proto may be any of:
            IP, IPv6, ICMP, ICMPv6, TCP, TCPv6, UDP, or UDPv6.
  -r        Displays the routing table.
  -s        Displays per-protocol statistics.  By default,
            statistics are shown for IP, IPv6, ICMP, ICMPv6,
            TCP, TCPv6, UDP, and UDPv6; the -p option may be
            used to specify a subset of the default.
  interval  Redisplays selected statistics, pausing interval
            seconds between each display.  Press CTRL+C to stop
            redisplaying statistics.  If omitted, netstat will
            print the current configuration information once.
```

nbtstat

For backward compatibility with some truly ancient local area networking (LAN) applications, Microsoft implements the NetBIOS over TCP (NBT) protocol in Windows. This manifests in a couple of ways. First, every Windows PC has a distinct NetBIOS name. My computer's name, for example, is Mike7. Second, you can use a specific utility to interact with other Windows computers on a LAN.

The *nbtstat* (NetBIOS over TCP/IP statistics) command enables a network tech to check information about the NetBIOS names. This includes viewing the names that have been registered by the local system (nbtstat –n), viewing the names registered by a remote system (nbtstat –A), and viewing the NetBIOS name cache (nbtstat –c), which shows the NetBIOS names and corresponding

IP addresses that have been resolved by a particular host. Here's some sample output:

```
C:\>NBTSTAT -c
Node IpAddress: [192.168.43.5] Scope Id: []

                 NetBIOS Remote Cache Name Table
    Name                Type         Host Address      Life [sec]
    =========================================================
    WRITERS      <1B>   UNIQUE       192.168.43.13       420
    DAN          <20>   UNIQUE       192.168.43.3        420
    VENUSPDC     <00>   UNIQUE       192.168.43.13       120
    GLEN         <20>   UNIQUE       192.168.43.2        420
    NOTES01      <20>   UNIQUE       192.168.43.4        420
```

When properly used, nbtstat helps network techs diagnose and troubleshoot NetBIOS problems, especially those related to NetBIOS name resolution.

Like netstat, nbtstat can provide a wealth of information using different switches. Here are some of the popular switches:

```
NBTSTAT [ [-a RemoteName] [-A IP address] [-c] [-n]
[-r] [-R] [-RR] [-s] [-S] [interval] ]

   -a  Lists the remote machine's name table given its name
   -A  Lists the remote machine's name table given its IP address
   -c  Lists NBT's cache of remote [machine] names and their IP
       addresses
   -n  Lists local NetBIOS names
   -R  Purges and reloads the remote cache name table
```

Exam Tip

Note that nbtstat enables you to purge and reload the NetBIOS name cache with the command nbtstat –R. Remember that, unlike most Windows command-line utilities, nbtstat is case-sensitive when it comes to its switches. Therefore, nbtstat –R and nbtstat –r are not the same command.

nslookup

The *nslookup* command provides a command-line utility for diagnosing DNS problems. All operating systems support this tool. Its most basic function returns the IP address, as shown here:

```
C:\>nslookup example.com
Server:  dns.example.com
Address:  192.168.31.211
Non-authoritative answer:
Name:  server1.example.com
Address:  192.68.67.12
```

The nslookup command also offers an interactive mode that enables you to specify a wide range of options as you diagnose and troubleshoot DNS issues. To see the full range of options, type ? at the nslookup prompt in Windows:

```
> ?
Commands:  (identifiers are shown in uppercase, [] means optional)
NAME            - print info about the host/domain NAME using
                      default server
NAME1 NAME2     - as above, but use NAME2 as server
help or ?       - print info on common commands
set OPTION      - set an option
    all                  - print options, current server and host
    [no]debug            - print debugging information
    [no]d2               - print exhaustive debugging information
    [no]defname          - append domain name to each query
    [no]recurse          - ask for recursive answer to query
    [no]search           - use domain search list
    [no]vc               - always use a virtual circuit
    domain=NAME          - set default domain name to NAME
    srchlist=N1[/N2/.../N6] - set domain to N1 and search list
                                to N1,N2, etc.
    root=NAME            - set root server to NAME
    retry=X              - set number of retries to X
    timeout=X            - set initial time-out interval to X
                             seconds
    type=X               - set query type (ex. A,ANY,CNAME,MX,NS,
                             PTR,SOA,SRV)
    querytype=X          - same as type
    class=X              - set query class (ex. IN (Internet),
                             ANY)
    [no]msxfr            - use MS fast zone transfer
    ixfrver=X            - current version to use in IXFR transfer
                             request
server NAME     - set default server to NAME, using current
                      default server
lserver NAME    - set default server to NAME, using initial
                      server
finger [USER]   - finger the optional NAME at the current
                      default host
root            - set current default server to the root
ls [opt] DOMAIN [> FILE] - list addresses in DOMAIN (optional:
                                output to FILE)
    -a                   - list canonical names and aliases
    -d                   - list all records
    -t TYPE              - list records of the given type (e.g.
                             A,CNAME,MX,NS,PTR etc.)
view FILE                - sort an 'ls' output file and view it
                             with pg exit  - exit the program
>
```

In UNIX/Linux/OS X you get the detailed nslookup options by typing **man nslookup** from the terminal prompt.

Using command-line utilities such as ping, tracert, arp, netstat, nbtstat, and nslookup, an experienced network tech can diagnose most TCP/IP problems quickly and begin working on solutions. If two hosts can ping each other by IP address but not by name, for example, the wise network tech knows to leave the routers alone and concentrate on name resolution issues instead.

To function effectively as a network tech, you need to learn TCP/IP. Supported by all operating systems, the TCP/IP suite provides excellent tools for integrating multiple operating systems within the same network. Its importance will continue to grow as the Internet continues to increase its importance in both business and everyday life.

arping

The *arping* utility is a popular UNIX/Linux/OS X command that combines the ping and arp commands together. When you use `arping` and specify the IP address to ping, it will return replies (like ping) if the system is up, but it will return the MAC address to you in the reply. Here is sample arping output:

```
ARPING 192.168.4.27 from 192.168.4.19 eth0
Unicast reply from 192.168.4.27 [00:1D:60:DD:92:C6]  0.875ms
Unicast reply from 192.168.4.27 [00:1D:60:DD:92:C6]  0.897ms
Unicast reply from 192.168.4.27 [00:1D:60:DD:92:C6]  0.924ms
Unicast reply from 192.168.4.27 [00:1D:60:DD:92:C6]  0.977ms
```

dig

In addition to nslookup, UNIX/Linux/OS X systems offer another DNS diagnostic utility called *dig*. The dig command has a number of useful switches, and the most popular uses of dig are listed here:

dig www.totalsem.com	Shows the IP address of the FQDN and shows the DNS server that gave the answer
dig www.totalsem.com +short	Displays the short answer—the IP address of the FQDN
dig –x 192.168.5.200	Does a reverse DNS lookup of the IP address and reports to you the FQDN of the system

The dig example shows the output of this command:

```
dig mx totalsem.com
```

This command says, "Show me all the MX records for the totalsem.com domain."

Here's the output for that dig command:

```
; <<>> DiG 9.5.0-P2 <<>> mx totalsem.com
;; global options:  printcmd
;; Got answer:
;; ->>HEADER<<- opcode: QUERY, status: NOERROR, id: 6070
;; flags: qr rd ra; QUERY: 1, ANSWER: 3, AUTHORITY: 0, ADDITIONAL: 1
;; QUESTION SECTION:
;totalsem.com.                    IN        MX
;; ANSWER SECTION:
totalsem.com.   86400   IN  MX  10
mx1c1.megamailservers.com.
totalsem.com.   86400            IN        MX       100
mx2c1.megamailservers.com.
totalsem.com.   86400            IN        MX       110
mx3c1.megamailservers.com.
```

mtr

The *mtr* command (UNIX/Linux/OS X) is a network diagnostics utility that combines the features of tracert and ping together. When you use mtr, it will send ping messages to each router along the route and report back to you diagnostics information, such as how long it took, how many packets were sent and received, and the percent of lost packets. Here's a sample of mtr output:

```
                          My traceroute  [v0.73]
totaltest (0.0.0.0)
Keys:  Help  Display mode  Restart statistics  Order of fields  quit
                                 Packets              Pings
Host                           Loss% Snt  Last   Avg  Best  Wrst StDev
1. Router.totalhome             0.0%   5  0.8   0.8   0.7   0.9   0.1
2. adsl-208-190-121-38.dsl.hstntx.s 0.0%  4 85.7  90.7  69.5  119.2  20.8
```

route

The *route* command is a Windows command used to manage the local routing table of a system. For example, to view the Windows routing table, you can use the route print command, and to add a route to your Windows routing table, you can use the route add command. Here's a sample of route print output:

```
================================================================
Interface List
8 ...00 1d 60 dd 92 c6 ...... Marvell 88E8056 PCI-E Ethernet Controller
1 ........................... Software Loopback Interface 1
================================================================
IPv4 Route Table
================================================================
Active Routes:
Network Destination        Netmask          Gateway    Interface         Metric
0.0.0.0                    0.0.0.0      192.168.4.1    192.168.4.27          10
127.0.0.0                255.0.0.0         On-link     127.0.0.1            306
127.0.0.1          255.255.255.255         On-link     127.0.0.1            306
127.255.255.255    255.255.255.255         On-link     127.0.0.1            306
169.254.0.0            255.255.0.0         On-link     192.168.4.27         286
169.254.214.185    255.255.255.255         On-link     169.254.214.185      276
169.254.255.255    255.255.255.255         On-link     192.168.4.27         266
192.168.4.0          255.255.255.0         On-link     192.168.4.27         266
192.168.4.27       255.255.255.255         On-link     192.168.4.27         266
192.168.4.255      255.255.255.255         On-link     192.168.4.27         266
224.0.0.0                240.0.0.0         On-link     127.0.0.1            306
224.0.0.0                240.0.0.0         On-link     169.254.214.185      276
224.0.0.0                240.0.0.0         On-link     192.168.4.27         266
255.255.255.255    255.255.255.255         On-link     127.0.0.1            306
255.255.255.255    255.255.255.255         On-link     169.254.214.185      276
255.255.255.255    255.255.255.255         On-link     192.168.4.27         266
================================================================
Persistent Routes:

None
```

Objective 12.02 Troubleshooting Network Performance

A number of logical network issues can arise when you're troubleshooting the network. Logical issues range from configuring a system with the wrong IP address or subnet masks to placing the system in the wrong VLAN. Here are some examples:

- **Port speed and duplex mismatch** If a system can't connect to the network, double-check that the speed and duplex settings of the card are set correctly.

- **Incorrect VLAN** Miscommunication can occur if you place a system on the wrong VLAN. Remember that a system on one VLAN cannot normally talk to a system on another VLAN unless you are routing between VLANs.

- **Incorrect or duplicate IP address** You may have mistyped the IP address of a system and thus the address you're trying to use won't work. A duplicated IP address won't let the duplicate node communicate, but always tells you that it's a duplicate address.

- **Wrong gateway** If you have trouble communicating off the network, it's typically a routing issue. Check the default gateway settings on all the systems to verify that they are pointing to the IP address of the router interface on your network.

- **Wrong DNS** If you can communicate by the IP address but not by the DNS name of a system, you most likely have a name resolution problem. Check the IP address you have configured on the system as the DNS server entry.

- **Wrong subnet mask** If you have the wrong subnet mask typed into the TCP/IP properties, this will cause miscommunication. When you check the IP address of a system, also verify that you are using the correct subnet mask.

- **Bad/missing routes** Even with dynamic routing protocols enabling routers to update routes without human intervention, human intervention happens at some stage of the process. An erroneous forwarding entry statically entered, for example, might become invalid later on. If the routers can't synchronize, they might report a missing route.

Protocol Analyzers

Things are getting a bit heavy when you reach for a protocol analyzer, because this means that you're checking out your network at a very fundamental level by analyzing individual data packets on the network. Software-based protocol or network analyzers (also called *packet sniffers*) include applications such as the Network Monitor (NetMon) provided with Windows Servers.

> **Exam Tip**
>
> The CompTIA Network+ exam calls both protocol and network analyzing tools *network sniffers*.

Use these tools when unexplained slowdowns occur on your network to help you determine which machines are possibly sending rogue or malformed packets. A *protocol analyzer* enables you to determine whether a broadcast storm (or just too much broadcasting in general) is occurring or whether a faulty NIC is installed in a machine that is flooding the network with malformed packets.

> **Travel Assistance**
>
> **Wireshark**   The protocol analyzer tool that every tech uses is called *Wireshark*. It performs beautifully and can analyze packets thoroughly. You can find it here: www.wireshark.org.

Protocol analyzers can serve many purposes: In addition to identifying faulty hardware, they can help determine whether any faulty software is on the network that might be sending out dodgy data, and sometimes they can even help trace intermittent faults, such as cabling problems (though other, simpler diagnostic steps can usually be taken first, employing some of the troubleshooting methods and tools discussed earlier).

Throughput Testers

Throughput testers enable you to measure the data flow in a network. Which tool is appropriate depends on the type of network throughput you want to test. Most techs use one of several speed-testing websites for checking an Internet connection's throughput, such as Speed Test at Speakeasy (Figure 12.1): www.speakeasy.net/speedtest.

Network Performance Optimization

A number of applications, such as VoIP or video-streaming applications, require a lot of bandwidth. And some applications, such as web servers and e-mail servers, can have performance optimized through caching features or through load balancing and high-availability solutions. The following features can be used to optimize performance of networking applications.

FIGURE 12.1 Speed Test results from Speakeasy

Caching

Caching is the process of storing data that someone asks for in the hope that someone else will ask for it again. Generally, odds are incredibly good that anytime anyone asks for anything on the Internet, either they or other folks on your LAN will ask for the same thing again—and that's why caching works so well in so many different ways. Caching reduces network workload by eliminating the processes required to reacquire data. Caching reduces network traffic and server workloads.

You can also employ dedicated cache servers on your network. These network appliances—CompTIA calls them *caching engines*—can work at just about any level, such as LAN or WAN, and reduce overall network traffic dramatically. One example is EngageIP Cache Server. Cisco has also produced these appliances, though now the caching is part of boxes with more integrated functions.

More commonly today, you'll find caching server functions as part of software services. Squid, for example, is a proxy and caching server that handles HTTP, DNS, FTP, and more. You can deploy Squid on multiple servers and use the *Cache Array Routing Protocol (CARP)* to load balance among them all, optimizing network performance (at least for HTTP).

Controlling Data Throughput

Former U.S. Senator Ted Stevens got a lot of teasing a few years ago by describing the Internet as "a series of tubes," but there's actually a strong argument for the idea of tubes when discussing the amount of data per second any given Internet connection may need. Unless your budget allows you to buy a "big tube" connection to the Internet, every network suffers from a limited amount of bandwidth that's rarely truly sufficient for everything your users need. Even if you're lucky enough to have good bandwidth today, ongoing network growth guarantees you'll eventually run into network slowdowns as demand grows.

There's no magic point at which a network goes from working well to working slowly. Most people are used to having to wait a bit for a webpage or a file transfer. Certain applications, called *latency-sensitive* applications, do not perform well when they lack adequate bandwidth. Some latency-sensitive applications require high bandwidth. Streaming video is a great example. Have you ever watched a video on YouTube that constantly stops and starts? At least YouTube enables you to pause the video so it can load more before you continue watching (Figure 12.2).

Try watching a video on Hulu.com (Figure 12.3) over an overly busy or slow connection. Hulu, unlike YouTube but like most other video sites, only caches a few seconds (to prevent people from stealing the video) and is all but unwatchable if there are constant stops and starts. Voice over IP (VoIP) applications are another great example. If every conversation is clipped...and... chopped...the beauty of VoIP falls apart.

Latency sensitivity takes on a whole new level of importance when you get into *unified communications (UC)*, where you roll all kinds of these services into one box: VoIP, instant messaging (IM), telephone service, video conferencing, and more. If you can't control the bandwidth, your network won't function properly.

When the size of your Internet pipe is limited, you need some method to throttle bandwidth so that in high-demand times, latency-sensitive applications get more bandwidth at the cost of reducing bandwidth to those applications that don't mind the wait. The CompTIA Network+ exam mentions two of the most common: Quality of Service (QoS) and traffic shaping, but I'll tell you about a few other solutions, as well.

FIGURE 12.2   Pausing a video on YouTube

Quality of Service   Quality of Service (QoS) is a procedure used almost exclusively on gateway devices to give certain applications priority when a connection reaches a certain amount of utilization. QoS works at layer 2 and layer 3 of the OSI model and works with 802.1Q trunks to prioritize traffic. QoS applies a *Class of Service (CoS)* priority (0 to 7) to a certain port. As traffic from that port goes through a trunk line, its priority defines how much bandwidth is allocated. The higher the priority of traffic, the more bandwidth it gets. This form of QoS is specialized when you have a high-priority file server or VoIP server systems connected to your network.

Exam Tip

QoS can also reduce jitter on VoIP connections.

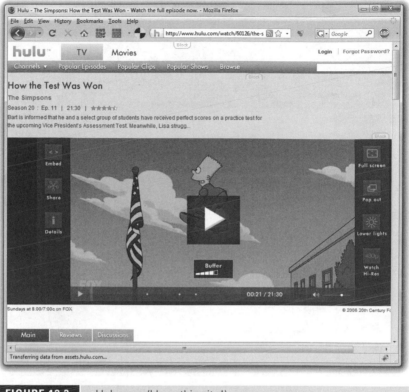

FIGURE 12.3   Hulu.com (I love this site!)

Traffic Shaping   Traffic shaping (also called *bandwidth shaping*) prioritizes traffic in various ways, such as by analyzing TCP/UDP port numbers or by examining the Application-layer information in packets. Traffic shaping works in one of two ways: by giving certain packets a priority or by directly assigning a fixed amount of bandwidth (in bits/sec) to packets from a particular application based on port number.

> **Local Lingo**
>
> When ISPs limit traffic based on applications to customers, it is called *bandwidth throttling.*

A typical setup of traffic shaping first requires you to tell the router the total upstream and downstream bandwidth of your connection. From there, you assign bandwidth to a particular application, as shown in Figure 12.4.

QoS and traffic shaping give you a number of tools to control traffic. You can control or prioritize traffic based on port/MAC address (QoS), IP address, or

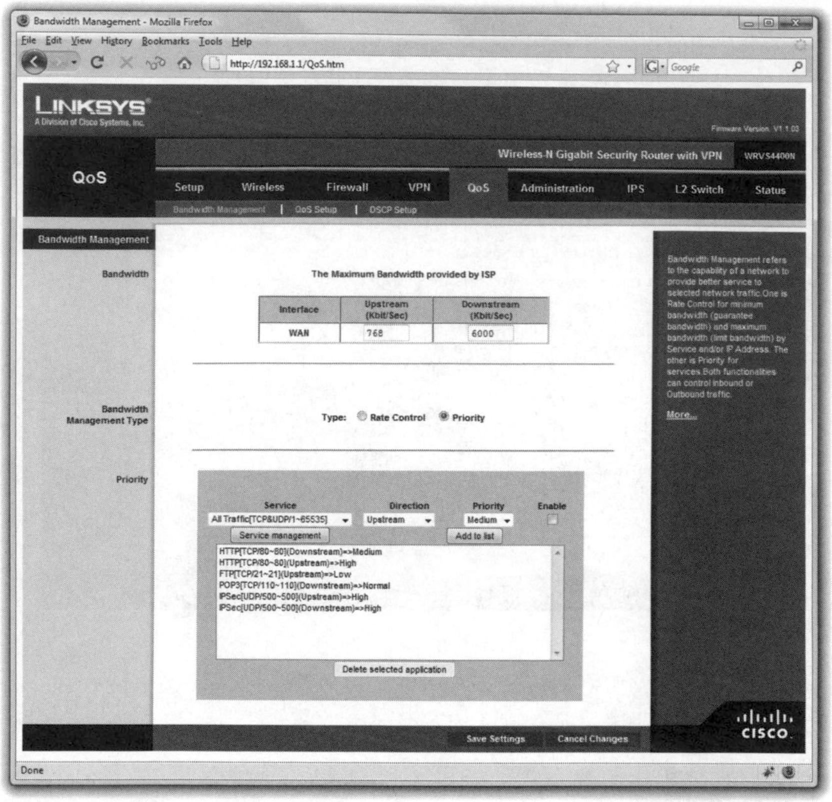

FIGURE 12.4   Traffic shaping on a SOHO router

application. The choice depends on the equipment you choose and the needs of your networks.

Load Balancing   Load balancing is used most by web servers. The administrator loads the website on multiple web servers and then uses load-balancing software to split the requests sent to that website between two (or more) systems.

DNS is an easy way to load-balance, but it still relies on multiple DNS servers, each with its own IP address. As web clients access one DNS server or another, they cache that DNS server's IP address. The next time they access the server, they go directly to the cached DNS server and skip the round robin, reducing its effectiveness.

To hide all of your web servers behind a single IP, you have two popular choices. First is to use a special multilayer switch that works at layers 3 and 4. This switch is really just a router that performs NAT and port forwarding, but also has the capability to query the hidden web servers continually and send HTTP requests to a server that has a lighter workload than the other servers.

The second option is to use a *content switch*. Content switches always work at layer 7 (Application layer). Content switches designed to work with web servers, therefore, are able to read the incoming HTTP and HTTPS requests. With this, you can perform very advanced actions, such as handling SSL certificates and cookies on the content switch, removing the workload from the web servers. Not only can these devices load-balance in the ways previously described, but their HTTP savvy can actually pass a cookie to HTTP requesters—web browsers—so the next time that client returns, it is sent to the same server (Figure 12.5).

Exam Tip

The CompTIA Network+ exam refers to a content switch as a *content filter* network appliance.

High Availability   High availability is a popular solution for e-mail and database servers. High availability means a spare server is ready to kick in when the primary server fails. This process is automatic and handled by the high-availability software, such as Windows Clustering and server farms.

Fault Tolerance   Fault tolerance ensures that the data is duplicated across multiple drives so that the data can still be retrieved if a drive fails. Most servers implement fault-tolerant solutions such as mirrored volumes or RAID 5 volumes.

ISPs and MTUs

I discussed the maximum transmission unit (MTU) in Chapter 6. Back in the dark ages (before Windows Vista), Microsoft users often found themselves with terrible connection problems due to the fact that IP packets were too big to fit

FIGURE 12.5   Layer-7 content switch

into certain network protocols. The largest Ethernet packet is 1500 bytes, so some earlier versions of Windows set their MTU size to a value less than 1500 to minimize the fragmentation of packets. The problem cropped up when you tried to connect to a technology other than Ethernet, such as DSL. Some DSL carriers couldn't handle an MTU size greater than 1400. When your network's packets are so large that they must be fragmented to fit into your Internet service provider's packets, we call it an *MTU mismatch*.

As a result, techs would tweak their MTU settings to improve throughput by matching up the MTU sizes between the ISP and their own network. This usually required a manual registry setting adjustment, although some older versions of Windows used third-party programs like Dr. TCP (Figure 12.6). This process is called "matching up" mismatched MTU settings.

Travel Advisory

Dr. TCP is an old program and does not work on Windows Vista or 7. Don't use it anymore; you don't have to, either, because of Path MTU Discovery.

Around 2007, *Path MTU Discovery (PMTU)*, a new method to determine the best MTU setting automatically, was created. PMTU works by adding a new feature called the "Don't Fragment (DF) flag" to the IP packet. A PMTU-aware operating system can automatically send a series of fixed-size ICMP packets (basically just pings) with the DF flag set to another device to see if it works. If it

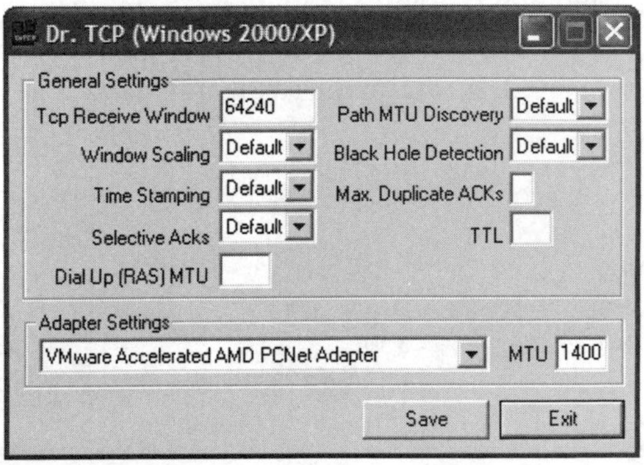

FIGURE 12.6 Adjusting the MTU settings in Dr. TCP

doesn't work, the system lowers the MTU size and tries again until the ping is successful.

You can imitate this feature by running a ping yourself. Open a command prompt and run the following command:

```
ping www.totalsem.com -f -l 1500
```

You should get results similar to the following:

```
Pinging www.totalsem.com [216.40.231.195] with 1500 bytes of data:
Packet needs to be fragmented but DF set.
Packet needs to be fragmented but DF set.
Packet needs to be fragmented but DF set.
Packet needs to be fragmented but DF set.

Ping statistics for 216.40.231.195:
    Packets: Sent = 4, Received = 0, Lost = 4 (100% loss),
```

Try running the ping command again, this time setting the MTU size smaller:

```
C:\>ping www.totalsem.com -f -l 1400

Pinging www.totalsem.com [216.40.231.195] with 1400 bytes of data:
Reply from 216.40.231.195: bytes=1400 time=81ms TTL=51
Reply from 216.40.231.195: bytes=1400 time=85ms TTL=51
Reply from 216.40.231.195: bytes=1400 time=134ms TTL=51
Reply from 216.40.231.195: bytes=1400 time=144ms TTL=51

Ping statistics for 216.40.231.195:
    Packets: Sent = 4, Received = 4, Lost = 0 (0% loss),
Approximate round trip times in milli-seconds:
    Minimum = 81ms, Maximum = 144ms, Average = 111ms
```

Imagine the hassle of incrementing the MTU size manually. That's the beauty of PMTU—you can automatically set your MTU size to the perfect amount.

Unfortunately, PMTU runs under ICMP; most routers have firewall features that, by default, are configured to block ICMP requests, making PMTU worthless. This is called a *PMTU* or *MTU black hole*. If you're having terrible connection problems and you've checked everything else, you need to consider this issue. In many cases, going into the router and turning off ICMP blocking in the firewall is all you need to do to fix the problem.

Exam Tip

The CompTIA Network+ objectives use the term *MUT/MTU black holes*. There's no such thing as "MUT" so, hopefully, CompTIA will have fixed this by the time you're reading this book.

Objective 12.03 Monitoring Networks

Networking technicians need to know how to use the tools that are available to monitor network performance and connectivity. A network administrator sets up the tools you use, but a tech needs to know how to use those tools to create baselines, monitoring utilities, and logs of various sorts.

Establishing a Baseline

The best way to know when a problem is brewing is to know how things perform when all's well with the system. Part of any proper configuration management documentation is a *baseline*: a log of performance indicators such as CPU usage, network utilization, and other values to give you a picture of your network and servers when they are working correctly. A major change in these values can point to problems on a server or the network as a whole.

All operating systems come with some form of baseline tools. A common tool used to create a baseline on Windows systems is the Performance Monitor utility that comes with all versions of Windows.

Performance Monitor

Administrators use *Performance Monitor* (also called PerfMon) to view the behavior of hardware and other resources on Windows machines, either locally or remotely. Performance Monitor can both monitor real-time performance and display historical data about the performance of your systems. Figure 12.7 shows the default Performance Monitor in Windows 7.

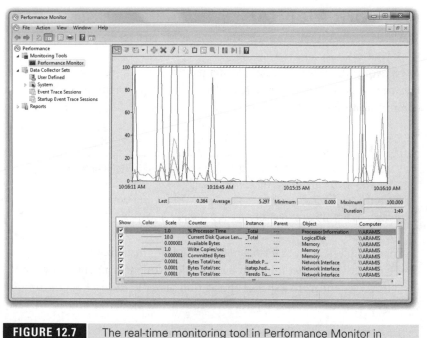

FIGURE 12.7 The real-time monitoring tool in Performance Monitor in Windows 7

Exam Tip

The CompTIA Network+ exam is not going to test you on using Performance Monitor or any other baselining tool. Just make sure you understand what a baseline does for you.

Windows 2000/XP calls the real-time monitoring section of Performance Monitor the System Monitor. Windows Vista/7 calls it Performance Monitor. Regardless of the name, this is the tool that enables you to view network performance.

Unfortunately, you can't just turn on Performance Monitor and instantly collect data. You'll need to choose what device or connection to monitor, how to monitor it, and how to display the data. If you want to record data for later use, you can configure Performance Monitor to log the data, too.

Network Monitor

The Network Monitor (another Microsoft tool) enables you to monitor network traffic.

Network Monitor is an example of a packet analyzer (see Figure 12.8), also known as a packet sniffer or LAN analyzer, that helps diagnose problems with communication over the network.

Exam Tip

A packet analyzer, also known as a packet sniffer, is used to monitor network traffic and view the packets that pass through the network. Microsoft's Network Monitor and a free program called Wireshark (www .wireshark.org) are examples of packet sniffers.

For example, let's say that you are responsible for installing a new sales application on each computer found in the sales department. This application, after installed, will connect to a special application server in the back room running the server part of the sales application. You install the server and client parts

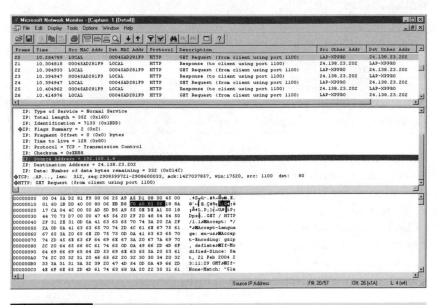

FIGURE 12.8 Looking at Network Monitor

without a hitch! You start up the client application on Sean's computer, but it is having trouble connecting to the server portion of the application.

You know nothing about this application, and you have followed the installation instructions—what can you do? One of the first things you can do is run Network Monitor and see what port on the server the client is trying to connect to—maybe the server port is configured incorrectly. This is the type of thing that Network Monitor is good at doing—monitoring traffic and displaying the contents of a discussion between two systems.

You can install Network Monitor on a Windows server through Add/Remove Programs. When in Add/Remove Programs, go to Add/Remove Windows Components and select Management and Monitoring Tools; then click the Details button. In the Details screen, select Network Monitor Tools.

Travel Advisory

The version of Network Monitor that comes with the Server versions of Windows enables you to capture data being sent only through the network card of the system doing the monitoring. For a free full-blown packet analyzer, check out Wireshark, which is similar to Network Monitor but can be installed on Windows clients, servers, and Linux systems.

Once you have the program installed, start it from the Administrative Tools menu. After the program has loaded, click the Start Capture button on the toolbar to start recording network traffic. While recording, generate the type of traffic that you want to analyze, and then stop recording by clicking the Stop and View Capture button. Now you can start analyzing your network traffic!

Exam Tip

Be aware that Network Monitor and Wireshark are also examples of network *traffic analyzers.*

Checking System Logs

Most network operating systems and modern client systems maintain their own log files, and it is important that you check these logs on a regular basis—once a day is a good idea, especially for servers. Checking the logs achieves two things:

It can tell you *why* a certain problem has occurred, and it can alert you to a problem that may get worse if not treated—for example, a log file can alert you to "timeout errors" from a hard disk that's having problems reading or writing data—*before* it dies!

Especially with a fault-tolerant server, examining the system logs regularly is vital because some component failures will be logged, but because the system has redundant items, the server may still run as if nothing bad has happened. It's both good and bad to discover that one of your mirrored drives actually failed several weeks ago without anyone noticing—good that the system kept running, but bad that no one realized that a disk replacement was needed to maintain full fault tolerance.

Logs and Network Traffic

Every operating system, and many applications, generate log files automatically that record events, actions, errors, and more. You can also use programs to generate custom logs. A skilled network administrator or technician can use various tools on log files to, among other things, analyze network traffic to determine problem areas.

> ### Exam Tip
>
> Most UNIX/Linux distributions and many Windows applications use *syslog* as the basic building block for logging messages and doing custom logs. Eric Allman developed Syslog in the 1980s as a logging program for e-mail, but it has grown into a general logging tool today.

Logs fall into several categories, such as general, system, and history. You see *general logs* in tools like Windows Event Viewer. These record updates to applications, for example, and aren't terribly interesting from a networking standpoint. Linux systems tend to have lots of logs, but most versions have a directory called /var/log where all of your logs (usually) reside. Mac OS X has roughly the same logs as Linux.

System logs display events such as login attempts, reboots needed for changes to OS files, and similar things (Figure 12.9). System logs (and security logs in Windows) can be important for finding security problems, but like general logs, they don't do much for network optimization.

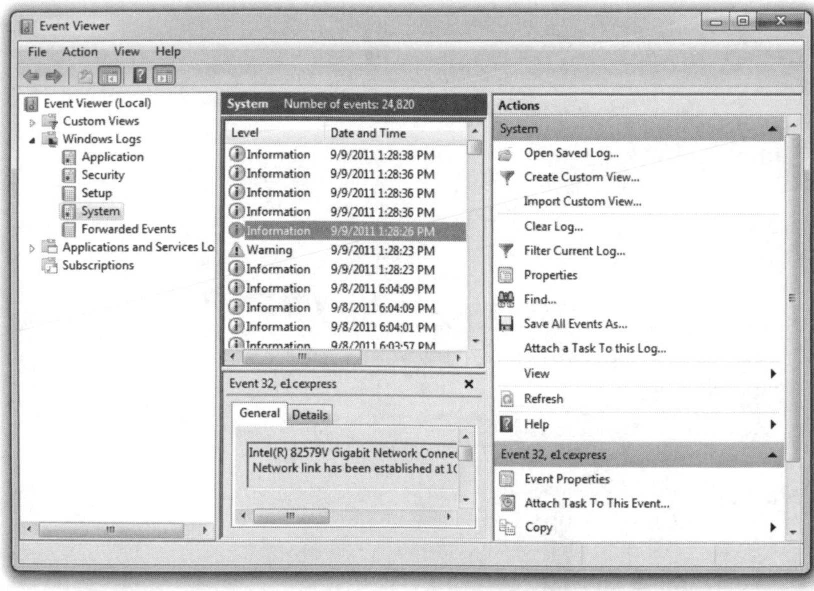

FIGURE 12.9 Event Viewer in Windows 7

History logs track the history of how a user or users access network resources, or how network resources are accessed throughout the network. Generically, you can use *traffic analysis* tools to chart HTTP use, for example, or discover when your network gets a spike in BitTorrent traffic.

SNMP

Most of this "logging" happens in a relationship between a router and a management server. *Simple Network Management Protocol (SNMP)* is a very popular method for querying the state of SNMP-capable devices. SNMP can tell you a number of settings like CPU usage, network utilization, and detailed firewall hits. SNMP uses *agents* (special client programs) to collect network information from a *Management Information Base (MIB)*, SNMP's version of a server. To use SNMP, you need SNMP-capable devices and some tool to query them. One tool is Cacti (www.cacti.net), shown in Figure 12.10. Cacti, like most good SNMP tools, enables you to query an SNMP-capable device for hundreds of different types of information.

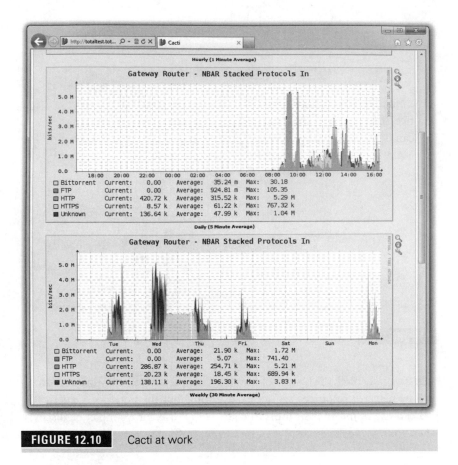

FIGURE 12.10   Cacti at work

SNMP is a useful tool for network administrators, but the first version, SNMPv1, sent all data, including the passwords, unencrypted over the network. SNMPv2 had good encryption but was rather challenging to use. SNMPv3 is the standard version used today and combines solid, fairly easy-to-use authentication and encryption.

CHECKPOINT

✔**Objective 12.01: TCP/IP Utilities**   The simplest, and often the most effective, software tools are the ones that come with your operating system. You can do a lot with ping, tracert, and the rest to diagnose network problems. Many common faults are protocol related; if you don't have the right protocols installed, or if they are misconfigured, you are not going to see all systems (or maybe anything) on your network.

✔**Objective 12.02: Troubleshooting Network Performance**   When your network feels a little under the weather, it's time for a tune-up. Protocol analyzers let you look inside packets to learn more about your network difficulties. You can optimize your network with features like caching, QoS, traffic shaping, load balancing, high availability, and fault tolerance.

✔**Objective 12.03: Monitoring Networks**   Don't forget that a server can tell you a lot about what's going on (or going wrong) if you take a look at its logs. The logs can also be used to preempt some problems and stop them from becoming reality. As well as being troubleshooting tools, the logs help you manage the health of your server before something nasty happens, so checking them should be a standard operating procedure.

REVIEW QUESTIONS

1. Which of the following commands will display the TCP/IP configuration of a system running UNIX/Linux/OS X?
   A. ipconfig
   B. ping 127.0.0.1
   C. ifconfig
   D. ipstat

2. Which of the following can be used to optimize performance of networking applications? (Select three.)
   A. QoS
   B. Switching loops
   C. Traffic shaping
   D. Load balancing

3. Which of the following programs can be used to view the error logs on a Windows server?

   A. Event Viewer

   B. PerfMon

   C. applog

   D. monitor.nlm

4. You notice that your system is running slowly, and you suspect that someone has planted a program on your system and is using that program to get unauthorized access. What command and switch could you use to troubleshoot this?

   A. ipconfig /all

   B. netstat –r

   C. nbtstat –A

   D. netstat –a

5. You are looking at your web server log files and you notice that a machine on your network with the IP address 192.168.3.2 has been sending a number of invalid requests to the web server. You would like to track down whose computer this is on your network. What command would you use?

   A. ping 192.168.3.2

   B. netstat –r

   C. nbtstat –A 192.168.3.2

   D. netstat –a 192.168.3.2

6. Which command shows you detailed IP information, including DNS server addresses and MAC addresses?

   A. ipconfig

   B. ipconfig -a

   C. ipconfig /all

   D. ipconfig /dns

7. Which tool uses ICMP packets to test connectivity between two systems?

   A. ARP

   B. arping

   C. netstat

   D. ping

8. If you want to see which other computers on your network are currently connected to you, what command should you use?

    A. ping

    B. nbtstat

    C. netstat

    D. tracert

9. Which Windows command displays the local system's routing table?

    A. route print

    B. print route

    C. tracert /print

    D. tracert /p

10. Which tools should you use to diagnose problems with DNS?

    A. Nmap or Wireshark

    B. nslookup or dig

    C. ping or arping

    D. tracert or arping

REVIEW ANSWERS

1. **C** Run the ifconfig command to display TCP/IP configuration information on a UNIX/Linux system.

2. **A, C, D** Switching loops are not used to optimize performance of networking applications and will typically bring the network down. All other choices are used to optimize performance of networking applications.

3. **A** Event Viewer is used to view the logs on any Windows server–based operating system.

4. **A** Using netstat -a, you can view the TCP and UDP connections and listening ports on your system.

5. **C** The nbtstat command with the –A switch is used to view the remote name table on a computer when you supply the command with an IP address.

6. **C** Running ipconfig /all displays detailed IP configuration information.

7. **D**   Only ping uses ICMP packets.

8. **C**   The netstat command shows your current sessions.

9. **A**   The route print command enables you to view and edit your local routing table.

10. **B**   The nslookup tool and the more powerful dig tool are used to diagnose DNS problems.

Career Flight Path

CompTIA Network+ certification generally serves as the follow-up to the immensely popular CompTIA A+ certification and is an important cornerstone for any number of career flight paths. Many IT companies see CompTIA Network+ certification as the foundation for networking expertise. After CompTIA Network+, you have a number of certification options, depending on the types or specific brands of network hardware you choose to support. Look at these four in particular:

- CompTIA Server+ Certification
- CompTIA Security+ Certification
- Microsoft Certified Technology Specialist Certifications
- Cisco Certifications

CompTIA Server+ Certification

CompTIA Server+ certification offers a more in-depth testing of your knowledge of PC and server-specific hardware and operating systems. If you plan to follow the path of the high-end hardware tech, CompTIA Server+ is a good next step—plus CompTIA Server+ is a natural lead-in to Cisco certifications. (See "Cisco Certifications.")

CompTIA Security+ Certification

CompTIA Security+ is a great starting point to learn about network security. CompTIA Security+ certification covers a wide range of security topics and technologies and is a great next step after you obtain your CompTIA Network+ certification. The CompTIA Security+ certification is also a great starting point to move on to other security certifications, such as the CISSP or the Security Certified Professional (SCP) certification.

Microsoft Certified Technology Specialist (MCTS) Certifications

Microsoft operating systems and server products control a huge portion of all installed networks, and those networks need qualified support people to make them run. Microsoft offers a series of certifications for networking professionals that naturally follow the CompTIA certifications. You can take a whole slew of certification tracks and exams, but I would suggest following Microsoft's recommended IT Pro track for networking professionals:

1. MTA Networking Fundamentals
2. MTA Security Fundamentals
3. MTA Windows Server Admin Fundamentals
4. MCTS Windows Server 2008, Network Infrastructure
5. MCTS Windows Server 2008, Active Directory

Once you've completed this MCTS track, you can continue on the Microsoft certification path and earn the more advanced Microsoft Certified IT Professional (MCITP) certification by passing the related exams in your product path. Check out Microsoft's Learning and Certification website for details on the different Microsoft certifications: www.microsoft.com/learning/certification

Cisco Certifications

Let's face it: Cisco routers pretty much run the Internet, not to mention most of the world's intranets. Cisco provides four levels of certification for folks who want to show their skills at handling Cisco products. Nearly everyone interested in Cisco certification starts with the Cisco Certified Entry Networking Technician (CCENT) exam. The CCENT exam is a darn easy way to slap the word *Cisco* on your resume! After the CCENT, you should decide on your desired specialty (Cisco offers tracks in a range of networking specialties, from routing and switching to storage networking) and follow that track. See the Cisco certification website at www.cisco.com/web/learning/index.html.

About the CD-ROM

The CD-ROM included with this book comes with an introduction video from the author, Mike Meyers; Total Tester practice exam software with two complete practice exams; a collection of Mike's current favorite tools and utilities for network management; a link to download the Secure PDF copy of the book; and a PDF Glossary. The software can be installed on any Windows 98/NT/2000/XP/Vista/Windows 7 computer and must be installed to access the Total Tester practice exam. The CD also includes a sample version of the Boson NetSim Network Simulator with a free lab.

Playing Mike's Intro Video

If your computer's optical drive is configured to auto-run, the CD-ROM will automatically start up upon inserting the disc. If the auto-run feature did not launch the CD, browse to the CD and click the Launch.exe icon.

From the opening screen you can launch the video message from Mike by clicking the Mike's Intro Video button. This launches the video file using your system's default video player.

System Requirements

The software requires Windows 98 or higher, Internet Explorer 5.5 or higher or Firefox with Flash Player, and 30 MB of hard disk space for full installation.

The Boson NetSim requires Windows 7, Windows Vista, or Windows XP. NetSim also requires Microsoft .NET Framework Version 3.5, 1-GHz Pentium processor or equivalent (minimum), 3-GHz Pentium processor or equivalent (recommended), 512 MB (minimum), 2 GB (recommended), up to 100 MB of available hard disk space, display capabilities for 1024 × 768, 256 colors (minimum), 1024 × 768 high color, 32-bit (recommended). The NetSim demo also requires an active Internet connection. NetSim is a Windows-based product.

Complete system requirements and product activation instructions can be found on the Boson website. A user guide is also available on the CD-ROM.

Installing and Running Total Tester

From the main screen you may install the Total Tester by clicking the Total Tester Practice Exams button. This will begin the installation process and place an icon on your desktop and in your Start menu. To run Total Tester, navigate to Start | (All) Programs | Total Seminars or double-click the icon on your desktop.

To uninstall the Total Tester software, go to Start | Settings | Control Panel | Add/Remove Programs (XP) or Programs and Features (Vista/7), and then select the Network+ Total Tester program. Select Remove, and Windows will completely uninstall the software.

Total Tester

Total Tester provides you with a simulation of the CompTIA Network+ exam. There are two complete CompTIA Network+ practice exams. The exams can be taken in either Practice or Final mode. Practice mode provides an assistance window with hints, references to the book, an explanation of the answer, and the option to check your answer as you take the test. Both Practice and Final modes provide an overall grade and a grade broken down by certification objective. To take a test, launch the program, select a suite from the menu at the top, and then select an exam from the menu.

Mike's Cool Tools

Mike loves freeware/open-source networking tools! Most of the utilities mentioned in the text are right here on the CD in the Mike's Cool Tools folder. You can access the folder from the menu by clicking Mike's Cool Tools from the list.

Please read the Cool Tools Descriptions.pdf file for a description of the utilities. Warning! While all of the tools are "Mike Meyers Approved," there is no guarantee they will work for you. Read any and all documentation that comes with each utility before using that program.

Secure PDF Copy of the Book

The contents of this book are available as a free download in the form of a secured Adobe Digital Editions PDF file, the Secure PDF.

The CD included with this book contains links to both Adobe Digital Editions and to the Secure PDF book download webpage. First, download and install Adobe Digital Editions on your computer. Next, follow the link to the Secure PDF download webpage. You are required to provide your name, a valid e-mail address, and your unique access code in order to download the Secure PDF.

Your unique access code can be found on the label that is adhered to the inside flap of the CD envelope. The CD envelope is inside the paper sleeve bound into the back of this book.

Upon submitting this information, an e-mail message will be sent to the e-mail address you provided. Follow the instructions included in the e-mail message to download your Secure PDF.

To download your copy, please visit http://books.mcgraw-hill.com/ ebookdownloads/9780071789066.

> **Note**
>
> The unique access code entitles you to download one copy of the Secure PDF to one personal computer. The unique access code can only be used once, and the Secure PDF is only usable on the computer on which it was downloaded. Be sure to download the Secure PDF to the computer you intend to use.

You need a copy of Adobe Digital Editions installed to open, view, and navigate the Secure PDF. You can download the latest version of Adobe Digital Editions for free from Adobe's website, www.adobe.com, or use the version included on the CD. Remember, it is highly recommended that you download and install Adobe Digital Editions before attempting to download the Secure PDF.

Boson's NetSim Network Simulator

This book includes a free demonstration version of Boson's NetSim network simulation software. Click the Boson NetSim 8 Demo button on the CD interface to install the NetSim demo.

The Boson NetSim Network Simulator is an application that simulates Cisco Systems' networking hardware and software, and is designed to aid the user in learning the Cisco IOS command structure. The NetSim labs do not directly address the CompTIA Network+ objectives, but all the labs/features/functions/ components of NetSim enable you to view simulated networks in a practice environment. Try the demo lab for free and see why NetSim stands in a class of its own.

NetSim uses Boson's proprietary Network Simulator, Router Simulator, and EROUTER software technologies, along with the Boson Virtual Packet

Technology engine, to create individual packets. These packets are routed and switched through the simulated network, allowing NetSim to build an appropriate virtual routing table and simulate true networking. Other simulation products on the market do not support this level of functionality.

Boson offers a NetSim for CCENT, CCNA, and CCNP. Each supports the technologies and skills you will need for the respective certification.

Boson NetSim provides more versatility and support than any other network simulation software on the market. NetSim software also includes a comprehensive lab menu that contains lessons and labs covering routing protocols, Cisco devices, switching, topological design, and much more.

NetSim is a Windows-based product and requires Windows XP, Windows Vista, or Windows 7 to run. System requirements and product activation instructions can be found on the Boson website. For technical support related to Boson NetSim, visit www.boson.com or e-mail supportissues@boson.com.

Technical Support

For questions regarding the Total Tester software, visit www.totalsem.com, e-mail support@totalsem.com, or e-mail customer.service@mcgraw-hill.com. Customers outside the United States, e-mail international_cs @mcgraw-hill.com.

Boson Technical Support

For technical support related to the Boson NetSim, please visit www.boson.com, or e-mail supportissues@boson.com.

Index

The Best in Security Certification Prep

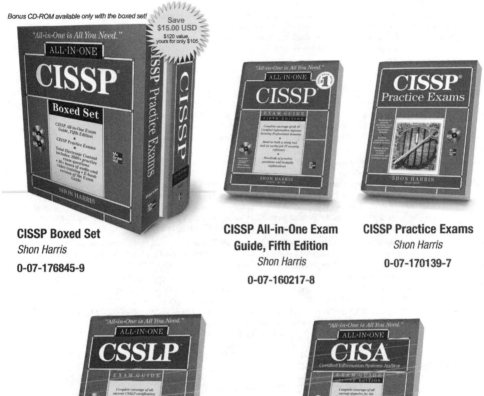